"CITY PLANNING is not only the design of physical spaces. Its essential elements include consideration and care for people, and including them in the planning process! Burnham's *Plan of Chicago* could have been a comprehensive one, but it wasn't. Every person—especially every city planner—who reads the 1909 *Plan of Chicago* should read this book. You will be nodding throughout and find yourself astounded that so much was missing."

—Karen L. Stonehouse, AICP, President, American Planning Association—Illinois Chapter

"*WHAT WOULD JANE SAY?* is not only an insightful historical work that highlights the work of Jane Addams and her progressive contemporaries, it is also a helpful guide that offers valuable lessons and ideas that planners and public-policy makers can apply today. If you are considering a career in urban planning, social work, or local government, *What Would Jane Say?* is a recommended read. There is much to glean from this book that speaks to why and how social factors should be incorporated in the crafting of any master development plan."

—Alderman Manny Flores, 1st Ward, Chicago

"JANICE METZGER'S RELENTLESS INQUIRY, integrity, and passion for the subject are evident on every page. The "Burnham" Plan was Chicago's gift to the world. *What Would Jane Say?* is a much needed expansion of the dialogue on the ingredients that make a healthy city, and it reminds us why place matters."

—Sylvia Ewing, Veteran producer and writer

"THE BURNHAM PLAN is often treated like a sacred text by urban planners. Its centennial is being celebrated in Chicago, the city it helped to define, with a reverential year-long tribute. Against this backdrop it's an illuminating relief to read Janice Metzger's *What Would Jane Say?* For me, the book exposes the nuances of the political and social conditions in which the Burnham Plan was forged. I was fascinated to learn how the seemingly innocuous frameworks of this regional vision were formed and reformed over the decades, casting for better and for worse, a long shadow over the shape and institutions of Chicago.

Had Metzger's history stopped there it would have been enough. Happily she dared to delve deeper, asking what *could have been* had the Burnham Plan included the voices of the female reformers of the day. And rather than simply catalogue these voices Metzger puts the reader right in the room with Jane Addams and her contemporaries as they debate subjects that dominate the Burnham Plan like transportation and open space as well as subjects glaringly absent from the Plan such as public health, juvenile justice, housing, and labor.

The conversations are historical fiction, cobbled together from the fragments that are known about the founding generation of Chicago's women leaders. Reading them, however, I'm struck by how so much of what was being debated 100 years ago continues to be discussed to this day, and how the social and economic divisions that existed then persist today. For me, through the imagined conversations of a century ago, it becomes clear that we still need to expand the regional vision. But not by making so-called big plans; rather by going small, which is inevitably a much harder, braver task. Metzger's work reveals not just the more liveable city that might have been, but creates a hopeful space for the Chicago that *could be* should we choose to open our eyes to the bigness of making small plans."

—Ben Helphand, Executive Director,
NeighborSpace

"IT APPEARS HISTORY CAN AND DOES repeat itself! As an elected official, I am struck by the comparisons of what Ms. Metzger writes of the days of Burnham's *Plan of Chicago* and Jane Addams's Hull-House, and life in Chicago as we know it today. As she notes, 'Chicago residents in 1909 suffered from corruption in government, inequitable taxation, overcrowded schools, unsanitary public hospitals, and a host of other social ills. Throw in gun violence and road rage and you've described Chicago one hundred years later! While the sad truth lies in what little has changed, this book offers hope for what can change. Let's hope leaders will soon start asking: *'What Would Jane Say?'!*"

—Kathy Ryg, Illinois State Representative,
District 59

"AFTER READING JANICE METZGER'S ACCOUNT of the work of Jane Addams and the remarkable women who shared her vision, I wonder not only what would Jane and her colleagues say now, but what Chicago and the region might have become if their words had been heeded, and their models followed through the years. Given the similarity of today's challenges to those they so bravely confronted a hundred years ago, this book suggests that it is not too late to revisit their world, and emulate their efforts.

Metzger has truly captured the spirit of Jane Addams and her associates in this fascinating story of how these women put their intelligence and compassion to work toward a creating a livable city for the people of Chicago. Unlike Burnham's "City Beautiful" Plan, these generous women not only recognized the needs of the people and identified practical ways to solve them, they put them into practice.

Metzger's own private and professional efforts to make the region more livable and beautiful have made her the perfect narrator for this engrossing book. She makes a compelling argument for a return the to the 'model of the collaborative, honest, and civic-minded network of women of all classes and races.'"

—Sheila H. Schultz, Past President of the
Village of Wheeling

"AFTER READING *WHAT WOULD JANE SAY?*, I felt the need to retrieve an old history of the Association House and read the names of the women who were involved. I had often walked the halls of our old building and wished that the women would speak to me. They have now. The impact of their wisdom and their struggles along with their successes continue to motivate the staff and leadership of modern day settlement houses and the communities we serve. This challenges me to do more and I hope that it will inspire others to do the same, after all, what *would* Jane say?"

—Harriet Sadauskas, President,
Association House of Chicago, Est.1899

"*WHAT WOULD JANE SAY?* is essential reading for anyone remotely interested in cities and urban planning today. What Metzger reveals happening one hundred years ago, through her research and insightful hypothetical narrative among women city-builders, continues to limit most mainstream planning in the US—a fervent belief that the design and workings of the city should strive to support business first, on the simple and misguided premise that this will benefit all people. As the women and men discuss in detail, this is not only misguided and narrow, it is a fundamentally unbalanced approach that ignores the real needs of the workers, their families, and the communities they live in, and more broadly the pursuit of social justice for all.

Moving beyond critique, Metzger provides insights from the past that can benefit all who today strive to plan with and for people of all classes, genders, and colors. Most pointed is the call to rethink the big plan and instead consider "visionary and broad-reaching" plans with "judiciously targeted small investments." Whether small or grand, we are reminded by this book that even the best plans are neither solution nor salvation if they are not implemented."

—Janet L. Smith, co-editor and co-author of
Where Are Poor People to Live? Transforming
Public Housing Communities.

What Would Jane Say?

City-Building Women
and a Tale of Two Chicagos

BY JANICE METZGER

First Edition

LAKE CLAREMONT PRESS
www.lakeclaremont.com
Chicago

What Would Jane Say? City-Building Women and a Tale
of Two Chicagos
Janice Metzger

Published August 2009 by:

LAKE CLAREMONT PRESS
lcp@lakeclaremont.com
www.lakeclaremont.com

Publisher's Cataloging-In-Publication Data
(Prepared by The Donohue Group, Inc.)

Metzger, Janice L.
  What would Jane say? : city-building women and a tale of two Chicagos / by Janice Metzger. -- 1st ed.

    p. : ill. ; cm.

  Includes bibliographical references and index.
  ISBN: 978-1-893121-90-4

  1. City planning--Illinois--Chicago--History--20th century. 2. Addams, Jane, 1860-1935. 3. Burnham, Daniel Hudson, 1846-1912. 4. Women social reformers--United States--History--20th century. 5. Social service--Illinois--Chicago--History--20th century. 6. Chicago (Ill.)--Social conditions--20th century. I. Title.

HT168.C5 M48 2009
307.1/2160977311
  2009927756

13 12 11 10 09   10 9 8 7 6 5 4 3 2 1

PUBLISHER'S CREDITS

Cover design by Timothy Kocher. Editing by Laurel Haines and Sharon Woodhouse. Editorial assistance from Therese Newman, Erik Germani, and Becky Straple. Interior design and layout by Charisse Antonopoulos. Indexing by Sally S. Kowalewski.

Table of Contents

	Introduction	v
1	A Comprehensive Plan for Business, a Shallow Plan for Chicago	1
2	Big Shoulders, Big Personalities	11
3	Herstory: Women with a Broad View	31
4	Bold Ideas and Major Movements at the Turn of the Century	53
5	Bringing All the Players Together	71
6	Parks	111
7	Transportation	137
8	The Heart of Chicago	171
9	Immigrants and Labor	193
10	Public Health	221
11	Housing and Neighborhoods	245
12	Education	267
13	Justice and the Courts	297
	Letter from Jane Addams	319
14	Can We Recover What We've Lost?	325
	Appendix A: Women Included as Participants in Meetings	345
	Bibliography	352
	Index	358
	Acknowledgments	371
	About the Author	373

Introduction

IN THE SEVENTY
YEARS AFTER ITS FOUNDING,
Chicago grew—without forethought—from five
thousand residents to a teeming metropolis of almost two
million. When Daniel Burnham wrote the *Plan of Chicago* in 1909,
a city plan was the exception, not the rule, in the United States.
He opened his plan with a justification of the benefits of growth
with forethought, not only for a city, but for a whole region. Chicago businessmen commissioned Burnham, one of the few men in
the United States who were trailblazing the new profession of "city
planner," to write Chicago's plan. Burnham, an architect by training, was proficient in visualizing present and future physical con-
figurations of the region. But his plan was deficient in the human
element. It failed to propose institutional or governmental systems
to improve quality of life for the people of the region. Chicago residents in 1909 suffered from corruption in government, inequitable
taxation, overcrowded schools, unsanitary public hospitals, and a
host of other social ills that the plan avoided.

Burnham's *Plan of Chicago* came to define planning for the next
hundred years as the rearrangement of the region's physical assets, but not the improvement of the residents' quality of life. One
might speculate that there were no local examples of city-building from a more humanistic point of view at the time Burnham
wrote the *Plan of Chicago*. But that would be wrong. Chicago had
a highly developed series of networks of women who worked to
build the city for its inhabitants, to clean it for those who suffered
from poor sanitation, to reform the school system, and to create
institutions like the Cook County Juvenile Court, the first juvenile
court in the nation. At the pinnacle of those overlapping networks
was Jane Addams, co-founder of Hull-House.

Jane Addams and Daniel Burnham were contemporaries. Both were city-builders although their approaches were very different. Addams was the Chicago and national leader of the settlement house movement. Burnham was the Chicago and national leader of the City Beautiful movement. The historic record seems to indicate that their paths crossed only infrequently, but their circles of friends and acquaintances overlapped with regularity. When the idea of writing this book to contrast the Addams and Burnham approaches to city-building occurred to me, it was hard to imagine that it hadn't already been conceived and written—the connections between their worlds seemed so obvious.

Perhaps it was the difference between her "think local" approach and his "think monumental" approach that kept Addams and Burnham from collaborating. As I wrote the book, I couldn't help but note the number of times the women in it—and there are many besides Jane Addams—made great changes with small resources, whether it was the first playground in Chicago (at Hull-House) or a dramatic reduction in infant mortality by bringing medical care out of impersonal and forbidding institutions and directly into immigrant communities. There are many such modest innovations with powerful results described in the pages of this book.

A good number of Chicagoans have heard of Jane Addams, but the specifics and importance of her contributions may have faded from memory. Most of the physical manifestations of her work—the Hull-House playground, the city's first bathhouse, the Hull-House complex itself—have been demolished (the two surviving buildings on the University of Illinois campus were once surrounded by eleven other buildings offering day care, a theater, meeting space, classrooms, a library, a coffee house, two museums, and other cultural amenities).

Daniel Burnham's *Plan of Chicago* had at least one asset Jane Addams's innovations never had—a promotional machine that began one hundred years ago and continues to this day. Although the 1909 plan was unauthorized, unofficial, and written only to represent the views of businessmen, all official plans developed subsequent to Burnham's mirror its focus and content. Wealthy businessmen not only controlled the crafting of the *Plan of Chicago*—they also controlled the early implementation of it. They were clear that the *Plan* was one to serve business interests and equally clear that they expected the taxpayers to pick up the tab.

In contrast, the settlement women were engaged in a different, more humanistic type of city-building. They created institutions to serve the public good and instigated reforms in public institutions through state and city legislative bodies, in spite of having no standing as voters. They often found, after securing a new law, that they had to pay for its implementation or volunteer to implement it themselves in the absence of state or municipal funding. Public funding usually followed their proof of the value of each innovation, but that was often a mixed blessing. Reforms of schools, public health facilities, courts, and other critical public institutions of the day were all threatened by patronage hiring and corruption.

The boundaries defining the limits of a city plan were flexible in this age. Some, including the businessmen of the Burnham era, would have denied that schools, public health, and other "software" of city-building or region-building were appropriate to a plan. The original promoters of a plan within the business community were primarily concerned with the consequences of rail traffic inefficiencies on their business prospects. Others, including Burnham himself, would have included urban institutions serving social needs, if given a free hand in developing Chicago's first plan. Sociology, the new discipline to study the behavior and needs of humans in group settings, developed on a track parallel to the discipline of city planning. At the early stages of development, sociology and urban planning were closely intertwined, as in the early efforts of New York settlement leaders to address "congestion" of housing through better urban planning in order to overcome a host of societal ills. City planning and sociology were closely linked in the first National Conference on Planning, which took place in Washington, D.C., in 1909, the same year the *Plan of Chicago* was released.

The business community of today, a more sophisticated breed than their predecessors of one hundred years ago, understands that the Chicago region's success does not rest solely on physical infrastructure. In fact, the *Metropolis 2020 Plan,* initiated by the Commercial Club and intended as an update to the Burnham plan, begins with a chapter on education, and takes on a host of controversial topics such as governance, inequitable taxation, racial segregation, and health care for poor children. This broadening of perspective is highly commendable, but now the challenge is to translate humanistic concerns into the region's official plan. The approaches, techniques, and accumulated wisdom the city-building women offered one hundred years ago were stamped out of any official processes long ago, to the disadvantage of all the region's residents. If we are to begin anew to build a regional planning process that incorporates their accumulated wisdom and addresses the human infrastructure needed for our region's continued success, we must honor more than the *Plan of Chicago.*

The region's official planning processes, up through the most recent plans, took the same approach as the *Plan of Chicago,* arranging and rearranging physical space and connectors like streets and rails. It is much easier to preserve open space, for example, than to attack poverty or injustice, although even preserving open space hasn't always been easy. Our challenge today, if we give *planning for people* our full attention, is to search out, assess, and promote the best models for a human-centered approach to regional planning. The seeds for the human-centered model were planted over one hundred years ago. We didn't nurture those seeds. In many cases we plowed them under, so that they are not available today without a good deal of digging.

The people who set urban and regional policy in northeastern Illinois have been and still are engineers and physical planners. The narrow lens established by Burnham has become narrower, not broader over time. The great majority of current planners with *official* decision-making authority bring expertise exclusively from the Illinois Department of Transportation, a limited perspective. Even with the best of intentions, they won't be able to absorb the amount of new material they need to master in order to plan for people.

This book came about because of the confluence of two events in September 2007 that fiercely affected me. The first was the decision of the Illinois State Toll Highway Authority to honor Jane Addams by renaming the Northwest Tollway after her. That struck me as an odd honor for a woman who lived locally and didn't drive! Three days later, at a "visioning" session with regional planners, three speakers repeated Burnham's quote "With things as they should be, every business man in Chicago would make more money than he does now." The first, historian Geoffrey Baer, used the quote in its proper historical context. The next two used it in reference to the preparation of a 2040 regional plan, seeing no apparent difficulty with planning exclusively for the benefit of business. Ironically, the twenty-first century business community has moved to a broad vision of regional well-being, but the official processes are still mired in the constraints of the 1909 plan.

My own history as a community advocate and organizer connected me to many of the issues the settlement house residents influenced, although my achievements are small compared to theirs. I fought for an active local park design, in contrast to a proposed Victorian garden. I supported affordable housing when my neighborhood was first threatened by gentrification. My children went to local public schools, although private school was easily an option. That day in September 2007, I knew, as a former board member of a modern-day settlement (Association House of Chicago), former leader of school reform under Mayor Harold Washington, and all-around advocate of social justice, that urban planning had to offer more than the vision of business success presented that day.

By the end of the month, I was compelled to respond and started to seriously research the women who I knew had made substantial contributions at the time. Where was Jane Addams's voice in the *Plan of Chicago*? What of the handful of other women's names that we still recognize today from that era? Where was the voice of Julia Lathrop, or Lucy Flower, or Ida B. Wells-Barnett? Who were the other obvious leaders and city-builders of the day who should have contributed to the *Plan* but had no voice in it? What might they have said? In what way would their scholarly sociological inquiries, reports, and published books and articles have informed and improved the *Plan of Chicago*?

Their books, reports, and articles began to "speak" to me as I read more and more of them. Soon I could imagine what some of their conversations might have been if they had been invited to contribute. I could imagine what they would have said about the chapters Burnham wrote. I could imagine what they would have said about the topics omitted from his plan. That is how the core of this book was conceived and how it is written. The eight central chapters are "speculative non-fiction"—heavily researched and documented opinions of the women (and the men who shared their purposes), threaded together by conversational strands that are plausible but not actual statements.

In the months I spent researching and writing about this topic, I was able to uncover a treasure trove of intersections and coincidences. Interesting parallels and contrasts between the work of city-building women and male-led institutions in Chicago at the turn of the century have been sitting unexamined for one hundred years, serving mainly as little anecdotes and vignettes in service to other theses.

The subject is nowhere near exhausted. I hope *What Would Jane Say?* will be read as an invitation to others to give the topic the scholarly attention it deserves. It is my fervent wish that scholars from the Chicago History Fair to the halls of academia will pick up the challenge to dig deeper, probe farther, and refine the connections that I have begun to mine here. I hope that planners will look at future regional plans and ask not whether they measure up only to the self-interested principles of the *Plan of Chicago,* but ask, *What would Jane say?*

OVERVIEW OF THE *PLAN OF CHICAGO*

By 1909, when the *Plan of Chicago* was published, Daniel Burnham held a national and even international reputation for his city plans as well as his building designs. Before completing the *Plan of Chicago,* Burnham had developed plans for Cleveland, San Francisco, and Manila, and had updated the park plan for Washington, D.C. He was probably best known in Chicago, however, as the superintendent of planning and construction for the 1893 World's Columbian Exposition. The Exposition, with its uniform, classical facades, was often called the White City, contrasting it to the grittiness of the real Chicago.

The Columbian Exposition was a grand success. Its commercial value to the city solidified business leaders' confidence in Burnham as the man to make big dreams bear fruit. Just a decade later, when businessmen began to envision the first plan for Chicago's future development, Burnham was the logical person to lead the effort. Talk of a plan for Chicago arose within two exclusive, male-only business clubs almost simultaneously. These were the Merchants' Club and the Commercial Club. The two clubs would eventually merge after the plan was begun, taking the name of the latter. The *Plan of Chicago* was designed to be a business plan from start to finish—a plan for business and business owners. It made no attempt to elicit the concerns, expertise, or experience of people from other classes or walks of life. The primary purpose of the *Plan* was to reconfigure space (especially roads, rails, terminals, etc.) to serve commercial interests, with a secondary emphasis on physical spaces like the lakefront and potential forest preserves. Besides the constraint of narrow business interests and perspectives, the fact is that Burnham was trained as an architect, not a city planner. The profession of city planning did not exist in the United States in the early 1900s. His plan was an *architect's* plan for the physical configuration of the city (although as I'll show later, there are indications that he would have preferred a broader mandate to address social aspects of urban life).

As he demonstrated in managing the World's Columbian Exposition, Burnham was a great promoter and public relations expert with an excellent eye for the power of imagery. The *Plan of Chicago* is a visually stunning document, even by today's standards. It is not hard to see how it could captivate the imagination of early Chicago leaders. One hundred and forty-two numbered plates grace the 124 pages of text. The plates range from precise diagrams and maps to misty, romantic drawings by Jules Guerin of the future city seen from a bird's-eye view.

The *Plan of Chicago* was important for a number of reasons. It proposed few original ideas, but integrated many existing ideas and plans into a unified package. The *Plan* enhanced the lakefront protection established by Chicago's early leaders. (Civic leaders in the first generation of Chicago set aside lakefront land with the "Forever Open, Clear, and Free" admonition.) Burnham incorporated existing proposals into his plan that would create forest preserves on the outskirts of the city. His vision for Michigan Avenue helped to turn it into the magnificent street we know today. Burnham's regional approach to planning was groundbreaking and original. In many ways, he set the standard for city planning in the United States, primarily through the *Plan of Chicago,* his best-known plan. Although the question considered in this book is what and who were missing from his plan, it is important to begin with an awareness of what he did accomplish.

The *Plan of Chicago* is comprised of eight chapters and an appendix on legal implications. In order to help readers of *What Would Jane Say?* understand the structure and recommendations of the *Plan*, a very brief summary of each chapter follows.

Chapter I
Origins of the Plan of Chicago

This brief chapter frames the argument for a plan. According to Burnham, men of the time were finding "formless growth" to be unsatisfactory. Among the themes introduced here and reinforced in the following chapters are that "disinterested" parties had initiated the *Plan*; the primary purpose was to improve business conditions; the success of the World's Columbian Exposition was a precursor to this plan and evidence of his qualifications; and order is a virtue of great magnitude for it promotes efficiency and civic character.

Chapter II
City Planning in Ancient and Modern Times

Burnham takes the reader on a survey of city-building from Babylonian times to the present, with accompanying diagrams and reproductions of paintings and etchings of architectural features in ancient cities. Planning in modern European cities is described in some detail, often including the cost of implementing the plans. Leaders in Paris, which originated city planning according to Burnham, turned a disorganized city of winding streets, crime, and vice into "the most beautiful of all cities" through planning that imposed order on the landscape. Burnham ended the chapter with images from Washington, D.C.; Cleveland; San Francisco; and Manila, other cities where he had city planning commissions. He ended by linking the common attributes of modern and ancient cities: convenient, healthful, attractive surroundings in a well-resourced, central location such as the Chicago region.

Chapter III
Chicago, the Metropolis of the Middle West

Chicago's exponential growth led Burnham, among others, to expect Chicago's population to be over thirteen million, the largest city in the world fifty years hence. Its location and excellent transportation resources, especially waterways, were seen as evidence of Chicago's impending greatness. However, Burnham writes, "thoughtful people were appalled" by the results of rapid growth. Burnham asks a series of questions, primarily about the business climate, and says, "(These) are the most pressing questions of our day, and everywhere men are anxiously seeking the answers." The idea of a planning commission that would have jurisdiction outside the city's boundaries is introduced in this chapter. He anticipates that these areas might be annexed into Chicago one day, but draws a very compelling vision for outlying towns of a town square with all the civic, governmental, educational, and recreational institutions clustered together in a "suburban civic center." The suburban area encompassed by the *Plan* is described as radiating sixty miles from the city's center. The greater portion of the chapter addresses suburban development, especially the role of highways. Burnham proposes a system of encircling highways in four arcs around the city, the longest beginning at Michigan City, Indiana, and ending at Kenosha, Wisconsin.

Chapter IV
The Chicago Park System

Burnham effectively makes the case that Chicago was woefully underserved with parks. He recounts the recent rise of the small parks movement and the rapid construction of seventeen parks on the South Side.[1] After offering European and East Coast examples of good park planning, Burnham turns to two of the contributions for which he is most famous: the lakefront and the forest preserves. He sets important standards in this chapter, insisting that the lakefront "by right belongs to the people" and "not a foot . . . should be appropriated by individuals . . ." This egalitarian impulse conflicts somewhat with the *Plan's* emphasis on the lakefront as a way to keep the wealthy spending their dollars in Chicago, with yacht harbors a key feature of the vision. (The emphasis on leisure activities of the wealthy over lakefront access by the "common people" is likely a result of Commercial Club objections to his original draft.) The chapter ends with several pages that suggest "forest spaces" should be purchased and preserved outside the city limits to the north, west, and south. Burnham states in the *Plan* that "He who habitually comes in close contact with nature develops saner methods of thought than can be the case when one is habitually shut up within the walls of a city."

---

1 At this time in Chicago's history, there were separate park boards for the South, West, and North Sides, and a newly formed Special Park Commission.

Chapter V
Transportation

In spite of the broad implication of its title, this chapter is about rail, both freight and passenger. Chicago's rail congestion was the impetus for this plan and this chapter is quite specific about remedies. The most significant recommendations are for relocation of all passenger terminals south of Roosevelt Road and/or west of Canal Street, and the consolidation of all freight yards southwest of the central business district. The *Plan* describes in some detail connections for downtown delivery through underground tunnels, a system of rail loops encircling the city and the business district, and two harbors, one each at the Chicago and Calumet rivers, where goods would be transferred from water to rail. Burnham proposes the passenger stations be at some distance from the central business district, and elevated, underground, and surface streetcar systems carry commuters to offices and stores. The *Plan* touched briefly on mail delivery and aggregation of utility plants. One of the *Plan*'s most widely quoted statements is in this section: "With things as they should be, every businessman in Chicago would make more money than he does now."

Chapter VI
Streets Within the City

Burnham's ideal plan for circulation on city streets would have involved a substantial number of diagonals, often linking the medium or large parks of the city, and radiating toward the central business district. Arcs within the city mimic the system of arced highways proposed earlier. Burnham calls these in-city arcs "circuits" and includes very specific text descriptions of the path of each circuit, in addition to maps highlighting the circuits. In this chapter he also introduces the idea of a new Civic Center at Halsted Street and Congress Street. He defines the specification of roadways as streets, avenues, and boulevards, giving due consideration to pedestrian travel. Burnham's conception of streets included the elevations of buildings alongside the streets, where he proposed architectural symmetry.

Chapter VII
The Heart of Chicago

The heart of the city, as defined in the *Plan,* was expected to grow to cover the area from Chicago Avenue to Twenty-second Street (now Cermak Road) and Ashland Avenue to the lake. The core of it was a center of business, entertainment, culture, and passenger travel. Traffic movement was the primary problem to be resolved, in Burnham's view. He proposes the widening of many streets to accommodate the new trend of private autos. Michigan Avenue is proposed to be a broad boulevard; Burnham describes it as "destined to carry the heaviest movement of any street in the world" and devotes eight pages to grade changes, bridge technologies, pedestrian counts, and other engineering specifications. Other topics covered in this chapter include the placement of rail passenger stations, the location and design of cultural institutions in Grant Park, treatment of other streets deemed significant by Burnham (Chicago Avenue, Congress Street, and Halsted Street), and a full description of his grand scheme for a new Civic Center replacing the immigrant neighborhood around the Hull-House complex.

Chapter VIII
Plan of Chicago

Burnham's priorities within the *Plan* are expressed concisely in this chapter: 1) improvement of the lakefront; 2) highways outside the city; 3) passenger and freight rail; 4) the outer park system; 5) systematic improvement of streets; and 6) intellectual life and civic administration. Past civic projects and their costs are presented as evidence that Chicago could afford to implement this *Plan,* although no estimates are given of what public resources the full *Plan* or aspects of it would require. Burnham goes on to discuss the urgent necessity to implement his plans and the low cost of some components. Where costs were high, he assures Chicagoans that property values would rise as a result.

Appendix
Legal Aspects of the Plan of Chicago, *by Walter Fisher*

Fisher determined that there were few legal impediments to the *Plan.* He reviews implications for Burnham's priority areas—parks, the lakefront, and various forms of transportation. He adds an additional topic, "congested areas." Fisher cautions that no matter how "unwholesome" an area might be, Illinois law did not allow eminent domain to claim land solely for the purpose of improving it. The city did have the power to claim land to construct wide thoroughfares and public parks however. The final section of the appendix is a discussion of the limitations on Illinois cities of the time in assuming debt to carry out capital projects. Fisher recommends legislative changes to increase the amount of bonding authority the city could use and to extend the repayment time over the twenty-year limit in effect then.

IMMEDIATELY FOLLOWING PUBLICATION OF THE *PLAN OF CHICAGO*

After the *Plan* was published, a non-governmental Chicago Plan Commission was formed almost immediately to execute the *Plan*. Its executive committee was comprised largely of members of the Commercial Club. The *Plan* was formally presented to the city by the Commercial Club in early 1910. Summaries for adults and children were developed, and for many years all eighth-graders in the Chicago Public Schools studied the *Wacker Manual,* the version designed for grade school students.

The first project proposed by the Planning Commission's executive committee in 1909 was the widening of Twelfth Street (now Roosevelt Road). City engineering studies began in 1910. The first forest preserve land was purchased in the teens. Michigan Avenue did become a grand avenue and other streets throughout the city were widened over time. The lakefront was preserved and enhanced.

Many other bold ideas were not enacted, for better or worse. Skyscrapers increasingly defined the Chicago skyline, in spite of Burnham's concept of uniform mid-rise buildings at a consistent height. Building the Civic Center was never seriously considered, nor was the system of diagonal streets. The railroad companies resisted attempts to make their privately owned systems connect more efficiently. All industrial harbor activity was moved to the Calumet River rather than a portion remaining near downtown at the Chicago River harbor.

1

A Comprehensive Plan for Business, a Shallow Plan for Chicago

CHICAGO WAS NOT THE ONLY NINETEENTH-CENTURY AMERICAN CITY experiencing a rapid influx of immigrants or severe shortages of housing and other basic necessities. But it was in some ways uniquely limited in its ability to deal with the disorder and dislocations inherent in massive change. The state of Illinois allowed Chicago no more authority than any other town of two thousand inhabitants. The city's ability to tax or issue bonds was severely restricted by state law. In contrast to East Coast cities, most of which Chicago eclipsed in size during the late 1800s, Chicago was still in many ways a frontier town without the culture, institutions, or inclinations of urbanity. Charges of political corruption accompanied one of the first official acts of the city (sale of school land) and corruption was alleged, and often proved, throughout the remainder of the century and beyond.

In this tumultuous milieu many reform efforts were undertaken by many different players. Suffragettes and anti-immigrant organizations, religious reformers and labor unions, prohibitionists and immigrants' rights organizations all attacked disorder and injustice with single-issue campaigns in order to reform the city. In the midst of these competing notions, two Chicagoans rose above others for their more comprehensive vision of the city. These two were settlement house[1] founder Jane Addams and famed architect Daniel Burnham. Burnham is credited with creating the first comprehensive vision for the physical shape of the Chicago

---

1 A settlement house was an early social service agency in which the workers lived in—settled in—the community with which they interacted on a daily basis.

region. However, his vision was restricted to physical manifestations, which could only have a limited impact on quality of life
for the region's residents. The other comprehensive view—Jane
Addams's—was a dedication to city-building by developing institutional capacity across a broad range of disciplines, including parks
and recreation, public health, and the justice system, to name just
a few. It is the region's loss that the first "comprehensive" plan
for future growth was limited to Burnham's plan for the region's
physical assets.

The 1909 *Plan of Chicago,* spearheaded by the private Commercial Club of Chicago and some of the most influential male leaders
of the day, was promoted and came to be known as the definitive
guide for development of the city of Chicago and the region around
it. Brought to life by Daniel Burnham, the plan, considered to be
one of the earliest and most influential comprehensive plans in
the United States, was developed around the concepts of the City
Beautiful movement, which assumed that a city that was attractive
and well-organized would serve to resolve urban disharmony. Chicago women from all walks of life were also engaged in city-building
efforts at the beginning of the twentieth century—efforts that still
resonate today, even if the women's names do not.

Most of the women who were active at the turn of the century
subscribed to a different theory—explicitly or implicitly—the theory of the "city as home." Resolving urban disharmony and blight in
their minds required investigating and reforming systems of urban
sanitation, juvenile justice, public health, industrial and labor relations, and education. The young city of Chicago was still debating
in 1909 whether public institutions or private commercial entities
should have responsibility for these tasks. The Commercial Club
generally advocated that most basic services could and should be
provided by the private market, but most of the active women demanded a municipal charter that assumed greater responsibility
for the health and welfare of the public.

Thirty years after the Chicago Fire, the conceptual differences
between men and women in Chicago's leadership were quite pronounced. One who never shied from pointing out those differences
was Jane Addams. In her book *Democracy and Social Ethics,* Addams observed that "well-to-do men of the community . . . are almost wholly occupied in the correction of political machinery and
with a concern for a better method of administration, rather than

with the ultimate purpose of securing the welfare of the people."[2] A similar appraisal could be made of the businessmen of the Commercial Club and the architects of the *Plan of Chicago,* who were concerned with the city as infrastructure and investment, not as children to be educated, immigrants to be *respectfully* acculturated, or workers to be invested with the full rights of citizenship. When the women focused on infrastructure it was to investigate or publicize the human cost of poor sanitation, overcrowded classrooms, corrupt inspections, or any of a host of other problems in Chicago at the time.

Women's suffrage was a wedge issue at the turn of the century. Although the state of Illinois gave women the vote in 1914, six years before national suffrage, the debates preceding Illinois's suffrage law were bitter. Jane Addams pointed out how nonsensical the patronizing justifications of male-only suffrage were when she wrote a satirical essay titled *If Men Were Seeking the Franchise.*[3] Her clever reversal of roles relied on a concept known as "municipal housekeeping" for one example of why women would be more responsible voters than men. She reasoned that men plainly cannot be depended upon to keep their businesses and factories clean—common dust, lead dust, inhalable metal filings, and other toxic particles covered the floors and surfaces of many workplaces—therefore, they can hardly be given the important responsibility of keeping the city or state clean, orderly, and well-functioning. Nor, Addams added, do businessmen protect children working in factories from loss of fingers or hands by investing in safety shields or other equipment to make machinery safe. She contrasts the business view of children in factories with the home-centered view of children in a family, and finds the former dangerously imprudent. Women's experience keeping children safe and homes clean, she figured, better qualified them to ensure public safety and sanitation.

The businessmen of the Commercial Club who paid for the *Plan of Chicago* were fairly isolated from Addams's thinking and other alternative views of the world. Their private intention was to create a document they hoped would have public implications. The

---

2   Addams, *Democracy and Social Ethics,* 222–223.

3   Elshtain, *The Jane Addams Reader,* 232–233. Addams's essay was written in 1913.

lack of an overall organizing strategy for growth of the city and the region had implications for their businesses and for business in general, especially, but not exclusively, for the railroad companies. The *Plan* was heavily focused on the lakefront, the central business district, and the suburban communities from which many club members commuted. The *Plan* contains little for the balance of the city, except the threat of wide-scale demolition for the erection of the new Civic Center and many new diagonal streets through existing neighborhoods to promote access to the downtown business district. The business community suffered under the mistaken notion that they were sufficiently diverse in their interests to represent the whole city. The businessmen had recently suffered rejection, by a two to one margin, at the hands of the electorate when their proposed city charter came to a vote in 1907. It seemed they took no wisdom from the experience, for the group crafting the *Plan* was even smaller and less diverse than the charter convention delegation.

The networks of activist women, by contrast, were more diverse in the ways we recognize today, often crossing race and class lines. This is not to say that these women had a contemporary sensitivity to such issues, but women leaders were in touch with and familiar with the lives and concerns of women richer and poorer than themselves, and with women of different races, ethnicities, and religions. There was communication and sometimes collaboration between women of widely different backgrounds.

The women were not the only group that could have added weight and breadth to the *Plan*. They were the group most familiar to the businessmen, however. Some of the subscribers to the *Plan* were married to activist women. A few subscribers *were* activist women, including Helen Culver and Mary Wilmarth. (Subscribers contributed financially to the *Plan of Chicago*.) In spite of the quality and quantity of the city-building women's achievements, they were virtually invisible to the men who believed they had sole rights to design the region.

THE *PLAN*—THE VISION OF A SMALL ELITE

The *Plan of Chicago* was revolutionary in its day, rightfully lauded for its beautiful illustrations, its consolidation of many disparate plans and projects into a coordinated whole, and its long-term, regional view. Judged by today's standards, however, Burnham's *Plan of Chicago* is limited in viewpoint and in content. The idea that public economic benefits would "trickle down" from a plan like this is generally discredited today, though it would seem that's what Burnham and most of the Commercial Club believed. The notion that one small demographic group (wealthy, white, male) could speak for a whole city has deservedly been quashed, in theory if not always in practice.

Some will say that since women did not yet vote in 1909, we shouldn't expect them to have been included in developing the *Plan of Chicago.* That view is only possible if the outstanding contributions Chicago women had already made to the city, county, and state by 1909 are disregarded. Their public policy and legislative agendas were shaped by substantial research, practice, and accomplishments that could have and should have informed the *Plan.* It is difficult to believe that Burnham and the Commercial Club were unaware that activist women in Chicago were deeply impacting the shape of the city, county, and state through reforms such as the new juvenile court, sweatshop and child labor legislation, investigations of corrupt inspectors, and advocacy for a new city charter, to name just a few achievements.

While Burnham and the male city-builders of the Commercial Club crafted a regional plan with the singular purpose of benefiting business, another group of city-builders asked themselves "not what your city can do for you, but what you can do for your city." The latter group was led by women and primarily comprised of women, but unlike the all-male business clubs of the day, city-building women gladly included reform-minded men in their work, their networks, and their settlement movement.

WHO PAID TO IMPLEMENT THE *PLAN?* WHO SHOULD HAVE PAID?

The most significant difference between the businessmen of 1909 and the city-building women, however, was in their approach to financial responsibility. A regrettable practice among many business owners in Chicago at this time was to underpay their taxes while taking full advantage of lucrative contracts and leases with the city and other public entities. The women will provide ample discussion of this pattern in later chapters, but for these introductory pur-

poses consider one example. The *Chicago Tribune*'s attorney served
as president of the Board of Education at a time of controversy over
leases of board property to private business for less than market
rates. The *Tribune* enjoyed a thirty-thousand-dollar per year lease
for school property at Madison and Dearborn streets, under a contract that lasted until 1985. The Board of Education leased back
one floor of the *Tribune*'s rented building for one thousand dollars
more than the *Tribune* paid for the whole property. Jane Addams
sat on a reform board that tried and failed to have the *Tribune* lease
voided in 1905.

Access to favorable leases on public property did not translate
into a sense of responsibility to help pay for public services. Social
commentator and Anglican minister William Stead, in his book, *If
Christ Came to Chicago*, included a list of what he called "curiosities
of Chicago assessments." He had come to Chicago for the World's
Columbian Exposition World Parliament on Religions and found
himself outraged about actual conditions in the city. On Stead's
list was the 1892 assessed property and actual tax for newspapers,
other corporations, and wealthy individuals. The *Tribune* was assessed on thirty-five thousand dollars of property, for a total of
less than three thousand dollars a year in taxes. Stead noted that
the price of one printing press was approximately fifteen thousand
dollars at that time. Governor John Altgeld accused the papers of
"waving the flag with one hand and plundering the public with the
other." The papers weren't necessarily any worse than other businesses, but some were aggressive in opposing what they saw as
wasteful educational "frills and fads." The *Tribune* alone published
thirty editorials in 1893 railing against innovations in the schools,
all while they skimmed profits from resources that should have
benefited the children.

In line with this ethic, the men who initiated and then promoted
the *Plan of Chicago* had Chicago taxpayers paying for improvements they had no say about, crafted primarily in the interest of
benefiting the business community, attracting the wealthy classes,
or easing the commute of the suburban businessman. The men
were right in thinking a regional plan should be publicly funded.
But there were two problems with their concept of public funding.
The whole region should have shared in funding the *Plan,* not just
Chicago taxpayers. Those who paid for a regional plan should have
had a voice in it, through appropriate representation.

WHAT DID WE LOSE BY SHUNNING
WOMEN AND THEIR IDEAS?

Just what were Chicago women's achievements and areas of expertise in this era? The women who will be described here saw the consequences of corruption and patronage and worked to ensure professional food inspections and adequate sanitation systems. They worked to make the existing system function properly, but could look beyond existing institutions to what was needed and then create it, in spite of their exclusion from the voting booth and legislative assemblies. These women understood immigrants far better than the businessmen; they had a much more nuanced and reasonable attitude toward labor unions; and they had within their ranks members with a great deal of expertise in issues of housing, playgrounds, public health, child labor, and public education. The omission of this wealth of information, as well as omission of the viewpoints and experience of the accomplished women on how to solve many of the most pressing issues of the day, account in large part for the *Plan* being a narrower document than what it could have been. It was designed to represent the businessmen and it does that job well. We can celebrate what it is, but should not mistake it for a comprehensive plan or a plan that benefited everyone in the region.

The one thing these women did not do well was promote themselves and their substantial work. On the other hand, promotion of the *Plan of Chicago* continues after one hundred years, with little or no critical thought about what and who are missing from its vision. One has to ask why we automatically celebrate the product of the undemocratic, exclusive club members who shirked taxes and abused government leases and contracts, while we continue to overlook their democratic, inclusive counterparts, women who made great public contributions to Chicago's early city-building, many times at their own expense.

We should celebrate the *Plan of Chicago* for what it is—a plan for physical space in the Chicago region, with an emphasis on enhancing business prospects. There is no shame in that. Our error has been in trying to impose this plan as a model for comprehensive planning for all the ages. If this defines "comprehensive," there is no need to turn to the plan that will address the welfare of the broadest number of people. We haven't asked if the businessmen's needs were served at the expense of others in the region because the value of the plan was not judged on whether it provided the greatest good for the greatest number of people.

We have in the *Plan of Chicago* proposals for monumental public spaces and broad thoroughfares, for example, without a plan for the neighborhoods or people of Chicago. For instance, the *Plan* doesn't evaluate the impact of the proposed new diagonal avenues on the communities that would experience substantial demolition in service to downtown accessibility.

The perceived need to demolish significant sections of city neighborhoods for the diagonals might have been an inadvertent, disinterested recommendation. It can also be interpreted as a deliberate attempt to dislocate populations that were unwanted or undervalued by business leaders. Walter Fisher's appendix reviewing legal aspects related to the *Plan* emphasizes the *Plan*'s proposed parks and thoroughfares as the only practical way to conduct slum clearance under Illinois law. This author happens to feel that the region should not target powerless communities for "urban removal." In this day and age there are environmental justice provisions in the law requiring evaluation of unfair impacts on poor or minority populations. What seems a bit duplicitous in the *Plan of Chicago* is to address slum clearance in a little-read appendix full of legalese and devoid of attractive drawings at the end of the *Plan.* As a practical matter, with Burnham's plan as our yardstick, it was business as usual to destroy many city neighborhoods to build interstates in the 1950s. It is not hard to imagine Jane Addams and her cohorts asking how to achieve the greatest access with the least dislocation.

But here is how the *Plan of Chicago* ultimately and most profoundly shortchanged Chicago: Because it was promoted as *the* model for planning, its limitations were perpetuated as well as its strengths. In a later chapter of this book, one of the women will express exasperation with the *Plan* by comparing it to a castle, a moat, and the surrounding hamlets whose residents are protected by the castle. In her example, downtown is represented by the castle, the suburbs by the hamlets, and the neighborhoods of Chicago by the moat—an empty area to be traversed. Holistic tendencies in planning, such as the inclusion of neighborhoods and people as well as city centers and big transportation projects, social infrastructure and issues as well as aesthetics and commerce, small-scale solutions as much as big visions, never had a chance to become a essential part of the mix. And these were the very things that early women city-builders practiced, created, and refined in their Chicago work.

A century has passed without anyone asking how the contributions of the city-building women might have improved the *Plan of Chicago*. Once the question has been posed, it is hard to fathom why it took so long. One possibility that must be considered is that the near-unanimous reverence toward Burnham's work left little room for alternate viewpoints. Another possibility is that we are still more enamored with visible, incontrovertible physical improvements than we are with quality of life improvements—we feel stronger as a region with a new eight-lane highway than with a higher graduation rate or lower infant mortality rate. A third possibility is that class still matters more than it should: Decision-makers may look more favorably on improvements benefiting the middle and upper classes—"people like us"—than those benefiting immigrants, the working class, or other "strangers."

2

Big Shoulders, Big Personalities

THE EARLY TWENTIETH CENTURY PRODUCED some of Chicago's most exceptional and creative leaders. Jane Addams and Daniel Burnham are names many Chicagoans recognize. The names and contributions of many other leaders of the time, especially those of outstanding women, are unfamiliar to most of us. In order to best grasp the era, we begin here by understanding a bit more about Addams, Burnham, and the city as it was one hundred years ago.

JANE ADDAMS—
THE MOST CONSEQUENTIAL OF A LARGE CONTINGENT

Jane Addams was the acknowledged leader of a large contingent of Chicagoans, including women and men living in settlements and other reform-minded individuals. Addams was a powerful theoretician, in spite of her emphasis on practical solutions to social and economic problems. In an essay, "The Subjective Necessity of Settlements," Addams observes that the business community lived a very insular life and failed to provide solutions that were within their means, in spite of their many advantages. She said:

> The people who might [remedy the dislocations of industrial society], who have the social tact and training, the large houses and the traditions and customs of hospitality, live in other parts of the city. The club-houses, libraries, galleries, semi-public conveniences for social life are also blocks away. . . . Men of ability and refinement, of social power and university cultivation, stay away from (the working class). Personally, I believe the men who lose most are those who thus stay away.[1]

---

1   Elshtain, *The Jane Addams Reader*, 16.

She was equally astute when evaluating necessary preconditions to sustain democracy. In *Twenty Years at Hull-House* she says, "The very existence of the state depends on the character of its citizens, therefore if certain industrial conditions are forcing the workers below the standard of decency, it becomes possible to deduce the right of state regulation."[2] This call for democratic institutions to respond to assaults on public health or workplace safety was a revolutionary idea at the turn of the century. It was also a very different approach from what would be offered by the Commercial Club and the City Beautiful movement in response to urban problems.

Jane Addams spoke eloquently for herself in numerous essays, articles, and autobiographical accounts. Many other authors have done admirable jobs of covering her life and her important contributions. Jane Bethke Elshtain, who has collected a large number of Addams's works in *The Jane Addams Reader*, says she was the first "public intellectual"—a social thinker who wanted to communicate with a mass audience. By the time the *Plan of Chicago* was produced, Addams had published *Democracy and Social Ethics* (1902), *Newer Ideals of Peace* (1907), The *Spirit of Youth and the City Streets* (1909), as well as several essays and articles.[3] Addams was a complex figure who has received more attention than the hundred-plus other women leaders active in Chicago at the time. For the purposes of this work, some of the most basic information on Addams's life, particularly the facets relevant to city-building, is summarized here to provide context.[4]

Jane Addams was born September 6, 1860, in Cedarburg, Illinois, into the solidly upper-middle-class family of Sarah Weber Addams and John Huy Addams. Her mother died when she was a toddler and her father remarried in 1868. Addams attended the Rockford Female Seminary and then, like many young women of her class, went to Europe. Between graduation in 1881 and the es-

---

2   Addams, *Twenty Years*, 134.

3   Elshtain, *The Jane Addams Reader*, xxv.

4   Jane Addams was influential until her death in 1935. Her audience expanded well beyond Chicago with national and international platforms. She was awarded the Nobel Peace Prize in 1931. However, this book focuses on achievements that Daniel Burnham and the Commercial Club could have reasonably been expected to know of, achievements before 1910.

tablishment of Hull-House in 1889, Addams seemed to suffer from bouts of soul-searching that ended in periods of depression. Her revulsion while watching the slaughter of a bullfight evolved into a broader humanitarian mission. The experience seemed to crystallize her response to the moral ambiguity she felt as an educated but "idle" young woman. The angst and soul-searching during her post-graduate period gave way to a clear vision of what she wanted to do. After visiting Toynbee Hall[5] in England, Addams was determined to bring the settlement house model to Chicago.

In 1889 she and Ellen Gates Starr, another graduate of Rockford Female Seminary, rented a house on the Near West Side of Chicago from Helen Culver. Culver inherited the house from her cousin, Charles Hull, who originally purchased a good deal of West Side land in the hope that affluent homebuyers would settle there.[6] Addams and Starr set about to create a unique institution, and succeeded, in very short order. The Hull-House charter described their desire: "To provide a center for higher civic and social life; to institute and maintain educational and philanthropic enterprises and to investigate and improve the conditions in the industrial districts of Chicago."[7]

Jane Addams and the residents strove to be good neighbors. In an 1892 address delivered to the School of Applied Ethics in Plymouth, Massachusetts, Addams said, "The good we secure for ourselves is precarious and uncertain, is floating in mid-air, until it is secured for all of us and incorporated into our common life."[8] The address was published the following year as "The Subjective Necessity for Social Settlements."

Fellow resident and close confidant Alice Hamilton described Addams this way: "Miss Addams was warm and magnetic, but she never tolerated the sort of protective, interfering affection which is so lavishly offered to a woman of leadership and prominence. Nobody ever ventured to refuse her to visitors, or even to take her telephone calls unless authorized to do so. She was impatient of solicitude, and her attitude brought about a wholesome, rather

---

5   Toynbee Hall in London was the first settlement house.

6   Glowacki and Hendry, *Images of America,* 10.

7   Addams, *Twenty Years,* 66.

8   Elshtain, *The Jane Addams Reader,* 17.

Spartan atmosphere."[9] She was a very formal person who expected to be referred to as "Miss Addams" by all but a small circle of friends.

In spite of the abundance of new political, social, and philosophical theories at the time, Jane Addams avoided fastening onto a specific ideology, which she felt would become a barrier to "reality." She lived the reality of the Near West Side. She wrote extensively about what it meant to her and the larger society. But she resisted becoming sidetracked by ideological debates that could have hampered the practical relief she and the residents afforded their neighbors, whether it was by establishing a labor law or providing day care for a child. Settlements, to Addams, allowed the merger of thought and action. If she belonged to any ideological school, it was to the school of pragmatism, which promoted intelligent, purposeful actions. Like some other early social scientists, Addams promoted practical approaches that relied on science, empiricism, evolution, and democracy.[10] But Addams was clear that the theoretical served the practical, rather than practice being in service to theory.

Addams, like Burnham, felt that the social ills the residents confronted came from a failure of leadership to organize resources properly. In *Twenty Years at Hull-House* she speaks of "our perplexity over the problems of an industrial neighborhood situated in an *unorganized* [emphasis added] city."[11] However, the remedy Addams proposed was very different from Burnham's. A beautifully ordered urban landscape was not the singular prescription for a harmonious city as far as she was concerned; fair access to basic necessities and to the resources that were needed to prosper in America were the keys to harmony. She said, "The Settlement, then, is an experimental effort to aid in the social and industrial problems which are engendered by the modern conditions of life in a great city" and "It is an attempt to relieve, at the same time, the overaccumulation at one end of society and the destitution at the other; but it assumes that this overaccumulation and destitution is

---

9   Hamilton, *Alice Hamilton, M.D.*, 61.

10   Deegan, *Men of the Chicago School*, 247.

11   Addams, *Twenty Years*, 88.

most sorely felt in the things that pertain to social and educational advantages."[12]

Addams promoted the idea that women were more humanitarian and down to earth than men and had distinctive assets to offer in social and political spheres.[13] Society was corrupt and unjust *because* women's influence was limited to the home. Although she did not choose to have children, Addams believed in a "maternal instinct"—and saw that instinct as a strength that extended beyond one's immediate family. According to Mary Jo Deegan, "Addams valued the female world and wanted it to be extended throughout society."[14] For Addams, urban housekeeping was not simply a matter of sweeping away the dirt that led to disease (although that might be a necessary first step), it was also a matter of nurturing the souls, psyches, and intellects of the city's inhabitants.

No overview of Jane Addams would be complete without reference to work she did outside of Hull-House. By 1909 she had personally:

- helped found the Civic Federation
- been appointed garbage inspector for the Nineteenth Ward[15]
- sought labor-industrial arbitration and reconciliation (she was on the Citizen Arbitration Committee during the Pullman Strike)
- served on the board of the Chicago Public Schools from 1905–1909
- chaired a federation of one hundred women's organizations
- defended anarchists and Russian émigrés the czar tried to extradite from the United States

---

12 Ibid., 75.

13 Deegan, *Men of the Chicago School,* 229.

14 Ibid., 227.

15 Davis, *American Heroine,* 121. Addams's campaign to clean up garbage and her appointment as garbage inspector for the ward, at a salary of $1,000, provided more national attention than anything she had done in the previous six years at Hull-House.

- engaged in the debate and lobbying on reform of the municipal charter for Chicago in 1906–07 and 1908–09

- helped secure legislation outlawing sweatshops and child labor (1893) and establishing the first juvenile court in the nation (1899)

- been nominated for an honorary degree by the faculty of the University of Chicago (1906). The nomination was vetoed by the university trustees, who considered her too controversial. Twenty-four years later, the University of Chicago conferred the honorary degree.

The last point is worth noting. Jane Addams's activities are hardly radical by today's standards, but she was viewed with suspicion by conservative elements of society. She personally avoided politics (she hated lobbying, but did it when necessary) and radicalism, yet she was constantly in contact with and learning from government reformers, labor, intellectuals, and radicals. She stepped boldly into labor confrontations, like the Pullman Strike, looking for a middle ground. Hull-House and Jane Addams became associated by proxy with the Haymarket affair by virtue of timing. Governor Altgeld, who pardoned the three surviving Haymarket defendants, also signed the first factory legislation into law around the same time, legislation with which Hull-House was closely identified.[16] Altgeld's pardon was unpopular and was a factor in his unsuccessful campaign for re-election as governor.

Mary Jo Deegan, in *Jane Addams and the Men of the Chicago School, 1892–1918,* lists Addams's many contributions to the developing field of sociology and to society in general. She has this to say about Jane Addams: 1) She was a major intellectual, a social theorist stigmatized as a radical; 2) She had a deep impact on sociology, which came to be dominated by men who selectively used her analyses but did not credit her; 3) Her role as a social thinker is under-analyzed and deserves re-examination; and 4) She was the leader of a complex network of women whose contributions have not been seriously studied.[17] In spite of Addams's own attempts to focus on the practical contributions she could make to daily

16   Addams, *Twenty Years,* 122.
17   Deegan, *Men of the Chicago School,* 13–14.

life on the Near West Side, her persona and her intellect were too large to avoid her also being seen as an intellectual and a theorist. Her emphasis on the practical helped her avoid being tied to any particular ideology or theory; she remained able and willing to see each new issue from multiple perspectives.

DANIEL BURNHAM—AN EARLY REGIONALIST

Daniel Burnham was a Chicago architect with a national and international following. He had already completed plans for Cleveland (1903), San Francisco (1905), and Manila (1905)[18] when businessmen selected him to craft a Chicago plan. As the manager of the World's Columbian Exposition, his profile in Chicago was very high, especially among the business class. His firm pioneered the design for park fieldhouses, a Chicago innovation, under contract with the South Park Commission. His architectural and managerial feats are substantial and well documented.

Burnham left the city to raise his children in Evanston. He saw the city, especially the city's density, as a source of disorder, vice, and disease. He believed that people who were in touch with nature "develop saner methods of thought."[19] This is a clear and direct contrast with settlement house residents who not only lived in the city, but in the kind of poor, immigrant neighborhoods that suffered most from disorder, vice, and disease. Rather than turning their backs on disorder and vice, or even working on the issues but retreating each night to some safer haven, the women and men of the settlements made the plight of the immigrants their own. They, too, sought opportunities for respite through contact with nature for themselves and their neighborhoods. They brought touches of nature to the neighborhood through small parks or country outings for children rather than by withdrawing personally.

Burnham's home was not only a place of rest. It was also intellectually active. He and his wife created an atmosphere that has been likened to a salon, and women artists, including one who will appear later in this book, were known to participate. Biographer Thomas S. Hine says of Burnham's wife, Margaret, that Burnham

---

18   Spain, *How Women Saved,* 53.
19   C. Smith, *Plan,* 101.

"delighted in her good looks, her wit, and social poise" but she "didn't have his own degree of intellectual curiosity."[20]

Burnham's assurance about the value of his own work is quite remarkable. He is sure that after implementation of his business-directed *Plan of Chicago,* "every one who lives here is better accommodated in his business and social activities"[21] largely due to the order he would impose and in spite of the wholesale condemnation of neighborhoods the *Plan* would require. He claimed his design of the World's Columbian Exposition "was the beginning, in our day and in this country, of the orderly arrangement of extensive public grounds and buildings,"[22] ignoring the contributions of people like Pierre L'Enfant, early designer of the Washington, D.C., street system, and others. In fact, the "design and arrangement of the World's Columbian Exposition, which have never been surpassed, were due . . . . secondly to the habit of entrusting great works to men trained in the practice of such undertakings."[23] The grandiosity of Burnham's self-descriptions became as much a part of the Burnham legend as the beautiful images in the *Plan.*

Burnham was no doubt a giant—in his own time, in his own mind, and in our time as well. Still, the limitations of his vision and the limited realm of his own experience affected the content and scope of the *Plan of Chicago* in ways that would leave a lasting imprint on the region. One of Burnham's claims, that it is "disinterested men of wide experience"[24] who crafted the plan, reflects his inability to grasp what a truly broad perspective would have been. In reality, it was men with very specific, and not "disinterested," motives who shepherded the *Plan* to completion. As members of Chicago's wealthy business class and the social and economic elite of the city, their experiences were quite uniform. Burnham was not the first to promulgate the myth that a business community alone could represent diversity within Chicago. The characterization of *businessmen* as a diverse group is consistent with other descriptions in early Chicago history of the members of the charter conventions and similar civic endeavors.

---

20   Hines, *Burnham of Chicago,* 252.

21   Burnham and Bennett, *Plan of Chicago,* 8.

22   Ibid., 4.

23   Ibid., 6.

24   Ibid., 2.

Wide and open gulfs on issues of social relevance existed between the businessmen and the immigrant communities, between
businessmen and labor, even at times, as we shall see, between
the businessmen and their own wives. To the extent that Burnham
recognized degrees of difference in opinion, he believed that his
version of "order" would indoctrinate newcomers in the values he
and his sponsors espoused.

Kristen Schaffer, in her introduction to the 1993 edition of the
Plan of Chicago, points out that Burnham looked to Lycurgus of
Sparta for social theory on the relationship of individuals to the
state. In addition to traditional Spartan values of self-sacrifice
and duty to the state, these principles from ancient Greece offered Burnham "a rational and secular means for inculcating a
diverse, multi-ethnic population within the values of the dominant
culture."[25] The more democratic view under which the settlement
community operated was that immigrants would benefit from exposure to the dominant culture *and* had unique and valuable traditions of their own to offer the larger culture.

The Burnham of the final *Plan of Chicago* seems unable to com-
prehend the lives of immigrants, factory workers, and their hard-
pressed families and is therefore naïve in his approach to their
problems. He repeatedly implies or states that men, women, and
children who work twelve to sixteen hours a day, six days a week,
in a dingy factory, and live in hovels without decent sanitary facilities, will be uplifted to good citizenship by the existence of parks,
wide thoroughfares, and pleasing railroad stations. Not only were
these facilities in most cases quite distant from their communities,[26] but they alone could hardly remedy the effects of grueling
work schedules and insufficient incomes on so many families.

Burnham's work did not reflect the emerging lessons of his day
on these topics. Social commentators had already pointed out that

---

25 Ibid., ix–x.

26 According to Kristen Schaffer, Burnham did request information on immigrant populations from University of Chicago professor Charles D. Buck and
the Chicago postmaster. The latter request was specific to the area bounded
by Halsted Street, Harrison Street, Ashland Avenue, and Kinzie Street. In
spite of his interest in the Near West Side there is no evidence that Burnham
requested information from Hull-House or consulted the *Hull-House Maps and
Papers.*

the failure of railroad magnate George Pullman's model town, for instance, was that an orderly and aesthetically pleasing city plan is no substitute for autonomy. Journalist-educator Richard Ely's articles spelled out the dissatisfaction of Pullman workers living in what might be charitably termed a benevolent dictatorship. Burnham doesn't seem familiar with Ely's assessment of the architecturally monotonous and intellectually stifling Pullman environment. He doesn't know or ignored William Stead's critique, *If Christ Came to Chicago,* and appeared oblivious even to the those elements of the business community that formed the Civic Federation and the City Club of Chicago, somewhat more reform-minded business associations, even though Walter Fisher, the *Plan*'s legal advisor, was prominent in several civic groups.[27]

Burnham's good intentions were restricted by a narrow lens— his own and his patrons' in the Commercial Club. Labor leaders, settlement house residents, municipal reformers, and even other businesspeople likely would have emphasized different issues than did Burnham and the Commercial Club. They certainly would have offered different remedies, even when agreeing with Burnham about which maladies needed treatment. Burnham says, "The growth of the city has been so rapid that it has been impossible to plan for the economical disposition of the great influx of people, surging like a human tide to spread itself wherever opportunity for profitable labor offered place. Thoughtful people are appalled at the results of progress; at the waste in time, strength, and money which congestion in city streets begets; at the toll of lives taken by disease when sanitary precautions are neglected; and at the frequent outbreaks against law and order which result from narrow and pleasureless lives. . . . How are we living? Are we in reality prosperous? Is the city a convenient place for business? It is [sic] a good labor market

---

27 However, in her article, *"Gender and Urban Political Reform: The City Club and the Woman's City Club of Chicago in the Progressive Era,"* pp. 1042–1043, Maureen Flanagan says: "Although the men of the City Club, unlike members of the more ardent antilabor business clubs such as the Commercial Club, did not advocate or condone police violence against strikers, they were loath to condemn it when it happened." The police violence to which she refers took place during a waitresses' strike, one in which Ruth Hanna McCormick (a member of the publishing branch of the McCormick family) walked the picket lines with the waitresses.

in the sense that labor is sufficiently comfortable to be efficient and content? Will the coming generation be able to stand the nervous strain of city life?. . . *They are the most pressing questions of our day, and everywhere men are anxiously seeking the answers* [emphasis added]."[28]

Perhaps these were the most pressing questions for the businessmen of the day, but they would not have topped the list for clergymen, suffragists, labor leaders, good government reformers, settlement workers, or many others. Most of these groups of people could have agreed with the businessmen that disorder was a contributing factor to some of the ills they sought to remedy. But many would have found the businessmen's prescription as bad as or worse than the disease. The plan that could have been developed with their participation might have been comprehensive in more than just the eyes of its promoters.

Above and beyond different interpretations of improving city life, a good deal of the *Plan of Chicago* is not about the city, but about the suburban commuter, his comfort, and access. Burnham says "These suburban residents are dependent on the city for a livelihood, and either directly or indirectly pay the taxes that support the municipality. They are vitally interested in adequate and convenient means of transportation, in the protection of life and property, and in well-ordered home surroundings. Thus it happens naturally that as the city grows, the functions of the various governing bodies are extended over areas outside the city limits."[29] Burnham pioneered the idea of looking at city, suburb, and exurb as part of an integrated region, and that is to his credit. But the *Plan* lacks clarity about who is to benefit and who is to pay for which of the improvements his vision is meant to offer. His confusion about suburban residents paying taxes to support the city is unfortunate and naïve. Those honestly paying property taxes on homes were paying to the suburb they lived in, not to Chicago. Those who were not honest in paying business taxes in Chicago—and the documentation indicates this included many leading businessmen—had little right to determine its future.

Likewise, Burnham offers a commendable vision of a suburban town plan with spaces for public schools, ample playgrounds, li-

---

28 Burnham and Bennett, *Plan of Chicago*, 32.
29 Ibid., 37.

braries, municipal buildings, and a public square. But he offers little in the way of a comparable vision for the hundreds of square miles of city neighborhoods outside the "Heart of Chicago" (defined as Halsted Street to the lake, and the main trunk of the river to Twelfth Street), other than the skeleton of roadways, rail, and park systems. Without understanding of and affinity for the "other" people of Chicago—people dissimilar from Burnham and the Commercial Club—he can't provide a vision to meet their needs.

BURNHAM AND CITY-BUILDING WOMEN

The first city-builder Burnham cited in the *Plan of Chicago* was a woman, Semiramis, queen of Babylon, who built a city on the Euphrates River, a city that was very hospitable to commerce. In spite of his admiration for Semiramis's foresight, Burnham's interactions with women in the course of developing the *Plan of Chicago* were minimal or not important enough to be documented. Women got an early preview (before 1898) of a new "lakefront scheme" when "very large drawings were prepared for a meeting at the Women's Club and the Art Institute and for a Merchants Club dinner at the Auditorium." A preview, however, is not at all like a participatory role. These drawings had already won the approval of the Commercial Club of Chicago and been presented to the West and South park commissions. Ten years later, when writing the *Plan of Chicago,* Burnham recalls, "This was the beginning of a general plan for the city."[30]

Beyond the lakefront preview for the Chicago Women's Club, there are very few other recorded interactions between Burnham and the city-building women of the time. Burnham's planners did consult with Jane Addams on the potential widening of Halsted Street. Addams said Hull-House would not oppose the widening if it was within the context of an overall plan for improvement. It is not clear whether or not she was given the full picture of the *Plan*'s vision for a new Civic Center or the potential impact the massive demolition required would have had on the Hull-House neighborhood.

One other meeting is reported to have occurred between Burnham and Addams. He consulted with her at a luncheon on De-

---

30   Ibid., 6–7.

cember 4, 1907, so that she might "see the plans and discuss the city's problems." Her only reaction, as recorded by Burnham's assistant, Edward Bennett, was her approval of an open lakefront and other parks, with the caveat that these should be a respite for the poor and immigrant populations.[31] According to biographer Thomas S. Hines, "Despite his commitment to himself and to Jane Addams that the waterfront should be designed to draw out the working classes, Burnham's ultimate recommendations alluded more strongly to another image, a return, in effect, to some of his original propositions of the 1890s." He saw the lakefront as an opportunity to attract "the cream of our earnings now spent in other lands" by designing the lakefront for the wealthy classes of the city rather than the masses.[32]

Historian Carl Smith asserts that women of the time didn't bother to get involved in the *Plan of Chicago*. He says, "What is remarkable, however, is the extent to which prominent people like Addams and even the mayor and governor seemed to concede the authority of Burnham and other members of the Commercial Club—who were a few dozen individuals in a small private organization—to propose major changes that affected all Chicagoans."[33] But the *Plan* had no real authority. The Commercial Club was planning to launch a monumental public relations campaign to try to "sell" its ideas to the general public after developing it in a well-insulated cocoon. Smith overlooks the fact that the process was closed as well as unofficial. Kristin Schaffer, author of the introduction to the 1993 edition of the *Plan*, gives a more realistic appraisal of the power of the *Plan* when she says, "The *Plan of Chicago* is an advocacy document, and it must be emphasized, one that was beautifully produced."[34] It was, in fact, a sales vehicle using imagery, clear language, and civic pride to sway the public to the businessmen's point of view, never an authoritative or official document.

To the women who will be profiled here, it surely must have seemed that the fight to gain the vote; the research to uncover the cause of localized typhoid outbreaks; and the development of groundbreaking innovations like playgrounds, public baths, and

---

31 Hines, *Burnham of Chicago*, 324–325.

32 Ibid., 332–333.

33 C. Smith, *Plan*, 78.

34 Schaffer, *Urban Ideals*, 402.

the juvenile court were infinitely more important than the paper and pencil exercises of the *Plan of Chicago.* Activist women were deeply involved between 1906 and 1909, however, in the debate about a new municipal charter for Chicago, a much more substantive consideration than the *Plan,* although one that failed due to the myopia of the business community. Had women been invited to participate in meaningful ways in developing the *Plan of Chicago,* some of them might have devoted some of their city-building energy to this vision. We will never know. But it will become quite obvious in the course of this account that they didn't have the time to fight their way into a process that must have seemed of questionable relevance in their era.

There was a fundamental difference in world view between the men of the Commercial Club (and their architects) and the women who were already actively engaged in building Chicago from the ground up (with credit to the men of the settlement house and reform movements who assisted). Women confronted the urban problems created by industrialization by working for the reform of factory and working conditions, better schools and housing, better municipal garbage removal, and improved public health. Many men—at least those actively engaged in major businesses—saw a private-market opportunity to make money from such goods and services. If it is too strong to say they profited from poverty, it is at least fair to say they had little incentive to increase low wages, upgrade poorly maintained real estate, or pay fair-market value for school board land they leased. Even Charles Hull, after whom Hull-House is named, was originally a speculator who purchased large swaths of land in the hope that wealthy families would choose to live there. By the time his cousin, Helen Culver, rented and then donated the house and land to the residents of Hull-House, the area was crowded with tenements and immigrants.

THE CITY
A Character in Its Own Right — A Living, Pulsing Organism

Chicago in the 1890s was a city of opulent mansions and horrific slums. City boosters touted the sophistication of Marshall Field's genteel department store, with its motto "Give the lady what she wants," while ignoring wide-open prostitution just outside the central business district. The 1893 World's Columbian Exposition (nicknamed the "White City") promoted a view of Chicago as clean, orderly, and modern—a vision true only inside the fairgrounds. The real Chicago was not much improved by 1904, when journalist Lincoln Steffens described Chicago as: "first in violence, deepest in dirt; loud, lawless, unlovely, ill-smelling, irreverent, new; an over-grown gawk of a village, the 'tough' among cities, a spectacle for the nation."

Political differences spiraled into violence several times near the turn of the century, most notably in the Haymarket (1886) and Pullman (1894) incidents. The open brutality (toward man and beast) of the stockyards became widely known when Upton Sinclair published *The Jungle* in 1906. But Chicago was also the source of some of the most humane movements in the nation, such as the settlement house movement and movements to abolish child labor and reform juvenile justice.

Chicago's dual nature one hundred years ago and more has implications for the present. What is the nature of the nineteenth-century foundation we are building on today? Is it a foundation established by humanitarian reforms of the Progressive Era? Or is it a foundation built on technical innovations in our physical space? Would it have been possible to build on both the human and the physical assets of the region? A century later, the city of contrasts is still with us. Education historian Dorothy Shipps summarizes the attitude of many toward modern-day Chicago: "The city is a clean, architecturally stimulating monument to human ingenuity and determination, and its citizens display an uncommon sense of civic pride. Yet, it is simultaneously the site of radically segregated ghettos lined with sterile rows of poorly constructed block-houses and high-rises, and neighborhoods with grossly inadequate schooling and other services."[35]

Maybe the only statement one can make about Chicago that will hold up as "truth" is that it was and is a city of contrasts.

AN IMMATURE CITY, POORLY OUTFITTED AND UNKEMPT

Chicago was incorporated as a town in 1833 and as a city in 1837. Chicago's population grew exponentially after incorporation. In 1840 the federal census found fewer than five thousand residents

---

35 Shipps, *School Reform,* 3–4.

in Chicago, 53 of whom were "Negro." Baltimore and New Orleans
at the time were both twenty times larger than Chicago; New York
was sixty times larger.[36] Three decades later, just before the 1871
Chicago Fire, Chicago's population had grown sixty-fold to almost
three hundred thousand. By the 1890 census, Chicago's population of over one million was second only to New York's. Seven hundred thousand Chicagoans had been in the city for one generation
or less in 1890. There was little common lore or tradition to bind
the populace to a unified set of beliefs.

Edith Abbott, in the 1935 study *The Tenements of Chicago,
1908–1935,* quotes another scholar of the time, Homer Hoyt, author of *One Hundred Years of Land Values in Chicago,* to express
the enormity of the change. Hoyt noted that Chicago's growth in
one century "compressed the population growth of Paris for twenty
centuries. From 1840 to 1890, the rapidity of its development out-
stripped that of every other city in the world."

Year	Population
1840	4,470
1850	29,963
1860	109,206
1870	298,977
1880	503,185

Chicago grew geographically as well as numerically in the late
nineteenth century as the rapidly expanding city annexed other
towns and open prairie. At the time of the 1840 census, Chicago
covered six thousand acres. Its boundaries were North Avenue to
Twenty-second Street and Wood Street to Lake Michigan. Incre-
mental annexations roughly doubled the city's size over the next
forty years. Then, between 1880 and 1890 the city increased its
land coverage fivefold[37] through annexation of several large areas
like the Town of Jefferson, City of Lake View, the Town of Lake, and
the Village of Hyde Park.

Annexation was one of many topics debated with vigor in the
city, and from many points of view. Some areas resisted annexation to maintain their autonomy. Some outlying communities were

---

36 Abbott, *Tenements of Chicago,* 16.
37 Ibid., 17.

alleged to seek annexation specifically to gain the help of the Chicago police in squelching labor unrest.[38] Business tycoons tried to influence the annexation debates for their own financial benefit. George Pullman, one of Chicago's most powerful tycoons, opposed annexation of his company town.[39] The Pullman Car Company discharged employees known to be in favor of annexation. The question of annexation was one of the rare instances when the people of Pullman were able to influence their fate; they voted for annexation.[40] Some businessmen opposed annexation because of the tax obligations city government would bring. Pullman had the additional incentive to try to maintain his ironclad control over his workers' lives as well as their livelihood.

Many of the newly annexed areas were nearly rural, but central city neighborhoods experienced grave overcrowding. Density for the city as a whole averaged below twenty people per acre for most of the 1800s. However, density per acre in the Nineteenth Ward (the ward in which Hull-House sat) was 92 persons in 1890, and 115 persons per acre in a nearby ward, while some of the newly annexed areas had only 1 or 2 persons per acre.[41] Since the majority of buildings were three stories or less in the late nineteenth century, high density was synonymous with severe overcrowding.

Ten years later, Robert Hunter, investigator for the City Homes Commission, surveyed Chicago tenement districts for a 1901 report (a report paid for by one of the city-building women) and found in one tenement area, dwelling units averaged under 300 square feet, divided into small, often unventilated rooms, occupied by large families and their boarders, so that an individual had on the average 28 to 32 square feet of space. At 457 people per acre, these areas were said to be the most densely populated in the world. In these dwellings, cooking was done in the main room, which was provided with a stove, also used for heating. This room might have a sink, but often shared sinks (or simply pumps) were in the halls or the back yard. Stinking basement privies were shared by an average of eight people; as many as half were illegal privies without proper sewer connections. Ninety-seven percent of the Chicago

---

38   Flanagan, *Charter*, 32.

39   Ibid., 16.

40   Karlen, *Crabgrass Communities*, 68.

41   Abbott, *Tenements of Chicago*, 16.

tenement units were without bathtubs, despite the fact that many
of the almost one million residents were employed in slaughter-
house work.[42]

After the 1871 Chicago Fire, housing had been quickly replaced,
with more attention to speed than durability. Post-fire regulations
called for buildings of four or more stories to use fire-resistant
materials. Three-story, multi-family buildings became the most
common way to maximize the use of land while minimizing construction costs.[43] According to an 1881 report by the city health
commissioner, tenements were built on speculation as an investment.[44] There was a general assumption that industry and the central business district would continue to expand outward and that
the tenement districts were temporary neighborhoods. Even before
commuter railroads accelerated the pace of suburban growth, Chicago households that could afford to tended to move away from the
central areas along the diagonal "plank roads."[45]

The central area of the city (except for the lakefront) was increasingly relinquished to new migrants to Chicago—Europeans and
southern blacks. According to Edith Abbott, who was a Hull-House
resident as well as a documentarian of conditions in tenement
neighborhoods, the Near West Side was a polyglot neighborhood.
Among the immigrant groups living there were Italians, Russian
Jews, Bohemians, Greeks, and Germans. Blacks had clustered
further east, near State Street and Harrison Street, until a fire in
1874 drove them further south.[46] All of these new arrivals had to
contend with a vice district that was just over the river, between
the tenement neighborhoods and the central business district.

In 1909 most prominent business leaders provided little leadership in addressing neighborhood conditions in the poorer parts
of the city. (Exceptional leaders like Julius Rosenwald will be discussed in a later section of this book.) Thomas Hines, a biographer
of Daniel Burnham, describes Chicago's problems of slums, pov-

---

42   Hayden, Delores, *Domestic Revolution,* 153.

43   Abbott, *Tenements of Chicago,* 64.

44   Ibid., 27.

45   The plank roads—Archer, Blue Island, Ogden, Milwaukee, and Clybourn—
     were long-distance roads built with raised wooden boards to allow carriage
     and wagon travel even during muddy periods.

46   Abbott, *Tenements of Chicago,* 10–11.

erty, ugliness, and inefficiency as a result of "rapid, unguided and haphazard growth." Real estate speculators and some members of the business community benefited from this rapid, unregulated growth. (So did some of the immigrant families who took in boarders or subdivided buildings they owned and lived in, aggravating already overcrowded and unsanitary conditions.) It seems that everyone was out to "make a buck," and government was unable or unwilling to rein in the excesses, or even to properly identify the source of threats to public health and safety.

Although there was a growing body of evidence that disease and epidemics were spread by poor sanitation facilities, Chicago's progress in combating epidemics in the nineteenth century was spotty at best. In poor neighborhoods, the city's sanitation systems (sewers, water pipes, garbage collection) ranged from non-existent to primitive. Corrupt inspectors worsened the situation. Biographer Louise C. Wade writes, "Chicago did not master the municipal science of garbage disposal until well into the twentieth century."[47] As the city developed, garbage was used as landfill, thrown in the river, or dumped in poor wards. In spite of the city's failure to provide an adequate municipal sanitation system, some in government found it more convenient to blame immigrants themselves for epidemics than to address the dark, crowded tenement conditions and inadequate sanitation that incubated disease.

Chicago's growing pains were perhaps greatest between 1889, when Jane Addams co-founded Hull-House with her friend Ellen Gates Starr, and 1909, when Daniel Burnham and his sponsors in the Commercial Club began promoting the *Plan of Chicago*. Those twenty years represented a dramatic growth spurt, doubling the population from one million to two million, or an average of fifty thousand new bodies to house, educate, and/or employ each year during that period. Both Addams and Burnham made efforts to fundamentally re-order conditions in the city. But their methods differed as much as their motives. The implications of their respective methods for the majority of individuals and families in the region differed greatly. Jane Addams and other settlement leaders chose to live in the neighborhoods and improve them from within, in collaboration with the people already living there. Burnham and the Commercial Club sought to impose "order" from afar, repre-

---

47   Wade, *Graham Taylor*, 55–56.

sented by bird's-eye views in the *Plan of Chicago,* beautiful but dehumanized representations of order requiring wholesale demolition of existing neighborhoods.

3

Herstory:
Women with a Broad View

IN SPITE OF THE LIMITATIONS ON WOMEN'S CIVIC ROLES, by the early twentieth century a substantial group of women was actively building city institutions, networks, and policies in Chicago. While Daniel Burnham and his sponsor, the Commercial Club, promoted monuments and thoroughfares they hoped others would fund and build, the women were hard at work, significantly reducing infant mortality, creating the first juvenile court in the nation, building the first playgrounds in Chicago, obtaining compulsory school attendance laws, investigating tenement conditions, and promoting legislation outlawing child labor and sweatshops. After securing these reforms, the women were often obliged to personally fund implementation of the reforms, because Chicago and Illinois had such a weak notion of municipal responsibility. There were even cases of new legislative reforms with specific prohibitions against state funding. This was the case with the state law mandating the first juvenile court in the nation, which also prohibited state funding.

Many histories of Chicago do an admirable job of covering the architects, academics, businessmen, and others who left grand buildings, grand theories, and big corporations as a legacy. An equally important piece of Chicago's history and of the history of city planning is often omitted from mainstream accounts and never makes it into our common knowledge. The missing piece is the contribution of women to building the fabric of our city, often in crucial but less tangible ways. The women left less in the way of buildings (or the buildings, parks, and other physical spaces they created were deemed less significant to preserve) and more in the way of institutional innovations and reforms that Chicagoans today benefit from but celebrate rarely, if at all.

A YOUNG CITY WITHOUT LEADERSHIP TRADITIONS

Chicago's leadership lacked tradition, maturity, and sophistication when Hull-House was established just half a century after the city was incorporated. Chicago's business ethic had sprouted as haphazardly as prairie grass and spread as quickly as a prairie fire. When entrepreneurial migrants from upstate New York or Massachusetts arrived in the frontier city of Chicago, they quickly shed any "gentlemanly" business ethics that had evolved in eastern cities. From its earliest days, a core component of Chicago's business tradition was to leverage public assets for private gain. Within two months of Chicago's incorporation as a town in 1833, a petition was presented by a contingent of citizens requesting that land conferred to Chicago from the federal government for future schools be sold, rather than being held in trust for the children of Chicago. Despite indications that some of the ninety-five signatures were fraudulent, the County Commissioner of School Lands, Richard Hamilton, was forced to sell the land.[1] Legal niceties were not allowed to slow the market for land in speculation-stoked Chicago, not even in 1833.

Following the World's Columbian Exposition, English reformer William Stead charged that "the plutocrats" in Chicago were worse than the aristocracy in Europe because they had no notion of noblesse oblige—the sense that obligations came with prosperity.[2] According to historian Kathleen D. McCarthy, wealthy Chicagoans were "disinclined to pass their time examining the minutiae of municipal management" but they did invest time and energy—and money—to bring European culture to Chicago.[3] Chicago business magnates created world-class cultural institutions in the 1880s and 1890s. The Chicago Orchestra held its first concert in 1891 (Marshall Field, Philip Armour, Cyrus McCormick, Jr., and George Pullman were prominent supporters). The Art Institute was built

---

1   Herrick, *Chicago Public Schools,* 22.

2   Stead, *If Christ,* 91.

3   K. McCarthy, *Noblesse Oblige,* 32.

in 1893[4] (Charles L. Hutchinson and Martin Ryerson built up the collection). In 1897 the Public Library, the new Chicago Historical Society building, and the John Crerar and Newberry libraries were built.[5] Cultural assets improved Chicago's national reputation and provided leisure activities for the upper classes, the same group Burnham hoped to keep in Chicago spending money locally, rather than on the Riviera. They benefited other classes too, particularly the free institutions. Charles Hutchinson, president of the Art Institute during this period in history, actively sought to bring art out of downtown and into communities, schools, and field houses.

Kathleen D. McCarthy makes the important point that conditions in turn-of-the-century Chicago shaped a particularly distinctive business and civic style. Tremendous wealth allowed Chicago businessmen of the Gilded Age to be isolated from other Chicagoans in ways their pioneer predecessors had not been.[6] Bitter labor disputes intensified the businessmen's sense of entitlement to rule their corporate domains with absolute authority. A civic tradition that municipal authority should defer to business acumen solidified businesses' sense of entitlement to speak for the city as a whole, even when representing only business interests. City government was weak, it was often corrupt, and government corruption was periodically exposed. Even the mayor in 1871 had little confidence in government when the Great Fire struck, as we shall learn below.

THE GREAT FIRE
A Chasm in Responses

The historic event most significant in molding a distorted ethos of civic involvement in Chicago—an ethos the activist women of this book would come to publicly dispute and refute—was the Great Fire of 1871. Most of the women profiled here were children at the time of the fire, and they might only have heard about it second-hand or in news accounts (for example Jane Addams, who was born in 1860, grew up over one hundred miles away in Cedarville,

---

4   The Art Institute was formed out of predecessor organizations existing from before the Chicago Fire.

5   Wade, *Graham Taylor*, 65–66.

6   K. McCarthy, *Noblesse Oblige*, 3.

The Chicago Fire destroyed businesses, government buildings, and many neighborhoods. (Chicago History Museum, ICHi-14894, Creator: R.P. Studley Company, St. Louis.)

Illinois), but they wrestled with its legacy for much of their adult-hood.

The catastrophic fire is well understood for its effect on the physical design of Chicago. The fire led to more stringent building codes, some of which activist women volunteers worked to see enforced or strengthened three decades later. What is not as well understood is how the weak municipal response left business interests in charge of rebuilding and deciding who was "worthy" of relief.

Although the fire did not dampen the growth of the city, it had short- and long-term implications for how people lived and supported themselves. The neighborhoods most severely affected by the fire were neighborhoods west of the central business district, which were primarily occupied by poor, immigrant families.[7] The O'Learys, whose cow has long been blamed for kicking over the lantern that ignited the blaze on October 8, 1871, lived at DeKoven and Jefferson streets, a few blocks south and east of where the Hull-House complex would later stand (Halsted and Polk streets). The fire swept largely to the east and north, wiping out industries and workers' cottages along both branches of the river, as well as

---

7   Wealthier families lost homes too, but were primarily clustered in a thin strip between State Street and the lake, while the immigrant neighborhoods covered the mile distance between State Street and Halsted Street.

leveling the central business district. In one evening, three hundred people lost their lives and tens of thousands of families lost homes and workplaces. The fire was catastrophic for individuals and almost beyond the city's collective ability to cope. Many seeds were sown in the aftermath of the fire that contributed to poor, over-crowded, and unsanitary conditions in future decades—conditions that Daniel Burnham and Jane Addams, among others, sought to remedy between 1889 and 1909.

Chicago's leadership, including its elected officials, did not trust local government to respond to the disaster. Instead, Mayor Roswell Mason authorized a private, business-led organization, the Chicago Relief and Aid Society,[8] to dispense almost five million dollars contributed to Chicago from across the nation for fire relief. The amount of corruption in early city government reduced public confidence in the ability of the city to manage relief itself. There was still, in early Chicago, a debate about whether government should be involved in areas like "charity." The donated funds came from individuals, organizations, and other municipalities, rather than from a single entity like a modern-day disaster agency, and had no disbursement guidelines. The businessmen of the Chicago Relief and Aid Society had to determine policies and procedures for dispensing the money. The policies they applied came from distrust and animosity toward workers and immigrants rather than from a desire to relieve and aid fellow Chicagoans.

Many women overtly and covertly disagreed with men about how to organize relief and who should be eligible to receive it. Even some of the wives of business leaders were active in their own charitable enterprises, and sought funds explicitly to circumvent the harsh and moralistic terms of the business-led charities.

The Chicago Relief and Aid Society, an organization controlled by Chicago's most successful businessmen, had dispensed charity since before the Civil War. As businessmen first and foremost, the society had a stake in maintaining a viable labor force, but no stake in bringing the labor force above subsistence levels. Many women might have preferred that the Northwest Sanitary Commission, a federal public health and relief agency that had been run by Mary Livermore until 1870, take on the task of fire relief, as the

---

8   C. Smith, *Urban Disorder*, 64.

commission had successfully provided relief during and after the Civil War.

The businessmen could not objectively fulfill civic and business roles simultaneously. Some businessmen opposed government rebuilding policies that would reduce their profits. For example, they opposed reducing the tariff on building materials to increase availability, because some of them owned undamaged stockpiles of materials stored outside the city limits. In relief distribution decisions their interest was less in addressing human needs and more about "maintaining the kind of stable and productive work force required by the unprecedentedly large-scale enterprises of the postwar period."[9]

At least fifty thousand[10] people were unable to find shelter in the aftermath of the fire, and winter was just a couple of months away. Moralistic concerns joined economic self-interest in driving reconstruction efforts, resulting in shoddy replacement housing. Relief money was more likely to be used to build small, cheap frame cottages than large apartment buildings, for example, based on the concern that large buildings would breed "promiscuous and involuntary association," disorder, and vice.[11] Relief leaders' own business interests were also better served by inferior housing with low property values and expendable buildings. Poor housing was no economic impediment to future expansion of industry and the central business district into tenement neighborhoods. The housing problems of two decades later, which would be addressed by Hull-House residents, were to a certain extent created by the decision to hastily build thousands of small, makeshift homes for one or two families, rather than build more substantial apartment houses.

Chicago's economy was in shambles after the fire, and its travails were compounded by a national depression in 1873. That year, ten thousand people gathered at City Hall on December 21, 1873, to protest the policies of the Chicago Relief and Aid Society and demand a public works program to provide jobs.[12] The society

---

9   Ibid., 73.

10   At least 50,000 more had lost homes but found shelter with friends or relatives, or left Chicago entirely.

11   Abbott, *Tenements of Chicago,* 19–20.

12   Ashbaugh, *Lucy Parsons,* 16.

continued to hold a substantial portion of the relief funds more than two years after the fire rather than using it to house, feed, or employ families that were still on insecure footing.[13]

The Chicago Relief and Aid Society was administered by the city's leading business titans, men like George Pullman, Marshall Field, Rufus King, and Wirt Dexter. There was no right of appeal of their decisions and there were no public officials within their ranks (except the mayor, who was an ex-officio member). They had already earned the enmity of many fire victims by requiring relief applicants to procure a written "endorsement" from a middle or upper class person to be eligible to receive relief funds.[14] Given the social separation between lower income individuals and upperclass men, this hurdle was insurmountable for many. The application process was also complicated and demeaning; and for many immigrants, the English-language forms were another significant barrier. The society did itself no favors by publishing a report in 1874 detailing its policies and expenditures. Along with details as inconsequential as the number of packages of corn starch distributed, were opinions on who suffered most from the fire. The society's sympathies were clearly with the formerly privileged—"the keenest sufferers of all. They were not accustomed to exposures and hardships which were easily borne by the laboring people."[15]

Other unpopular policies of the society clearly indicated the businessmen's interest in the labor force's immediate availability rather than the stability and security of individuals and households. Relief was withdrawn from all men, boys, and unmarried women only fifteen days after the fire to ensure their rapid re-entry into the labor pool, even though most people had lost their jobs as well as their homes.[16] It is not hard to see why the businessmen's stewardship of the funds came under question from the public, especially since some of their wives discreetly operated relief efforts

---

13   The official report of the Chicago Relief and Aid Society shows a balance of $591,328.66 remaining in 1874. Critics claimed that the society used the last $600,000 to build a headquarters, and suspended fundraising for a decade. Another account says society funds were invested in the board members' companies at low interest rates.

14   Ashbaugh, *Lucy Parsons,* 16.

15   Report of the Chicago Relief and Aid Society, 198.

16   C. Smith, *Urban Disorder,* 74.

of their own with different approaches. Katherine Medill (wife of *Chicago Tribune* owner and mayor-elect Joseph Medill) handled as much relief on her own as possible. Aurelia King, the wife of Chicago Relief and Aid Society president Henry King asked out-of-town friends to send donations directly to her rather than to the society. Activist church women directly challenged the Chicago Relief and Aid Society in a more public way than the wives had and gave to a broader class of recipients. A church-based network responded to the direst cases without scrutiny. The YMCA objected specifically to the Chicago Relief and Aid Society's punitive attitudes about fire victims' situations.[17]

The Chicago Relief and Aid Society was not unique in its analysis of potential causes of and responses to poverty, although it was more forceful in its self-styled "scientific" administration of aid ("scientific" in this case meant based less on benevolence and more on business management principles). Similar organizations, including the Charity Organization Society, held that poverty was primarily due to individual and hereditary defects, except for the "worthy poor" like wounded Civil War veterans or widowed mothers, for example.[18] The Charity Organization Society merged in 1887 into the larger and stronger Chicago Relief and Aid Society. But by that time, organized groups of women were starting to provide visible and viable alternatives that attempted to lift immigrants and other marginalized populations above subsistence levels with less demeaning requirements.

During the decade after the fire, Chicago women began to organize into clubs and to demand that municipal government provide responses to urban problems. They also lobbied for the right to vote to better influence public policies.[19] The Chicago Women's Club was established in 1876 by upper-class women who had the expressed desire to be "socially useful" (the club changed its name to the Chicago Woman's Club in 1895).[20] As the women gained experience, they began to tackle municipal problems and provide a female point of view on key public roles. They successfully advo-

---

17   Sawislak, *Smoldering City,* 110–112.

18   Getis, *The Juvenile Court,* 14–15.

19   Flanagan, *Hearts,* 9.

20   Schultz and Hast, *Women Building Chicago,* 994.

cated for a woman on the board of education and a woman doctor at the county insane asylum.

LABOR ORGANIZATIONS AND BUSINESS RESISTANCE

Two of the most tumultuous events in Chicago history were labor struggles that took place around the time Hull-House was founded. The 1886 Haymarket incident, which has come to be seen by most historians as a police riot, offers more unsolved than solved questions. What is known is that seven policemen (and an unknown number of civilians) were killed when a bomb was thrown at the end of a peaceful demonstration. Four labor activists were executed for the police deaths in 1887, after a trial with questionable witnesses and charges of judicial misconduct. Three of their co-defendants were later released. All eight, including one who committed suicide in prison,[21] were later pardoned by Governor Altgeld. By 1889 public sentiment had swung toward a more sympathetic view of labor, partly because of the perceived overreaction of the police and business agents.[22] Economic forums were held in Chicago during the winter of 1888–89 to try to bring business and labor together. This slight liberalization of attitudes coincided with the founding of Hull-House.

However, not much later, the year after the World's Columbian Exposition, the shining new reputation Chicago enjoyed because of the fair was sullied again, this time by the Pullman Strike (1894), which spread from Chicago to cripple the national railroad system. Police and federal troops used force to end the strike. The Chicago Federation of Labor was organized shortly thereafter in 1896 to provide an umbrella for peaceful organizing. In addition to its primary mission in the labor organizing arena, the Federation was also actively involved in civic reform efforts, such as the push for a municipal charter for Chicago and other populist reforms.

Business's organized response to labor came through an organization known as the Citizens' Association. The organization's original purpose was to promote a good climate for business and an efficient government. By the period after the fire, the Citizens' Association turned its attention to labor strife in the city. A com-

---

21   Louis Lingg committed suicide rather than go to the gallows.

22   Ashbaugh, *Lucy Parsons,* 175–176.

mittee of the Citizens' Association was formed by Philip Armour, Marshall Field, and George Pullman in the aftermath of the Haymarket tragedy. The Citizens' Association volunteered its services to the police, and pledged and raised over $100,000 each year until 1891 to help stamp out "anarchy."[23] It is possible that anarchy was the product of the Citizens' Association rather than just its target. The police responded more readily to business benefactors than to civil authorities. Some histories suggest that the Citizens' Association induced the violence at Haymarket. The police captain, John Bonfield, who gave the order to charge the crowd defied Mayor Carter Harrison's instructions to simply oversee the end of the demonstration. Harrison was on hand for all but the final portion of the protest.[24] (Bonfield, who was dismissed from the force in 1889 for corruption, had a long history of beating workers. Whether or not he acted on orders from the Citizens' Association is a source of speculation, but not fact.)

Others point to potential business interference in the judicial process: one of Marshall Field's salesmen was the foreman of the Haymarket jury, while Field was outspoken in his contempt for the defendants.[25] It is unlikely in today's court system that a person whose employer had publicly declared the defendants' guilt would be seen as unbiased and able to serve on the jury in that case, let alone as its foreman.

Business leaders acted individually and collectively to stamp out labor activism. Marshall Field convinced the Commercial Club to donate land to the federal government for Fort Sheridan (after strikes in 1877), and the Merchants' Club donated land to build the Great Lakes Naval Training Station.[26] The business leaders wanted troops nearby and used their clout and connections to secure bases for the troops. Once troops were nearby they wielded their clout to usurp the powers of the city and state when they deemed it necessary. After Governor Altgeld and Chicago Mayor Hopkins refused to call out the National Guard during the Pullman

---

23   Flanagan, *Charter,* 31.
24   Ashbaugh, *Lucy Parsons,* 77.
25   C. Smith, *Urban Disorder,* 130.
26   Flanagan, *Charter,* 29.

Strike, business leaders used their national connections to have President Cleveland declare an emergency.[27]

Not every business leader was willing to twist the law or trample rights to defeat the labor unions, but many of the most powerful Chicago businessmen were the most vehemently anti-union. A moderate business leader, Lyman Gage, called a meeting after the Haymarket tragedy and tried to get the business community to oppose the death penalty. Marshall Field spoke in favor of the death penalty (this is, remember, the same case his salesman sat in judgment on). The group voted with Field, but many confided to Gage afterward that they went along fearing business retaliation.[28]

URBAN FORM
The White City or the Real City?

The 1890s were a particularly productive time for developing early responses to problems that persisted into the 1900s. The 1893 World's Columbian Exposition (also known as the White City), built under Daniel Burnham's direction, may be the most famous symbol of that decade, but it was not the only important social force. Burnham biographer Thomas S. Hines lists Chicago's challenges in 1893 and some of the responses offered, including that of Jane Addams, her *Hull-House Maps and Papers* and what Hines calls her "social laboratory on Halsted Street." In contrast, Hines says, "The world's fair . . . under Burnham's leadership had signaled the beginning of a different kind of civic reform."[29] Hines is one of few historians who consider Addams and Burnham in the same context, and his reference is regrettably brief, as he returns almost immediately to the impact of the fair on Chicago's form and future.

Hines is correct in pointing out that *Hull-House Maps and Papers* (which were written the year after the fair) provided a view of the real city, of its immigrant and poor residents, of working conditions for adults and children, even complete with maps of nationality and income by *housing unit*. Another chronicler who specifically contrasted the real city to the White City was Englishman William Stead who came to Chicago because of the fair's congress

---

27 Flanagan, *Charter*, 32.

28 Wade, *Graham Taylor*, 63.

29 Hines, *Burnham of Chicago*, 313.

Roots of Chicago Women's Activism in the World's Fair

Meetings and events related to the fair had ramifications for the future of women in city planning:

- **Jane Addams** led a meeting at the fair of settlement workers from Boston, New York City, and Chicago. By the fall of 1894, Hull-House, Chicago Commons, and four other settlements established the Chicago Federation of Settlements. A National Federation was started in 1911.

- **Bertha Palmer**, president of the Board of Lady Managers and wife of Potter Palmer resisted efforts to include black women in the Women's Pavilion and resisted feminists on the board (who were called Isabellas in honor of Spain's queen) who did not want to segregate women's achievements in a Women's Pavilion.

- **Ida B. Wells** wrote an eighty-one page pamphlet – "The Reason Why the Colored American Is Not in the World's Columbian Exposition" and formed the Ida B. Wells Club to continue her advocacy activities.

- **The National Association of Colored Women** was formed in reaction to the exclusion of black women from the fair, on the grounds that they had no national organization.

- **Fannie Barrier Williams**, a light skinned African American who was part of Chicago's black aristocracy was appointed Secretary of the Art Department after uproar about a white woman being named to a different post, purportedly to represent black women's interests at the fair.

- **Sophia Hayden**, the first woman architect to graduate from the Massachusetts Institute of Technology, won the right to design the Women's Pavilion over the objection of some male architects. Her building won the Artists' Medal for Design, but she never designed another building after the fair.

on religion. His book *If Christ Came to Chicago* is a scathing indictment of the crime, corruption, and despair he found. A national depression descended on Chicago just as the fair ended, creating even greater hardship in the "real city." Stead gave an impassioned speech in 1893 that galvanized reform elements to form the Civic

Federation (which is still in existence, addressing municipal fiscal issues). The Civic Federation began with a broad charter to improve schools, fight for public health and sanitation reforms, and conquer political corruption, an approach more in keeping with the settlement women than with Burnham and the businessmen. The Civic Federation, with substantial male leadership, straddled both worlds though.

The fair itself had some unintended consequences for organizing later efforts to work on the problems of the real city. Women had a limited role in Burnham's fair. But the fair did prove to be a meeting ground for diverse actors in the ever-expanding networks built and maintained by women. Most city-building women (and their male allies) were deeply engrossed with efforts to build and improve the real city. The year of the World's Columbian Exposition was particularly turbulent and portentous. The Illinois General Assembly passed anti-sweatshop legislation and child labor prohibitions in 1893. Municipal investigations of lodging houses were begun, partly because housing pressures created by the fair greatly increased overcrowding in some areas.[30] A fierce battle raging in the Illinois General Assembly over increased representation for Chicago's rapidly growing population (which presented a serious threat to downstate control) was at fever pitch. The judicial system came under attack from the state's executive branch when Governor John Altgeld pardoned the surviving Haymarket prisoners[31] with a denunciation that the Haymarket trial was biased.[32] Mayor Carter Harrison I was assassinated late in the year, on the last day of the World's Columbian Exposition, just before the national depression that gripped Chicago along with the rest of the nation.

Innovations that would shape Chicago at the turn of the century came in rapid succession. The first playground in Chicago was built at Hull-House in 1894. The Chicago Arts and Crafts Society was founded in 1897 at Hull-House, celebrating handcraftsmanship and creating a style that influenced architectural ornamentation and furnishings of the period. Cook County became the site

---

30 Abbott, *Tenements of Chicago,* 53.

31 Of the eight men convicted, four were executed in 1887; one committed suicide.

32 Ashbaugh, *Lucy Parsons,* 189.

of the first juvenile court in the nation, after activist women and male allies succeeded in securing court reform legislation in 1899. The rest of the nation came to know more of the dark underbelly of Chicago with the publication of American literary classics such as *Sister Carrie* and *The Jungle* in 1900 and 1906.

A DIVIDED REFORM MOVEMENT

Because municipal government was weak under Illinois state law, voluntary organizations sprang up in Chicago when local government failed to provide essential services. Debates raged in governmental and private bodies over the causes of poverty and whether "blame" was to be placed on the individual or society. Other debates revolved around the proper role of government in providing basic services such as sanitation, or whether private enterprise could do a better job. Some Chicago debates paralleled a national debate—often led or instigated by women—about whether poverty should be addressed with compassion, science, or practical help. Chicago's statutorily weak municipal government complicated the issue, since government was not only unwilling, but also unable to act aggressively. The women of the settlements and the broader city-building networks attacked poverty from a variety of fronts. They advocated for a broader view of government responsibility. Where responsibility existed (as for health and safety inspections) but corruption reduced government's effectiveness, they produced exposés. They created original research like the *Hull-House Maps and Papers* and formed academic organizations like the one that began as a settlement project and eventually became the School of Social Service Administration at the University of Chicago. They accepted roles as ward garbage inspector and state factory inspector to do the job themselves, when necessary.

During the decades between the Chicago Fire and the *Plan of Chicago,* the old prescriptions of groups like the Chicago Relief and Aid Society and the Charity Organization Society began to disappear or be drastically revised to serve new purposes. By 1907 these older charitable organizations were folded into a new United Charities, with professional employees and a board that included city-building women and progressive businessmen like Julius Rosenwald. While this reduced the humiliation applicants had to face, it did not resolve the problem of the private agencies having to

Business, Labor, Civic, Organizations 1850–1910

- ❧ Chicago Relief and Aid Society (1857)

- ❧ Citizens' Association (1870s)

- ❧ Chicago Woman's Club (1870s)

- ❧ Commercial Club (1877, merged with the Merchants Club in 1907 to become the Commercial Club of Chicago)*

- ❧ The Charity Organization Society (1883)

- ❧ The Chicago Relief and Aid Society and the Charity Organization Society merged in 1887 and eventually became United Charities (with a board influenced by board members Addams, Bowen, Blaine, and Rosenwald)

- ❧ Municipal Order League (1892)

- ❧ National Organization of Colored Women (1893)**

- ❧ Ida B. Wells Club (1893)**

- ❧ Civic Federation (1893)

- ❧ Immigrant Protective League (1907)

- ❧ Municipal Voters League (1896)

- ❧ Municipal Improvement League (1894)

- ❧ Chicago Federation of Labor (1896)***

- ❧ Merchants Club (1896)

- ❧ City Club of Chicago (1903)

- ❧ Woman's City Club of Chicago (1911)

*The Commercial Club is discussed in detail in Chapter 1, as the organization that initiated and funded the Plan of Chicago.

**Both organizations were started in response to the exclusion of blacks from the World's Fair.

***There were many more labor organizations, but the CFL was an important umbrella organization involved in general reform movements.

compensate for a weak and often corrupt municipal agency. The privations of poverty were still worsened, rather than reduced, by municipal policies that left many streets in poor neighborhoods filthy and festering and made county health agencies unhealthy institutions.

There were as many definitions of reform swirling around Chicago around the turn of the century as there were groups claiming to be reformers. Some wanted to protect children, women, or immigrants. Some wanted a city more hospitable to business. A few wanted genuine reform of the political process and others wanted control of the political machinery. Many voluntary groups that are familiar to today's Chicagoans were organized during this fertile time in Chicago's history (see the chart of organizations on p. 45). Some background on the spirited civic debates of the time provides context for the activities of the people to be profiled in later chapters.

Business associations and the charities controlled by business titans dominated the city until the 1890s. The Civic Federation and the Municipal Voters League were both formed in the 1890s. They defined reform more broadly than did the business groups. While the Citizens' Association, of which George Pullman was a member, looked for governmental force as a response to the Pullman Strike, the Civic Federation sought business-labor peace as a benefit to the city and as good for business. The Civic Federation was born from a mass meeting in 1893, called by William T. Stead, the reformer who wrote *If Christ Came to Chicago*.[33] Civic Federation leaders were not advocates for labor interests but sought a middle ground and set up an arbitration committee that attempted to intervene in the Pullman Strike.

When reform groups could agree on an appropriate role for municipal government in solving urban problems, they found themselves hampered by the city's very limited charter. In response to that barrier, the Civic Federation promoted a plan in 1902 to study whether Chicago had outgrown the statewide general incorporation act for all towns with a population over two thousand. The most important issues, upon which many reformers could agree, were

---

33   Jane Addams was on the first Civic Federation Steering Committee. She later
      parted ways because the Federation's view of the working class and the prob-
      lems of unemployment seemed to her unnecessarily restrictive.

the inability of the city to set its own policies on issuing bonds, establishing an adequate tax rate, and control over schools and parks. These were state matters at the time rather than municipal matters. The Civic Federation's study sparked a spirited debate on the municipal charter that took place during the time the *Plan of Chicago* was drafted. This debate was directly relevant to city-building and city planning. Charter reform consumed the energies of many reformers from 1899 to 1909, including settlement workers, businessmen, women's clubs and networks, the Chicago Federation of Labor, suffragists, ethnic organizations, and good government proponents.

THE CHARTER DEBATE

During the time the Burnham *Plan of Chicago* was under development, two "charter conventions" were held to draft legislation that would have significantly improved Chicago's ability to govern itself. The two conventions (1906–07 and 1908–09) attracted the intense interest of activist women, who made several appeals for inclusion. The businessmen who held the majority of seats in the charter conventions were as sure as the Commercial Club that business voices alone could provide a "representative" sample of the populace.

Women had many reasons to be invested in the results of the charter conventions. First, municipal housekeeping tools were very limited without municipal authority to clean up specific problems. Second, many of Chicago's problems were intractable without sufficient tax revenues, and the existing law put most taxing authority in the hands of the state. Third, activist women were lobbying to include women's suffrage in a city charter.

Without a municipal charter there was no organizing principle for city/county/special district governance of the municipal spaces women were most interested in creating, like schools, parks, and libraries. The city could not issue bonds to construct public buildings without a charter. Taxes could not be raised to build essential sewers and drainage systems, even as the city grew by leaps and bounds. The city had to create a patchwork of new entities, like the Metropolitan Sanitary District (now known as the Metropolitan Water Reclamation District), to provide crucial sanitation systems. The city was limited not only in the amount of taxes it could collect or the bonds it could issue, but also in how it could allocate funds and coordinate other tax entities like the public school system and park systems.

Illinois's laws regulating municipal authority were written before large cities existed in Illinois. The laws were much more suited to small- and medium-sized towns. The federal constitution gives to states all responsibilities not specifically claimed under federal authority under Article Ten of the Bill of Rights. Illinois's constitution did not allow a similar flexibility for municipalities, which could only exercise power when specifically authorized to do so by the state. To compound the political problems Chicago faced, downstate antagonism toward Chicago grew as the city grew. By the turn of the century, downstate legislators had made several attempts to cap the number of legislators the growing powerhouse would send to the General Assembly. The continuing fight over apportioning legislative districts did not bode well for charter reform.

Maureen A. Flanagan has written a comprehensive history, *Charter Reform in Chicago,* which is fascinating reading on a little-known chapter of Chicago history—a chapter that has had major ramifications for municipal government and reform in Chicago. The summary here comes primarily from her research.

Although neither the first, full-fledged (1906–07) nor the second pro-forma (1908–09) attempt at charter reform was successful, Flanagan believes the debate itself had positive side effects. The charter debate caused Chicagoans to think beyond their own self-interest or group interest. The vigorous and extended debate is indicative of the importance given the topic even though the delegates and the general public couldn't come to a unified vision for the city.

Women's suffrage was unpopular with many of the convention delegates, and not only because of prejudices or preconceptions about appropriate roles for women. Class came into the equation, too. The addition of large numbers of working-class women to the rolls of voters was especially and explicitly feared by the businessmen who were barely able to maintain their favorable balance of power as immigrant populations grew, became naturalized, and produced native-born sons and daughters—citizens with the same rights as the businessmen. The businessmen who had unilaterally controlled Chicago for its first sixty years were faced with threats to their control on several sides—not only the swelling immigrant tide, but women who equaled or exceeded the number of men in

Chicago, and lastly, the most despised group of all, labor union members. The businessmen couldn't change the conditions of citizenship, but they intended to keep both labor and women outside the councils of power for as long as they could.

Unfortunately, the businessmen involved in charter reform didn't perceive how narrow their group was, any more than the previous generation understood that the paternalism and moralism of the Chicago Relief and Aid Society was counterproductive. The charter convention had one German delegate (who was a lawyer and a director of Republic Steel and Iron), one black businessman, and one Jewish businessman. Two representatives of the Chicago Federation of Labor, one professor, and a minister were also members. Fifty-eight members were lawyers or businessmen; most were from a handful of business organizations with overlapping club membership. Small nuances of difference between each business or civic group represented "diversity" to them, and because their worlds were so constricted, they were unaware of other groups' legitimate claims to other reform agendas. At the convention's inception, the *Chicago Tribune* pronounced the membership "a really representative body. There is no prominent organization, municipal, individual or political which will not be represented."[34] At the close of the convention, its chair Milton Foreman crowed, "An inspection of the membership will disclose the fact that they represent every walk and condition and poll of thought in life."[35]

This insularity had disastrous consequences, for the recommendations of the charter convention had to be ratified by the electorate. The men of the charter convention were sure the voters would follow their lead. Although Chicagoans of many backgrounds and interests were expressing themselves frankly to the convention, the delegates were unable or unwilling to hear.

There was organized opposition to the leadership of the business community, even when it acted in a civic capacity. The Independence League and the Municipal Ownership League challenged the Civic Federation, the City Club, and other business-led groups. They laid responsibility for the city's financial woes at the feet of the businessmen, many of whom paid less than their fair share of taxes.

---

34   Flanagan, *Charter,* 50.

35   Ibid., 96.

Non-partisan reform groups had each defined reform in its own image. Now party politics began to be defined in those terms too, increasing the confusion. Although all sides claimed non-partisan intentions, the mayoral election of 1907 had been a bitter fight that saw a Republican elected mayor. If a new charter could be established during his term, Mayor Fred Busse and his business allies could seize the opportunity to institutionalize their view of city administration. Busse became a liability, however, because his purge of the Board of Education in the spring of 1907 energized the electorate in opposition to the mayor and his allies.

Another significant factor, but one that won't be discussed in length here, was the fierce debate over whether charter reform would mean restrictions on alcohol consumption. The charter convention, an almost exclusively Protestant, middle-class organization, was perceived by many immigrant and ethnic organizations as inclined toward prohibition of liquor sales on Sunday, the only day most laborers had for relaxation and celebration of ethnic traditions. For the Germans in particular, but also for other ethnic groups, the consumption of alcohol became a political issue as well as a class issue. The charter debate was viewed with great skepticism by the immigrant community.

After much internal debate, but none in which women played any role, the delegates hammered out a platform for charter reform. On the three issues most important to Chicagoans—bonds, taxation, and control of schools and parks—the charter draft was either exceptionally weak or was weakened when proposed to the General Assembly. Some of the provisions, such as a limit on property tax rates, were seen as benefiting wealthy landowners and shifting more of the burden to small taxpayers.

The delegates, however, were very pleased with the charter and were taken by surprise when the charter faced vehement opposition from the public. Milton Foreman, the chairman of the convention who declared its membership represented "every walk and condition and poll of thought in life" also stressed that the delegates had no self-interest in the outcome. These same two points—the diversity and disinterest of the businessmen—are made in the *Plan of Chicago*.

Women had taken an altruistic and a selfish interest in the charter. The city needed the tools and authority to carry out municipal housekeeping, so they supported the charter for "good government" reasons. They also inserted the issue of women's suffrage into the debate. They were never allowed to present their point of view to the assembly during the first charter convention, although they did present their argument for suffrage to a committee—which voted 5–4 against adding suffrage to the charter.

The women consciously promoted the breadth of their networks, which stood in contrast to the narrow reach of the businessmen's organizations. Addams, in a speech opposing the first charter convention's draft, noted the many backgrounds of the women in opposition: "Organizations of working women . . . federations of mothers' meetings . . . property-owning women . . . professional women . . . women's clubs interested in municipal reform." The women's groups lobbied the men of many classes. The Woman's Trade Union League asked the Chicago Federation of Labor to support a charter with suffrage for women. The Chicago Woman's Club advocated for suffrage; many of their husbands were businessmen. If only we had records of their pillow talk . . . Jane Addams, as head of a one-hundred-group federation of women's organizations, spoke out at many stages of the debate.

Mayor Busse, a German who was expected by the businessmen to bring the ethnic vote into the fold, was unpopular for his school board purge and for his earlier decision to grant the long-term lease of a transit line to an unpopular rail baron. By the time Chicagoans voted on the charter in September of 1907, liquor laws, schools, and transit franchise reform were all more important reasons to disapprove the charter than was women's suffrage.

Charter reform was probably doomed that year anyway, but last-minute re-designation of the vote as a "special election" rather than a "general election" by the Republican-controlled election board was seen as a blatant attempt to keep working men from the polls. The custom of the time was for men to be given time off work to vote in general elections, but not in special elections. Thirty thousand people protested against the charter in Grant Park the Sunday before the election. The final vote was two-to-one in opposition to the charter.

An attempt was made during the following two years to hold a second charter convention. While the details of that effort differed slightly from the first, the result was the same or worse. Animosity grew. Proponents of charter reform assailed the motives of the opponents. Opponents accused the delegates of being tax-dodgers and labor-baiters. Women were allowed to speak to the convention the second time, but suffrage was still unpopular with the delegates. Rather than submitting a comprehensive charter package, the convention split the platform into many individual bills that the General Assembly could consider piecemeal (including suffrage). Charter reform died,[36] after consuming a great deal of the public's attention for four years, the same year the *Plan of Chicago* was unveiled.

CITY FATHERS AND THEIR PROGENY

The blatantly aggressive businessmen in turn-of-the-century Chicago were a dying breed near the turn of the century. A shift in expectations of civic leadership began around the time the *Plan of Chicago* was crafted, but was still a minor influence on the prevailing civic-business ethic. According to McCarthy, some second- and third-generation members of the wealthiest families identified themselves as members of the Progressive movement. McCormick, Crane, and Pullman descendants were serving on settlement house boards or helping to fund other charitable institutions. These sons and daughters generally had less influence on the city than their fathers had in 1909, but it is interesting to consider whether the Plan would have been significantly different if this generation had led the effort to craft it.

---

36   A third attempt to reform Chicago's charter failed in 1914–1915.

4

Bold Ideas and Major Movements at the Turn of the Century

THE STRUGGLES OF WOMEN TO INFLUENCE THE CIVIC SPHERE in Chicago took place against a backdrop of larger forces. Chicago at the turn of the century was fertile ground for movements and ideologies that swept the nation, including the benevolence of progressivism and the excesses of the Gilded Age. The simmering stew of players, points of view, and classes was seasoned by newly evolving professions like city planning[1] and sociology, both of which were strongly influenced (many would say conceived) in Chicago. Business and labor vacillated between uneasy peace and outright warfare. Chicago's collective psyche had been shaped in part by some of the most violent business-labor-police clashes in the nation. The ten years before 1900 and the ten years after were witness to innovations in a broad array of fields.

The men who crafted the *Plan of Chicago* and the women who built the city through settlement house work operated in a chaotic but intellectually bountiful time in Chicago. Anything was possible. The young city had little in the way of tradition to hold it back and much in the way of brash innovation to move it forward. Two important movements, the City Beautiful and the City Livable, were fermenting. Their separate and unequal trajectories— one with the power and resources of the business elite behind it, the other a handful of reformers with a constituency of the dispossessed—could have informed and augmented each other. The *Plan of Chicago* could have been a better plan if it had extended beyond Burnham's opinion that: "With things as they should

---

1 For the purposes of this discussion, city planning and urban planning will be used interchangeably.

be, every business man in Chicago would make more money than he does now."[2] A plan to improve quality of life in the region for everyone could have accomplished many of the physical changes he proposed *and* improved schools, reduced infant mortality, and safeguarded the juvenile court without the shame brought on the institution by untrained and uncaring patronage employees.

THE CITY BEAUTIFUL AND THE CITY LIVABLE

The City Beautiful movement, exemplified in the architecture of the White City, did not take a broad approach to cities or address the social ills or inequities highlighted by literary, social, and civic reform movements, at least not in Chicago. Charles Mulford Robinson, a journalist who popularized City Beautiful concepts in a 1903 book, wrote that "statues, monuments and skylines can wait," but people could not.[3] Mulford, who understood the significance of "small" projects was in touch with women in Chicago, Brooklyn, Baltimore, and Colorado Springs, who were planting trees, building playgrounds, and improving parks. Mulford's conception of the City Beautiful did not prevail in Chicago where Daniel Burnham was largely responsible for promoting the movement, and Mulford himself moved toward more grandiose designs before his death in 1917.

In Chicago, the City Beautiful movement hypothesized that a visually pleasing, well-organized city would create harmony, in and of itself. It didn't attempt to actually cleanse the city, but to build over the problems. Burnham expected that civic order and a better moral climate would be the natural outgrowth of improved aesthetics and increased civic pride. Monuments, plazas, wide thoroughfares, and classical building styles dominated Daniel Burnham's application of the City Beautiful philosophy, as represented by the White City and Jules Guerin's eye-catching illustrations in the *Plan of Chicago*.

The City Livable theory of activist women of the period took a more practical approach to city-building. A livable city had to be clean and safe first and foremost. Order was desirable, but they were less concerned with uniform building facades than with clean

---

2   Burnham and Bennett, *Plan of Chicago*, 76.

3   Spain, *How Women Saved*, 53.

streets, functioning sewers, and adequate numbers of classrooms. They were not so naïve as to believe that monuments and buildings would create enough civic pride to quell disorder that festered in injustice. Rather than trying to create broad parkways for fine carriages (or the new motor vehicles) or lakefront parks to attract and retain the wealthy, most of the women volunteers active at the time were directly and deeply in touch with the grittier side of Chicago and the need to help residents create "order" of a more fundamental sort.

Maureen Flanagan in *Seeing With Their Hearts: Chicago Women and Their Vision of the Good City, 1871–1933*, tells of Anna Nicholes, resident of the Southwest Side Neighborhood Settlement House, who had a vision of "a city of homes, a place in which to rear children."[4] In the "good city," the soot and smoke from industry was not allowed to permeate homes and neighborhoods, as it did in Chicago at the turn of the century. Food and laundry were not contaminated by Chicago's filthy air. The "good city" was like a home but created by public policy rather than by a parent or householder.[5] These two approaches to one factor—soot—says volumes about the different approaches of the businessmen and settlement leaders.

The business leaders, some of whom were surely responsible for the industrial soot that fell across Chicago, had no plan to attack their own pollution or alleviate its impact on human health in the *Plan of Chicago*. The "dirtiness" of the city was blamed by some on the immigrants who were crowded into substandard housing on streets with inadequate or non-existent sewerage systems. Even those whose professional experience should have told them otherwise found the immigrant tenements to be easy targets of blame. Chicago's Health Commissioner in 1867 called tenements "nurseries of every contagious form of disease, and of perpetual epidemics."[6] He proposed sanctions against building owners and tenants to address the sanitary conditions inside the homes of the "laboring class." It doesn't appear that he proposed greater municipal responsibility for the sanitary facilities outside the homes though—the ones the city should have maintained. The commis-

---

4   Flanagan, *Heart,* 1–4.
5   Flanagan, *Heart,* 194.
6   Abbott, *Tenements of Chicago,* 45.

sioner's prejudice had little effect on public health policy though, since the city was unprepared to take an aggressive role in municipal sanitation even twenty years later.

The question of order, disorder, and dirt, what they meant and how they should be addressed were viewed differently by the businessmen and the settlement women. Daphne Spain, in *How Women Saved the City*, explains that at the turn of the century (and perhaps many other eras), disorder was considered comparable to dirtiness. By virtue of their newness, strangers—immigrants—were out of place. If out-of-place people represent disorder, disorder equals dirt. Therefore, some could say the polluted air and the poor sanitation system were not the cause of filth and disease in the city. It was strangers themselves, who were blamed as "dirty." When Hull-House opened its doors in 1889, one of its earliest achievements was to investigate and act on municipal sanitation problems.

All of Chicago, including its businessmen, benefited when the independent, activist women defused potentially antagonistic situations by helping immigrants become less "the stranger" and improved worker health (and productivity) through sanitation or housing reforms. These contributions to the public good, tangible and intangible, hint at the high quality of contributions women could have made to the *Plan of Chicago,* had they been included.

The premise of this book is that the *Plan of Chicago* would have been much richer if it had embraced the theoretical and practical achievements of the activist women of that time, who consciously worked toward urban constructs of "the City as Home," or "municipal housekeeping." The ways in which that is true will be shown shortly in an overview of the women's achievements, and in later chapters, which look at specific aspects of the *Plan* (and its missing elements) from the point of view of woman leaders of the time.

The table below is a brief glossary of terminology, characteristics, and issues of these competing notions of the city. The story of how the different views of urban life evolved through the very different life experiences of the businessmen and the women volunteers is as interesting as the story of how those differences played out in Chicago in 1909.

	Plan of Chicago— **BUSINESSMEN**	*City-Building—* **WOMEN VOLUNTEERS**
Names	City Beautiful	City Livable
Characteristics	Competitive	Municipal Housekeeping
	Business-oriented	The Good City
	Wealthy	Cooperative
	Males Represented	Broader in race and class associations
Issues, Concerns	Monuments	Redemptive spaces
	Parks (primarily lakefront and forest preserves and large destination parks)	Playgrounds (small, close neighborhood parks)
	Transportation infrastructure—freight rail and boulevards	Streets—safety and sanitation
	Central business district	Working conditions, labor
	Wealth	Justice for juveniles, immigrants, the poor
	Legal aspects of implementing the *Plan of Chicago*	Education
		Public health

MUNICIPAL HOUSEKEEPING AND "REDEMPTIVE SPACE"

The City Beautiful movement operated as if wide streets and uniform but graceful buildings would magically disperse the soot in the air, the chaotic tenements poor people endured, and the "otherness" of new immigrants. Municipal housekeeping and its companion theories were generally, but not always, a more benign response to the dirt and disorder of the city. The municipal

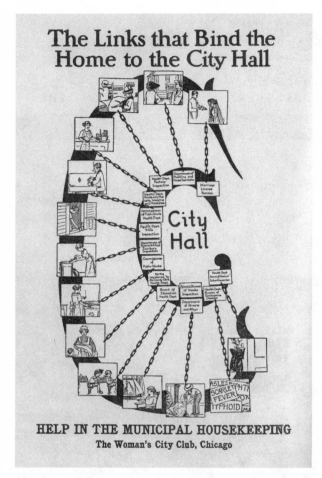

The Links that Bind the Home to the City Hall

City Hall

HELP IN THE MUNICIPAL HOUSEKEEPING
The Woman's City Club, Chicago

This illustration from the 1915 yearbook of the Woman's City Club shows the many ways City Hall must be maintained like a home. (Chicago History Museum, ICHi-28546, The Links That Bind the Home to City Hall, Woman's City Club, Yearbook.)

housekeeping movement was national in scope, as women in cities across the continent became more involved in civic affairs. In the city of Chicago, Hull-House defined municipal housekeeping in an intense and personal way. Its definition was one of "settling" with and becoming one with "the others."

The Hull-House residents' relentless research and advocacy focused on the need to cleanse public services and policies, and demanded more from municipal government. Sometimes this meant finding the source of a break in the sewer system that was contaminating the community because the city didn't. Sometimes it meant uncovering corruption in sanitation inspections. Simultaneously, they gently offered parks, public baths, day care, and other public health essentials to help "the others" (immigrants) assimilate. Their means and methodologies will be discussed in further detail in Chapter Five, but it is particularly important to note that the settlement residents quickly learned it was much more effective to gently lead or offer amenities to immigrants than to try to impose mainstream customs.

Burnham used space to flaunt monumental structures, whether it was in the White City or the *Plan of Chicago*. Burnham's approach to public space symbolizes what urban planning would come to be all about—the rearrangement of large units of structure or infrastructure to effect some physical change over a given territory. The architects of the *Plan of Chicago* represented the profit-making sector. As Daphne Spain points out, it was the profit-making sector across the nation that dominated the Gilded Age (1870–1900) and shaped physical space in ways that overshadowed all other contributions.[7] As she notes in her introduction, "Architecture, planning and urban histories recognize the significance of this period and document the accomplishments of men who built skyscrapers, city halls and department stores."[8] The contributions of Chicago's city-building women of the time were certainly overshadowed by the profit-making sector, and in fact most of the physical manifestations of their work—the "redemptive spaces" they built—have been destroyed.

The concept of redemptive space rather than monumental space neatly dramatizes the differences between the views of settlement house residents and the business community. Although we have few surviving examples, many redemptive spaces by their very nature are familiar types. Redemptive spaces were places that were open and welcoming to people who knew they were strangers. Redemptive spaces didn't confer order with their sheer grandeur as City Beautiful proponents expected from their monuments, but offered tangible benefits because they helped "strangers"—immigrants and migrants to the city—assimilate the values and customs of their new home.

Redemptive spaces allowed the weary mother, innocent farm girl new to the city, or mischievous immigrant adolescent safe space to experience the bounty and boundaries of the city in a setting where helping hands were nearby if needed. It wasn't just immigrants that benefited from redemptive spaces. Redemptive spaces

---

7   Spain, *How Women Saved*, 12.
8   Ibid., xii.

such as settlement houses allowed unmarried women to set up a cooperative housekeeping arrangement to ensure their own good reputation, even as they carved out radical new roles for women. Spain reminds us that "redemptive places emerge as sites where significant issues of the day were actively negotiated."[9] In Chicago, redemptive spaces included not only the settlement houses, which fostered very broad discussion and debate, but many sites like the playgrounds, coffeehouses, and bathhouses (often initiated by settlement houses) where people congregated in small-scale, some-what personal, and home-like atmospheres.

Chicago was not very different from other cities in failing to preserve historic examples of its redemptive spaces. Bathhouses, playgrounds, and even most of the Hull-House complex fell victim to "progress" in the twentieth century. Spain points out the irony of this loss: "Women volunteers provided an orderly system by which to assimilate newcomers and in the process they cleaned up. This was unglamorous work compared with building grand monuments. In the end, however, more cities were influenced by the creation of redemptive places than by skyscrapers or City Beautiful plans."[10] Spain says the "oversight is especially puzzling in the case of Chi-cago, where Jane Addams and the Woman's City Club had such high profiles." Spain offers a potential answer in quoting historian Peter Hall "who found 'alas, almost no founding mothers' in his intellectual history of urban planning and referred to Jane Addams as a 'do gooder.'" [11] In other words, the answer to the question of why redemptive spaces and the women who created them seem to have disappeared lies partially in the failure of historians to re-count their value to and impact on "mainstream" history.

SOCIAL SCIENCE, URBAN PLANNING, AND POLITICAL REFORM

Along the philosophical continuum with the businessmen and the settlement women were several other variations on civic and economic reform. Populists and progressives, socialists and social Darwinists, even anarchists, contributed to an ideological outpour-

9   Ibid., 237.

10   Ibid., 238.

11   Ibid., 250.

ing of ideas at the end of the nineteenth century and the beginning of the twentieth. Even when common ground on defining problems could be found, there were often differences on causes and solutions. For example, "urban housekeeping" was a mainstay of progressivism. A city was like a large home to them and most progressives agreed that to protect family, one had to influence the outside forces that threatened family health and welfare. Families that had to trudge through streets covered with slimy offal from the stockyards were going to have difficulty keeping their homes clean. Mothers who were forced to support their families through long hours of factory work had to leave many home duties untended. These practical matters were self-evident to most progressives.

Most progressives were native-born, well-educated Americans. Many were not familiar with immigrants in any sense but the intellectual. Most progressives did assume that immigrants had to be assimilated—for their own good as well as the nation's. But there was a range of points of view, including some progressives with overtly anti-immigrant or condescending attitudes. Jane Addams, a progressive leader in Chicago, took a characteristically practical approach, although not without first stumbling a few times in her approach to her neighbors. Her approach was, first and foremost, respectful of her neighbors.

Whatever the nuances of difference among reformers on issues of immigration, they had a shared faith in scientific approaches to problems. Their "scientific" inquiries were not about the physical sciences, but used an impartial approach to researching problems and recommending solutions. This was the beginning of "social science" as a discipline. They conducted scientific inquiries into problems, advocated for public policies and laws to strengthen families as well as the city, and then tried to ensure the impartial administration of new (and old) laws by "experts." Reforms like civil service protection for qualified employees (as opposed to the patronage system of employees whose primary or only qualification was acquaintance with an elected official) were an attempt to ensure both fairness and appropriate expertise to solve problems. Implicit in these assumptions about the necessity of scientific inquiry and appropriate expertise is the notion that government could and should have a positive impact on the lives of its people. If some, in government and elsewhere, blamed immigrants for epidemics, the women intensively studied the real causes of epidemics (transmis-

sion by contaminated water, transmission by insects, and transmission by clothing produced by very sick workers). If government
dodged responsibility for solving the problem, they disclosed which
inspectors had failed in their duties or, in one case, actually entered a garment factory and removed and destroyed contaminated
clothing. The focus on government and science had implications
not only for the voluntary reform movements, but also for the newly developing professional fields like urban planning, social work,
and sociology.

This scientific approach spurred new ways of assessing antiquated customs. For example, until the latter years of the nineteenth century, American law gave fathers ultimate authority for
their children, as if they were his property. Progressives, settlement workers, and other reformers promoted the concept of the
"best interest of the child" and of parents (mothers as well as fathers) as trustees, rather than owners, of a child. If the parents
were unable or unwilling to care for the child, he or she became
society's responsibility. This may seem obvious today, but it was
radical a century ago. Reformers were explicit about why the nation had a vested interest in the adequate care of children, and
neatly tied national tranquility to domestic tranquility. For example, John Shoop, an assistant superintendent of Chicago schools
said: "When the home is right, the city is right; and when the cities
and homes are right, the state is right; and when the state is right,
the nation is right; and when the nations are right, the world is
right."[12] Ensuring that society had an agreed-upon role in family
law was contextual groundwork for creating the juvenile court system, one of the most outstanding contributions made by Chicago's
city-building women. One logical extension of the "best interests of
the child" approach was protecting children from industrial situations injurious to their health and development.

Chicago's turbulence stimulated and shaped new professions for
the middle class. Social work and sociology arose out of the work
of Hull-House and other settlement houses and was adopted later
by academics and university departments. Urban planning as it
evolved in Chicago was primarily a male domain; its City Beautiful
roots were fed and watered by Daniel Burnham and his colleagues.
As sociology and urban planning were beginning to arise in other

12   Getis, *The Juvenile Court,* 24.

places, primarily along the East Coast, the two professions were intertwined. Chicago could have adopted the East Coast model. Instead, shortly after the period discussed here, urban planning separated itself from sociology at the national level, in deference to the promoters of the City Beautiful movement. The loss of a humanistic perspective in planning was not only Chicago's loss but eventually the nation's too.

CITY-BUILDING WOMEN, WORKING-CLASS WOMEN, AND WOMEN OF COLOR

Chicago was the site of well-known examples of business-police-labor clashes. There are many good histories of the labor movement in Chicago, so this brief overview will simply describe the broadest outlines of the labor movement and the ways in which women were influenced by and beginning to influence the labor movement at the turn of the century.

Poverty was rampant in Chicago during the latter half of the nineteenth century. Worker wages were as likely to go down as to go up; wages were lower in 1886 than in 1882 for instance, leading to severe deprivation and sometimes to strikes. The average daily wage for men in 1886 was less than $2, for women it was $1.11, and for children it was 70 cents.[13] The Pullman Strike of 1894 can be attributed to a reduction in wages at the Pullman Palace Car Company factory, while George Pullman maintained the rent levels in his company town,[14] squeezing workers past their limits. By the turn of the century, tenement dwellers earned about 16 cents an hour on average and worked 60 hours a week.[15] Child labor laws came into existence in Illinois in 1893, after Hull-House residents conducted investigations of the conditions under which children labored and discovered children working long hours, in unsafe conditions, at repetitive tasks that maimed their developing bodies.

---

13   Ibid., 48.

14   By all accounts the Pullman town was a clean and aesthetically pleasing environment, in stark comparison to the living conditions of most industrial workers at the time. But it was also a profit-oriented venture and needed to "pay its own way," even when the Pullman Car business was depressed.

15   Getis, *The Juvenile Court,* 9.

Labor historians note that the fledgling labor movement of the late nineteenth century was not one but many philosophical movements debating contrasting operational models. Should the movement focus on class consciousness or a vision of producer/consumer cooperatives? Can the democratic system be made to provide justice for working people or do they have to go outside the system? Should disputes between labor and capital be resolved by arbitration or strikes?[16] Different unions took different approaches and a number of theorists and journalists debated the fine points of each of these possibilities. The Chicago public's sentiment about the labor movement vacillated as much as the debate within the movement did.

Historian Maureen A. Flanagan's research shows that in spite of male historian's implicit or explicit assumptions that women followed the politics of their husbands or fathers, activist Chicago women between 1871 and 1933 "made common cause in politics despite differences of class, race or ethnicity" and "frequently took public stands that diverged from those of the men of their race and class." There was solidarity in the understanding that one woman's vulnerability was a threat to all. Settlement women, members of the large network of women's clubs, and women labor leaders knew each other, largely through networks that either began at or intersected at Hull-House.

The network of women's clubs was very large at the turn of the century. Most were clubs for white women, but the black middle and upper class in Chicago was substantial enough to support many clubs of its own. Middle- and upper-class clubwomen made common cause with women in other classes. Chicago Woman's Club members took an interest in the problems of working women, for example, even though most of them were not in the workforce. They published an exposé of working conditions at Marshall Field's department store and supported the Chicago teachers (who were primarily women) in their advocacy for a pension.

The relationship of settlement house workers to the labor movement is a good example of the ways in which nineteenth-century boundaries of class and ethnicity were breached by activist women. Settlement house workers came predominantly, at least at the beginning, from middle-class backgrounds, and were intimately

---

16   Ashbaugh, *Lucy Parsons,* 49.

woven into the fabric of the women's clubs. Settlement residents had firsthand experience of the abuses suffered by industrial workers because of their investigations, including the very early ones published in the *Hull-House Maps and Papers*. Hull-House in particular took a position strongly in support of the rights of workers to organize, but also kept lines of communication open to business leaders. This stance required a delicate balance and absolute impartiality since Addams's "constituency" was from the laboring classes, but some of Hull-House's donors were from the business class.

Support for working women was especially strong at Hull-House. Unions representing female bookbinders, shirt-makers, and cloak-makers originated at or were very closely tied to Hull-House, and the Dorcas Federal Labor Union (a federation of women's unions) was also formed there. Corollary organizations, like the Jane Clubs (see Chapter Five), were developed at Hull-House to help sustain working women during periods of economic hardship.

Although many middle- and upper-class women formed alliances across boundaries of class and race, some boundaries, especially racial boundaries, remained in the first decade of the twentieth century. Initial steps were taken before 1909 to reach across racial barriers, without removing the barriers completely. Jane Addams was a leader in these early openings, inviting women of color to Hull-House, working with the residents of settlements in the black community on issues of common concern, advocating for inclusion of black women's clubs within the larger club network, and helping to found the National Association for the Advancement of Colored People. But Hull-House's programs were not desegregated for several more years.

As imperfect as the women's racial tolerance might seem to us today, their experience with women of different classes, races, and ethnic groups was generally much broader than that of their husbands or of the Commercial Club. This is another dimension in which they had much to offer in building a plan for the region's future.

THEORIES OF "HOME," CHICAGO SETTLEMENT HOUSES, AND COOPERATIVE VALUES

In the decades following the Civil War, American middle-class women and women labor activists sought avenues for civic involvement before they gained civil rights. It was radical for women to take civic roles at that time, in the sense of being uncommon. Many of the earliest (post-Civil War) independent women couched their work in conservative religious and domestic terms. "Women alone," i.e., women without husbands and children of their own, were especially suspect under the conventional role definitions of the time. By the turn of the century, Chicago's trailblazing women began to create voluntary organizations and new cooperative living arrangements for themselves at the same time that they created physical and intellectual spaces to enable public discussion of public issues.

The settlement women benefited from earlier and contemporary attempts to redefine the roles of women. Two theoretical constructs were especially useful in defining settlement residents' relationship to their households and to each other. The theories were "material feminism" and "cooperative housekeeping." Material feminists tried to redefine the terms of work and motherhood within a very political paradigm (see box). Cooperative housekeeping was less dogmatic, but no less intent on finding alternatives to the isolation of work at home in an industrial society.[17]

Women volunteers in Chicago benefited from this nationwide wave of interest in reconsidering the household roles of women. Material feminists and proponents of cooperative housekeeping calculated the economic value of household labor and considered alternative ways to structure such work. Both movements were often presented as solutions to the middle-class problem of finding household help, although some middle-class women were not in a position to hire household help and sought a more rewarding and collaborative way to accomplish their own work.

These theorists and practitioners developed unconventional options for how women might live and work. One group developed floor plans for a cooperative workplace where cooking, laundry,

---

17   In farm households or craftsperson households, two or more adults were likely to work in and around a homestead.

Material Feminism in Brief

Material feminists advocated for a change in economic conditions for women, including the payment of wages for domestic work. They also called for changed spatial arrangements to allow for different concepts of home and work.

Material feminists wanted housework and child care socialized in both the economic and interpersonal senses. They wanted reasonable pay for the critical work they did, but they also wanted to work in a less isolated setting.

Material feminists said women should "assert control over the important work of production which they were already performing." They rejected the challenge of some men that women could only be equal if they participated in what was traditionally men's work.

Material feminists believed society would evolve from capitalism to socialism. They, along with many archi-tects and urban planners, believed the industrial city would liberate women through mechanization of tasks and through services that brought products to their doorsteps. They did not foresee that the industrial city would result in suburban isolation of families and ever-larger and more impersonal corporations.

Material feminists' demand for housework pay paralleled architects' promotion of collective urban residential space in Eastern cities. Both were eclipsed by red-baiting and finally the Hoover Commission report, *Home Building and Home Ownership*, which led to construction of fifty million single-family houses. "It was a decisive ideological defeat for feminists and for architects and urban planners interested in housing design."

From: Hayden, Delores, *The Grand Domestic Revolution: A History of Feminist Designs for American Homes, Neighborhoods and Cities*

clothes-making, and mending could be efficiently accomplished, at pay scales representative of skilled (male) laborers, with the co-operatively-produced goods sold back to households at fair market value. Architects on the East and West Coasts tinkered with radically different styles of housing. Several designs for single-family households clustered around a shared, communal kitchen were promoted, but not built.[18] Cooperative apartment buildings were

---

18   Similar plans in Europe led to actual construction of cooperative housing de-

built in Boston and New York, although they proved controversial. An editor of *Architectural Record*, who was clearly unnerved by unconventional domestic arrangements, opined in 1903: "While the apartment hotel is the consummate flower of domestic cooperation, it is also, unfortunately, the consummate flower of domestic irresponsibility. It means the sacrifice of everything implied by the word 'home'. . . . It is the most dangerous enemy American domesticity has yet to encounter."[19]

At the same time that women began to look at housework in political and economic terms, some began to describe public policy in domestic terms. During the Progressive Era, attempts to re-define women's roles were less likely to invoke religion and morality than earlier eras. For instance, settlement house women opposed bars and prostitution for pragmatic, rather than moralistic reasons— to protect community peace and order and to protect vulnerable newcomers to the city. Crusades for schools, parks, and housing regulations were undertaken to make the city comfortable and welcoming for all. One of the ways women of the time described this view was through the theory of "municipal housekeeping." And at the most literal level, the soot that Anna Nicholes described falling from smokestacks onto the food and laundry of industrious housekeepers could only be dealt with at a societal level.

Hull-House and its allies blended a response to these new theories of household and municipal management. These educated women, without traditional roles themselves and few female role models in the working world, shared household duties, freeing up their time to undertake municipal housekeeping. (They also avoided the dangers to character and to physical well-being inherent to women living alone in that time.) Educated, middle-class women benefited from the cooperative household model as an alternative to the limited role their peers had as wives and mothers. Poor and immigrant women benefited from the child care, youth programs, cultural activities, and the health and nutrition advocacy of the settlement house workers. The city and all people living in it benefited from these efforts to build a safe and healthy environment where everyone could thrive.

---

velopments.

19 Hayden, *Domestic Revolution,* 192–193.

Many of the intellectual currents discussed in this section were closely associated with or originated from spaces created by women, like Hull-House. Issues that were omitted or excluded from the *Plan of Chicago*, such as poverty, child welfare, work conditions, public sanitation, and other concerns of a rapidly industrializing society were addressed in both word and deed by Chicago women, largely but not exclusively through the settlement movement (an active network of women's clubs provided allies on most issues too). As Rima Schultz says in her modern-day introduction to the ground-breaking *Hull-House Maps and Papers,* "Hull-House was at the cutting edge of major initiatives that collectively defined progressivism by the 1900s. It had literally and figuratively mapped those initiatives by 1893, the year the settlement celebrated its fourth birthday."[20]

By 1909, a distinctly "woman's" view of Chicago resonated across many topics, largely through networks of women's organizations and the growth of settlement houses. Men were always a part of the settlement house movement, and their contributions will be recognized here. But the unique men who participated directly in the settlement houses publicly declared their allegiance to cooperative rather than competitive values. For purposes of simplicity, the settlements' cooperative values will be discussed here as "feminine." Although it may not be universally true that men are more competitive, the distinction is a reasonable shorthand given the aggressive business and development environment of Chicago at the turn of the century.

The settlement workers' attitudes were a radical departure from those of the Charity Organization Society, the Chicago Relief and Aid Society, and other business-backed philanthropies. The settlement residents, who benefited and learned from firsthand experience in immigrant neighborhoods, generally held that social conditions rather than individual "defects" were the root of poverty and disorder. The Charity Organization Society studied individual human behavior in order to change ("improve") it. The settlements systematically gathered social data to enable individuals and neighborhoods to change the social conditions that limited their opportunities. These were fundamental differences that led to very different approaches to civic reform.

---

20   Residents of Hull-House, *Hull House Maps and Papers,* 1–2.

5

Bringing All the Players Together

SETTLEMENT LEADERS AND ALLIES

IF WOMEN HAD
BEEN AT THE TABLE WHEN
THE *PLAN* WAS DEVELOPED, how might
it be different? The purpose of this book is to speculate on
how city-building women might have broadened the scope of the
Plan, although we will never know for sure what difference they
could have made. The settlement women were diverse in their interests, professional skills, and backgrounds. They created and
expanded economically and racially diverse networks to facilitate
coalition-building. They were socially innovative, whether they
were carving out new roles for unmarried, educated women or
responding to perplexing public health problems. They were flexible. Jane Addams described the harm that might be done when
philanthropists are "good to people" rather than "with them."[1]
In this case, she was writing specifically of the inflexible patriar-
chal employer, George Pullman. In a clever essay, she compared
Pullman's inability to understand his workers to King Lear, who
couldn't understand his daughters' ingratitude and unwillingness
to comply with his wishes.

The men who participated in developing the *Plan of Chicago* had
common goals for the city. Their goals were molded by their experience in business and by their position in the wealthier classes.
Maintaining order, keeping the moneyed classes in or near the
city, creating a strong business climate, restructuring the transportation network, and linking their suburban homes to their central business district offices were the primary goals informing their
plan. Their unified vision resulted in a plan that was notable for
its uniformity—if Chicago had been built as the *Plan of Chicago*

---

1 Elshtain, *The Jane Addams Reader,* 172.

directed, we would not have seen the architectural innovation Chicago is known for, let alone the social innovation needed for a successful region.

There is a regrettable lack of scholarship linking city-building achievements by women of the time to the *Plan of Chicago*. Historian Carl Smith shows a glimmer of insight in *Urban Disorder and the Shape of Belief* in pointing out that "When Jane Addams and Ellen Gates Starr moved in September of 1889 into the 'hospitable old house' that Charles J. Hull had built in the West Division in 1856, they were just as concerned about the state of urban society as were the businessmen who secured Fort Sheridan, but they had a very different conception of the best way to head off social cataclysm. They chose this location because they believed that what happened to the Hull home and its neighborhood in three decades demonstrated the problems posed by urban growth and change." He goes on to say, "As pioneers in the settlement house movement, which directed middle class energies back into the city that others were ready to abandon, Addams and Starr were hardly free of cultural blind spots, but they were dedicated to the idea that the urban social order was something of immense human value and could be better held together with mutual understanding than with force."[2] Hopefully, the modest exploration represented by this book will inspire an outpouring of academic research in a generally overlooked area.

If there is debate about whether or not the women's insights would have improved the *Plan*, there should certainly be agreement that the *Plan* would have been *different*, had the women's expertise, interests, and networks been brought to bear on its recommendations. What specifically might these activist women have brought to a plan in general terms?

- In-depth knowledge of conditions and needs in city neighborhoods
- Thorough, groundbreaking research on municipal issues of sanitation, public health, neighborhood development, and economic conditions

---

2   C. Smith, *Urban Disorder*, 221–222.

- Skills and resources sufficient to build many civic and social institutions like parks, public baths, hospitals, and schools

- Wise counsel on the unrecognized strengths of poor and immigrant families, the ability to translate "foreign" habits in a benign, or at least neutral, context

- Innovative, practical, and successful model programs to help working-class people participate fully in civic life

- A passion for democratic ideals

- A commitment to offer the gifts of democracy to the newest of immigrants, to ease the transition to citizenship

- A strong community arts and intellectual tradition that often linked to the downtown cultural institutions, but was also very robust at the settlement houses themselves

- The ability to organize broad-based coalitions

The last point on the list presents an interesting paradox. If the activist women had been drawn into the planning, if their expertise had been respected and trusted, they might have rallied broad support for the *Plan*. Certainly these women proved over and over that once they rallied behind a cause, they could make the impossible possible. Their absence was a slight to their capabilities, but on a broader level their absence left the *Plan* where it remains today: It stirs men's souls, to paraphrase Burnham, but only certain men and women with limited professional and business interests. People may like parks and the lakefront, but most don't thank Burnham, because planning is invisible to most residents of the region. The *Plan* established an exclusive approach and didn't address many of the issues most critical to Chicagoans of the time. The extent to which the region can overcome one hundred years of planning for influential populations is part of the challenge this book presents to modern-day planners.

JANE WAS NOT ALONE
Other Leaders and Their Ground-Breaking Work

Jane Addams had a unique ability to attract highly competent and innovative women and men to the settlement and networks she led.

While she may be the best-known woman of her generation in Chicago, her real genius was in managing relationships that led to so many productive contributions to city-building. Many more women will be introduced in the chapters that follow, but the information here provides context on some of the members of Jane Addams's most trusted confidantes. For a more extensive list of city-building women of the time, see *Women Building Chicago: 1790—1990*, edited by Rima Schultz and Adele Hast.

A significant portion of Addams's inner circle was called to larger platforms because of the outstanding contributions they made while at Hull-House. Alice Hamilton, after twenty-two years as a resident, became the first woman on the faculty of Harvard Medical School. Florence Kelley moved to New York to head the National Consumer League. Julia Lathrop and Grace Abbott were each called to head departments of the federal government in Washington, D.C. In 1909 Florence Kelley was the only key contributor who had already left Chicago. However, she was still in constant communication as part of a growing national network of settlements. In addition, her eight years at Hull-House (1891–1899) were so seminal in establishing the house's research and advocacy style, they cannot be overlooked.

By 1895 the residents of Hull-House had conducted several innovative research studies and published them as the *Hull-House Maps and Papers*. Florence Kelley, Julia Lathrop, and Jane Addams were among the major contributors, but it was Kelley who outlined the rigorous methodological standards, as well as provided a significant amount of the content.[3] The studies included exposés of the sweat-shop and child-labor systems of production; comparisons of laborer wages in Chicago and New York; ethnographic studies of Jewish, Bohemian, and Italian populations; a description of Cook County charities; articles on the labor movement; and a "sketch" or description of the many programs at Hull-House in 1895. Among the most astounding features of *Hull-House Maps and Papers* are the painstakingly hand-painted, building-by-building maps, which rival the complex layers of today's computer-generated maps.

In her introduction to the 2007 edition of *Hull-House Maps and Papers*, Rima Schultz writes:

---

3   Deegan, *Men of the Chicago School,* 57.

Hull-House residents made a dramatic statement about their shared values and understanding of the nature of social science knowledge and its usages in a democratic society when they made the decision to put together a collaborative work of sociology based on their experiences as residents of Chicago's near West Side. They were certain that publishing maps with explicit information about the wages and conditions of the working poor in the Nineteenth Ward would educate the public and lead to much-needed reforms. The belief that an enlightened citizenry could be mobilized for reform causes was part of the Progressive era's faith in the efficacy of social science investigation to produce solutions for society's problems. HHM&P [the acronym is used], the first study of its kind in the United States, directly influenced subsequent social surveys that also emanated from settlement houses rather than from universities.[4]

It is entirely in keeping with the spirit of the settlement that the "author" is "The Residents of Hull-House" rather than an individual editor.

Collective action was characteristic of Hull-House efforts. In the early years of the settlement, residents built and managed the first public playground in Chicago; built the first public gymnasium and first bathhouse in Chicago; offered the first college extension courses in Chicago; and experimented with cooperatives, including a community coal-buying club and residential cooperatives. They conducted a multitude of studies and investigations, including a midwife investigation, a truancy investigation, a shared investigation on behalf of newsboys who were not covered by child labor laws because they were legally defined as "merchants," a study of infant mortality by nationality, and studies for the U.S. Departments of Agriculture and Labor on diets and the impact of food cost on immigrants.

Other women (and men) contributed to Hull-House's growing stature. A few residents who were active between 1889 and 1909 and who played leadership roles in establishing Hull-House's reputation are briefly profiled here to give a flavor for the depth and breadth of expertise and commitment that resided at Hull-House.

---

4   Residents of Hull-House, *Hull House Maps and Papers*, 4.

Additional residents will be featured in the chapters that discuss how the *Plan of Chicago* might have been improved by the participation of city-building women.

Ellen Gates Starr was a college classmate of Addams and co-founded Hull-House. Starr was a teacher, arts supporter, and labor activist, who was much more strident in her support for labor than Addams. She was a proponent of the Arts and Crafts movement, and she founded the Public School Art Society to bring art into the schools.

Dr. Alice Hamilton was a physician and epidemiologist, and the first woman appointed to Harvard Medical School faculty in 1919. Hamilton's typhoid study resulted in almost half of the city's health inspectors being fired for inadequate or corrupt inspections. Hamilton conducted other studies on tuberculosis, midwifery, and infant mortality. Her eventual area of medical specialization was industrial medicine.

Florence Kelley was a Hull-House resident from 1891 to 1899. Kelley was the scholar behind the *Hull-House Maps and Papers*. After passage of Illinois labor law reforms, Mrs. Kelley was appointed the first state factory inspector. Kelley moved to New York in 1899 to head the National Consumer League.

Julia Lathrop was the first woman appointed to the State Board of Charities (1893), co-founder of the Chicago School of Civics and Philanthropy, co-founder of the juvenile court, and first head of the federal Children's Bureau (1912), making her the first woman to lead a federal agency. She was by all accounts a generous spirit and a quick wit.

Hull-House is the best known of the several settlement houses that provided physical space devoted to the affairs of city-building. Its success was largely due to Jane Addams's success as an administrator, writer, speaker, and charismatic leader. Other settlements with leading roles in city-building and municipal reform movements were the University of Chicago Settlement (led by Mary McDowell), Chicago Commons (led by Graham Taylor), and the Northwestern University Settlement (led by Harriet Vittum). By 1900, only eleven years after Hull-House opened, fifteen settlement houses were operating in Chicago neighborhoods, responding to the dual pressures of an arrogant industrial sector and a detached municipal sector.

Most settlement residents were similar to the businessmen in their economic, ethnic, and political status. Settlement house folks (as well as most other progressives and reformers) were largely middle-class, white Anglo-Saxon Protestants, generally leaning toward the Republican Party, which was still closely associated with Abraham Lincoln. The characteristic that most distinguished settlement house workers from some other reformers, as well as from the businessmen, was their willingness to settle with, learn from, and appreciate the cultures of populations that were shunned by so much of middle-class society.

HULL-HOUSE
A Creative Environment That Spawned Innovation

The residents themselves were surely the greatest asset Hull-House possessed. However, the environment within the Hull-House complex came to be larger than the sum of its parts, and was a force for creative ideas and unconventional activities. It attracted stimulating and innovative people from well beyond the neighborhood.

Journalist Henry Demarest Lloyd called Hull-House "the best club in Chicago."[5] Although nowhere near as elegantly appointed as the downtown clubs, Hull-House seems by all accounts to have had the finest intellectual accoutrements of the time in Chicago. Settlements, especially Hull-House and Chicago Commons, drew authors, artists, politicians, civic leaders, academics, and other members of the intelligentsia to open forums on controversial topics (Chicago Commons ceased sponsoring controversial forums in 1902, but Hull-House continued).[6] The cross-fertilization among Chicago's most highly educated thinkers and some of the self-taught or informally trained radicals, immigrants, and labor leaders made for the broadest possible range of ideas and viewpoints. This fertile ground was an asset to Addams and her networks in shaping new public policy. It also solidified bonds between disparate types of people. According to at least one report, Hull-House residents were as physically active as they were intellectually active. Alice Hamilton reports that residents organized bicycling trips

---

5   Davis, *Heroine,* 95.

6   Feffer, *The Chicago Pragmatists,* 112.

on Sundays along the North Shore or to Palos Park, distances of twenty or more miles.

Five years after opening Hull-House to Near West Siders, the residents had built a significant core constituency among their neighbors. In 1894 social commentator William Stead (author of *If Christ Came to Chicago*) reported that two thousand people visited Hull-House each week.[7] Expansion of the physical facility began almost immediately after Hull-House's founding. The Butler Art Gallery, the second building at Hull-House, opened in 1891. By 1893 the residents succeeded in building the coffee house and a gymnasium. The Jane Club residential building was built in 1898. A new coffee house and theater were built in 1899.

The Hull-House Labor Museum opened in November of 1900 "to display the industrial arts and crafts of the many immigrant cultures found on the near west side."[8] This was a physical manifestation of the residents' evolution from teaching appreciation of mainstream culture to learning and sharing appreciation of folk cultures. By 1906 Helen Culver donated the original rental house to the settlement, including the surrounding land on a full city block. A thirteen-building complex was completed in 1907, designed by Irving and Allen Pond, architects who were also instrumental in fostering the Arts and Crafts Movement at Hull-House.[9]

The activities conducted in this complex spanned most of human cultural, intellectual, and recreational activity: art, music, debates, lectures, sports, day care, sales of pure milk, ethnic dance, crafts, citizenship/naturalization classes, millinery and dressmaking, manual trades instruction, homemaking and hygiene, cooking, bookbinding, pottery, metalworking, and printmaking, to name a few. There were civic clubs, kindergartens, and a coffee shop.

Hull-House had to be managed on two levels. There were public programs, classes, and activities like those listed above, that required staff and financial support. Some residents worked full time at the settlement, teaching, coaching, counseling, and performing a multitude of other duties to meet the needs of neighbors; others had outside jobs and carried out settlement duties on evenings and weekends. Outside employment consisted of "the secretary of

---

7   Spain, *How Women Saved,* 228.
8   Feffer, *The Chicago Pragmatists,* 130–131.
9   Glowacki and Hendry, *Images of America,* 20.

the City Club, two practicing physicians, several attorneys, newspaper men, business men, teachers, scientists, artists, musicians, lecturers in the School of Civics and Philanthropy, officers in the Juvenile Protective Association and in The League for the Protection of Immigrants, a visiting nurse, a sanitary inspector. . . "[10]

Women like Louise de Koven Bowen, who gave over three-quarter million dollars[11] to Hull-House, or Mary Rozet Smith, Jane Addams's long-time companion, were major donors and original members of the board of trustees. Bowen Hall bears its donor's name; the Children's Building was built by Smith. Julius Rosenwald was one of many men who consistently contributed, beginning in 1902. By 1912 he was a member of the Hull-House board of trustees.[12]

There was a household to support too. Residents paid room and board to a "cooperative club" that was managed by a committee.[13] Although most residents paid their own room and board, Addams did solicit "fellowships," generally $50 a month, to help support the household.[14]

HULL-HOUSE AS ASSISTED
BY A BROAD NETWORK OF WOMEN

The achievements of Hull-House residents in their first twenty years of operation were significant. But it would be unfair and unwise to omit the contributions of a host of city-building women who were not residents at Hull-House. It was often the concerted effort of large networks of women that ensured success for settlement house initiatives. Too often, legislative "victories" could only be implemented with donations from the wealthy women in the network, while Hull-House provided research, organizing strategies, and staff support. Labor and immigrant colleagues informed the work with living examples of the need for reform of factory conditions and hours or the havoc wreaked on families when a mischievous child ended up in an adult prison. In the case of their

10 Hayden, *Domestic Revolution,*171–173.

11 Davis, *Heroine,* 107.

12 K. McCarthy, *Noblesse Oblige,* 109–110.

13 Costin, *Two Sisters,* 43.

14 Getis, *The Juvenile Court,* 16.

By 1907, the Hull-House complex included sixteen buildings. (Chicago History Museum, ICHi-17807, Photographer: Kaufman and Fabry.)

drive to make the juvenile court a reality, private donations were collected to pay for probation officers, a detention home, and even the judge's salary. Other women who were not wealthy but comfortable enough to volunteer in-kind services provided free housing for probation officers or worked as unpaid probation offers. In another act of private benevolence, the cost to post visiting nurses in Chicago public schools was originally covered by Louise de Koven Bowen and other donors. Only when the benefit of school nurses became indisputable did the Board of Education begin to pay their salaries.

Among the wealthy women critical to Hull-House's success was Louise de Koven Bowen, a member of a Chicago pioneer family, the largest donor to Hull-House, and a close friend to Jane Addams. Addams died at Bowen's home in 1935. Bowen was a strong advocate for racial justice and active in the founding of the juvenile court. Anita McCormick Blaine, daughter of the inventor of the McCormick Reaper, was a socialist education reformer and funder of many civic studies, including a major study of housing conditions. Ellen Martin Henrotin was a clubwoman and wife of the Stock Exchange president. She had served as vice president of the World's Fair Board of Lady Managers and was a strong advocate for labor and women's rights. She nominated Fannie Barrier Williams to be the first black member of the Chicago Woman's Club in 1894. Helen Culver, a real estate developer and the donor of the Hull-House building, was one of the wealthiest women in Chicago. Hull-House was only one of many philanthropies she supported.

As other settlements were organized, Hull-House could draw on the support and assistance of a network of other settlement leaders. Mary McDowell, a former Hull-House teacher, became head resident of the University of Chicago Settlement and a strong ally of Hull-House. She was a founding member of the National Women's Trade Union League, a co-founder of the Playground Association of America, and a founder of the Chicago Federation of Settlements and the National Federation of Settlements. Minnie Low, co-founder of the Maxwell Street Settlement, and Harriet Vittum, head resident of Northwestern Settlement House, were also important allies.

Another critical group of allies included women in the labor movement. Jane Addams and Hull-House plainly empathized with the struggles of labor, although they did not endorse all the tactics or strategies employed in confrontations. Labor leaders with strong ties to Hull-House included Mary Kenney who started the Jane Club before moving to Boston, Bessie Abramowitz Hillman of the garment workers union, and several members of the Women's Trade Union League, the Chicago chapter of which originally met at Hull-House.

Many more women interacted with Hull-House sporadically or through the network of women's clubs and civic reform initiatives. These women, some of whom will play roles in future chapters, included architects, businesswomen, lawyers, educators, physicians, journalists, and more. Many were founders of schools, hospitals, and other critical institutions. Elizabeth Harrison and Alice Whiting Putnam, for example, founded the Chicago Kindergarten Training School (now the National College of Education). Lucy Flower helped found the Illinois Training School for Nurses and the juvenile court. Fannie Barrier Williams helped found Provident Hospital and Training School.

ACTIVIST WOMEN AND NEW ROLES & RESPONSIBILITIES

The settlement house was not the only venue for activist women at the turn of the century. (Some women worked exclusively on suffrage; others formed temperance associations to fight alcohol abuse. These endeavors were different from the city-building work discussed here, although many city-builders were secondarily suffragists.) However, Hull-House was such an important institution, a philosophical and residential innovation created by women that it has to be given a primary role in the story of women's activism. Hull-House in Chicago and the College Settlement in New York both opened in 1889; both were "firsts." By 1911 there were nearly three dozen settlements in Chicago.[15] Many of the women leaders of time lived in settlement houses for at least some period of their lives. Clubwomen, businesswomen, artists, and intellectuals who lived outside the settlements attended meetings, concerts, lectures, and other events at settlement houses or provided financial support to them and their reform initiatives. The settlements, therefore, were central to the work of women in Chicago, and Hull-House was central to the settlement movement.

The settlements were neutral ground for the broadest spectrum of ideologies. Hull-House was a place where the radical Lucy Parsons, the black widow of a white Haymarket martyr, would find political support from Jane Addams after police violence during a demonstration. The deputy chief of police accused Addams of being an anarchist for supporting Parsons's right to protest.[16] At the opposite end of the spectrum, Jane Addams worked closely with Anita McCormick Blaine (of the McCormick Reaper, later International Harvester, family). Lucy Parsons's husband, Albert Parsons, was executed following a labor demonstration (some call it a police riot) against the McCormick Reaper Works in 1886. Between those extremes of class were scores more women (and some men too) who crafted collaborative, nurturing institutions; who built spaces

---

15 Feffer, *The Chicago Pragmatists,* 107.

16 This incident actually took place in 1915, after the *Plan of Chicago* was written. In most cases, historical examples will reflect the period before 1910, or will be noted as after the *Plan.* This example is indicative of Jane Addams's support for free speech throughout her life; the quote of the deputy is what establishes the lengths to which Addams was willing to extend her good offices.

to improve human health and well-being; and who engaged in civic and institutional reforms that were unprecedented at the time.

The women profiled in this book took a pragmatic rather than moralistic approach to cleaning up the city. For instance, Hull-House created public spaces that were alternatives to saloons, because people needed places to socialize, enjoy a beverage, and relax. Rather than railing against the use of alcohol, Hull-House created alternatives such as the coffee house, a debating society, and many special-interest classes, lectures, and concerts. The activist women also explicitly refuted Darwinian and capitalist notions of survival of the fittest. They refused to lay the blame for dirt, disease, or even depravity on individuals who were more likely victims than perpetrators of some of the evil they saw around them. Earlier women reformers felt compelled to couch their calls for change in religious terms. The settlement house women largely rejected sin and sinning as the basis of their critique and focused on the social and industrial conditions that created disorder and disease.

Although there were opportunities for all ages and genders to engage in constructive social activities at Hull-House, some activities were gender-specific. One example of innovative space promoted by Hull-House was the Jane Club, cooperative apartments where young working women shared expenses. (The Secretary of the U.S. Department of Labor claimed he had never seen women cooperate successfully before visiting the Jane Club.)[17] These shared living arrangements helped sustain young women who were occasionally out of work or on strike, so they could avoid those who preyed on women in economically vulnerable positions. Even women who worked full time were not safe. Wages for young clerks were set so low in some stores that women were expected to "supplement" their incomes to survive.[18]

The settlement house took cooperative housekeeping as its own model, with residents who lived together, worked together, and shared chores. Hull-House grew from two resident women and a housekeeper in 1889 to thirty-one women and twenty men in 1911. That settlement house women embraced a cooperative model of working and living was not a purely altruistic stance on the part

---

17   Hayden, *Domestic Revolution,* 168.
18   Stead, *If Christ,* 245.

of the women who organized the living arrangement. Cooperative living freed women from isolated domestic routines that had kept women out of the intellectual mainstream for centuries. Cooperative housekeeping also gave them social "cover" to a certain extent. Although their status as women without husbands and children was seen as odd (making them one of the groups of "strangers" that occupied big cities of the time), their conduct was also considered entirely respectable. Over time, women such as Jane Addams came to be seen as above reproach on any "moral" basis, even if one disagreed with her on an issue. Younger women who lived in the settlement households could be assured of preserving a high reputation even as they maintained their independence from family and expanded their interaction with the larger world.

Hull-House and other settlements offered support for a range of shared living arrangements, but respected the more conservative family traditions of their neighbors and did not preach cooperative living. Cooperative living was for them a functional arrangement rather than a movement to espouse. They were too busy promoting factory reforms, juvenile courts, and sanitation improvements to try to impose their style of living on others.

Women took the cooperative approach into their work partly because it was familiar and had worked in their personal lives. Cooperative values permeated the women's civic work, which was largely accomplished through a network of over one hundred groups. Jane Addams was at the forefront of many of these groups in Chicago and the nation. The groups coalesced around issues with varying degrees of fervor and involvement, and built coalitions around common issues. Some, like suffragists, worked primarily on "women's issues." Others worked on children's issues in general, or in specific children's arenas like child labor laws, education, or juvenile justice. There were wealthy women who funded social innovations and cultural institutions. There were African American, Jewish, and Eastern European women who overcame barriers of gender, class, and race/ethnicity to improve their own lot and that of their peers. Labor leaders, especially female labor leaders, created their own unions but also interacted with women in the other networks. At a time when business and labor were often involved in bloody clashes, when the male-dominated business world was a white, upper-class preserve and male unions were becoming more, not less, segregated,[19] women persevered in cooperating. There were less-than-perfect examples of cooperation, but the attempts, however imperfect, were made.

Cooperative networks and structures helped to promote and bring about change, but Addams and her allies knew the limits of voluntary cooperation in trying to institutionalize change. Delores Hayden speaks of Addams and her counterparts as having "a much keener and more realistic sense of class interests than any of the reformers who preceded them, and this knowledge ultimately showed itself in mistrust of voluntary cooperation. These women tended to prefer forms of organization that emphasized the partnership of the state and the skilled professional, the latter usually an idealistic, university-trained woman who saw herself as an advocate for the needs of poor women and children, especially the single women and married women in the paid labor force who were concentrated in city slums."[20] Though the belief that only women like themselves were up to such reform tasks was less than admirable, Jane Addams and her peers' desire to ensure the survival of their reforms beyond volunteerism through institutionalization and state-sponsorship was a bold leap for the time.

One way in which the women of Hull-House in particular differed from the mainstream culture of the time was in their flexibility. The choice of residence alone made by these educated, middle-class women—to live in "tenement" communities—establishes their flexibility. Hull-House residents created a reciprocal learning environment in which they learned from their neighbors, while sharing with them their own ideas about democracy and Western culture. In other words, they were open and flexible about learning from the less formally educated immigrants.

Several short anecdotes help to illuminate this flexible, reciprocal learning environment. One poignant episode involved a sickly, abandoned baby brought to Hull-House from County Hospital. The residents tended to the baby and secured medical attention for it, but to no avail. When the baby died, the residents caused distress among their neighbors by trying to return the body to the county for burial. The immigrant mothers' traditions called for a proper and demonstrative funeral, whereas the residents felt the care they

---

19 The American Federation of Labor stopped organizing black workers in 1893.

20 Hayden, *Domestic Revolution,* 153.

lavished on the infant in life was the important element.[21] Another example begins with the Hull-House residents' desire to improve their neighbors' nutrition level, particularly for immigrant families where the mother was working and unable to cook. Their experiment in introducing Eastern and Southern Europeans to "Yankee food," as it was called by at least one unappreciative immigrant, was a spectacular failure, but a failure from which they learned. The Hull-House coffee house, which was substituted for the nutrition program, more successfully met the needs of their neighbors.[22] And as Hull-House evolved, the residents learned the value of celebrating the holidays, music, attire, and culture of its neighbors, presenting Western culture in an unassuming context alongside others in an appealing cultural smorgasbord. As Addams herself said, "The experience of the coffee house taught us not to hold preconceived ideas of what the neighborhood ought to have, but to keep ourselves in readiness to modify and adapt our undertakings as we discovered those things which the neighborhood was ready to accept."[23]

CONFRONTING THE MOST COMPLICATED ISSUES

Some of the most complicated issues of the early twentieth century involved race and class. Most of the activist women of the time, whether at Hull-House or elsewhere, were on the forefront of those challenges, although not always with a unity of purpose. There were some examples of refreshing openness and others of shortsightedness. For example, the campaign to admit Fannie Barrier Williams to the Chicago Woman's Club (initiated by Ellen Martin Henrotin in 1894) took over a year.

The immediate Hull-House neighborhood did not include an African American population, and Hull-House did not serve a black constituency. However it was one of the sites in Chicago where blacks were invited to speak on issues important to their community.[24] The Jane Club apartments were not integrated until after the first decade of the twentieth century. This may have been why

---

21   Longo, *Why Community Matters,* 54.

22   Addams, *Twenty Years,* 78.

23   Ibid., 79.

24   Diner, "Chicago Social Workers," 399.

Louise de Koven Bowen said Hull-House lacked "warmth" toward black women even as residents spoke of "the race problem" in Chicago.[25] It is unclear whether her remark reflected on Jane Addams or Hull-House residents generally. Bowen knew that Addams's attitudes and work in the area of race relations were quite progressive. In 1909, Jane Addams was a founding member of the National Association for the Advancement of Colored People (NAACP) and was contributing articles to black publications like *The Crisis* and *Opportunity.*[26]

In part, the opportunity to collaborate on forming organizations like the NAACP came about because white and African American clubwomen had formed coalitions to address local issues. Jane Addams, Louise de Koven Bowen, and Mary McDowell worked closely with African American women on the issues of housing discrimination, African American children in juvenile court, and suffrage.[27] Jane Addams helped found the Wendell Phillips Settlement (1907) to serve a racially mixed neighborhood. She hosted a lunch for the National Association of Colored Women at Hull-House. In 1902, at the National Convention of Women's Clubs in Los Angeles, she spoke for the inclusion of African American women's clubs in the federation.[28]

African American women faced multiple barriers in developing community institutions like settlement houses. Cooperative housing arrangements could seem like another affront to African American men or to the endangered status of the black family.[29] Although Chicago had a black elite, financial support for settlements and other agencies was problematic, given the great need. The focus of settlement work in African American communities was more heavily on "uplift," or religion; education; and economic development. Settlements were seen by African American leaders and constituents as missionary or charity work rather than scientific or progressive-era institutions.[30]

---

25   Spain, *How Women Saved,* 119.

26   Ibid., 119.

27   Knupfer, *African American Women's Clubs,* 46–47.

28   Davis, *Heroine,* 129.

29   Knupfer, *African American Women's Clubs,* 16.

30   Ibid., 95.

The first interracial settlement house was the Frederick Douglass Center (1905) on the edge of a black community, founded by
Ida B. Wells and Celia Parker Woolley, a white Unitarian minister.
The Phyllis Wheatley Home (1908) and Old Folks Home sustained
themselves for a significant time, but most efforts succumbed to
funding shortfalls after a while. Fannie Barrier Williams pointed
out the reliance on the "dominant race" for financial support.[31]
Other neighborhood centers like Emanuel House and the Abraham
Lincoln Center were formed in the mid- to late-1900s. In addition
to the complications cited of funding, of black women needing to
avoid undermining black men, and the need to solicit mainstream
involvement, African American settlements faced a final, and in
many cases, fatal barrier. National institutions like the NAACP
and the Urban League began to absorb smaller, community-based
institutions at a time when African American settlements were
barely on their feet. Ida B. Wells, for one, was skeptical of the motives of the national organizations, fearing the loss of local voices
in advocacy and policy-making.[32] In an unfortunate irony, after the
death of Wells's former collaborator Celia Parker Woolley, Woolley's
husband gave the Frederick Douglass Center building to the Urban
League.[33]

The relationship between labor and settlement houses was no
less complex. Most labor union activists, even women, were in-
stinctively wary of the middle-class women's motives. Mary Kenney, a bookbinder, had to learn to trust Jane Addams: "It was that
word 'with' from Jane Addams that took the bitterness out of my
life. For if she wanted to work with me and I could work with her,
it gave my life new meaning and hope."[34] Winning the trust of labor allies once did not guarantee that future collaboration would
be smooth. In a wrenching break, Jane Addams fell into a serious
dispute with allies Margaret Dreier Robins, of the Women's Trade
Union League (WTUL), and her husband Raymond Robins over a
series of votes when Jane was a school board member. The Robinses urged Addams to take a harder line than she was willing to
take after a mayoral purge of progressive school board members

---

31   Ibid., 44.
32   Ibid., 45.
33   Schultz and Hast, *Women Building Chicago,* 994.
34   Davis, *Spearheads,* 139.

and a clumsy attempt by the superintendent of schools to initiate secret evaluations of teachers. The disagreement resulted in a break in their relationship, although not a permanent one. Dreier Robins led a cleverly staged *coup d'etat* to move the Chicago WTUL from meeting space it had used at Hull-House since its founding to the Chicago Federation of Labor offices.[35] The Chicago branch of the WTUL was founded at Hull-House with Mary McDowell as president and Jane Addams as vice president.[36] Addams would continue to work with both of the Robinses in future years, but this particular schism is important because it comes shortly before the period discussed here.

Mary McDowell took on the dual challenges of race and class. When she began her tenure at the University of Chicago Settlement in 1894, the only labor unions in the stockyards were small and secret; they thought the settlement workers were spies.[37] As McDowell worked to earn the trust of the unions, she also actively sought to convince stockyard unions to admit blacks.[38]

For Addams and many other settlement workers, there was clear congruence with their goals and those of labor unions, but not always with tactics, especially militant tactics. Arbitration was favored by settlement workers, but there were times when labor did not want to arbitrate or did not want to accept terms proposed under arbitration. In spite of any reservations about tactics, Addams was strongly in support of the unions in her public comments. She spoke out for workers in the Chicago Building Trade Strike (1900), the National Anthracite Strike (1902), and the Chicago Stockyards Strike (1904).[39] The year after the *Plan of Chicago* was completed, she supported striking textile workers, even though Joseph Schaffner and Harry Hart (of the textiles firm Hart, Schaffner and Marx) were donors to Hull-House.[40] In *Twenty Years at Hull-House,* Addams comments on the balancing act required to maintain Hull-House's independence and keep it solvent. From the time of Addams's participation on the Citizen Arbitration Com-

---

35   Payne, *Reform, Labor, and Feminism,* 61–67.

36   Ibid., 64–65.

37   Davis, *Spearheads,* 113.

38   Diner, "Chicago Social Workers," 402.

39   Davis, *Heroine,* 114.

40   Ibid., 115.

mittee, which tried unsuccessfully to resolve the Pullman Strike, funding complications arose from Hull-House's support for the labor movement. Some residents felt that money from industrialists was "tainted," and some donors did seek leverage in return for their contributions.[41]

SETTLEMENT LEADERS' CONTRIBUTIONS TO SOCIOLOGY

The following chapters will offer many examples of specific city-building contributions made by the residents. It is important to note that these women also helped establish the field of sociology, which evolved at roughly the same time as urban planning. Sociology, settlement work, and urban planning arose as responses to many of the same challenges. Over time they each began to offer unique solutions, differing in their emphasis on the importance of such things as research typologies, attitudes toward physical space, and theories of human development. One hundred years ago the boundaries between the three professions and fields of study were still somewhat fluid.

The story of how academia and city planning shunned the settlement model and values is largely a tale of gender politics. In both cases, men defined or redefined professional protocols to be less human-centered. In the case of sociology, the practical application of sociology was demeaned, even to the extent that collection of statistical information was seen as "women's work" and not sufficiently theoretical to be of significance.[42]

For reasons that didn't become apparent until well beyond the 1909 horizon of this discussion, sociology became an academic sphere dominated by men who preferred theoretical approaches over Jane Addams's pragmatic, hands-on approach. An earnest battle within the sociology department of the University of Chicago took place between men (and a few women) loyal to the work of the settlement houses, and theoreticians who wanted to remake the new science. One sociologist even claimed a variety of firsts for himself where Hull-House had already blazed a trail.[43] According to Mary Jo Deegan, the authors of the *Hull-House Maps and Papers*

41   Addams, *Twenty Years,* 82–84.
42   Deegan, *Men of the Chicago School,* 46.
43   Ibid., 64.

differed from male sociologists as a whole in the following ways: they stressed the impact of economic dislocations on individuals and families, studied art as a function of life, studied women and their issues, advocated government intervention and social change, and eschewed conflict as a methodology.[44] The earliest male sociologists were most likely to know and respect Hull-House trailblazers. Later sociologists ignored or suppressed their contributions, while relying on many of their research methodologies.

The direct relationship between Hull-House and sociology can be followed in the careers of two Hull-House residents: Edith Abbott and Sophonisba Breckinridge. During their earliest years at Hull-House, Abbott, Breckenridge, Florence Kelley, Jane Addams, and others produced a large quantity of scholarly studies on the practical problems associated with poverty. For instance, between 1895 and 1935, the *American Journal of Sociology* printed over fifty articles by residents who could be easily identified with Hull-House and reviewed twenty-seven books written by Hull-House residents.[45] Their quantitative evaluations of sanitation conditions, typhoid outbreaks, housing conditions, infant mortality, and ethnicity by residential lot established a scholarly standard for the developing field of sociology. Their protocol for high standards of scholarship was of secondary importance to the women; the primary purpose of the studies was to make practical improvements in the social and public health status of neighborhoods inhabited by poor people.

Residents of several settlement houses founded the Chicago School of Civics and Philanthropy to sustain their research activities. Eventually Edith Abbott moved the school to the University of Chicago, where it became the School of Social Service Administration, with Abbott as dean (the move came in 1924, long after the period under discussion here). From the beginning, there were opposing notions of sociology and social work within the faculty at the University of Chicago, with many of the differences following gender lines. The gulf between female and male sociologists became wider over time, with the more theoretical and abstract approach of male academics eventually dominating sociology departments at the University of Chicago and elsewhere. Hull-House methodology

---

44   Ibid., 62.
45   Ibid., 47.

represented a multi-pronged approach that balanced its need to maintain benefactor relations with the imperative to fully expose neighborhood challenges, no matter how controversial. At many universities the disapproval of business donors drove sociology departments away from the kinds of controversial inquiries that had originally spawned the field. Jane Addams felt the difference directly in sociology's earliest days when the faculty of the University of Chicago voted to give her an honorary degree in 1906 but the trustees overruled the vote, largely because of her support for organized labor.

SETTLEMENT LEADERS' CONTRIBUTION TO THE YOUNG FIELD OF PLANNING

At the time the *Plan of Chicago* was written, most people would not have recognized the terms "city planning" or "urban planning." The architects of the *Plan* were, literally, architects. Settlement workers in Chicago and elsewhere were advocating for better planning in journal articles, speeches, and exhibitions. When the split between city planning and settlement work came, it was much more rapid and forceful than the split between sociology and settlement work.

The first national conference on city planning was held only a few months before release of the *Plan of Chicago*. The conference was convened by New York City's official Committee on Congestion of Population. The leadership of the Committee on Congestion of Population included former Hull-House resident Florence Kelley, Addams confidant Lillian Wald, and Mary Simkhovitch, head resident of Greenwich House. Their solution to the overcrowding of people was to provide or improve schools, parks, playgrounds, housing, and transportation.[46]

The National Association of City Planning was born of the conviction of these women that social planning and physical planning are intrinsically linked.[47] Simkhovitch, who was the theoretician of the group, subscribed to the vision of "the City Social," a vision of neighborhoods that offered self-determination, organization, and integration of social services. She saw these attributes

---

46   Davis, *Spearheads,* 71–72.
47   Sies and Silver, *Planning,* 56.

as the foundation from which one could move to urban design and policy-based planning. She and other leaders were explicit that the City Beautiful movement was inadequate to address a full range of urban issues. The Committee on Congestion of Population popularized its case with a traveling exhibit with the theme "Every City Needs a Plan Now."[48]

The First National Conference on Planning was held in Washington, D.C., May 21–22, 1909. Mary Corbin Sies, in her history of city planning, reports that "Concerned more with economics than aesthetics, conference participants called for an urban planning process based on sociological research."[49] They also emphasized a regional perspective.

In spite of the importance of the role of the Committee of Congestion of People, Simkhovitch was the only woman to speak at the conference. She advocated a campaign to introduce city planning across the nation. While decrying the negative effects of "congestion" on people, she was cognizant of the appeal of urban density: "The reason the poor like to live in New York is because it is interesting, convenient, and meets their social needs. They live there for the reason I do; I like it."[50] She was also clear-headed about the importance of ensuring community support, saying, "no matter how good a plan looks from the point of view of a sound economy, it is not a good plan unless the people like it."[51]

Despite this hopeful start, by the next year, the second annual conference of the National Association of City Planning was completely dominated by architects and engineers and consumed with the physical aspects of planning. Hull-House resident George Hooker and others tried to keep a comprehensive focus, but the national conference turned its focus to beauty for the well-to-do rather than improvements for tenement dwellers.[52] Simkhovitch and others organized the National Housing Association, which held its first conference in 1911, as a more focused alternative for addressing their issues.[53]

---

48   Ibid., 67.
49   Ibid., 70.
50   Ibid., 71–72.
51   Ibid., 73.
52   Davis, *Spearheads,* 72–73.
53   Sies and Silver, *Planning,* 75.

MEN WHO SHARED THE SETTLEMENT ETHIC

The businessmen of Chicago in the period between the Chicago Fire and first decade of the twentieth century operated under a unique blend of *laissez-faire* capitalism and Wild West bravado. While the businessmen benefited from a weak, corrupt political system and from private contracts to perform municipal services, other groups of men (and even some businessmen) allied themselves with settlement house residents working for improved parks, schools, sanitation, and municipal reform. Some of the most significant male allies of the settlements are briefly introduced here.

One of the most intriguing of these men happened to be an architect, Allen Pond. Pond was one of the first people to meet Jane Addams and Ellen Starr when they arrived in Chicago. Pond heard Addams speak early in 1889 at a meeting of the Armour Mission board and offered to introduce Addams and Starr to others in the city.[54] He became a long-time friend to Hull-House. Pond designed the thirteen-building Hull-House complex and was an original member of the Hull-House board of directors. He played a similar role with the Chicago Commons settlement, designing the Commons building and serving on the board.[55] Pond was a proponent of the Arts and Crafts movement, which influenced settlement ideology about craftsmanship as an alternative to mechanized production. He played a role in various municipal reform movements and was a member of cultural and literary groups like the Little Room, which brought together artistic, intellectual, and settlement house professionals.

William Kent, an ally of Pond, owned a tenement near Hull-House that was the subject of concern from residents. After offering to turn the building over to Hull-House (they declined because of the poor condition of the building), he agreed to demolish the building and donate the land for Chicago's first playground. Kent became a lifelong advocate of parks and playgrounds,[56] a leader of many municipal reform efforts and eventually an alderman. Kent was a subscriber to the *Plan of Chicago*.

---

54 Davis, *Heroine*, 54.
55 Wade, *Graham Taylor*, 143.
56 McArthur, "Chicago Playground Movement," 379.

One of the men Kent worked closely with was Walter L. Fisher, the lawyer who wrote the *Plan of Chicago*'s appendix on the legal aspects of implementation. Fisher was Secretary of the Municipal Voters League. He moved up in leadership of the League (with Charles Crane) to replace Kent and Pond in 1900.[57]

Charles Crane, son of an early Chicago plutocrat, funded many good government, settlement house, and arts programs. Charles convinced his father to donate $100,000 to Hull-House for a nursery, which was named in memory of his mother, Mary Crane.[58] He was also on the Chicago Commons board of directors.

Another progressive business leader was Charles L. Hutchinson, a banker, who became president of the Art Institute in 1882. Hutchinson wanted to bring art to the streets, as in European cities. Furthermore, he personally helped to bring art to the neighborhoods, loaning some of his own art to Hull-House, arranging for Art Institute works to be displayed in field houses, and helping the Public School Art Society build a collection for the schools.[59] Later in life, Hutchinson became a trustee of Hull-House.[60]

A woman leads children in exercise on the roof of the Mary Crane Nursery, an open-air school. (Chicago History Museum, DN-0008025, Chicago Daily News *negatives collection, Chicago Historical Society.)*

57 Steffens, *Shame of the Cities,* 180.

58 K. McCarthy, *Noblesse Oblige,* 120.

59 Schaffer, *Urban Ideals,* 133.

60 Ibid., 124.

Several male educators, sociologists, and reformers were closely tied to Hull-House, including John Dewey, Albion Small, George Mead, Charles Henderson, Charles Zueblin, Henry Demarest Lloyd, and Richard T. Ely.[61] The cross-fertilization among city, settlement house, and academia was powerful. Upton Sinclair, author of *The Jungle*, lived in a room near the University of Chicago Settlement in the stockyards, and took his meals at the settlement while collecting information for his book.[62] Historian Charles Beard lived at Hull-House in 1896 and was influenced by his experience there.[63] Educator John Dewey, who arrived in Chicago in 1894 as the Pullman Strike began, was affected by his initial experiences in the city. In the first few days of his tenure in Chicago, thirteen people died in labor unrest and $80 million worth of property was destroyed (including buildings remaining from World's Fair, which were burned on July 6).[64]

Several of these men collaborated with settlement house workers to develop the school of social work that eventually became the School of Social Service Administration at the University of Chicago. In its early days, the school was known as the Chicago Institute of Social Science and offered college-level classes in settlement houses. It became the Chicago School of Civics and Philanthropy in 1908 and finally became the School of Social Service Administration. The early board included men such as Graham Taylor, Edward L. Ryerson, Charles Crane, Allen Pond, Victor Etling, Judge Julian Mack, Julius Rosenwald, Richard Ely, and William Kent. Jane Addams, Julia Lathrop, Louise de Koven Bowen, Anita McCormick Blaine, and Ethel Sturges Dummer were also on the early board.[65]

Another network of men connected to the settlement houses could be found in civic reform efforts. Walter Fisher, secretary of the Municipal Voter League, organized the City Club of Chicago in mid-1903 as a discussion forum. By December, 175 progressive businessmen, journalists, and other professionals joined, including Victor Lawson, Medill McCormick, Graham Taylor, George Hooker,

---

61   Davis, *Heroine,* 97.

62   Davis, *Spearheads,* 117.

63   Ibid., 171.

64   Feffer, *The Chicago Pragmatists,* 91.

65   Wade, *Graham Taylor,* 168–169.

Raymond Robins, Charles Merriam, John Dewey, and Charles Zueblin.[66] Women were not allowed to be members. Paradoxically the City Club of Chicago voted against admitting women in 1906, at the same meeting where they accepted a report on municipal reform written by Charles Merriam and financed by Helen Culver.[67] (The Woman's City Club was formed in 1911.)

Although settlement houses were generally established and operated by women, many prominent men were residents of settlements in Chicago and firmly integrated into the work of the settlements. Men living at Hull-House had their own living quarters by 1896 on the third floor above Butler Art Gallery.[68] Raymond Robins came to Chicago in 1901 after careers on the West Coast as a lawyer and gold miner. He began his settlement career at Chicago Commons and moved to Northwestern University Settlement in 1903.[69] Robins and his wife, Margaret Dreier Robins, head of the Women's Trade Union League, were prominent in many reform movements in Chicago. Raymond Robins was a member of the charter convention and the Chicago Board of Education.

George Hooker, director of the Chicago City Club and an expert on city planning, was a Hull-House resident whose work had real relevance to Burnham's work although there is no evidence he was invited to contribute.[70] Hull-House didn't lack residents with business acumen either. Resident Gerald Swope, who went on to become president of General Electric (his future wife was also a resident), taught an early Hull-House class on electricity and magnetism.[71]

Graham Taylor, a minister and theology professor who established the Chicago Commons, was nearly as prominent in reform activities in Chicago as was Jane Addams, although he was somewhat less able to hold his ground when faced with vigorous dissent. Taylor came to Chicago from Hartford in 1892. He was one of many Chicagoans shocked by the abrupt change from the majestic facade of the World's Columbian Exposition to the desperate con-

---

66   Feffer, *The Chicago Pragmatists,* 195–196.

67   Schultz and Hast, *Women Building Chicago,* 204.

68   Ibid., xxxv.

69   Wade, *Graham Taylor,* 132–133.

70   Davis, *Heroine,* 75.

71   Glowacki and Hendry, *Images of America,* 22.

dition of the depression that followed. He called it a "transforming experience."[72] By 1894, he had founded the Chicago Commons
on the near Northwest Side of the city. Chicago Commons offered
many of the same programs (kindergarten, day nursery, clubs, and
classes) offered by Hull-House. But it differed in two significant
respects. The German, Scandinavian, and Irish population nearby
was predominantly English-speaking, and the leadership of the
Seventeenth Ward was not nearly as entrenched as the leadership
of the Nineteenth (Hull-House) Ward. While Hull-House failed and
ultimately ceased trying to oust the Nineteenth Ward alderman,
Taylor had some success with local political reforms.[73]

Taylor's greatest contributions to settlement work came in the
area of promulgating the settlement ethic and the movement's
news. He founded a magazine covering settlement house issues,
The Commons (1896–1905), which merged with *Charities* magazine
in 1905 to become *Charities and the Commons*. Taylor also wrote a
weekly column from 1902 to 1938 in the *Chicago Daily News*.[74] The
latter platform was particularly important since the *Chronicle* and
Inter-Ocean newspapers tried to smear the settlements as socialist.
The *Inter-Ocean* was originally owned by Charles Yerkes, one of the
least reputable businessmen in the city, and used as a vehicle for
promoting his anti-reform agenda. Victor Lawson, editor of the *Chicago Daily News*, supported Taylor and the settlement movement,
even under trying circumstances.[75] When Hull-House and Chicago
Commons came to the aid of unpopular outsiders, the *Chronicle*
and *Inter-Ocean* accused them of being anti-American apologists
for anarchists. The *Chicago Daily News* and the *Chicago Post* defended Jane Addams, Graham Taylor, and the settlements.[76]

Taylor was a member of the Civic Federation, Municipal Voters
League, and Vice Commission, among other civic and reform initiatives. He served on the Chicago Public Library Board and became
a member of the Chicago Plan Commission.[77] His strong ties to
more conventional, predominantly male reform groups may have

---

72   Wade, *Graham Taylor,* 72.
73   Ibid., 133.
74   Ibid., 3.
75   Ibid., 100–101.
76   Wade, *Graham Taylor,* 135.
77   Ibid., 7, 125, 196–197.

made Chicago Commons, under his leadership, less open to all expressions of thought than what was customary at Hull-House. Taylor was not always decisive in supporting unpopular positions or groups. On one occasion the well-known and controversial anarchist, Emma Goldman, was to speak at Chicago Commons but her invitation was withdrawn.[78] He criticized striking meatpackers in 1904 for not accepting an arbitration decision and returning to work. Mary McDowell, head resident of the settlement in the Stockyards District, struggled with their stance, but stuck by the union and its right to self-determination. Eventually as conditions worsened, she got Cornelia deBey, a prominent physician and reformer, and Jane Addams to help intercede with the packinghouse owner, J. Ogden Armour.[79] Taylor also had a mixed record on racial issues. He rebuked African American strikebreakers, as if they were the cause of labor's difficulties rather than another set of victims in the labor-capital battles of the day. However, he also rebuked the city of Springfield for conditions leading to the race riot in 1908. Taylor lauded Julius Rosenwald's philanthropic interests in blacks but essentially saw blacks as "depraved" and in need of uplift by whites.[80]

Julius Rosenwald, one of the founders of Sears, Roebuck and Company, was singular in his ability to look beyond his own self-interest. Rosenwald was born in Springfield in 1862 to German-Jewish immigrant parents. He probably gave away $60–70 million in his lifetime and did so under unconventional conditions. He wanted input from social scientists on what was needed and wanted to match other funds in order to avoid the potentially autocratic power of a sole donor. The lengths to which he would go to be impartial are suggested by this anecdote: When Hull-House resident Grace Abbott was late to join garment workers who were picketing *his* factory, Rosenwald had his chauffeur drive her to the site.[81]

Rosenwald began supporting Hull-House financially in 1902 and joined the board in 1912. However, his greatest interest was in race relations. He supported YMCAs serving blacks across the nation. In Chicago he was a contributor to Provident Hospital, which

78 Davis, *Spearheads,* 110.

79 Ibid., 118–119.

80 Wade, *Graham Taylor,* 401.

81 Davis, *Spearheads,* 108.

served the black community, and provided many scholarships for black students.[82]

It is hardly surprising that a city as large and diverse as Chicago would include business and civic leadership with diverse viewpoints. It is unfortunate that the ethics and priorities of men like Rosenwald (who was a subscriber to the *Plan*), William Kent (also a subscriber), Allen Pond, and other reform-minded men influenced the *Plan* as little as the women of the settlement houses. Subscribers, people who contributed financially to the production of the *Plan*, were a separate group from the Commercial Club members who actually determined its content.

THE BUSINESSMEN OF CHICAGO

William Stead castigated a "trinity" of capitalists in *If Christ Came to Chicago* (1893): Marshall Field, George Pullman, and Philip Armour.[83] These giants of Chicago commerce died only a few years before the *Plan* was developed, but their influence was still widely felt. Although the business community suffered occasional setbacks in implementing its vision of Chicago, such as the rejection by voters of its proposal for a new municipal charter, the hubris and reach of the trinity had not yet been curbed. Commercial Club members took upon themselves such "noble" civic guardian roles as fighting gambling, drugs, and prostitution. At the same time, most businessmen blithely benefited from substantial assessor-granted tax breaks, a tradition practiced by the trinity, who paid taxes on total property values of $5,000 (Armour) to $20,000 (Field).[84] It was accepted custom in Chicago for the assessor to allow the most powerful and wealthy people to pay absurdly low taxes, in some cases, as Stead pointed out, no more than the madame running a reasonably successful brothel. Another source of morally questionable business practices included real estate deals that undervalued public school property,[85] as the example of the *Chicago Tribune* illustrated, or contracts for municipal services.

---

82 K. McCarthy, *Noblesse Oblige,* 109–111.

83 Stead, *If Christ,* 72.

84 Ibid., 214.

85 Herrick, *Chicago Public Schools,* 18.

William Stead's critique disclosed that forty of the sixty Commercial Club members lived within five blocks of each other in 1893, in the Prairie Avenue area south of the business district, which he referred to as "the Mecca of Mammon."[86] A notorious vice district lay between their homes and the central business district.[87] Presumably, several of the *Plan of Chicago*'s improvements would have eliminated the vice trade and replaced it with expanded businesses, a widened Twelfth Street, and the Twelfth Street Train Station (about which Burnham boasts specifically, "No more modern or perfect plan could be devised").[88] South of Twelfth Street Burnham proposed "a great meadow developed as an athletic field, with central gymnasium, outdoor exercising grounds, swimming beaches, and such other features as have been found advisable in playground parks."[89] The degree of detail in the *Plan* about this one geographic area, although it is interspersed throughout the document and not immediately obvious, is explained by the personal stake Commercial Club members had in the Prairie Avenue area. As Michael P. McCarthy says in his article, "Chicago Businessmen and the Burnham Plan," "But the planners were not entirely altruistic. A number of them lived in the fashionable neighborhoods close to the lake. The prospect of nearby parks with such features as lavish restaurants and yachting facilities delighted many businessmen, especially those on the South Side who were then cut off from the lake from Twelfth Street to Jackson Park by the tracks of the Illinois Central Railroad."[90]

The standard established after the Chicago Fire, that the business community could legitimately take municipal authority and that the citizenry should be grateful for their involvement,[91] was unchanged by setbacks at the hands of the voters. The City Beautiful movement seemed to offer an antidote to those municipal problems most troublesome to the business community: the need for greater order, civic pride, and aesthetic upgrades. They didn't ask what the rest of the populace found most troubling, although they

---

86 Stead, *If Christ,* 71.

87 Hoyt, *One Hundred Years,* 205.

88 Burnham and Bennett, *Plan of Chicago,* 73.

89 Ibid., 112

90 M. McCarthy, "Chicago Businessmen," 244.

91 C. Smith, *Urban Disorder,* 73.

did expect the taxpayers to fund their proposed plan. The World's Columbian Exposition was seen as a great boon to business and to Chicago's reputation, so the businessmen naturally turned to Daniel Burnham to develop a plan for Chicago.[92] They seemed not to have absorbed the lesson of George Pullman's failed experiment in creating an aesthetically pleasing, but autocratically governed, company town.

Critiques of Pullman's town were circulating even before the bitter strike that exposed its limitations. The town of Pullman offered workers housing, stores, schools, and churches, without saloons or other establishments considered by some to be morally questionable. All issues within the town were decided by George Pullman or his company, not by the town's residents. Journalist Richard Ely wrote a lengthy, balanced account of Pullman in 1885 after spending ten days talking to residents as well as managers. (He was one of few who interviewed residents; many writers considered the residents' opinions insignificant or unintelligent.) His assessment of Pullman's physical form was that it was "monotonous, and rather wearying to the eye," presaging later critiques of the Burnham *Plan of Chicago.* According to historian Carl Smith, "In Ely's opinion Pullman was a city that paid a very high cost in human rights for its beauty and order." Some workers described it as "camping out" because residents had no civic role, no autonomy. Ely said, "The idea of Pullman is un-American."[93]

The business community had difficulty understanding civic benefit as anything other than what they would design for the city, such as the Pullman model. Journalist Lincoln Steffens interviewed Chicago businessmen for his 1904 exposé, *Shame of the Cities*, and found them unwilling to support municipal reform, let alone feel a sense of obligation to the larger community. "Anarchy" and "socialism" were the terms the business interviewees used to describe reform. Steffens observed, "Though reform may have been a benefit to the city as a community of free men, it is really bad; it has hurt their business!"[94] Few reforms in Chicago—other than changes to the physical environment—could be considered without running up against the conditions of the working class, the abusive leases

---

92   Ibid., 225.

93   Ibid., 205–206

94   Steffens, *Shame of the Cities,* 188–189.

of school property, and the corruption inherent in awarding city contracts to businessmen. The business community didn't want to bring extra attention to any of these issues.

The idea to create a plan for Chicago's future is generally credited to two energetic businessmen, Frederic A. Delano and Charles D. Norton, both of whom were in Chicago a relatively short time. Delano was president of the Wabash Railroad and wanted a plan that would offer efficient, coordinated terminals.[95] Norton, an insurance executive, and Delano were members of the Merchants' Club when they first approached Burnham about crafting a plan for the city.

In a parallel effort, Franklin MacVeagh led the Committee of Nine for a Chicago Plan within the Commercial Club. They recommended in 1904 that city planning be taken on as a major club project. Although a decision was delayed at that time,[96] by April 1907 a reorganized Commercial Club adopted the plan project after merging with the Merchants' Club. Norton, Delano, Charles H. Wacker, and Walter H. Wilson were in charge of the planning committee.[97]

Businessmen had a limited view of what constituted civic improvement but shored up that view with generous resources. The *Plan* was started with $50,000 in pledges, half of the estimate of total funds needed to complete it. In order to raise additional funds, the argument that parks for the poor had served to protect the general public was put forth as a "sales point." The more grandiose plan would foster civic pride, bring business dividends and help preserve peace.[98] Historian Michael McCarthy describes Burnham's success in securing political support as well. "Burnham convinced influential leaders such as Mayor Fred Busse and Alderman 'Bathhouse' John Coughlin of the need to reshape the city. Indeed, Coughlin so completely aligned himself with the cause that at one planning meeting he remarked, 'If Chicago cannot vote

---

95   After the plan was developed, Norton was instrumental in forging an agreement with Illinois Central Railroad to extend the shoreline by several hundred feet to accommodate a new park and the railroad's existing lines.

96   M. McCarthy, "Chicago Businessmen," 229.

97   Ibid., 233.

98   Ibid., 232.

for the millions needed to carry out this plan, it is a city of yokels and deserves to take a back seat.'"[99]

THE MYSTERY OF THE *PLAN OF CHICAGO*

There is strong indication that Burnham originally created a plan with broader parameters than the one for which he became famous. Kristin Schaffer, an eminent scholar on Burnham and his plan, has studied an earlier draft and presents an interesting mystery. Large sections of the draft, primarily those dealing with education, public health, and related topics, were removed after meetings of the Commercial Club on December 13, 1908; January 28, 1909; and March 14, 1909. During the December meeting, the committee expressed concern that the *Plan* be presented as a *business proposition* (original emphasis). The March meeting, which lasted five hours, was summed up in minutes that were two sentences in length.[100] These minutes were in contrast to other well-documented meeting deliberations.[101] Schaffer, after studying Burnham's handwritten outline and draft said, "Had the draft version been published the *Plan of Chicago* would hold a very different position in the history of American city planning."[102] And Burnham would most likely be credited with developing a more robust and comprehensive style of planning.

The draft documents show another side to Burnham. As Schaffer says, "What exists in the draft but is omitted from the plan, however, are simple and direct statements of concern that the lakefront really be accessible and usable to all citizens. . . . For instance, when describing the recreational use of the waterways, Burnham, in the draft proposes that the fee for rental craft be so low that many can benefit from this form of enjoyment."[103] She also points out that Grant Park was to be the "Place of the People" in Burnham's draft. Burnham proposed free bathhouses and restaurant fare priced at many levels. In the draft, transit was proposed

---

99   Ibid., 236.

100 Schaffer, *Urban Ideals,* 335–338.

101 Burnham and Bennett, *Plan of Chicago,* xiii.

102 Ibid., vi.

103 Schaffer, *Urban Ideals,* 372.

so all Chicagoans could reach the lakefront at little cost; in the final plan, transit's purpose was to give "decided value" to parks.[104]

Schaffer is uncertain whether the plan committee omitted sections of the draft or whether Burnham censored himself. Some of his draft statements are uncharacteristically critical of the elites with whom he associated socially and professionally. Among the list of "intolerable" evils presented in the preliminary outline of the draft plan were: the herding of people by nationalities, the increase of wealth among the few and enormous power ill-used, the tendency to separate classes, and the rapid increase in fortunes without social responsibility.[105] Recommendations that could have reduced the autonomy or profitability of business interests included supervision of public utilities by government to make them a safe investment (omitted from the final plan) and smoke pollution (which was mentioned but not elaborated on in the final plan).[106] In a direct critique of abuse of civil authority, Burnham's draft included a section about designing police stations to be open and visible, to temper the instinct to use unnecessary force. "To sum up, the stations should be arranged so that the policemen can do nothing to any prisoner while hidden from view." In the final *Plan of Chicago*, his only station reference is to one of many buildings in the suburban civic center, Schaffer reminds us.[107]

The distinction between what the *Plan* became and what it might have become if Burnham's additional sections were maintained is an important one. Excerpts from Schaffer's introduction to the 1993 edition of the *Plan of Chicago* summarize many of the ways in which Burnham's draft plan would have differed from the published one:

In [the] second half of the draft, Burnham takes on topics of a more technical nature, or a narrower scale. Here he is more concerned with the provision of services, and perhaps less with the city's representational "face." Burnham discusses mail delivery and the postal service, central power plants, public utilities and utility lines, and smoke pollution. He notes manufacturing and future business districts in brief.

104   Ibid., 375–376.
105   Ibid., 379.
106   Ibid., 390–391.
107   Ibid., 393.

He concerns himself with schools, hospitals, police stations, foundling homes, cemeteries, and "public comfort" facilities. Some items from this second half of the draft find their way into the text of the published version as small asides, imbedded in chapters devoted to related topics. . . .

Of particular interest are those topics entirely omitted from the final version, or so reduced as to be effectively nullified. These show a very different side of Burnham and challenge conventionally held assessments of the *Plan*. They greatly expand our perceptions of his conception of the city, his sympathies, and his concerns. They define the role of the state—that is, the city government—in shaping and improving the life of the individual. In the draft, for instance, public utility companies are considered, and not only in their relationship to the physical fabric of the city. He writes of public utilities, "All of them for every purpose should be operated by private corporations, under supervision of the government. The government should not only supervise, but encourage and foster them in order that they may, first, do their work perfectly as servants of the public, and second, that their securities issued under strict government supervision, may become and forever continue to be absolutely reliable." He is concerned not only with the provision of utilities to the city, but also that these companies offer a safe investment for Chicago's citizens.

Burnham discusses hospitals in the draft, not only as facilities, but also in terms of their coordination and the provision of services. This topic is entirely omitted from the published *Plan*. . . .

Only brief remarks are made on schoolhouses in the *Plan*, and they are buried in Chapters III and VI, but in the draft Burnham discusses their design and location extensively. Burnham argues that schoolhouses should be located in the neighborhoods of the populations to be served, and that the plans of the buildings and playgrounds should be carefully considered. He is particularly concerned with the provision of adequate amounts of sunlight and fresh air. . . .

In the draft, Burnham discusses the needs of families who cannot care for their children and work at the same time, and for children who are given up . . . Burnham recommends the establishment of day-care centers, what he terms crèches
. . . .

He addresses the city's interaction with the citizen in very fundamental ways. He is well aware that the most basic of human functions must be accommodated. . . . "Public stations should be provided liberally, nor should they be for men alone, or of the minor functions of his need, but should be for both sexes." [108]

Burnham considers the World's Columbian Exposition an achievement relevant to his credentials for the *Plan of Chicago*; the exposition did offer day care,[109] an indication that left to his own devices he had more to offer than what we see in the *Plan of Chicago*. The optimistic vision of Burnham seems to be a man who was embedded in the wealthy class and shared many of its sensibilities, but did not necessarily share all its worst fears and animosities. He may have inhabited a position in the intellectual middle between the business ethic of the time and the settlement house ethic, at least in broaching questions of education, public health, and safety.

However, his own grandiose notions of his work and his sense of entitlement to make decisions for others, even if the decisions were benign, separate him from the settlement ethic. For example, his view of Americanization was much less reciprocal than theirs. The *Plan* tends to come across as imposing order *on* people rather than *for* people. He failed to grasp the impact on Chicagoans of the demolition required to build the Civic Center and diagonal avenues.

Burnham's *Plan* fails to deal with many of the important civic debates of the day, like a new charter for the city and tax reform. In fact, he defined the important issues primarily from the business point of view. He seems unable to reach across the chasms of class, and in fact could not reach across the chasm of gender, even within his own class. His apparent ignorance about the civic institutions and innovations coming from the settlements, at a time when places like Hull-House were the intellectual hub of the city, is hard to fathom.

Today's observations about the final *Plan* can only be made on the basis of what is there, not what might have been. Although it is unfortunate that the *Plan* was limited to physical features of

108 Burnham and Bennett, *Plan of Chicago,* viii–xi.
109 Spain, *How Women Saved,* 221.

interest to the business community, it did result in preservation of and access to the lakefront, a vast forest preserve system, a transportation network that encouraged the growth of the metropolis, and the development of a world class central area. For some that was and is sufficient.

The question posed here is whether inclusion of city-builders who worked in areas of municipal reform, access to decent housing, sanitation, health, education, and justice, for example, would have made for a better plan and a social fabric to match the physical fabric of the region.

In answer to "What would Jane (or Ellen or Alice or Julia) Say?" about a plan for Chicago's future, these women would have been likely to propose building on the practical examples of city-building work they had already accomplished. Their physical accomplishments like playgrounds, the juvenile court, and the settlement houses themselves (in Hull-House's case a multi-purpose complex) were augmented by a multitude of programmatic innovations in areas like public health and education. The physical and programmatic achievements were complemented by a host of other municipal reforms like investigations into inept or corrupt inspectors, passage of child labor and factory legislation, and broad municipal reform efforts.

In the next eight chapters, the potential contributions of specific women to major aspects of the *Plan of Chicago* will be proposed, in a format that is heavily researched but includes speculative conversations based on their words and deeds. The historic record they left has been combed to suggest how they *might have* commented on Burnham's chapters on parks, transportation, and the central business district. These first three chapters are "conversations" they might have had at three different committee meetings on those topics—had they been asked. Since their purview was much broader than the purview of the *Plan of Chicago*, they could have offered good counsel in additional areas, such as immigrant and labor rights, public health, housing and neighborhood development, education, and justice and the courts. Five more chapters include their insights from the historical record in these areas, also in conversational form. Their views are offered as examples of what a truly comprehensive plan could have been in 1909.

Chapters 6 through 13 propose conversations that *might have* occurred at Hull-House if Daniel Burnham had invited city-building women to comment on the *Plan of Chicago*.

The opinions expressed in these chapters are based on research and are characteristic of opinions the women are known to have held. Creative license has been used in imagining these specific gatherings that *did not actually take place* and to create links in the conversational format.

Footnotes indicate opinions that can be verified.

6
Parks

First (middle, maiden) Name	Last Name	Brief Biographical Information	Approximate Age
Jane	Addams	Founder and head resident of Hull-House, leader of civic and progressive organizations.	40s
Neva Leona	Boyd	Chicago Kindergarten Institute graduate; settlement volunteer; set model for park activities, starting in 1909 at Eckhart Park; established Chicago Training School for Playground Workers in 1911.	30s
Rose Marie	Gyles	Hull-House resident, first gymnasium director at Hull-House (1893–1907), taught high school gym in Berwyn after 1907.	40s
Mary Wood	Hinman	Introduced dance at Hull-House, promoted folk dance as a new art.	30s
Mary	McDowell	Taught Hull-House kindergarten, headed University of Chicago Settlement House, founding member of National Women's Trade Union League.	50s
Ada	McKinley	Founder of South Side Settlement House, 1918.	40s
Rosamond	Mirabella	From the Clark/Polk Italian neighborhood; attended Froebel Kindergarten College, graduated 1906; taught kindergarten in Bohemian neighborhood.	20s

Lea	Taylor	Daughter of Graham Taylor, grew up at Chicago Commons (founded 1894), assistant to her father through 1910s when she began research on her own.	20s
Harriet	Vittum	Political activist, head resident of North-western University Settlement House from 1904–1947, pasteurized milk for babies.	30s
Charles	Zueblin	Hull-House resident, a former University of Chicago sociology professor, founder of Northwestern University Settlement.	40s

THE YEAR IS 1909. The location is a drawing room in Hull-House, a cozy space nearly filled to overflowing with the ten people preparing to discuss Daniel Burnham's proposals for parks in the *Plan of Chicago*.

Jane Addams began the meeting with a statement of its purpose:

> We have the duty and honor today to review a draft plan for the future of Chicago which has been drawn up by the esteemed architect, Daniel H. Burnham, at the direction of the Commercial Club of Chicago. I called this sub-committee meeting to review the Parks chapter in the proposed *Plan of Chicago*. We may suggest additions or modifications of the *Plan*, based on our practical experience working directly with residents of Chicago neighborhoods. We expect the architects of the *Plan of Chicago* to seriously consider and to incorporate ideas from citizens, organizations, and experts on each topic.
>
> I personally had one meeting with Mr. Burnham and his assistant, Mr. Edward Bennett, in 1907 when they invited me to comment very generally on their concept for the *Plan*. Mr. Bennett was accurate in[1] reporting my approval of his plan for an open lakefront, with the caveat that parks should be available for the poor and immigrant populations. To be perfectly honest, I am not sure they were happy to know of

---

1   Hines, *Burnham of Chicago*, 324–325.

*Jane Addams.
(Library of Congress,
LC-USZ61-144, Prints
and Photographs
Division.)*

my support for people from all walks of life using the parks regularly, but I appreciate the accurate report. Mr. Burnham has a difficult task, trying to reflect the views of his patrons in the business community along with other segments of the city.

We are somewhat concerned that the playground movement may find it difficult to co-exist with the City Beautiful movement, of which Mr. Burnham is a leader. The question of passive versus active space, which we thought had been negotiated to a truce several years ago, seems to reappear these days. Our friend, Mr. Charles Mulford Robinson, who was an early champion of playgrounds and small parks, has been moving toward the definition of City Beautiful that sees playgrounds as diversions of funding from larger parks and monuments. We will want to put forward our most tactful, yet most persuasive arguments for why small parks and play lots play an important role within the City Beautiful movement.

Many of you have worked together on playground issues before. I see that many of our settlement house friends are with us today. I believe we all know each other from a host of collaborative projects over the years.

Let's begin our deliberations by reviewing the draft we have before us to determine the degree to which it best serves the interests of all Chicagoans. Miss Taylor, you volunteered to summarize Mr. Burnham's plan for us.

Lea Taylor, slightly intimidated in the presence of the more experienced settlement workers began haltingly, but gained confidence as she spoke:

Mr. Burnham's plan is beautifully illustrated with maps and sketches that help the reader understand his ideas. His focus in the chapter on parks is primarily on the lakefront, the ring of boulevards, and a proposed system of forest preserves near or beyond the city limits. He provides a great deal of background about the importance of parks and how they have been developed and designed in great European cities and in some East Coast cities. He makes a clear and unequivocal statement that the lakefront is an asset that belongs to all the people and should not "be appropriated by individuals to the exclusion of the people." I liked the democratic sound of that section very much.

He makes very interesting points about how the city has grown rapidly and often without forethought to preserve land for parks. Of particular importance to us, he points out that in congested neighborhoods there are over five thousand people to each acre of park space, when the standard "for health and good order," as he puts it, should be one hundred persons per acre of park space.[2] This fact would seem to warrant vigorous action in the most congested neighborhoods, but in all honesty I could not find a sense of urgency in the *Plan* about addressing needs of congested communities for either active or passive green spaces.

Unfortunately when he does, in fact, begin to reveal the details of the plan for the Chicago Park System, his emphasis is not on uses that would be beneficial to our communities. He shares our positive assessment of the work of the Special Park Commission in building small parks with field houses but he is unclear about their future location, saying at one point they should be clustered near the boulevards lining the city and at another point that small parks may be clustered away from the boulevards to serve neighborhoods. Other than

---

2   Burnham and Bennett, *Plan of Chicago,* 44.

endorsing the 1904 report of the Special Park Commission, he offers no suggestions about expanding the desperately needed neighborhood parks. He does include an occasional sentence suggesting that "wage-earners" should be able to reach the lakefront or the woodlands, but with relatively little elaboration.

He is very clear, on the other hand, in wanting to appeal to "people of means." He proposes a lakefront park system that will keep them close to home, spending their money locally, which is not all bad, but I daresay he has no plan for how people of means will share the parks with people of little or no means. As we know from other experiences in our fair city, once the middle and upper classes claim an area, there will be no intermingling with the poor. His emphasis on yachting and yacht harbors made clear in my mind that his plan is exclusive to the wealthy classes.

From the lakefront, he moves to the ring of forested areas that are primarily outside the city of Chicago, or on its boundary. I was surprised to find that the boundaries of the city are so fluid in his mind. He writes of places I've never seen—Glencoe, Glenview, River Forest, Riverside, DuPage County, the Palos region, Lake Zurich—as if they are Chicago neighborhoods.[3] I am inclined to believe he is wise to suggest setting aside land for park space before it is built up. But I think our greatest service will be in proposing parks, field houses, bath houses, and other public facilities in existing neighborhoods. Most city neighborhoods are more than a mile from the great lakefront parks or from the boulevards. He actually offers us a model in an earlier chapter, when he describes the way suburbs should be developed. Let me read it to you:

> In each town plan spaces should be marked out for public schools, and each school should have about it ample playgrounds, so that during all the year the school premises shall be the children's center, to which each child will become attached by those ties of remembrance that are restraining influences throughout life. Next to the school the public library should have place; and here

---

3   Ibid., 54.

again the landscape setting should be generous and the situation commanding. The townhall, the engine-house with its lookout tower, the police station with its court of justice, and the post-office, all naturally form a group of buildings that may be located about a common or public square, so as to form the suburban civic center.[4]

I think that is a lovely image, and one we might strive to bring to our city neighborhoods—a clustering of buildings used for civic and recreational purposes. It is in many ways what Miss Addams has brought to the Hull-House neighborhood, except for the police, fire, and governmental offices. She has created a civic center with a library, art gallery and studio, gymnasia, meeting rooms, coffee house, kitchen, classrooms, and so much more. Wouldn't it be lovely to expand Mr. Burnham's image and Miss Addams's reality to every community in Chicago?

Jane Addams thanked Lea Taylor for her summary and asked if Mary Hinman would make notes of the discussion. With that business detail dispatched, Miss Addams called on Rose Marie Gyles to report on what Hull-House had learned since Hull-House residents opened the first playground in Chicago in 1894. Miss Addams explained that others would speak briefly on innovations since that time, up through the first congress of the Playground Association of America, which was held in Chicago in 1907.

Rose Marie Gyles began:

At Hull-House our gymnasium is ample and athletic programs are many. But children and adults need spaces with fresh air, sunshine, and room for active play. We had no idea when we built the first playground that a playground movement would arise from it and grow so quickly. Some of us had heard about or seen the "sand gardens" built for children in Boston,[5] even before Hull-House was founded. But most parks in Chicago, and in other cities, were built as passive, contemplative spaces. Parks were not always in the places where they could

---

4   Burnham and Bennett, *Plan of Chicago*, 35.

5   Spain, *How Women Saved*, 79.

most easily be used, especially by children or by families too poor to afford streetcar fare.

Children were playing in streets and alleys in tenement neighborhoods like ours, exposed to open sewers, piles of garbage, and the threat of moving carts and vehicles. In some of the most congested communities, there were no vacant lots for unsupervised play. Hundreds of people crowded into every square acre of the poorest communities, and overcrowding inside the tenement buildings was even worse.

Several of us, including Charles Zueblin, Miss Addams, Ellen Gates Starr, and other early residents felt we could create a model that would be useful in many communities. We set about to construct a playground where children could safely play while they gained the additional advantages of sunshine, fresh air, and exercise.

We had two barriers to overcome. The first was that the idea was new and untried. The second was a philosophical difference that needed to be worked through with people who saw parks as artistic arrangements of plantings and gardens, rather than active spaces to be used.

Our first play lot was built near Hull-House on a piece of land that was donated by Mr. William Kent. We had complained to Mr. Kent of the condition of tenements on the land and he agreed they were beyond repair. Mr. Kent demolished the buildings and gave the land to Hull-House.[6] Since that time, Mr. Kent has been a consistent supporter of playgrounds and the playground movement.[7] I was happy to see that Mr. Kent is a subscriber to the *Plan*. I hope, given his early support for our playground, that he will be supportive of a stronger section on small parks in the *Plan*. He knew we hoped to create a model that could be easily and economically applied in many neighborhoods, and it seems the idea has begun to catch on across the city.

This seems like a good time to turn this summary over to Mary McDowell to talk about the larger playground movement that has grown beyond our initial, local effort.

---

6   Philpott, *Slum and the Ghetto*, 92.

7   McArthur, "Chicago Playground Movement," 379.

Mary McDowell, a member of the Chicago Playground Association, thanked Miss Gyles and carried the history forward in time:

When Hull-House was founded, there were only seven parks
between Fullerton Avenue and Roosevelt Road. There were
three large parks: Douglas, Garfield, and Humboldt. And
there were four smaller parks: Union, Vernon, Jefferson, and
Wicker. I think all of the small parks were on land donated
by developers rather than purchased by the city, so their
being there at all was serendipitous. Hull-House was so far
advanced when it built a playground[8] in 1894. It was another
case of Miss Addams sensing just the right reform at just the
right time. The idea has taken hold here in Chicago in less
than a decade and we are now part of a national playground
movement.

Many other organizations quickly followed suit and built
neighborhood or settlement house playgrounds. Business
groups often helped to fund individual efforts.[9] In my own case
at the University of Chicago Settlement, the local alderman
gave me $25 to find a way to keep the neighborhood boys
out of mischief. I bought a swing and sandbox for a vacant
lot. The success of that modest venture sent me to Boston to
study their playgrounds. Boston had been experimenting with
playgrounds and play lots longer than most cities and had
many ideas to offer.

Other settlement houses that built playgrounds include
Chicago Commons, Northwestern University, Forward
Movement, Olivet Institute, and Association House.[10]
Settlement residents were among the strongest proponents
of playgrounds. Several people in this room deserve credit
for the rapid adoption of the playground movement at their
settlements.

In this case we also had help from city government. Mayor
Carter Henry Harrison II created the Special Park Commission
in 1899 to hasten the development of municipal playgrounds
in crowded neighborhoods. The Special Park Commission

---

8   Spain, *How Women Saved,* 229.

9   Ibid., 25

10   McArthur, "Chicago Playground Movement," 379.

focused its efforts on the Chicago Public Schools and the three existing park[11] commissions to try to quickly add playgrounds to school and park property.[12]

Early commissioners of the Special Park Commission included social reformers like Lea's father, Graham Taylor, and our good friend, Charles Zueblin. Other members included businessman Clarence Buckingham, Prairie School architect Dwight H. Perkins, and landscape architects Jens Jensen and Ossian Cole Simonds. Perkins and Jensen wrote an influential report for the Special Park Commission in 1904 that called for establishment of a Forest Preserve District,[13] an idea Burnham has carried into the *Plan of Chicago*.

The South Park Commission[14] was quick to embrace the small park and playground movement. It is noteworthy that the South Park Commission was so much more innovative than either the West or Lincoln Park Commissions. The South Park Commission members are named by the judges of the Cook County Circuit Court and can claim a tradition of integrity and professional interest.[15] The other two commissions are named by the governor, in a more political process. The South Park system created an innovation that is now becoming quite popular throughout the city—the park field house.

The South Park Commission hired the Olmsted brothers and Daniel Burnham's firm to design active parks and field houses in landscaped settings. McKinley Park was the first, in 1902; ten more were built by 1905, with over five million visitors in one year. Small parks had innovations like local libraries, public bathing, wading pools, food, and health services.[16] The South Park Commission and its architects based park plans on a canvass of needs. They found that over

---

11 Chicago did not have a unified park district. It had a South Park Commission, a West Park Commission, and the Lincoln Park Commission at this time.

12 Grossman, Keating, and Reiff, *The Encyclopedia of Chicago,* 621.

13 Bachrach, *The City in a Garden,* 12.

14 Chicago had three separate park boards, the North Division, the South Division, and the West Division. Each had its own board, tax rate, and administrative and maintenance systems.

15 McArthur, "Chicago Playground Movement," 382.

16 Bachrach, *The City in a Garden,* 12–14.

half the population within the South Park District territory had no access to parks of any kind. That included as many as 350,000 people![17]

In a very short time, new organizations sprang up in Chicago and across the country devoted exclusively to expansion of the playground and parks movement. What had seemed like a conflict between people who preferred active parks and people who preferred passive parks was diminished by 1904 when a compromise design for an active park with contemplative spaces was developed.[18] Reformers and park advocates promoted the view that open space and fresh air were imperative to the development of healthy, well-rounded citizens in a democratic society. Advocates emphasized that children, whose behavior was being shaped by the rough and tumble of the streets, would be better citizens if they experienced teamwork and orderly, structured activities.

Field houses quickly gained popularity too. Park programs became one tool to be used by a democratic society to help assimilate immigrants and migrants from rural areas. Ethnic and Americanization activities were held in field houses. Field houses became meeting halls for issue forums and neighborhood meetings. Meeting halls and classes in field houses offered shared space that was not "private" as in a home, but was "public" primarily to neighbors and others in proximity to a neighborhood park.

As parks and field houses began to grow rapidly, advocacy groups rose to spread the good news. The Playground Association of America was founded in 1906 by some of the people in this room, notably Jane Addams, Graham Taylor, and myself,[19] working in cooperation with progressives from other cities. The Chicago Playground Association was born at Hull-House in 1907.[20] The Playground Association quickly earned the support of prominent Chicagoans. Two McCormicks served on the eighteen-member Chicago Playground Association board, Harold and Anita. Judge Julian Mack, Jens Jensen,

---

17   McArthur, "Chicago Playground Movement," 382.

18   Grossman, Keating, and Reiff, *The Encyclopedia of Chicago,* 621.

19   Spain, *How Women Saved,* 79.

20   McArthur, "Chicago Playground Movement," 384.

Children standing on a sandy beach at the lagoon in McKinley Park. (Chicago History Museum, DN-0000583, Chicago Daily News *negatives collection, Chicago Historical Society.)*

settlement workers, and other businessmen and professionals also devote time to promoting the playground movement.[21]

As you all know, because I think most of you were there, the Playground Association of America recently held its first congress in Chicago.[22] The goals set for the association's first year were to investigate existing needs and conditions; form neighborhood booster groups; and immediately put vacant lots to use for playgrounds.[23] Exciting innovations in park design and management were showcased at the congress. Future steps to build the movement were planned for or begun.

The people who started the playground movement were often the same people who were creating settlements, public health programs, and other civic institutions. The papers read at the first national playground convention made clear the link between playgrounds and other issues of the day, including good citizenship, prevention of juvenile delinquency, and prevention of tuberculosis to name a few.[24]

21   Ibid., 385.

22   Schultz and Hast, *Women Building Chicago,* 397.

23   McArthur, "Chicago Playground Movement," 384.

24   Ibid., 386.

Charles Mulford Robinson, a journalist, wrote *Modern Civic Art, or, The City Made Beautiful* (1903), considered by some to be the "bible" of the City Beautiful movement. Originally a proponent of small, active parks, by 1909 Robinson adopted the prevailing architectural and engineering definition of City Beautiful.

He started with the premise that "(s)tatues, monuments, and skylines can wait but bodies and minds must be fed; aesthetic improvement comes last." He was explicit that: "The playground is a bit of land seized from the builder's clutch and set apart for the children, consecrated to their use to help them keep their souls pure though they soil their hands. It may or may not be beautiful."

But by 1909, Robinson wrote "the whole playground conception has heretofore been wrong. We have taken as our ideal a bare city lot equipped with paraphernalia for children's exercise. The truer ideal would be an acre or so of natural looking country."

Robinson was, however, one of few men to acknowledge the work of women: "It is well that (the women's clubs') appreciation of the desirability of beauty as an element in civic development should reach small matters as well as large. Grand schemes for vast public improvements with parks, drives, and boulevards naturally stir enthusiasm and allure to effort; but these smaller plans for making a city attractive are also discussed and promoted." (Daphne Spain, *How Women Saved the City*)

Miss McDowell nodded to Jane Addams to indicate she had completed her historical review.

Miss Addams redirected the group to the task for the day:

We have made great progress, but the movement for playgrounds and neighborhood parks is not yet so firmly established that we can assume it is safely launched and needs no further oversight from us. Rather, it is more like an adolescent, needing our oversight from a distance and with an eye to releasing it from our protection in the near future.

It is important that we succeed in expanding parks and play lots to all neighborhoods of the city. They have an important function within a democracy. In a supervised setting children learn to play together, to put their individual wishes aside for the good of the group. These are the skills needed for democracy—skills not learned on the street, where might makes right. As centers where groups from many nationalities gather, small parks help create tolerance and respect for the customs of others. "Many Chicago citizens who attended the first annual meeting of the National Playground Association of America, will never forget the long summer day in the large playing field filled during the morning with hundreds of little children romping through the kindergarten games, in the afternoon with the young men and girls contending in athletic sports; and the evening light made gay by the bright colored garments of Italians, Lithuanians, Norwegians, and a dozen other nationalities, reproducing their old dances and festivals for the pleasure of the more stolid Americans."[25]

For young adults, the difference between an evening at a field house and an evening at a dance hall or bar means prudent spending and prudent behavior. The well-appointed rooms at a field house serve as "municipal drawing rooms" with free rent and reasonably priced food.[26] During the day "Well considered public games easily carried out in a park or athletic field, might fill both the mind with the imaginative material constantly supplied by the theater, and also afford the activity which the cramped muscles of the town dweller so sorely need."[27] When we consider the rapid growth in use of the new neighborhood parks, the relatively modest investment and the great good to the mind, body, and spirit of Chicagoans, one would expect Mr. Burnham to cover the city with a robust network of small parks.

There is much more we could say about the playground movement but I think we have covered enough of the essentials of the movement and Mr. Burnham's plans for park improvements. I think we should be ready to move to discussion of the *Plan* and our suggestions for it.

---

25   Addams, *Spirit,* 102.
26   Ibid., 97.
27   Ibid., 95.

Ada McKinley started, becoming more impassioned as she spoke:

I found the chapter on parks to be intellectually dishonest.
His title is "The Chicago Park System." He includes pictures
of Chicago parks. Yet his emphasis in planning for the future
is only on an upper-class playground on the lakefront and
the suburban park system. Not only does he disregard over a
million Chicagoans living in the great mid-section between the
lakefront and the forests, but he insults city residents by saying
those in close contact with nature develop "saner methods of
thought than can be the case when one is habitually shut up
within the walls of the city." I think we are quite sane and in
fact if Mr. Burnham came out to the communities to see the
innovations of the settlements he would learn a thing or two.

I'm not sure we should even participate in this exercise.
It sounds to me like another of the business community's
attempts to grab public resources for their own use, and leave
the rest of us to pay the bill. These men have been shown
over and over again to be paying less than their fair share
of taxes. Remember in 1894, when many of you helped to
set up the Civic Federation? One of the issues thoroughly
uncovered by Mr. Stead[28] was the thievery of the businessmen
who paid a pittance in taxes in spite of their opulent mansions
and fancy carriages. Until the Civic Federation, or someone,
solves that problem I say we can't give credence to the plan
the businessmen devised to take more out of our pockets to
put in theirs!

Rosamond Mirabella was next to speak:

I agree that taxes are an issue that must be dealt with in this
plan, but don't agree that we should forego this opportunity to
try to improve the *Plan*. Perhaps the chapter on parks is not the
place where tax policy can be resolved. I would like to suggest
that we make note of the ways the tax system is a barrier to

---

28 She refers to William Stead, an English clergyman who wrote *If Christ Came to
    Chicago*, an exposé of the many municipal and social ills of Chicago in 1893.
    Stead listed the actual tax assessment of most of the wealthy men of the city to
    show that all were paying unreasonably low taxes.

good public policy, but defer any attempts to resolve the tax question for a later time. At some point we should go back and look comprehensively at the equity and sufficiency of the tax system for schools, parks, and other essential services. The kindergarten where I teach is also severely underfunded.

The funding situation is so wretched that the Chicago Woman's Club, working with the Civic Federation and Associated Charities, had to fund the early vacation schools to provide wholesome recreational activities to children during the summer months.[29] Vacation schools, as you remember, are summer programs in congested communities in which schoolchildren undertake nature studies, music, practical arts, and physical training. Most, but not all vacation school programs, have been held at public school facilities.

Fortunately, Superintendent Albert Lane was receptive to good ideas from people outside the system even when he had no funds to implement them. The Board of Education is reluctant to fund summer programs because there is not enough money to support the standard school year and they believe taxpayers are generally not happy with paying for the education of other people's children, let alone paying for summer recreational programs.[30] Anita McCormick funded a vacation school program at the University of Chicago Settlement. Hull-House and Northwestern University settlements also had vacation schools, funded by other Woman's Club donations.[31]

After the first year of funding vacation schools, the Chicago Woman's Club assessed their benefit and practicality. They found that for a total of $1,400 per year, three schools with fifty teachers could serve fifteen hundred children. This included a group of deaf, blind, and crippled children.[32]

The Chicago Woman's Club report exonerates the school system for their failure to fund vacation schools and other programs, saying, "We cannot blame the lack of (kindergarten) upon our Boards of Education or the executive officers of our

29 McArthur, "Chicago Playground Movement," 380.

30 Playground Committee of Chicago Women's Clubs, "Chicago Vacation School," 1.

31 Herrick, *Chicago Public Schools,* 73.

32 Playground Committee of Women's Clubs, "Chicago Vacation School," 2.

schools systems, but upon those who insist upon having kindergartens, etc., in the more cultured districts where they are least needed."[33] Mr. Burnham's plan is an opportunity to discuss what level of funding is necessary to ensure a democratic society.

Harriet Vittum offered a very practical perspective:

We need to be realistic. The big parks and the forest preserves are attractive to the businessmen for a lot of reasons. First, they hope to live where they can see and use natural areas. Second, many of them are major landowners, and private land becomes much more valuable when a large public park is built at taxpayer expense. I'm familiar with the area around Humboldt Park, which is the largest park near our settlement. Do you know that land prices went from $250 per acre to $5,000 per acre in just four years when the park was new?[34]

I'd like to remind everyone that there are drawings in the *Plan* illustrating possible park designs for Chicago neighborhoods. These drawings stand alone with no text to describe them, but I think we should discuss whether the designs meet the needs of our communities. Most of the parks he depicts are a mile to a mile and a half on each side. The one exception is Sherman Park which is only two blocks by three blocks. I feel that what is lacking is a plan for small parks in all communities, parks at which children can congregate and which families can reach without the expense of a streetcar ride. I hope the smaller parks will be less likely than the very large ones to encourage land speculation in the surrounding neighborhoods.

I believe we should ask Mr. Burnham to include some drawings for play lots and small neighborhood squares. Building these parks as cultural complexes adjacent to schools, libraries, and other civic institutions would be just as advantageous for city residents as suburban residents. In addition, I believe he should express some set of principles about how we begin to approach the figure of one acre for every one hundred persons, when we are so far from it now. Perhaps he should suggest that a certain amount of park

33   Ibid., 5.
34   Hoyt, *One Hundred Years,* 107.

acreage be purchased in the city of Chicago by 1920 and 1930, and specify how much of it should be in small parks within neighborhoods.

If Mr. Burnham is willing to take the logical next step, it would be advantageous if he would spell out the possibilities inherent in the cultural complex. The opportunities to present community theater, adult education, debates and civic dialogues, and other activities in such a complex would be a genuine asset to communities. Programs that straddle more than one sponsoring agency would be administered more efficiently when administrators are in immediate proximity to each other. Vacation schools are but one example of the need for collaboration between public schools and public parks.

Mary Wood Hinman offered a more positive assessment:

I agree there needs to be more emphasis on the neighborhoods of Chicago. But I think we need to realize how far-sighted Mr. Burnham is to think of the city and the suburbs as one region. There are over a quarter million people in Chicago's suburbs, and many suburbs are growing very rapidly. It will be to Chicago's advantage to encourage a cooperative working relationship with those suburbs, especially on issues like preserving some of the land as parks and nature preserves for future generations.

Neva Leona Boyd spoke from her experience as a teacher stationed at a small park:

Regional cooperation is an admirable goal as long as existing neighborhoods are not left behind or forgotten. There does seem to be some danger of that in this document, so I think we need to be forceful in making the case for what Chicago neighborhoods require before we invest in expanding beyond the city limits. My experience teaching classes at the new park on Chicago Avenue and Noble Street increases my commitment to the notion that these neighborhood parks are essential for the health of the children and an important source of civic engagement for the adults. This is the first of the small parks built by the West Park Commission. It hasn't even been named yet. They call it Small Park #1.[35] Yet it is overflowing with children and adults every day, in every season. You know it was designed by Jens Jensen,[36] who has great talent at arranging local plantings and designing naturally featured grounds and play equipment. It really is a lovely respite for the families living in crowded conditions.

Harriet, this new park is near Northwestern University Settlement. I believe it was you who told me that even the police were extolling the benefits of the neighborhood park—that a local police official, Lieutenant Kroll, exclaimed, "We're going to make this a fine place! Not less than fifteen lives have been saved from the electric car since the establishment of the playground and juvenile arrests have decreased fully 33.3 percent."[37] Those are very impressive statistics. Coming from the police rather than from us, they should carry extra weight with the business types.

Charles Zueblin, author of scholarly articles on parks, had much to say:

But the three park commissions hold a mixed record on building new, small parks. The South Park Commission has already built ten new small parks. They led the way in defining and designing field houses. After building their first small park with a field house, McKinley Park, they built nine more in three years and can hardly keep up with the demand.[38] The West Park Commission has only built three small parks. Unfortunately, the Lincoln Park Commission didn't start building small parks and field houses until last year.[39]

The South Park Commission hired Daniel Burnham himself to design the field houses. I find they are both attractive and functional. I don't understand why he doesn't seem to value that work or see how useful it would be to build many more neighborhood-centered parks.

---

35   West Commission Annual Report, 1907, 11–12. Small Park #1 was eventually named Eckhart Park.

36   Chicago Park District Web site.

37   American, " Small Playgrounds," 163.

38   Grossman, Keating, and Reiff, *The Encyclopedia of Chicago,* 621.

39   Bachrach, *The City in a Garden,* 19.

He did include a brief discussion of the Special Park Commission and neighborhood-centered park philosophy. But I can't agree with his emphasis on establishing new parks on or near the boulevards because the boulevards are at the edge of the built-up neighborhoods. Even he recognizes this isn't adequate for the congested areas when he acknowledges "The smaller play parks disregard to some extent the above principles, because these are in the strictest sense neighborhood centers."[40] But that is the extent of his discussion of small parks, simply to say that they don't follow his principles in the main.

It's a shame Mr. Burnham wasn't here at the Hull-House Municipal Science Club meeting in 1898 to hear Jacob Riis[41] speak on the need for parks.[42] People were so inspired by Mr. Riis they began promoting the idea of the Special Park Commission, which was formed by Mayor Carter Harrison in 1899. Mr. Riis also spoke at several businessmen's meetings, including the Merchants' Club in 1898. The twenty-one aldermen present at the meeting were so inspired that the city council followed with a $100,000 appropriation. Unfortunately their inspiration exceeded their prudence. Since the city didn't have sufficient funds, the appropriation was reduced to $11,500.

The momentum for small parks grew rapidly. Even the business community was won over by the strong arguments for small parks. The Merchants' Club began buying and donating land for small parks.[43] Frederick Bancroft, president of the Merchants' Club, said after hearing Jacob Riis speak, "This is not Socialism, not anarchy, not the preaching of a new course of municipal action, but it is common sense applied to actual conditions."[44] Reformers positioned the playground movement as a way to teach self-discipline and teamwork,

---

40   Burnham and Bennett, *Plan of Chicago,* 44.
41   Jacob A. Riis was a New York City social reformer and author of many books on urban issues.
42   Bachrach, *The City in a Garden,* 11–12.
43   McArthur, "Chicago Playground Movement," 380–381.
44   Ibid., 390–391.

a way to control excess energy, all qualities of use to the business community.

We saw immediate results in children learning to cooperate and share. Where new playgrounds were installed at public schools, parochial school children in the neighborhood sometimes thought they couldn't use the parks. It was a challenge to get children from different backgrounds playing together, to overcome the habits accumulated by playing only in streets and alleys, to get children involved in organized play.[45] Children who learn teamwork early in life will ultimately make better employees as adults.

Unfortunately, I don't see the *Plan* as responsive to the business community's interest in this regard. They indicated support for small parks and playgrounds. They even committed some of their own resources to constructing local parks. But the *Plan*'s focus on large, distant parks ignores the difficulty and cost of traveling to those parks. "A complete chain of parks and boulevards encircling the city, it was thought originally would satisfy the need of the growing population. This supposition was based on the following assumptions: the streets connecting with the boulevards will be available for private vehicles; private vehicles will be available to a substantial number of households; the street railway system will be adequate; every man, woman and child possesses ten cents. None of these assumptions being true, the park system is in so far imperfect. The inevitable misfortune was that no city large enough to need and support such a system of encircling boulevards and parks could afford to dispense with a central boulevard system and numerous small parks."[46] "Even if the streets were all good and the transportation arrangements adequate, a city of a million and a half inhabitants, under present conditions always contains a large mass of overworked, underpaid, and densely crowded people. This class can rarely, if ever, visit the distant parks. Another very large class can go but seldom, and needs for hygenienic [*sic*] reasons, space for recreation within easy access of their homes. These classes in Chicago are found chiefly in the river districts. If one traces

45   Zueblin, "Municipal Playgrounds," 154.
46   Ibid., 146.

the two branches of the river on the map, from the northwest and southwest to the point at which the river enters the lake, it will be seen that they pass through a parkless region. . . . Between six and seven hundred thousand people live more than a mile from any large park."[47] There is no point in having a section of the *Plan* on transportation and a section on parks, if there is not a realistic relationship between the two. I'm not sure that Mr. Burnham, living in the world in which he lives, understands the challenges of families in our communities. Coming up with two street car fares for every member of a family for a recreational outing may not be a realistic choice.

Harriet Vittum thought it was time to make a transition to a new topic:

I couldn't agree with you more, Charles. Assuming there is no disagreement with your remarks, I would like to move to a somewhat different point. From the beginning, the activities conducted in the field houses bore some relationship to the modes and methods of settlement houses. In fact, Henry G. Forum, president of the South Park Commission, is a frequent visitor at Hull-House and Chicago Commons forums and events. He prefers to hire settlement residents as employees for his park field houses because their experience closely matches the active, community-building model the South Park District is promoting.[48]

Unfortunately though, the park leadership in this part of the city is not comparable in experience or creativity to that of the South Park Commission. The West Park District here in the center of the city was hampered by its corrupt board until 1905. Since Governor Deneen replaced the West Park Commissioners,[49] it seems the new ones are trying to catch up, but it will take several years before we see significant results. In its 1897 Annual Report, the West Park Commission called on the wealthy to donate land for parks.[50] Two years later, because of continuing financial problems and an inability to

---

47   Ibid., 146.

48   Davis, *Spearheads,* 81.

49   Bachrach, *The City in a Garden,* 15.

50   Annual Report of the West Chicago Park Commissioners, 1897, 28.

maintain the parks already under its jurisdiction, the West Park board called for the city to close some infrequently used streets and put a "heavy coating of sand" down to create cheap play areas.[51] The new commission president, Bernard Eckhart, seems very committed to small parks, but the difficulties of finding land in our congested section of the city will be difficult to overcome, and financing them seems even more difficult.

There are some larger problems that need to be addressed. We are almost forced to return to the taxation question to talk about land acquisition. The $1 million bond issue the General Assembly approved in 1905 for the West Park Commission will not last very long with land prices escalating so rapidly in the center of the city.[52] And how will the commission pay for maintenance of these parks as we add more?

Do we want to even discuss the problem of the General Assembly holding all power in regard to Chicago taxing and bonding authority? How can the city manage its business without the authority to pay its expenses?

Jane Addams added:

That is a problem, but again I would like to suggest that we come back to the question of taxation under a different discussion so we can concentrate on parks here. What should be the role of the Small Parks Commission in all this? Should Burnham's plan propose a more comprehensive approach to neighborhood parks? There are at least four park boards now, and the newly annexed areas have the legal authority to set up their own boards if they so choose. How can we establish a system of city parks if there is no coordination? That seems like an important question for a plan to consider.

Neva Leona Boyd addressed a vexing problem:

Another very difficult problem we need to raise is the balance between open space and the need to demolish some homes in crowded communities in order to obtain that open space. There are areas with no substantially-sized vacant plots of land. This plan should look at neighborhood land uses

---

51   Annual Report of the West Chicago Park Commissioners, 1899, 24–25.

52   Annual Report of the West Chicago Park Commissioners, 1905, 15–16.

comprehensively and recommend ways to minimize the loss of housing and to compensate families that are forced to move for the benefit of the general public. Usually it is the poorest families, in the most decrepit tenements, who are displaced to build the parks. I'm in favor of the parks, but even here at Hull-House we were appalled to find ourselves responsible for the resettlement of many families when our playground was built. I have heard it was a painful time.

I hear that cities in the east are discussing requirements that each subdivider set aside a certain amount of land for public space[53] so that we will not repeat the same problem over and over as new areas are built up. Do you think we should recommend such a policy for consideration?

Rose Marie Gyles shook her head as she responded:

We must remember that the primary sponsors of the *Plan* are businessmen. Even businessmen who are inclined to donate land of their own volition will not be inclined to write into their plan a requirement that private property be appropriated for public uses.

Mary McDowell was not so discouraged:

Our most effective tools are the persuasive power of facts on health and well-being. I saw a map in the West Park District's annual report almost ten years ago that showed deaths for one month in relation to the park system,[54] actually just the large parks and boulevards. Perhaps the map caught my eye because of the Hull-House maps. Maps were so unusual in 1894, when you published *Hull-House Maps and Papers*. They were very powerful explanatory tools. The mortality map published by the Park District had the same effect of making the case immediately obvious and transparent. The map seemed to show many more deaths on blocks far from parks than on blocks near to parks. The accompanying text said police report more juvenile problems where no playgrounds exist. We can make a very strong argument, based on these

---

53 Annual Report of the West Chicago Park Commissions, 1899, 20.
54 Ibid., 1899, 18.

reported facts, that parks and playgrounds within easy reach of city residents will reduce other costs.

Mary Hinman saw other potential allies:

There are so many other good arguments that can be made for an abundance of parks. Do you remember Charles Hutchinson, the banker who was one of the first to donate art to the Hull-House gallery? He is now a South Park commissioner and advocates field houses as locations to rotate art from the Art Institute through communities.[55] He is also on the list of subscribers to the *Plan of Chicago*. Parks possess great potential as cultural resources. And they can help people learn to appreciate the delicate balance of nature and the relationship of humans to the natural world. I hope Mr. Hutchinson will make the case within the businessmen's meetings for more attention to neighborhood parks.

Neva Leona Boyd saw positive and negative possibilities:

Frederick Law Olmsted and Calvert Vaux believe urban parks are not only a refuge but a social leveling site where classes mingle. They are working for the South Park Commission, putting some of those ideas to work.[56] I wish Burnham would incorporate those ideas into his plan . . . but perhaps the businessmen would not look kindly on the classes mingling.

Jane Addams brought this part of the discussion to a close:

We need to summarize our ideas and areas of agreement. I think we have substantial agreement on most points. Mary, can you read the major points the group made today from the notes you took? With that quick review I think we should be ready to fashion our recommendations. We should limit ourselves to just a few recommendations on the most important issues, keeping in mind that there are seven other groups meeting here at Hull-House. And hopefully Mr. Burnham is soliciting ideas from other civic organizations around the city too.

Mary Hinman gave a summary of the main ideas the group had covered: access to parks, small parks, the challenges of

---

55   K. McCarthy, 112.
56   Bachrach, *The City in a Garden*, 7.

disconnected park boards, field houses as community centers, unfair taxation, and the role of parks in building teamwork and democratic principles. The group discussed their priorities and fashioned a unified statement for Chicago parks, based in part on Daniel Burnham's own vision of a community complex. They also approached, but did not attempt to resolve, the issue of taxation. The recommendations they agreed to were stated as follows:

Recommendation One:

The *Plan of Chicago* should promote a park of two to five acres for each square mile of the city that is primarily residential. This park should be modeled on the South Park Commission model with field houses, similar to those designed by Mr. Burnham, offering a full palette of recreational and cultural activities. Wherever possible, the park and field house should be adjacent to the local grammar school and library, in order to create a cultural complex. The staff of the park and field house will be well-trained civil service employees competent in numerous disciplines.

Recommendation Two:

The *Plan of Chicago* must address the complicated issues of taxation and municipal self-determination if it is to have any value to future generations. The statewide incorporation act for municipalities with more than two thousand in population is outdated and detrimental to a city the size of Chicago. We urge the Commercial Club to work with the Civic Federation and other groups to build a broad coalition to secure municipal legislation for a twentieth-century region. We offer our own networks and organizing skills as resources in winning these reforms.

7

Transportation

First (middle, maiden) Name	Last Name	Brief Biographical Information	Approximate Age
Jane	Addams	Founder and head resident of Hull-House, leader of civic and progressive organizations.	40s
Louise de Koven	Bowen	Probably the largest donor to Hull-House, inherited a fortune from pioneer grandfather who owned much of what became the central business district; involved in a wide range of civic reform efforts; early proponent of racial justice.	50s
Fannie Hagen	Emanuel	Physician, supported Frederick Douglass Settlement, founded Emanuel Settlement .	30s
Marion Lucy	Mahony (Griffin)	Second woman to graduate MIT architecture school, a "community planner," shared work space with Pond brothers, was primary designer for Frank Lloyd Wright.	30s
Annette E. Maxson	McCrea	Landscape architect of railroads and depots.	50s
Catherine Waugh	McCulloch	Friend of Jane Addams from Rockford Female Seminary; admitted to Illinois bar in 1886; represented women (Rockford); helped write 1905 law on rape and age of consent; Justice of Peace in Evanston, 1907–1913, to stay near children.	40s

Anna	Nicholes	Resident of Neighborhood Settlement House (Southwest Side) from 1899; social worker; president of Federation of Chicago Settlements, 1901.	40s
Margaret Dreier	Robins	President, Women's Trade Union League, Executive Board of Chicago Federation of Labor from 1908.	40s
Raymond	Robins	Municipal reform activist, tied closely to settlement movement, member of charter convention.	30s
Marion	Talbot	Home economist, University of Chicago professor, sent students to settlements, sanitary scientist with a focus on public and home sanitation.	50s

THE YEAR IS 1909. The location is the library at Hull-House. An intense group of activists is gathered around a library table at the center of the room.

Jane Addams began the meeting by explaining the purpose of the meeting and introducing two special guests:

We are invited to discharge an important responsibility. Mr. Daniel Burnham and his colleagues have been retained by the business leaders of the Commercial Club of Chicago to create a forward-looking *Plan of Chicago.* Mr. Burnham is very knowledgeable about Chicago's downtown, about its suburbs, and about the transportation connections between the two. Our job is to speak for neighborhood interests in Chicago. This sub-committee will look especially closely at the transportation needs and requirements of residents in Chicago neighborhoods to help ensure the *Plan* meets the needs of everyone in the region. At the end of this discussion we will fashion recommendations if we feel that there are omissions or misunderstandings in the *Plan.*

You had a slightly larger assignment than some of the other committees. Mr. Burnham has a chapter entitled

Jane Addams. (Chicago History Museum, ICHi-17894, Photographer: Moffet.)

"Transportation," which is primarily about railroads, and another chapter called "Streets Within the City." I hope you read both of them for today's meeting so that we can discuss them together. We have neither the business experience of running a railroad or traction[1] company, nor the experience of a road-builder. But virtually everything we work toward requires access and connections at a reasonable cost to our community members. So we are certainly expert on the consequences of poor streets and transportation systems!

We are honored to have Marion Mahony and Annette McCrea with us today to assist us in this endeavor. They each bring essential experience and knowledge to the discussion. Miss Mahony is an architect, the second woman to graduate from MIT's architecture school, working in the office of Frank Lloyd Wright.[2] Miss Mahony describes herself as a community

---

1   The private passenger rail companies were called "traction" companies. Some of the traction lines are part of the CTA rail transit system now.

2   Bernstein, "Rediscovering."

planner. Mrs. McCrea has established a reputation designing landscape elements at railroad stations.

Because of the complexity of this topic, we asked everyone to do some advance preparation. I will give an overall summary of the plan, which will be followed by a review of the freight and economic development components by Louise de Koven Bowen. Her position among the elite business families of the city gives her insight into the needs of the freight and railroad companies, and we do want to give fair consideration to the needs of businesses. Fannie Hagen Emanuel worked on a summary of Mr. Burnham's section on the conditions of streets.

Mrs. Emanuel will be followed by Raymond Robins on the complications of the traction franchise system. Mr. Robins has been much involved in movements to reform city governance, including the question of long-term leases for the traction companies. Mrs. McCrea and Mrs. McCullough have focused on the commuter rail system and stations, Mrs. McCrea from a professional landscape point of view and Mrs. McCullough as a resident of Evanston who uses the commuter rails.

Finally, Marion Talbot, Anna Nicholes, and Margaret Dreier Robins will assess the likely costs for average families to make use of these transportation options, and the potential regional impact of a system that is either inadequate or overly expensive. After this rapid but extensive review of the *Plan*, we will want to ask "What is missing?" and that is a question to which we can all contribute. Are there any questions? Good, we will begin our work.

Let me begin. I must confess I had more difficulty with Mr. Burnham's chapters on Transportation and Streets than I had with some of his other chapters. He tends to see the city as primarily "a center of industry and traffic." His limited vision yields limited results. Where we tend to see a city of faces, and wonder if the persons behind those faces are healthy, gainfully employed, safely housed, adequately educated, and able to realize their aspirations, he sees the city as lines on a map needing rearrangement to promote efficiency and business growth. He acknowledges that the "problems of transportation have been viewed entirely from the standpoint of the paramount interests of Chicago as a commercial city."[3] He has a simple—I would allege simplistic—belief that what benefits business is what is good for the city as a whole.

I must say I had to question the whole premise of his chapter on streets, that premise being that the vast expanses of lake and prairie mean that "the people of Chicago must ever recognize the fact that their city is without bounds or limits." That statement seems to be to be patently unwise and filled with hubris. If we expand our city thoughtlessly we will pay a price in the future. That price may manifest itself in inefficiency, in loss of natural assets, in inequitable distribution of civic benefits, or in all those worries and more! I think before we accept his view that the region is without limits, we need to ask what an efficiently organized, compact community needs to maintain itself without great expenditure of time or resources. We need to look not only at efficiencies for businesses, but at efficiencies for families in the region. What will bring about the greatest efficiencies (and consequent happiness) in the daily life of communities? Is it more efficient for children to be in local schools and parents at local jobs, or to build roads and rails that facilitate the longer and further separation of families during the day? Is it better to concentrate all retail business downtown and have customers travel there? Or is it better to encourage local commercial areas to which people can walk? The neighborhood shopping areas on Madison Street, Milwaukee Avenue, and 22nd Street, for instance, declined in value since the mid-1890s, after the new elevated lines were built.[4] Transportation that is good for our downtown and for the grand commercial emporia like Marshall Field's may not be good for neighborhood businesses. If the business imbalance becomes severe, people will need to travel long distances for essentials, further eroding the prospects for conducting essential daily business close to home. I'm sure it is better for families not to bear long commutes to reach jobs. I suspect that long commutes are not advantageous to

3   Burnham and Bennett, *Plan of Chicago,* 78.
4   Hoyt, *One Hundred Years,* 182.

business either, since the possibility for employee absenteeism and tardiness increases with long and complicated travel.

Efficiency and business growth are important goals, but they need to be balanced with the needs of workers and families so that the whole region prospers together and so the many don't suffer dislocations for the benefit of the few. Although we feel passionately about these issues, we must dispassionately assess Mr. Burnham's suggestions for growth, focusing on costs and benefits to the whole community. In the early years of Chicago, employers and employees lived near each other. After the Chicago Fire, the wealthy clustered together in areas like Prairie Avenue, which is now losing stature to even more exclusive communities near the north lakefront[5] and in the distant suburbs.

Our friends at the national Charity Organization Society in New York are noting that this social distance increases distrust between the classes and distrust breaks out in animosity.[6] We have had our share of ugly and violent strikes in this city. We must consider the possibility that the hardening of positions by both labor and capital is a result, at least in some part, of their spatial distance from each other. If we are to move from a city of walking neighbors to an anonymous regional behemoth we must take care to find new ways to know and understand each other. I think Mr. Burnham would do a much greater service if he could concentrate somewhat less on the roads sixty miles from the center and concentrate a bit more on avenues that promote social intercourse and civic engagement throughout the center and midsection. The more we spread out physically, the more urgent is the need for common meeting ground to bind us philosophically.

If I was too impassioned in my recitation of concerns, please forgive me. We do want to offer an analytical response and some of my concerns are hard to quantify. How much common meeting ground or shared philosophy is sufficient? No one knows. But I fear we *can* be sure of the loss of good will if no bonds of neighborliness connect this expanded region.

---

5   Ibid., 190.

6   K. McCarthy, 131.

I will turn the meeting over to my dear friend Louise de Koven Bowen, who will give you a more dispassionate review than I managed. Louise has reviewed Mr. Burnham's suggestions on freight and economic development for us.

Louise de Koven Bowen began with a reference to Jane Addams's closing statement:

Please do not apologize to us for your fine impulses. You have been an interpreter between working men and women and the people who lived in luxury on the other side of the city. This question of how we live together in the future is certainly as important as how we travel away from each other.

I must begin with a caveat, lest anyone misunderstand my role. I developed some experience in reform movements, settlement houses, and children's issues. I am not expert in the needs of manufacturing businesses, or in how to move their goods from place to place. However, my husband Joseph is a banker and manufacturer, and I have access to the thinking of the captains of industry. Mr. Bowen also serves as one of the "subscribers" to the *Plan* and is in general support of the concept of a plan for the region's development. I think it is fair to say that Mr. Bowen and I hope to find the greatest good for the greatest number of people. Improved economic conditions will benefit the workers and their families. This question of freight traffic is of utmost importance to the economy of Chicago—it really is the reason Chicago has grown and become prosperous, as Mr. Burnham points out.

However, I believe it is fair to challenge Mr. Burnham on his statement that the present problem is how to increase efficiency and lower the cost of using rail transport. That may be one part of the problem. He is probably correct in saying that we need a traffic clearinghouse for freight. It will be to Chicago's benefit to improve the terminal situation so that cars are not stranded for days in congested loading areas. We do not want to lose this important industry to another city—it produces too many jobs. However I believe we should pose some questions about how this is done to ensure that business *and* the neighborhoods benefit from any changes.

His freight clearinghouse diagram proposes a belt line and clearing yards a good distance west and south of downtown and includes provision for many warehouses along the railroad right-of-way. This will undoubtedly improve efficiency for the benefit of the railroads and the businesses they serve. But Burnham does not discuss the implications of that proposal on surrounding neighborhoods or on workers who may have to travel significant distances to reach the new warehouses, depot, and loading platforms. I think we must ask him to expand his plan to include the human cost-and-benefit equation. Here are some of the questions that easily come to mind: Will established communities be razed to make way for the new platforms and warehouses? Will there be sufficient, safe, and sanitary housing near those jobs at affordable prices for the workers? If Mr. Burnham does not foresee adequate housing nearby, are there other plans for worker access to these jobs? Will the smoke nuisance disappear from the central area, as he predicts, only to befoul another neighborhood? If the freight yards near the central area are abandoned, and riverbank land becomes available, will it be used for the good of all or for another group of businesses that contaminate the water? The river is a cesspool now, with industrial and stockyard waste pouring into it.

It only gets more complicated after those five questions. Mr. Burnham proposes that the railroads share in building the common transfer station. Most of these railroads have been in direct competition with each other since the system was established in the 1840s. An almost casual mention of cooperation buried within a plan will not change the essence of capitalism. If Chicago is to be a well-organized freight-handling center for the future—and Mr. Bowen and I believe it should be—we need to consider a radically different structure of public and private investment. I know this may sound ill advised, when we can observe the current example of the traction company franchises creating governmental corruption and turmoil. But we have to begin to envision municipal functions as assets, not liabilities.

If the railroads are critical to Chicago's economy, the city should consider investing in the transfer station. As a practical matter, the railroads, which are investing heavily to raise the tracks above street level in most of the city, possess neither the resources nor the collaborative will to build a shared facility. Even if some of them come to agreement on a location, it would not necessarily be planned with the interests of the city, the neighborhoods, and the workers in mind. This is a critical question which should be debated and decided by many more voices than the railroad owners alone.

Mr. Robins, I know you have been intimately involved in the question of reforming the franchise system to fight official corruption and promoting municipal reform.[7] I look forward to hearing your review of the *Plan*'s sections on streetcars and traction franchises in the hope that we could conceive of a new system that will work for both the streetcar system and this freight rail conundrum.

Jane Addams thanked Louise de Koven Bowen, who was quite worn out with the study of unfamiliar material and with trying to foresee how new systems could potentially be organized. They all agreed it was a difficult and complex subject that needed to be debated throughout the city. Then Miss Addams introduced Anna Nicholes and Marion Lucy Mahony.

Anna Nicholes spoke first:

I would like to focus initially on the condition of our existing streets. Miss Mahony has many good ideas about possibilities for the future that she will share with us. Chicago had almost three thousand miles of streets in the early 1890s, but fewer than one-third were paved; the ones that were paved were mostly in the central area and affluent residential areas. Only the largest streets had stone sidewalks, others had "rickety and worm-eaten planks." European visitors to our city, like Rudyard Kipling and the crown prince of Belgium, were appalled at the primitive condition of our streets.[8]

We need to find a reasonable balance of improving and caring for the assets we built already and planning for new municipal investments. I cannot agree with Mr. Burnham when he says, "Congestion within the city demands new and enlarged channels of circulation," and "New streets must be created at whatever the present cost." We will be building irresponsibly if we do not take care of what we have first. And

---

7   Flanagan, *Charter*, 125–126.

8   Wade, *Graham Taylor*, 61.

it is very clear to neighborhoods all over the city, as well as to European visitors, that we are not maintaining our existing resources responsibly.

You all know me as someone who espouses this idea of "municipal housekeeping" which owes much to Hull-House. It was Jane Addams who said in 1907, "May we not say that city housekeeping has failed partly because women, the traditional housekeepers, have not been consulted as to its multiform activities?"[9] Caroline Hunt, a former Hull-House resident and influential home economist published a book recently called *Home Problems from a New Standpoint,*[10] which carries the question of women's roles as producers and consumers much further. Clearly Hull-House has been in the forefront of defining municipal housekeeping. It is in this context that I react to Mr. Burnham's *Plan of Chicago.*

Burnham alludes to the problem of poor maintenance when he says, "Noises, ugly sights, ill smelling as well as dirty streets and workshops or offices tend to lower average efficiency." The unfortunate truth is that filthy streets create more than efficiency issues. They harbor disease, degrade living conditions, limit mobility for the very old and the very young, and in some cases can actually cause injury when they are slippery with offal, as are many streets near the stockyards. The federal Neill-Reynolds report to Congress, submitted on June 4, 1906, pointed to extremely unsanitary street conditions in the Stockyards District, including "use of paving materials which could not be properly cleansed" and became "slimy and malodorous when wet."[11]

Even where the slaughter of livestock is not an issue, we see streets on the West Side near Hull-House that are old and in poor repair. Some sections of the city such as the Milwaukee/Division/Ashland area, Chicago Avenue neighborhoods,[12] and the Bohemian areas on the near Southwest Side are built below the street level. Houses are even more unsanitary where light cannot reach but seepage can.

---

9   Hayden, *Domestic Revolution,* 175.

10   Ibid., 175.

11   Abbott, *Tenements of Chicago,* 132.

12   Ibid., 106.

The unspoken issue, at least unspoken in Mr. Burnham's plan, is that there are terrible inequities and corruption in the way we currently maintain the streets. The stockyards area still has unpaved streets,[13] in spite of the one thousand miles of streets resurfaced between 1899 and 1893 to prepare for the World's Columbian Exposition.[14] In that case, only certain areas benefited, and usually not the areas most in need. Burnham doesn't need to dwell on the sorry record of past decisions and poor maintenance. He should simply put the city and region's best foot forward and propose a better system for making these decisions.

There is a fairly long record of proposals Burnham could draw on for his own recommendations. Women have attempted to remedy the deplorable condition of streets. More than fifteen years ago, Ada Celeste Sweet founded the Municipal Order League to lobby for municipal street cleaning rather than leaving this important function in the hands of private contractors.[15] Women were not alone in the quest for sanitary streets. It has been over a decade since the election in which Carter Harrison II charged our businessman-mayor George Swift with leaving streets unclean and garbage uncollected in the neighborhoods while keeping downtown quite clean.[16] Reform of municipal street sanitation functions meets strong resistance. This year, when the Civic Federation tried to simply consolidate all street cleaning, repair, and inspection into one department, opponents were able to see that action was delayed.[17]

Mr. Burnham himself includes a footnote in reference to the Street Paving Committee of the Commercial Club and its 1904 report stating that streets are always improved with quieter, more durable paving where wealthy people live, or "where luxury and comfort demand it."[18] How does Mr. Burnham propose that we maintain new streets if we have

13   Ibid., 130.
14   Flanagan, *Charter*, 18.
15   Schultz and Hast, *Women Building Chicago,* xxxiii.
16   C. Harrison, *Stormy Years,* 117.
17   Sutherland, *Fifty Years,* 28.
18   Burnham and Bennett, *Plan of Chicago,* 83.

not yet learned to fairly and prudently care for the streets we have already built? Mrs. Emanuel, you look like you have an urgent wish to add to this discussion.

Fannie Hagen Emanuel was clearly relieved to be offered the opportunity to break in:

Thank you, Anna, I appreciate your generosity. As a physician, I am concerned about the sanitary aspects of our streets and their overall condition. Anna has done a good job of summarizing those challenges. Before we leave the question of streets though, I would like to briefly discuss the tension between streets and communities as proposed by the *Plan of Chicago*. These comments have less to do with being a physician than they do with being a citizen of the region.

Mr. Burnham opines that in Chicago "there are no buildings possessing either historical or picturesque value which must be sacrificed to carry out plans necessary to provide circulation for a growing metropolis." He is short-sighted in his conclusion that those are the only two criteria for preserving buildings. Even if they were the only valid criteria, today's innovation is tomorrow's history. What if the Hull-House complex were razed because it is not yet old enough to merit historic significance? To destroy these buildings would be a tragedy, given what they mean to the thousands of people who come here every week, what they mean to the history of the settlement house movement and to several other reform movements in the city of Chicago and in the nation.

Uncharacteristically, Jane Addams interrupted Dr. Emanuel:

You are probably all aware that Mr. Burnham consulted with me on the question of widening Halsted Street and that I had no serious objections as long as it was within a well-conceived plan.[19] At the time of that discussion I had not seen his plan for the Civic Center. Now that I have seen the drawings in the *Plan*, I understand that widening Halsted Street is a minor matter, compared to the destruction Mr. Burnham envisions for all of the communities on either side of Halsted. The Civic Center and the new boulevard system to serve it might leave

---

19   C. Smith, Plan, 78.

Hull-House intact, but the surrounding neighborhood would be gone. I am flattered that Dr. Emanuel offers our buildings as an example worth preserving, but without our neighbors we would be without purpose, merely a lesson in history or architecture.

I'm sorry Dr. Emanuel, for interrupting the flow of your comments, but I feel very strongly that the Civic Center proposal is a direct threat to our neighbors.

Dr. Emanuel picked up where she left off:

I agree with you wholeheartedly and am glad to defer to you on a subject of such consequence to Hull-House. Your comments are a good segue to my last point, that this is not a plan for Chicago. It is a plan for the wealthy of Chicago. He expends no effort thinking of the interests of the million and a half Chicagoans who live far from the lakefront or the boulevards. He expends great effort to promote a Civic Center of questionable utility or wisdom. Mr. Burnham goes to great lengths to describe boulevards with fine dwellings, limited light traffic, statues, fountains, and continuous playgrounds for children.[20] He spends equally great amounts of time advocating for a large system of diagonal streets, without making a very strong case for why the demolition necessary to build the diagonals is justified. His recommendations for communities like ours seem to rest heavily on demolition but say little about enhancing or improving what our existing assets.

When Dr. Emanuel finished her remarks, Jane Addams introduced Marion Mahony:

Thank you Dr. Emanuel. I couldn't agree more. Now I have the pleasure of introducing Marion Mahony who, as the first woman licensed to practice architecture in Illinois, is one of few women as qualified as Mr. Burnham to design new communities. Miss Mahony is a lead architect in the firm of

---

20 Burnham and Bennett, *Plan of Chicago*, 85–86.

Frank Lloyd Wright, a founder of the Prairie School style[21] and of the Arts and Crafts Society.[22]

Marion Mahony thanked Anna Nicholes, and let her eyes drift slowly over the heads of the committee members, at the walls of the library.

I feel very much at home at Hull-House, where I have attended many meetings of the Arts and Crafts Society. I am at home too, because Irvin and Allen Pond's Arts and Crafts style[23] fairly sings to me from the walls. And I feel at home because of the wonderful women, friends of my mother, who are so much a part of your work. Mary Wilmarth, who was one of the earliest supporters of Hull-House, helped me prepare for college,[24] and Ella Flagg Young, the reform-minded educator, helped my mother resume her career in education after my father's death.[25] So as you can plainly see, I am very indebted to women like you who have been engaged in city-building work for many decades. And of course we are all grateful for the men like Raymond Robins and the Pond brothers who always worked side-by-side with women to build a better city.

Your training and experience finely tunes your ear and your heart to the human voices of the city. My training, like Mr. Burnham's, focuses the eye on the structural aspects of buildings, streets, and cities. I can appreciate the visual effect he desires to bring about, but like you I hope we can find a middle ground that is beautiful yet safe, respectful, and functional for existing communities. Thank you for inviting me to join you. It is a real honor to contribute to your deliberations.

Some of what I want to suggest to you is very speculative. This discipline of city planning is very new. I don't believe we have decided with certainty what we want for the present, let

---

21   Supplement to The Magic of America, Pregliasco.

22   The Magic of America, Timeline.

23   Glowacki and Hendry, Images of America, 20.

24   Griffin, Marion Mahony. The Magic of America: Electronic Edition. Art Institute of Chicago: n.d., 152.

25   Ibid., 137.

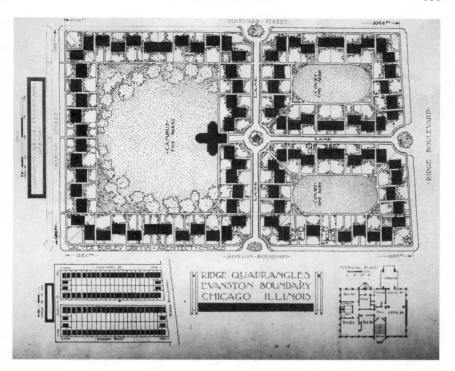

Mahony designed the "Ridge Quadrangles," four blocks in Evanston, Illinois. (Collection of The New York Historical Society, from Magic of America, p. 188, Chapt. Ref. IV.08.187.)

alone determined the right answers for the future. Personally, "I was awakened to the magic that can lie in town planning if it escapes from the boundaries of what is being done"[26] today. Much of the Burnham plan relies on designs of the past. It is not surprising the plan fails to address today's city problems. I hope we can entertain some new ways of thinking about streets, neighborhoods, and city planning here today and propose useful amendments to the *Plan of Chicago.*

If we assess streets for the ways in which they serve communities *and* serve the central business district, we might suggest some modifications to Mr. Burnham's plan. There is too much emphasis on the geometry of streets in my opinion and too little emphasis on the human cost and

---

26   Ibid., 192.

consequences of adding angles, arcs, and loops. The street pattern of Chicago has its strengths, such as predictability and easy navigation. Those benefits accrue to both downtown and communities. But we could propose modifications of the grid that will protect children in neighborhoods from through traffic. I have been sketching some ideas for blocks with large, shared interior parks surrounded by homes and apartments facing the streets. "In this subdivision there is ample provision for thorough [sic] traffic in the exterior roads. The domestic uses to which the property is put renders the cross road unnecessary for rapid traffic and becomes purely a menace to children, an expense in useless pavement, a nuisance in barrenness and dust."[27] I brought an example so that you might see the vision I am trying to work through.

As you can see from the sketch, the buildings facing the street are staggered, maximizing the amount of light that reaches the building interiors. This particular design is based on the street system of Evanston. Areas that need alley access through the center of the block could use a modification of this plan, with a narrow brick alley having a very slow speed limit. The irregularity of the brick itself would serve to keep the speeds low.

The predictability of the rectilinear street pattern is preserved here, but the park-like space behind the buildings provides a safe play space for children unprecedented in our cities. The ring at each intersection offers a spot for art or vegetation and also forces vehicles to proceed very slowly, whether turning or continuing to travel forward. This is one potential modification of street design to serve the needs of families and communities. I'm sure it is not the only one. If architects, planners, and civic-minded people set our minds to it, we can certainly come up with many more ways to provide safety and preserve connectivity.

I would like to comment on other aspects of Mr. Burnham's street geometry. His diagonals offer a nice symmetrical effect on paper, but there are at least four complications in applying

---

27 Ibid., 186–188. These drawings are from a period later than 1908, but the premise here is that Mahony was already experimenting with this type of configuration.

such a plan in the city today. The first and most serious is that huge swaths of land must be cleared, neighborhoods brutally cut through, many households displaced. In the context of his proposed boulevards, thoroughfares, loops, and ring roads he speaks of "improvements the necessities of which have been universally acknowledged," but I am not clear on the size or composition of his universe. I don't imagine it includes the citizens of the communities that are to be leveled in order to build the wide roads.

The second problem with the extensive system of diagonals and angled ring roads is that they reduce the advantage Chicago has with its very regular north-south, east-west axes. Chicago is exceptionally easy to navigate for residents, visitors, and deliverymen alike. It is useful to include a certain number of diagonals to make trips more direct on high frequency routes. Perhaps we need more diagonals than what we have now. But diagonals can dismantle our simple, intuitive street grid if they are over-built. We need to weigh the advantages against the disadvantages of each diagonal.

My third concern in this area is that Mr. Burnham has little to say about what vehicles he foresees using these grand highways. Is the primary purpose for a more extensive streetcar system? For deliveries? For private autos? For carriages? The License Department of the city of Chicago recorded five thousand motor vehicles registered in the city last year.[28] We don't know what the implications are for future growth of private motor vehicles, but I would recommend that we address that question directly in a plan for the future. There are a great number of implications in the decision to collectively allocate public investments. If we reduce our attention to streetcars, trolleys, and interurbans, more people will purchase cars to use the roads we are investing in. As Miss Addams pointed out, the shape of our cities is being changed by the residential dispersion of well-off and poor populations. Neighborhoods that barely support businesses within walking distance now could easily lose their remaining retail trade. It's obvious that this will strand many residents who don't possess the means to travel elsewhere for their daily goods.

28   Hoyt, *One Hundred Years*, 205.

Mr. Burnham and the businessmen don't assess the social impacts of their plan. That is their right, to look at it from a business point of view. But I can't understand why they don't see that miles and miles of abandoned commercial areas in the neighborhoods will weaken rather than strengthen Chicago's economic position.

Finally, his recommendation to maximize use of the underground tunnels in the central business area for deliveries is a sound one, but I take exception to his proposal to build double-decked roads in the central area. This will darken and dirty the very area he and the businessmen hope to promote.

Perhaps I am too hard on Mr. Burnham. I must confess to having a long-standing aversion to what he did with the World's Columbian Exposition, with "the whole nation being seduced by the superficial beauty of that wanton thing."[29] This plan is an entirely different work, although he relies heavily on the fair in presenting his credentials in his opening statements of the *Plan* and in many design elements, particularly the monumental and monotonous buildings. I tried to judge the plan on its own merits, but thought it only fair to let you know of my fixed opinion of his previous work.

Jane Addams stood to thank Marion Mahony and introduce the next topic:

Thank you, Miss Mahony. You confirmed some of our instinctive reactions with your professional perspective. It is good to hear that professionals like you are at work on plans to develop safe, self-reliant communities with good access and connectivity to other parts of the city and region. We look forward to watching your career unfold and hope the next time Chicago undertakes a plan that you will be in the forefront of the effort.

We have three distinctive points of view to present now as we discuss streetcars and passenger rail. Raymond Robins is one of the leading civic reformers in the city. He has worked for years to reform the traction franchises for the benefit of riders and the businesses served by transit. Catherine McCulloch

---

29   Mahony, *Magic of America,* 276.

is an old friend of mine and a resident of Evanston who will contribute from the perspective of suburban commuters. Annette McCrea is, like Miss Mahony, a professional whom we invited specifically to assist with this section of our response. Annette has completed many railroad station commissions as a landscape architect.

Raymond, would you like to start?

Raymond Robins gave a brief squeeze to his wife's hand, a curt nod to Miss Addams[30] and stood to address the group:

I must say from the outset that the question of how Chicago and other large cities administer their transit systems is a complex one that cannot be easily summarized in a brief statement. If you will accept my comments as evidence that we need much more investigation of future possibilities, rather than as a specific antidote to any of the myriad problems with the traction franchise system, then our cause will be well served.

Chicago's public transportation systems offer a number of benefits for the city. At present, we have eighty miles of elevated track in Chicago and hundreds of miles of streetcar lines.[31] The first cable car was built on State Street in 1882, and the first elevated line was built ten years later, in Jackson Park, for the World's Columbian Exposition.[32] The elevated loop around downtown was finished shortly before 1900. The elevated lines to Englewood and Ravenswood were completed by 1907. Last year, the Northwest line was extended from Wilson to Evanston. Several commercial centers emerged at the termini of elevated lines.[33] One of the negative effects of the elevated system is that it opened up new areas for development, which allowed or hastened the abandonment of areas close to downtown that were older or had come to be seen as undesirable.[34]

---

30 Robins and his wife might have been uncomfortable at Hull-House in 1909, after a significant falling out with Jane Addams the previous year.

31 Flanagan, Charter, 13.

32 Wade, Graham Taylor, 57.

33 Hoyt, *One Hundred Years,* 200–216.

34 Ibid., 144.

We are just beginning to understand the new dimensions of urban development in an industrial society. While cities evolved over thousands of years, moving people around cities by mechanical means is a very new phenomenon. I agree with Mr. Burnham's recommendation that we should expand the subway and elevated lines, but I think there is much he left unsaid that needs saying.

First, I should like to say that the streetcar system should not be overlooked. Streetcars are important feeder routes for the elevated and subway systems. They are critical for neighborhood mobility outside of the central business area. Looking to the future, as we start to see traffic lanes filling up with private automobiles, we might consider a separate guideway for streetcars that can also be used by emergency vehicles for rapid movement in congested areas. Toronto has instituted such a system. Emergency response times, neighborhood shopping, and worker commute patterns are all good reasons to devote more thought to the future of streetcars in Chicago.

The most serious omission however is in the lack of discussion about who will administer the transit system or systems in the future. This is not an obscure topic. It has been a central issue in most of our recent mayoral and city council elections. The corruption of the city council is inextricably tied to the corruption of the franchise system for public utilities in Chicago. You have all heard of the "gray wolves" who sell street franchises to the highest bidder, leaving the public to pay the high costs that are passed along.[35] You know of workers who must pay two or more transit fares to reach work because the lines are individually owned and not a coordinated system. Even where one company owns two lines, passengers are charged separately for each trip.[36]

On a related matter of political reform, several of you valiantly tried to open the recent charter conventions[37] to the opinions and wisdom of women. As one of the few "reform-

---

35   Flanagan, *Charter,* 20.

36   Ibid., 26.

37   Raymond Robins served on the first and second charter commissions, 1906–1907 and 1908–1909.

minded" members of the convention, I strongly supported that motion. I wish we could "bring you to the table" so to speak, for discussions on the franchise system, as well as other municipal obligations. The businessmen, who made up the vast majority of delegates to both conventions, are firmly opposed to any public ownership of public utilities. They try to smear supporters of municipal ownership, like the Chicago Federation of Labor and other reform groups, as radicals who would harm the system and the city. We managed to make only the smallest of reforms a part of the charter reform package—in reality we agreed only to reforms that were aligned with recent or pending state laws.[38] I am afraid that Mr. Burnham's plan, if carried into the future, will only solidify the control of businessmen, railroads, banks, and utility franchises over the fate of the city.

Consider this: Once the original franchises were extended for twenty years in 1883,[39] the city had little leverage over the traction companies. But that wasn't enough! Traction line owners tried to extend their franchises to ninety-nine years. We can go back fifteen years and listen to that great reformer, William Stead, who wrote in 1894 that among the "predatory rich" in Chicago, one name stands out, that of Charles T. Yerkes. Yerkes was a corrupt businessman who controlled a substantial number of traction lines. The corrupt city council at that time practically gave franchises away. Franchises for tunnels under the river were negotiated for less than the cost of building them.[40] Mayor Carter Harrison II decried the franchise system and the rampant land speculation that accompanied it virtually every election after his first, when he learned from his opponent how compelling the issue was.[41] He spoke to the Chicago Woman's Club in late October 1898 regarding public utilities, offering the radical notion that streets belong to the people and there should be no use without full compensation to the city. Early on, Mayor Harrison hoped to evolve to public

---

38 Flanagan, *Charter,* 91–93.
39 Young, *Chicago Transit,* 49.
40 Stead, *If Christ,* 108.
41 C. Harrison, *Stormy Years,* 101–111.

ownership of utilities,[42] but he was never able to develop enough political support for that reform.

Nevertheless, Harrison was aggressive in pushing for elevation of railroad tracks to prevent a continued high death toll at rail and road crossings. Two people a day, on average, were killed by trains at the end of the last century.[43] During his first year in office, Harrison was able to convince the city council to appoint a special committee and hire an engineer, John O'Neill, to press for rapid completion of the work. In six years, 286 grade crossings were separated and fifty-five miles of track were elevated.[44]

The traction franchise system has been an issue in virtually every mayoral election since 1897.[45] The Municipal Voters' League, much to the chagrin of businessmen who were its original sponsors, fought long and hard against the corruption common to the franchise system. William Kent and Allen Pond were among those instrumental in the victory over corruption that finally drove Charles Yerkes out of Chicago.[46]

The local alderman in Hull-House's area, Johnny Powers, chaired the city council finance committee. He personally gave millions of dollars in railway franchises to Yerkes and associates. Hull-House was also at "the center of much of the agitation and protest against Yerkes's attempts to extend the streetcar franchises to ninety-nine years. . . . The celebrated group of Chicago settlement workers made trips to Springfield to lobby against the bills, held mass meetings, and organized a protest."[47] Reformer Henry Demarest Lloyd came to Chicago in 1903 and made Hull-House the headquarters for a municipal ownership campaign. A referendum the next year received an overwhelming majority of votes for municipal ownership. Support was especially high in working-class neighborhoods.[48]

---

42   Ibid., 173.
43   Miller, *City of the Century,* 184.
44   Green and Holli, *The Mayors,* 24.
45   Steffens, *Shame of the Cities,* 174–177.
46   Ibid., 179–180.
47   Davis, *Spearheads,* 91.
48   Ibid., 191.

Although Yerkes was the predator from Pennsylvania, with no long-standing ties and no reputation to protect here, Chicago's most prominent local business captains were also deeply, if more discreetly, involved in the franchise machinations. Marshall Field, Levi Z. Leiter, Henry A. Blair, Erskine M. Phelps, George H. Wheeler, and Samuel W. Allerton were all happy for Yerkes to be the public face of the franchise debate, but their interlocking directorates of banks and railroads gave them all a stake in the questionable deals. Banks and real estate syndicates were making money on land speculation related to rail expansion.[49]

Mayor Harrison had a sophisticated and nuanced approach to traction reform, which the public didn't always understand or appreciate. He promoted five conditions for future traction agreements: service and safety improvements; adequate compensation to the city; complete abandonment of ninety-nine year provisions; a clause specifying the city's right to purchase and operate the system in the future; and finally, a public referendum to approve, or disapprove, the contract conditions.[50] Harrison was unable to conclude negotiations with the traction companies by the time he left office in 1905. Negotiations and court battles about the traction agreements went on for four years, from 1903 to 1907.[51] The terms of the extension did include some of the principles Harrison fought for, including upgraded equipment, the right of the city to purchase the lines, and a public referendum on the terms of the extension, which was held and approved in April of 1907.[52]

The battles to prevent ninety-nine year franchises and to uncover the graft that accompanies the traction agreements have been time-consuming and distracting. Thankfully, Mayor Harrison and others held the line, but year after year we invested time and resources in trying to squelch the forces of corruption. Our friend William Kent was a leader in the city

---

49 C. Harrison, *Stormy Years*, 138.
50 Green and Holli, *The Mayors*, 27.
51 Young, *Chicago Transit*, 49.
52 Green and Holli, *The Mayors*, 27.

council fight to resist these abuses.[53] If Mr. Kent and other reformers were not always engaged in battles to keep the public from being swindled, they could move the city forward. It seems that every time we are close to winning the battle, a new challenge arises. The election of Fred Busse as mayor two years ago presents new opportunities for the business community to bend the city's municipal transactions to its will.

I would like to close with a plea that we convey to Mr. Burnham and the members of the Commercial Club that a plan for the future must address the structural, financial, and legal status of an integrated transportation system. It is not merely matter of showing on a map how one might move freight or passengers from one point to another or circle around certain points, but how will we manage, organize, coordinate, and financially sustain the systems that our city and its residents are so reliant upon.

Jane Addams rose and thanked Raymond Robins for his impassioned and pertinent statements. She then introduced architect Annette McCrea:

Annette McCrea is someone I want to introduce to you as an architect who designs the landscape and area around rail stations. She can offer some ideas for how transportation facilities can be integrated into the urban landscape and serve the aesthetic, economic, and even natural assets that people value and need. Annette is new to our circle and we are very indebted to her for sharing her expertise as we learn more about her field.

Mrs. McCrea began by referencing sections of Burnham's plan:

In listening to the discussion today, I understand your frustration about what this plan does not do. However, in terms of the visual effects landscaping will have on transportation facilities, Mr. Burnham's plan is quite commendable. I am glad he references European railroad stations, which provide excellent models to reproduce here. Mr. Burnham also understands that it is not just the plantings which make

---

53   C. Harrison, *Stormy Years,* 112–113.

a station or train line attractive. Plazas at stations provide visual relief as well as comfortable and safe waiting areas for travelers. Designing viaducts that are architecturally pleasing as well as functional is a benefit to the communities through which the lines pass. He overlooks one of the most important features of viaduct design, which is to allow natural light to penetrate the viaducts, or to light them artificially. Otherwise, neighbors must traverse dark, forbidding, and dangerous caverns under the railroad tracks.

Mr. Burnham references well appointed stations on East Coast lines, particularly the Boston and Albany and Pennsylvania Railroads. He makes the unfortunate reference to increasing the pleasure and comfort of the suburban traveler again here,[54] and I certainly understand why you object to his singular focus on that constituency and his lack of concern for the neighborhoods of Chicago through which these lines cut. For my own part, I am disappointed that he could find no local examples of station areas to recommend. I have been designing landscaped stations for the Rock Island Railroad since 1901 and could have offered him several examples to consider, had he expressed an interest. It seems that my work is invisible to many of my architectural colleagues, who only cite the work of other men. I know many of you often experience the same disappointment.

The new stations I designed have been well received by their host communities, however. It appears that they are used as informal gathering and meeting spaces by local people as well as by rail travelers. It also appears that businesses are clustering near the stations, as the foot traffic there offers a potential customer base. The plazas, statuary, and vegetation that I designed or selected for the station areas create an open and hospitable hub of activity. My intention is to create outdoor drawing rooms that encourage people to arrive early or tarry a while on their way home.

My one regret is that my work has been focused on stations, and those are primarily in suburban locations. I would relish the opportunity and challenge to improve the viaducts along

---

54 Burnham and Bennett, *Plan of Chicago,* 77.

the lines, to make them less of a barrier to neighborhood travel in the city.

I had a very interesting conversation with Catherine McCulloch before this meeting started, and think she can help me to summarize how design techniques become living elements of your communities and assets to movement and social intercourse rather than barriers. I would like to turn the floor over to her to close this section.

Catherine McCulloch smiled at the trust of her new acquaintance and began slowly:

I have known Miss Addams since our college days at Rockford Female Seminary. Although I have not been intimately involved in the work of Hull-House, I am very honored to be a part of your deliberations. After I was admitted to the Illinois bar twenty-some years ago, I spent several years representing women. I helped write a new state law on the age of consent and rape in 1905.[55] So I share your passion for justice and for safe and uninhibited movement by women and girls.

The opportunity to collaborate with you about how to strengthen our whole region is a very exciting one. My statement is not lengthy. I believe Mrs. McCrea may have liked it more for its brevity than for its verbosity. I am now a resident of Evanston, where I can work near my home and children, as justice of the peace.

It is clear from my vantage point that the rail lines moving people between the city and the suburbs will continue to grow and expand. Well-planned, efficient communities built compactly around the suburban train stations are an asset to the residents of those communities. The recommendation Mr. Burnham proposes for town centers with green space, civic institutions, schools, and surrounding businesses and homes can only be substantially improved in two ways that I can think of.

One recommendation is for every station area or community center to contain not only the economic and governmental institutions we commonly might expect to see clustered around a town square, but also the kinds of institutions of civic life

55   Schultz and Hast, *Women Building Chicago,* 561.

that Hull-House has pioneered to promote democracy, debate, adult learning, art, community theater, and all that makes life worthwhile. This may seem a non-essential item, but as our region grows we will need to be linked in new ways, in order to be thoughtful and deliberate about the implications, benefits, and burdens of growth. Hundreds of autonomous communities may turn inward if left to their own devices. Space for thought is as essential to regional health as space for commerce. This may be idealistic, but I would like to propose a Hull-House complex for every community and an interlocked net of traveling discourses about life throughout the region! Let us use the train lines to spread and share ideas as well as to spread commerce!

Second, and on perhaps a more realistic note, I hope Mrs. McCrea and the railroads will give thought to the city neighborhoods through which the lines pass, enhancing rather than dividing neighborhoods where possible, providing a judicious number of in-town stops so that city dwellers might have the option of using the rail system for their travel. Within those city neighborhoods, safe passage over, under, and around the rail lines by foot or vehicle is a critical concern, even for those who will never ride the rails but must cross them daily. Elevating many of the rail lines in the city above street level is proving to be effective at preventing conflicts with street traffic, but the dark and foreboding corridors create terrible hazards to personal safety for women, children, older people, and often even for able-bodied men, forcing people to limit or curtail essential trips, or to take very long and expensive trips around the rail barriers. The kind of work Mrs. McCrea does at stations—creating plazas, open spaces, and green oases—could be expanded to a series of "way stations" for passing and crossing safely and pleasantly at reasonable intervals throughout the city, with a very modest investment of rail capital. We are not talking about large expenses or heavy equipment. The railroads are already making those big capital outlays. I am suggesting well-lit safety enhancements along and across the right-of-way to allow other forms of travel to flourish at the same time. Natural plantings that do not require maintenance would be an inexpensive asset too.

That is my perspective and although I am in no way an expert on transportation planning, my years of experience helping women and children who have been victimized by inadequate legal and civic safeguards give me passionate concern that we plan for the future of all in the region, from the largest corporation to the smallest child trying to walk across her neighborhood.

Jane Addams arose and thanked Catherine McCullough for her insightful and unique perspectives. She outlined the closing discussion, which would be led by sanitary scientist and home economist Marion Talbot, professor at the University of Chicago:

Miss Talbot will provide an overview of the costs and benefits of this plan from the point of view of home economies, rather than just the regional economic view. We believe this is an area the plan has fallen far, far short on. Miss Talbot has collaborated with Fannie Hagen Emanuel[56] to better understand the economic impacts on communities like the Negro[57] communities of Chicago, and Margaret Dreier Robins,[58] of the Women's Trade Union League, to provide perspective on the economic challenges faced by other working and immigrant families.

Marion Talbot began with a very broad outline of "municipal housekeeping":[59]

I must begin with a word of gratitude to Ellen Swallow Richards, the first woman to graduate from the Massachusetts Institute of Technology and now a faculty member there. Mrs. Richards is my mentor and an author of several books on home economics and municipal housekeeping. She is president of the new American Home Economics Association. I

---

56 Early supporter of the Frederick Douglass Center; founder of Emanuel Settlement.

57 In keeping with the customs of the time, African Americans will be referred to as "colored" or "Negro" in sections of this book that propose conversations the women might have had.

58 Dreier Robins was also on the executive board of the Chicago Federation of Labor.

59 See Chapter Two for additional information on municipal housekeeping.

encourage anyone who finds this overview too brief to consult her work for more detail. I should also warn you that it may seem that I travel a bit afield from the question of streets and transportation to discuss municipal housekeeping, but I vow to return and tie the pieces together to make the relationships clear.

Women began to express themselves in civic discourse during and after the Civil War. Many women assumed administrative and organizational roles in that time of great stress, proving their capabilities. After the war, not all the women were willing to return exclusively to home and hearth.

Although most women were not holding the levers of power, they began to invent ways to organize their personal and civic lives to influence the larger world and to do it from a distinctly feminine point of view. There has been a broad national movement toward municipal housekeeping in cities across the United States led by women of substance, sometimes assisted by men of vision.

Many of these efforts were directed at municipal sanitation, like Hull-House's efforts to reduce epidemics through better public streets and sanitation systems, to keep children out of dirty streets, and to reduce the impacts of the soot problems that come from the factories and the vehicles on our streets. Women overcame vigorous opposition to their engagement in civic affairs by pointing to the impossibility of keeping their homes clean and their families safe if the external environment was a constant threat to families.

A rich and diverse collection of ideas has developed over the last half century that I can do no more than touch on as food for thought about the future. Cities in the United States, unlike in Europe, were newly building in nineteenth-century America. Newcomers of all stripes were flocking to large, disorganized, transitional settings with few amenities and fewer safeguards. Even the older Atlantic seaboard cities struggled to manage rapid growth outside their historic, stable cores. The railroad cities of the interior had fewer stable institutions and little in the way of custom and order to cushion the entry of newcomers, especially those who arrived destitute and ripe for exploitation.

Part of the campaign undertaken by women volunteers was to help create municipal order to benefit those newcomers.[60] The alternative, Draconian view was that urban disorder and filth was the result of the immigrants themselves, that unsanitary conditions needed to be avoided by established society, but not alleviated. The question of who pays to pave and clean municipal assets is of course at the heart of the question for the business community.

Mr. Burnham and his team operate under the City Beautiful rubric, which is in direct contrast to a City Livable viewpoint, which could include concepts of municipal housekeeping, or "the city as home." Women began by trying to scrub the physical setting clean but realized they needed to clean up the corruption and mismanagement in city government first. Many of you were actively involved in the recent conventions to reform the city charter. My hat is off to you especially, Mr. Robins, for your service as a delegate in that crucial but inconclusive debate. Mr. Burnham's plan must address these fundamental underlying problems of municipal management and upkeep if the future is to be an improvement on the past.

But I digress. Let's return to the *Plan*. Mr. Burnham begins with a very good statement of concern, to which we can all ascribe. "Men are becoming convinced that the formless growth of the city is neither economical nor satisfactory; and that overcrowding and congestion of traffic paralyze the vital functions of the city. The complicated problems which the great city develops are now seen not to be beyond the control of aroused public sentiment; and practical men of affairs are turning their attention to working out the means whereby the city may be made an efficient instrument for providing all its people with the best possible conditions of living."[61]

But what are those conditions? That is the crux of the question we ask today and the crux of the question Mr. Burnham has not really begun to answer. The first and most obvious omission we notice is that not only "practical men of affairs" entertain an interest in the region's future, but

60   Spain, *How Women Saved,* 13.
61   Burnham and Bennett, *Plan of Chicago,* 1.

women like ourselves or working men and women and their families also have an interest in the question. We might frame it differently though. We might put more emphasis on the safe passage of women and children, as we heard several times today. We might recommend that as mechanized vehicles increase the speed of traffic, pedestrians and bicyclists need dedicated right of way and safe crossings. As a matter of economics, I would like to point out that not only is pedestrian and bicycle travel the least expensive for the traveler, it is also, by far, the least expensive type for which society might provide right of way.

I don't see much in the *Plan* to benefit the average household. What will be the impact on the streetcar, elevated, and railroad systems of the growing use of private automobiles? How will we allocate future capital expenditures between public transit and private transportation? Will Mr. Burnham's wide thoroughfares and boulevards be clogged with traffic? If more neighborhood shopping areas are weakened by the dominance of the central area, will more people travel farther and at greater expense to obtain their daily needs?

Another visionary active in Chicago right now, Frederick Law Olmsted, describes improvements in paving materials, utilities, and sewer systems that will increase the ease of and access to homes of the future. He sees a future in which the network of streets will enable postmen and other deliverymen to provide goods and services previously crafted in isolation in homes, freeing more women to take a place in civic society.[62] I'm afraid I don't see anything in Mr. Burnham's plan that speaks to the current or future role of women in our region. Dr. Emanuel, Mrs. Robins, what would you add to the discussion?

Fannie Hagen Emanuel responded, with obvious vexation:

I'm afraid I don't have anything more positive to offer. Every question you raised, every situation you described is more complicated in the Negro community, not less. We usually travel farther for jobs, since there are fewer businesses investing in our communities. That usually means a higher cost to reach

---

62   Hayden, *Domestic Revolution,* 11.

work, especially because each transit line charges a separate fee. A proposal to coordinate all the transit lines would be an especially welcome component of a regional plan, from my point of view.

We often must travel farther to accomplish our daily errands because there are fewer shops and services in our communities. That is an additional burden in time and money. There are fewer places where we can find an open door to health care and other essential services. Except for those who live near Provident Hospital, a long and expensive trip is likely to be the first step in responding to a health care emergency.

The condition of streets and alleys in our part of town is almost always worse than in other parts of town. I don't expect that Mr. Burnham can solve that problem, but it needs to be acknowledged in order to become part of a long-term solution. While our streets and alleys may be somewhat worse than other communities, I think the overall lack of attention to maintenance in working-class neighborhoods is color-blind.

Margaret Dreier Robins nodded sympathetically and had more to add:

I have to take exception to Mr. Burnham's ideas about who should pay for municipal improvements. He says, "On residential streets the city should not be burdened unnecessarily with the cost of street construction and maintenance."[63] It is the very people who live on those residential streets who are paying for the business-backed investments he proposes.

I would like to reinforce the need for a strong system of public transportation to enable workers and their families to move freely about the city and region. Mr. Burnham's diagonal throughways, circles, and arcs are a potential threat to the communities they will cut through. But the larger question is the preservation and expansion of public transportation investments. The emphasis in this plan on new road construction, especially roads to the farthest reaches of the region, indicates to me that this is not a plan for Chicago's people. We need to bring the focus back to what the two million people living here in Chicago need, which is the question of

63   Burnham and Bennett, *Plan of Chicago*, 88.

how they can most economically travel to the greatest range of places.

In listening to the discussion today, I have been struck by the degree to which Mr. Burnham's grandiose plans seem foreign to our notion of what is practical, necessary, and desirable. While he wants to tear up neighborhoods to build wide thoroughfares, we simply want reliable sanitation systems on existing streets. While he attempts to reorganize the system of freight transfer and delivery, we are concerned with the safe movement of bicyclists and persons on foot. He wants to demolish the Hull-House neighborhood to build a Civic Center; we would simply like safe passage under dark viaducts. While he wants to build expensive roadways to distant, lightly populated portions of the region, we express the need for a coordinated system of public transportation.

Do you think the problem is his edict "Make no small plans"? Perhaps we should recommend a new planning principle: "Consider all small, inexpensive, and efficient improvements in a system before recommending grandiose additions to that system." It appears that that is the fundamental difference between our view of the world and his. Perhaps it is because we are in close and constant communication with the people who pay for these improvements that we are more circumspect with their money. Certainly Mr. Burnham's sponsors historically shifted the burden of funding public investments onto the shoulders of other Chicagoans.

Jane Addams was clearly very impressed with Margaret Dreier Robins's summary:

Margaret, your statement is so clear and so compelling that I hesitate to suggest any amendment to it. However, I want to ensure that everyone has an opportunity to contribute to our final recommendation. May I suggest that we use your statement as the basis of the recommendation, but give leave to others to add to it?

Margaret was pleased by the suggestion and others nodded their assent. After another hour of discussion, the group agreed on the following statement:

The *Plan of Chicago,* with respect to transportation and streets, should consider investments in order by size and expense, with the goals of nurturing neighborhoods and the central business district and providing transportation options that are inexpensive and accessible for users. The first priority should be to maintain or upgrade existing public infrastructure, including basic sanitation practices. The second priority should be for safe travel by means that create no cost to the user and little cost to the public treasury. This includes making all areas safe for bicycling and walking, or providing separate right-of-way for walkers and cyclists. For those who must travel some distance to work, school, recreation, health care, and other necessities of life, the public transportation system should be coordinated, especially with regard to fares. Where bicycling, walking, and transit are not feasible travel options, and in order to provide delivery vehicles access to businesses and homes, the judicious use of new thoroughfares is the option of last resort, given the high construction cost, impact on community cohesion, and high cost to purchase private vehicles for use on public roads. The citizens of Chicago will see their taxes used much more efficiently and their lives enriched by completing the simplest and least expensive improvements first.

8

The Heart of Chicago

PLAYERS

First (middle, maiden) Name	Last Name	Brief Biographical Information	Approximate Age
Enella	Benedict	Hull-House resident, artist, link between Art Institute of Chicago and Hull-House, involved in Arts and Crafts Movement.	50s
Louise de Koven	Bowen	Probably the largest donor to Hull-House, inherited a fortune from pioneer grandfather who owned much of what became the central business district; involved in a wide range of civic reform efforts; early proponent of racial justice.	50s
Helen	Culver	Donated Hull-House building and land, subscriber to the *Plan*, real estate developer with progressive business and racial practices.	70s
Harriet	Monroe	Poet laureate of World's Columbian Exposition, briefly a resident at Hull-House, started *Poetry* magazine in 1912.	40s
Anna	Morgan	Drama and speech teacher, helped found (in 1890s) an arts club called the Little Room—members included the Pond brothers, Howard Van Doren Shaw, Jane Addams, and Harriet Monroe.	50s

Edith	de Nancrede	School of the Art Institute student, then Hull-House resident in 1898; led Boys' Club; directed Hull-House plays, including a play (1905) by Harriet Monroe.	30s
Mollie	Netcher	Chicago's "Merchant Princess," owner of the Boston Store—almost four thousand employees, some benefits uncommon at the time, such as generous commission (small salary), lunchrooms, classrooms, tennis court on roof.	40s

● THE YEAR IS 1909. The meeting takes place in a cozy corner of Bowen Hall, the large room that served as a theater, lecture hall, and dance floor for a variety of Hull-House events. The meeting was opened by Louise de Koven Bowen, namesake of the hall:

Thank you for joining us today. Miss Addams asked me to convene this committee to discuss Mr. Burnham's *Plan of Chicago*, with particular respect to what he calls the Heart of Chicago. As one who is not a resident of the house, I am particularly honored to be given this important leadership role. I hope we will be able to contribute a vital perspective to improve the plan. We have a broad range of experience in this room, including the business community, the arts community, and municipal reform proponents. I believe you all know each other.

Miss Addams tells me that in some of the other meetings, she asked for formal presentations on the topics at hand, some of which required specialized expertise or historic background. In this case, since we are all familiar on many levels with the center of the city, we will dispense with background briefings and begin with a general discussion of your observations and concerns. We do want to ensure before we finish that we cover certain topics. Please indulge me while I list the three primary center-city functions for your consideration: government, business, and cultural. Within those areas we will want to consider whether the *Plan* addresses the fairness and sufficiency of taxes and assessments for supporting

*Louise de Koven Bowen.
(Chicago History Museum,
ICHi-09570, Photographer
unknown.)*

government services, business practices in relation to the public and taxpayers, and cultural institutions and how to increase their benefits to the general public.

Those of you who reviewed Mr. Burnham's chapter on the Heart of Chicago will note some differences between his emphases and ours, but I think you will agree we have a great deal to offer in these arenas. I'd like to suggest we discuss the governmental functions first. Helen, you are one of a handful of women who will be listed as a subscriber to Mr. Burnham's *Plan*. We are glad to hear that you are represented there. Would you like to start?

Helen Culver clearly had much on her mind and was eager to share it:

Thank you, Louise. I think we need to look at the last two sections of the *Plan* as well as the chapter on the Heart of Chicago to understand the implications of what Mr. Burnham has and has not recommended. Some of what is omitted is as important as what is included. Mr. Burnham assures us in his summary in Chapter VII that public funds can be found, must be found, to immediately begin to implement his plans. He says the economic benefits the region will realize from the plan justify the increased tax burden, but does not quantify either the cost or the benefit.

Our good friend Walter Fisher, who has led so many efforts to reform the municipal charter, solve municipal tax problems, and strike out municipal corruption in utility franchises[1] is oddly complacent in his review of the *Plan*'s legal implications, which is an appendix to the document. Although this section is very dry, as lawyers are wont to be, it is also very telling.

One important point that comes through clearly only in Mr. Fisher's essay is that wide thoroughfares and parks enjoy legal standing which makes them attractive to planners for reasons that have nothing to do with transportation and recreation. In Illinois, municipalities cannot condemn land simply because it is congested or used for unattractive purposes. As Mr. Fisher says, the only recourse under Illinois law if one wants to appropriate multiple parcels for public use is to build "wide thoroughfares and avenues through congested districts, or take the heart of the district for a public park."[2]

In principle I support many of the recommendations Mr. Burnham makes about the importance of impressive boulevards, especially his recommendations for Michigan Avenue, which serves as the spine of our city center. I am, after all a businesswoman, with a large financial stake in the continued growth of our real estate and business markets. As someone who has supported Hull-House from the first days I rented my cousin's former home to Misses Addams and Starr, I am concerned that the current residents of the West Side will not be the ones to benefit from wide thoroughfares built to replace Twelfth Street and Congress Street for example. After reading Walter Fisher's chapter, I can't help but read the *Plan*'s recommendations for wide thoroughfares as an objectionable and roundabout way to do away with certain neighborhoods.

Harriet Monroe spoke up:

I had a similar concern about Mr. Burnham's recommendations for Halsted Street. And I feel conflicted in many of the same ways Helen feels, in my loyalty to Hull-House and also to members of the business community with whom I have friendly

---

1   Flanagan, *Charter*, 69, 91–92, 142.

2   Burnham and Bennett, *Plan of Chicago*, 151.

relations. I know you are all aware that I was a resident at Hull-House briefly, but don't know if you are all aware that my sister was married to Mr. Burnham's late partner, John Wellborn Root. I have been a guest in Mr. Burnham's home many times. My friendly relations with Mr. Burnham go back a long way, all the way back to 1893 when I recited my poem "Columbian Ode" at the opening ceremony for the World's Fair and was appointed laureate of the White City.[3]

Nevertheless, I shuddered at his plans for the civic complex, which will ultimately require all the land around this beloved building, and more. Do you realize how many functions he proposes aggregating at the civic center? He sees municipal headquarters, school headquarters, hospitals, the asylums, morgue, courts, police, and an arsenal as well as all county and federal offices[4] amassed in one location.

Enella Benedict broke in to make another point:

I wonder if Mr. Burnham even understands the long battle to keep the schools from business and political influence in awarding school contracts. Putting the superintendent and board offices right in the civic center would be the end to independence, on the rare occasions that the board shows any.

Harriett Monroe continued:

Artistically, I have another confession to make about Mr. Burnham's work. Although he unabashedly touts his uniform designs, I find them aesthetically sterile. Worse yet, they strike me not as harmonious but as representing brute uniformity and repression of artistic expression. While it is true as he says that "art everywhere has been a source of wealth and moral influence,"[5] I don't believe that the purpose of art is to serve commerce or conventional morality. I fear that his heavy style represents "the general foulness of feudalism and pessimism which permeates worn activity. I believe a reaction is near; but how near it is difficult to estimate. Until the trusts,

3   Williams, *Harriet Monroe*, 8–9.

4   Burnham and Bennett, *Plan of Chicago*, 115.

5   Ibid., 112.

and special privilege, are overthrown, democracy in any walk of life will have but little to show, and a democratic art least of all."[6]

Edith de Nancrede said:

I resent the way he describes our beloved neighborhood, which he calls a "district inhabited by a mixture of races living amid surroundings which are a menace to the moral and physical health of the community."[7] I don't hear in his statement a concern for our neighbors' welfare but a fear of them, as if they are the cause of dirt and disease. We know from our own experience with the city sanitation department that inspection is almost always indifferent and frequently corrupt. The insistence of the business community on private contracts for municipal sanitation services belies this plan's concern for the neighborhoods. It is about profit and profit alone.

Helen Culver reminded the group:

We do need to view this from Mr. Burnham's own promise that "with things as they should be, every business man in Chicago would make more money than he does now."[8] Our task is to discover how to preserve our city's economic advantages but moderate or alleviate the high costs to specific communities and populations.

Louise de Koven Bowen broke in to redirect the conversation:

With your leave, I'd like to move the discussion to our thoughts on the proper role of municipal government and how a plan like this should outline the issues and challenges. This is a big topic; I suggest we try to focus on efforts to root out corruption and to adequately and fairly fund municipal services. There might be some who say it is unrealistic to expect corruption to be addressed, much less remedied, by a plan, but I for one think we can't ignore it.

6   Williams, *Harriet Monroe,* 11.
7   Burnham and Bennett, *Plan of Chicago,* 107–108.
8   Ibid., 76.

Enella Benedict, a longtime resident of Hull-House took up the challenge:

Chicago has a long history of trying to keep government weak on the theory that it is so corrupt its functions must be restricted. Why, Mayor Medill even took steps to limit the tax rate to two percent to keep elected officials from "stealing" from the public.[9] We have seen two attempts in this decade to reform the municipal charter so that Chicago might tax itself adequately and fairly, among other improvements sought. Neither charter convention was successful. I would venture to say that the charter conventions suffered from a problem that will affect this plan too. The businessmen controlling the charter reform process were out of touch with the general public and arrogant about their right to speak above all other interests. The vote they lost in 1907 went against them by two votes to every one for the charter.[10] Their high-handed antics created distrust in the very voters who were needed to endorse the charter proposal. Mayor Busse increased suspicions by playing politics with the Board of Education just as the charter vote came to a head.[11] The planners and Commercial Club would do well to remember past struggles to keep the schools free of political interference.

Over the years, we have watched from Hull-House as many honorable men struggled to start one municipal reform movement after another. Occasionally they included women in their reform efforts. I can't help but smugly suppose that when women finally get the vote on more than school board elections, we can help our male allies tip the balance toward good government. Still, it won't be easy. The Civic Federation tried. When they were stymied, they started the Municipal Voters' League, populated by many of the men who are so integral to Hull-House and the settlement movement, men like Allen Pond and Graham Taylor.[12] William Kent, who donated

9   Stead, *If Christ*, 172.

10   Flanagan, *Charter*, 134.

11   G. Harrison, *Anita McCormick Blaine*, 125.

12   Steffens, *Shame of the Cities*, 168–169.

the land for the Hull-House playground, tried as an alderman[13] and through various civic groups to reform the city council. The City Club is another example. Walter Fisher has played a prominent role there, as has Hull-House resident George Hooker; Raymond Robins of Northwestern Settlement; and Charles Zueblin, John Dewey, and others from the University of Chicago.[14]

I've even heard that there were quiet attempts by businessmen to regulate the graft, to move it from outright blackmail to more manageable bribery. Even Charles Yerkes, king of the traction grafters, was rumored to have pushed the city to mobilize against the worst excesses as being bad for business.[15]

I know you remember the incident just a few years ago when Raymond Robins was severely beaten after completing a study for Mayor Dunne investigating the records and qualifications of aldermanic candidates.[16] This is serious business with serious implications for those who try to bring about improvements, if those improvements threaten to limit graft.

The struggle against corruption has been long, hard, and rarely successful. Without the vote, our task is even harder than that of the men who tried their hand at reform.

Edith de Nancrede spoke up:

The cost of graft and inefficiency may be high to business, but it is so much higher for the public. Some say the loss of six hundred poor souls in the Iroquois Fire in 1903 would not have happened in a city that had adequate and honest inspection systems to protect public health and safety.[17] We must try.

Louise de Koven Bowen saw an impasse arising and moved swiftly to head it off:

---

13   C. Harrison, *Stormy Years,* 141.

14   Feffer, *The Chicago Pragmatists,* 195–196.

15   Steffens, *Shame of the Cities,* 165.

16   Davis, *Spearheads,* 192.

17   C. Harrison, *Stormy Years,* 236.

Let me suggest that we review some of the problems with the system of municipal taxation, as a less highly charged way to grasp the possibilities. Anna, you told me you would like to present some information from a book you recently read.

Anna Morgan clutched a small volume and smiled:

Yes, thank you, Louise. I have been rereading William Stead's book *If Christ Came to Chicago*. Mr. Stead was an Anglican minister who came to Chicago for the World's Columbian Exposition's Congress on Religion.[18] What he found was the dark underbelly of Chicago far from the Midway. He and Graham Taylor used to walk the streets of the Levee[19] late at night and then come to Hull-House for a cup of hot chocolate and a chat with Miss Addams.[20]

Mr. Stead's book reads like a series of sermons on municipal integrity and accountability. What I find most interesting in the context of this discussion however, is a series of tables he printed in his book, listing the actual taxes paid by various Chicagoans of the day. Inequity fairly leaps off the page. Let me read to you from the sworn records of assessors stating the total valuation of property, including buildings, carriages, pianos, and horses for prominent businessmen. Marshall Field owned property valued at $20,000, his son Marshall Field, Jr.'s property was valued at $2,000. Philip Armour had only $5,000 of property in total, and George Pullman, another man of substantial means, was listed as being worth $12,000. The infamous Charles Yerkes was only taxed on $4,000 of property and Potter Palmer on $15,000.[21] Carrie Watson, the owner of a vice house on Clark Street had property assessed at four times as much as John R. Walsh, president of Chicago National Bank and owner of the Herald. Her property was valued at $4,000 and his at $1,000.[22] Stead points out that the total assessments for property and real estate for many

---

18   C. Smith, *Urban Disorder,* 248.
19   The Levee was the vice district.
20   Wade, *Graham Taylor,* 72.
21   Stead, *If Christ,* 214.
22   Ibid., 29.

of the newspapers was equivalent to the price of one printing press.[23]

It wasn't just the businessmen who took advantage of the situation. Among sixty-eight aldermen, fifty-five had no assessed personal property at all. Another thirteen had property with a combined assessed value of $1,550.[24] Stead observed that "The result of the Chicago system is too ludicrous for belief if it were not so cruel and unjust to stifle laughter."[25]

Some of the faces have changed since Stead was here in 1893. Marshall Field, Philip Armour, and George Pullman have died. But essentially the same group of people who brought us the World's Columbian Exhibition, Mr. Burnham and Chicago's business leaders, now want us to believe that wide avenues and monotonous facades will pay for themselves and solve complicated problems in the process!

Helen Culver returned to the complications of the tax system:

I think most of you remember, and some of you were probably at the Central Music Hall in 1893, when Mr. Stead gave a thundering address about corruption in Chicago. His challenge to Chicago's leadership resulted in the founding of the Civic Federation. Since that time, the Civic Federation secured legislative changes to do away with township assessors and to create a board of review.[26] As the city kept growing, particularly some of the annexed areas, the revenue increased, but never really kept up with the needs.[27] Mayor Harrison's comptroller researched the city's tax options less than ten years ago. While the city's geography had increased 420% from 1888–1900 and population increased 110%, tax revenue was only up 35%.[28] It is not possible to serve a larger population and provide services to a vastly expanded geography with such a small increase in resources. The Federation's 1907 *Summary of the*

---

23   Ibid., 218.
24   Ibid., 219.
25   Ibid., 217.
26   Sutherland, *Fifty Years,* 18.
27   Ibid., 29.
28   Green and Holli, *The Mayors,* 24.

Reports of State Tax Commissions offers many alternatives, some of which could offer useful guidance for this plan.[29] I am sorry that the work of the Federation was not incorporated in Mr. Burnham's *Plan.*

Enella Benedict broke in to say:

I think we must look at who benefits from the existing system. Not only are the assessments too low on properties in the Heart of Chicago, but rental of much public land is established by the artificially low assessment levels, robbing the public twice. Some of the worst abusers are the railroads and the newspapers, especially the *Chicago Tribune.* The Board of Education signed leases at deflated assessment rates in 1892, which will deprive the public of its rightful returns for ninety-nine years![30] The *Tribune* attorney was, at the time, the president of the Board of Education. Even Governor Altgeld was powerless to stop the transaction. He accused the papers of "waving the flag with one hand and plundering the public with the other."[31] What really seemed most shameless to me was that the *Tribune* ran thirty editorials opposing educational "frills and fads" in the same year they pursued land negotiations with the board.[32] Perhaps if the schools were not cheated out of funds they needed to operate, educational enhancements would be the norm, not a "frill." Let me tell you about a maddening example of the unfairness of this leasing system. The Board of Education leased one floor of a *Tribune* rental property at Dearborn and Madison. The Board paid $1,000 more in rent to the *Tribune* than the paper paid the Board for rental of the whole property! Unfortunately the *Tribune*'s lease is locked in until 1985, like so many others.[33] It seems to me the whole question of the land leases must be reopened by the legislature, along with further reform of the assessment system.

Mollie Netcher looked uncomfortable as she began:

---

29 Sutherland, *Fifty Years,* 29–20.
30 Herrick, *Chicago Public Schools,* 75–76.
31 Ibid., 77.
32 Ibid., 73–73.
33 Ibid., 105.

I have to reluctantly agree with you. Much of the property Mr. Netcher and I assembled to build and expand the Boston Store was school board property we leased.[34] We never received terms as favorable as the *Tribune* achieved, but I don't think we paid the fair market value either. Businesspeople will not pay more than the price asked, even if they feel sheepish taking advantage of a regrettable system. That is why it is so important for the municipal plans and policies to be firm and fair.

I would like to move to another topic, with your leave. As a businesswoman, I am concerned about the lack of detail in the *Plan* as to cost. Mr. Burnham airily dismisses the need for hard figures with the statement that the *Plan* "can be executed without seriously increasing present burdens."[35] From what I hear today, burdens are not fairly shared now. Major increases in capital investment will surely require increased taxes. If the Heart of Chicago, its businessmen, and its wealthy residents are not sharing the burden, then that burden is heavier for all other Chicagoans. While I would like to say I care about fair taxation as a matter of principle, you will surely see through that simple statement of altruism. My success in operating the Boston Store is based on the ability of tens of thousands of Chicagoans to make discretionary purchases. Shortages in their pocketbooks become shortages in my cash registers.

Mr. Burnham says the cost of the outer parks will be "considerable" and must be borne by the public. His street plan will be very expensive, but he doesn't share with us how expensive.[36] Mr. Fisher has taken a very narrow course in his chapter, defining only those laws that limit the plan's implementation. Mr. Fisher has extensive knowledge from the municipal charter discussions and from his civic reform work that could help identify new sources of revenue to pay for these investments, simply by applying the law fairly in many cases. It is truly telling that neither Mr. Burnham nor Mr. Fisher allude to that possibility.

------

34   Corwin, "Mollie Netcher Newbury," 35.

35   Burnham and Bennett, *Plan of Chicago,* 119.

36   Ibid., 123–124.

Louise de Koven Bowen nodded and picked up the thread of conversation:

Thank you, Mrs. Netcher, your points are very well taken. Let's move directly into a discussion of what we see as the role of business in the Heart of Chicago, and how that differs from the views expressed in the plan. I hope we can live up to the spirit of Miss Addams. She has been "an interpreter between working men and women and the people who lived in luxury on the other side of the city and she also gave the people of her own neighborhood quite a different idea about the men and women who were ordinarily called "capitalists."[37] It is in that spirit that I hope we can bridge some of the chasms between the view of the businessmen and the views of the neighborhoods.

Mrs. Netcher herself provides us with one excellent example of how business might conduct itself in the best of circumstances, especially in relation to employees. The Chicago Woman's Club published a report of working conditions in Marshall Field's and other stores, some years ago.[38] Some of the downtown commercial emporiums pay their clerks so little that young women are forced to "supplement" their incomes or find they cannot pay for stable housing and are in jeopardy for their reputations.[39] Our sisters in the colored women's clubs tell us that most of the big department stores, and especially Marshall Field's, practice segregated employment policies, refusing to hire Negro women and often refusing to wait on them.[40]

Your approach with several thousand employees[41] has been different. Can you tell us a little about your business philosophy, Mrs. Netcher?

Mollie Netcher replied:

---

37   Bowen, *Growing Up,* 93.
38   Flanagan, *Charter,* 40.
39   Stead, *If Christ,* 245.
40   Knupfer, *African American Women's Clubs,* 59.
41   The Boston Store employed almost four thousand people sometime in the teens.

Well, in one sense it is probably very similar to that of my male counterparts. "I was drawn to (Mr. Netcher) just as he was to me" by our mutual interest in business. "I abstained from parties, clubs, dinners, company, and everything of that kind so as to devote myself to him, and the result was that he talked everything over with me. All this has been an invaluable business training for me which I seem to have absorbed unconsciously."

However, I may differ from the owners of other emporia in managing people. I am not chummy with employees, but neither do I wish to take advantage of them. I believe their loyalty to the Boston Store is likely to be improved if they perceive the store as loyal to them. I have embarked on an expansion plan that will take the next decade to complete, but will eventually include classrooms and recreational spaces like reading rooms, a billiard room, and a tennis court on the roof. I am negotiating with the public library to include a branch library in the store.

My customers will also appreciate my concept of full service. I will eventually offer a playroom with attendants for the convenience of mothers, a barber, telegraph office, post office, bank, and small hospital for emergencies. Some floors will be devoted to factories making candy, cigars, and baked goods right here on the premises. Drugs and toilet articles will be tested here to ensure their safety.

I am able to provide these amenities and still make money using policies that are foreign to most department store owners. I never waste money on frills like business entertaining, which only drives up the cost of goods. And most importantly, all transactions are in cash. I buy from suppliers with cash and only accept cash from my customers. The system of operating on credit is sure to bring businesses to a sorrowful end.[42]

---

42 All information in this section is from one article: Margaret Corwin, "Mollie Netcher Newbury: The Merchant Princess," *Chicago History* (Spring, 1977). Molly did build her store to include all the specifications outlined here. By 1916 she bought a summer resort with cottages that she rented to employees. However, a series of poor business decisions in the 1920s, coupled with her continued resistance to credit transactions, caused the business to decline, and the Boston Store closed in the 1940s.

State Street, viewed toward the north from Madison Street, with the Boston Store on the west. (Chicago History Museum, DN-0003432, Chicago Daily News *negatives collection.)*

Louise de Koven Bowen graciously thanked Molly Netcher and began a new direction:

I would like to make a few observations about the McCormick family, their business style and their role in Chicago business history. They seem to me to offer a fascinating study of how leadership style influences business and civic practices. But first, I think Edith has a lovely little story about the McCormicks that will help to set the tone. Edith, will you share the story?

Edith de Nancrede smiled and nodded to indicate her agreement:

Are you all aware of Anita McCormick Blaine's insistence that her property be fairly assessed? She marched into the assessor's office in 1899 to say that even though her property at one million dollars was the largest on the Cook County rolls, it was woefully underestimated. Her rationale was, "those able to pay the taxes should pay them" and she brought the assessor a more careful estimate.[43] Shortly thereafter, her mother, Nettie Fowler McCormick followed suit.[44] The two women were, and probably still are, the largest taxpayers in Cook County.

Louise de Koven Bowen chuckled at Edith's clear delight with the story and continued:

The McCormicks are particularly noteworthy because of their rapid progression from the firm most closely associated with the Haymarket tragedy to a firm notable for good civic citizenship. Cyrus McCormick's daughter, Anita, is the most visible example, but I think it begins with her mother Nettie, who was especially influential on company policy after Cyrus Sr. died, although it was her son, Cyrus Jr., who actually ran the company. Nettie's worldview is focused more on religious than civic life, but her values imbued the children with a strong sense of responsibility to others. Let me give you just a few examples from their lives and works.

Stanley proposed to his brother Cyrus in 1902 that they develop a profit-sharing system for International Harvester[45] employees, with Anita strongly in support.[46] Cyrus Jr. was won over by business arguments that he could encourage loyalty and discourage union activity within the company.[47] Stanley is a good friend of the settlement movement, especially the Gads Hill Settlement near their plant.[48] In another innovation, John Dewey of the University of Chicago placed a student in a Harvester plant to operate a social welfare department.[49] Of course, it is Anita who has caused the most consternation, and I would say, done the most good. You may remember

---

43   G. Harrison, *Anita McCormick Blaine,* 145.

44   Ibid., 146.

45   McCormick Reaper became International Harvester Company in 1902.

46   Anita McCormick Blaine, Nettie McCormick, Louise de Koven Bowen, and Jane Addams are known to have influenced Cyrus Jr.'s business practices in 1912, after the period of this meeting. They went to his office to protest unsanitary conditions in a New York twine mill. Cyrus responded with changed practices and new machinery.

47   G. Harrison, *Anita McCormick Blaine,* 148.

48   K. McCarthy, *Noblesse Oblige,* 113.

49   Feffer, *The Chicago Pragmatists,* 227.

when she was called a socialist by the *Baltimore Sun* simply for putting her household help on eight-hour days![50] But we all know she has taken her civic duty more responsibly than most and used her wealth in the service of Chicago and its people. She paid for the 1901 City Homes Association report on housing conditions,[51] for a City Club report on vocational education,[52] and funded several innovative schools.[53]

Now, some may say these are private practices having little to do with the conduct of the city's business. But I believe we should look at the tone set by the business community. If they want to marshal the city's resources to serve business interests, it is entirely fair that we ask what is being offered in return. Do we receive an offer of fair leadership, innovation, and long-term commitment to the city? Or are we being asked to continue to pay for business benefits that business won't pay for itself?

This discussion of business leaders' responsibility to the larger community is fascinating and necessary, but I fear I must move us to an entirely different, but equally important, topic. We are fortunate to have several people with us today who are involved in the cultural life of the city. Before we move to the question of recommendations for the *Plan of Chicago*, we want to consider the cultural role of the downtown district.

Harriet, as an art critic and columnist[54] you have had the opportunity to gain broad perspective on the role of culture in the city. Do you see ways in which creative endeavors could be fostered by a plan for the city's future?

Harriet Monroe was obviously pleased to bring her passion for the arts to this discussion:

I do see opportunities that Mr. Burnham overlooked. Furthermore, I think that the arts can be a great unifying

---

50   G. Harrison, *Anita McCormick Blaine,* 147.

51   Philpott, *Slum and the Ghetto,* 94.

52   Herrick, *Chicago Public Schools,* 118–119.

53   G. Harrison, *Anita McCormick Blaine,* 123.

54   Williams, Harriet Monroe, 9. Monroe was an art critic and columnist for the *Chicago Tribune, Chicago Times Herald, New York Sun, Leslie's Weekly,* the *Atlantic, Chicago American,* and *Chicago Evening Post* over the period 1889–1912.

force, an especially important bridge between the business community and some who are antagonistic to the businessmen. I myself am drawing on business support to try to raise money for a magazine I hope to start.[55] I am working toward a goal of one hundred business supporters, each of whom pledges fifty dollars a year for five years, until the magazine is self-supporting.[56] I expect there is a good degree of overlap between my list and the list of subscribers to the *Plan of Chicago*.

There is great variety in the cultural life of this city and we can only improve upon our region by creating more cultural opportunities. I fear that Mr. Burnham and his sponsors see culture as only that version that begins with a capital "C" and is housed in a large, classical-style building. It is less about sculpture, or dance, or opera, and more about the monumental buildings that house the activities. Although we can boast a rich literary history in Chicago, little in this *Plan* promotes literary activity. This plan doesn't reflect the breadth and depth of cultural life in Chicago, because the businessmen are indifferent to cultural associations like the Little Room. I think most of you are familiar with the Little Room, but in case some are not, let me explain that the Little Room is a group composed of architects, novelists, settlement residents, poets, sculptors, and dancers. In short, anyone involved in creative endeavors might join us at our weekly session in the Fine Arts Building. It is simply a discussion group, committed to fostering cultural activities throughout the city. It is distinctly cultural with a small "c." We promote no grandiose plans for buildings or monuments. We possess a desire to fertilize across artistic specialties and especially hope to provide a link between cultural activities downtown and in the neighborhoods. For instance, some of the plays written by members of the Little Room are first performed on settlement house stages.[57]

Anna, you are one of the settlement house members of the Little Room. Why don't you describe the role of the settlements in the cultural life of our city?

---

55 Monroe started *Poetry* magazine in 1912.

56 Williams, *Harriet Monroe,* 15.

57 Grossman, Keating, and Reiff, *The Encyclopedia of Chicago,* 483–484.

Anna Morgan was happy to oblige:

The settlements function as cultural societies for a number of reasons. The settlements are themselves creative institutions, organizationally and in their programmatic activities. Let me read you an excerpt from a theater review written by Loredo Taft in the *Chicago Daily Record*. He is speaking of the Hull-House production of *Odysseus*. He reminds us that Jane Addams felt that showcasing artistic works of various groups would result in greater respect from all segments of society, a view he endorsed. He reported that the audience was "packed too closely for comfort with the most cosmopolitan crowd I have ever seen. Everybody that I know was there or had been on the previous evenings, and there were several hundred present variously from the Lake Shore drive and the Nineteenth Ward whom I did not know. For a couple of hours all distinctions were forgotten—the millennium was here . . . we were all brothers and sisters again." Taft understood the purpose of having Greek actors enact classical Greek plays. Greek immigrants took pride in the work while the audience would never "think of (neighborhood Greeks) in quite the same way as before."[58]

Cultural activity is not something restricted to large institutions in the downtown area. Indeed, some of the most creative activity is undertaken far from the influence of conventional cultural institutions, which tend to be very conservative, like their donors. The businessmen tried to apply a veneer of culture to Chicago by purchasing European artwork[59] and housing it in monumental buildings. I would suggest that there are underappreciated groups of artists of all types here in Chicago, and that they are spread throughout many different neighborhoods of the city.

Chicago could become a truly exciting place by cultivating its own artistic community—a cultural capital offering our own population and visitors a potpourri of visual, performing, and literary arts. We could do this by linking the downtown arts world to the neighborhoods. I offer as one example the

---

58   Residents of Hull–House, *Hull-House Maps and Papers,* 32.

59   K. McCarthy, 32.

work that Charles Hutchinson is doing to bring visual art from the Art Institute to schools, settlement houses, and park field houses.[60] He defines his role as president of the Art Institute very broadly. The physical edifice in which the Art Institute sits is not the wellspring of culture. Rather than passively waiting to see who will visit his institution, he brings art to the places people are most likely to see it and enjoy it in their everyday lives.

The settlements promote the dispersion of culture, and they offer a very broad variety of cultural activities, largely due to the diversity of ethnic groups that inhabit their neighborhoods. Think of the educational, cultural, and even economic benefits this region could derive if we committed significant resources to a program like Charles Hutchinson's in theater, in literature, and in the rest of the arts.

Edith de Nancrede wanted to add to the discussion:

Miss Addams has just published a new book, *The Spirit of Youth and the City Streets*. She proposes that art be brought out onto the streets, with marching music, festivals, orchestras in the parks "with the magic power they all possess to formulate the sense of companionship and solidarity."[61] She speaks of the benefits to youth, who would be offered an alternative to cheap dance halls and five-cent theaters. She speaks also of the benefits to immigrants who appreciate their own culture anew when presented with dance, storytelling, or other art forms from their homeland. I would venture to say that other beneficiaries would include the business community which might see increased retail sales in areas hosting festivals, both in the neighborhoods and downtown. Think of the possibilities if the rest of the nation looked at Chicago as a city of arts and festivals rather than as a city of strikes and tenements.

Louise de Koven Bowen reluctantly broke in:

This has been a fascinating discussion to participate in. I daresay we covered a broader range of topics than any of the other groups will, but I think that is fitting. The center city is

---

60   Schaffer, Urban Ideals, 125.

61   Addams, *Spirit*, 98.

the core of our region. There is a symbiotic relationship between the activities of the core and activities of the neighborhoods. But now we must find a way to synthesize this into a coherent statement about our vision for the central business district.

It seems we covered at least three primary ideas here. The first was the governmental functions associated with the center city, specifically the problems caused by the out-dated and too-often-manipulated tax assessment system. The second was business culture, including some alternatives to aggressive business practices that treat employees as adversaries. The third portion of our discussion was about the downtown as the nucleus of a cultural network linked to neighborhoods and to more outdoor cultural celebrations. Perhaps we should break into three groups and ask each group to present a recommendation.

Your gestures seem to indicate agreement. Can we reconvene as one group in a half hour, with a recommendation from each group?

The recommendations each group offered were as follows:

Taxation: Ellen Culver, Enella Benedict

Convene a new charter convention that is truly representative of the city as a whole to propose an adequate and fair system of taxation, and to give municipal government more authority and responsibility for municipal services. Include a strong civil service system to abolish patronage hiring. Publish the terms of all contracts, including the ownership of all businesses benefiting from each contract.

Business culture: Molly Netcher, Louise de Koven Bowen

Establish a business-labor-community consortium at the Armour Institute or another university to promote harmonious relations and to work out practical solutions to potential conflicts between business and other groups.

Arts: Harriet Monroe, Anna Morgan, Edith de Nancrede

Apply Charles Hutchinson's model of disseminating art such as the performing arts and literature throughout the city. Create a cultural commission to uncover or create opportunities for cross-fertilization between downtown arts institutions and neighborhood institutions.

9

Immigrants & Labor

PLAYERS

First (middle, maiden) Name	Last Name	Brief Biographical Information	Approximate Age
Grace	Abbott	Led investigation of employment agencies and child labor, headed Immigrant Protective League.	30s
Bessie	Abramovitz (later Hillman)	Arrived in United States in 1905 from Russia as a teen; attended night school at Hull-House; organized a walkout at a coat factory in 1908, blacklisted; after 1909 organized Hart, Schaffner & Marx strike (1910).	Late teens
Florence	Kelley	Social scientist, first woman factory inspector in Illinois, head of National Consumers' League, headquartered in New York after 1899 but retained strong ties to Hull-House.	50s
Elizabeth Chambers	Morgan	Immigrated to Chicago from England in 1869; worked to protect women and children from industrial abuses and to increase requirements for compulsory school attendance; investigated sweatshops, labor conditions in prison industries, abuse of prostitutes by legal system, and poor work conditions of teachers.	50s
Othelia Mork	Myhrman	Co-founder of Swedish National Association (1893) after a Swede was killed by police without provocation (police were found guilty); ran the Swedish Free Employment Bureau during and after the depression of 1893–94; supported bureau with ethnic festivals, cultural celebrations.	50s

Agnes	Nestor	Organized female glove makers; joined Chicago Women's Trade Union League in 1904, elected to national WTUL board by 1906; third president of Chicago WTUL and first from working class; involved in suffrage and educational advocacy as routes to improve worker status.	20s
May Wood	Simons	Socialist, publisher of "Woman and the Social Problem" (pamphlet), friend of Jane Addams and Mary McDowell, many socialist publications, resident of Evanston.	40s
Ellen Gates	Starr	Co-founder of Hull-House, teacher, arts supporter, labor activist.	50s
Mary	Wilmarth	One of earliest supporters of Hull-House, first president of Hull-House board, involved in many civic and social justice causes, subscriber to the *Plan of Chicago*.	70s

THE YEAR IS 1909. The women, a mix of labor leaders, immigrant leaders, and Hull-House residents and supporters, are gathered around a table in the Labor Museum. Ellen Gates Starr, co-founder of Hull-House, leads the meeting.

Ellen Gates Starr welcomed everyone and began with an introduction to the purpose of the meeting, followed by some general remarks about the evolution of the relationship between labor, immigrants, and the settlement movement:

Thank you all for coming. Your individual experiences provide a wealth of information that will be invaluable to this task. We are especially grateful that Florence Kelley, who played such a large role in Hull-House's early work on labor and immigrant issues, is able to join us for this discussion.[1]

---

1   Kelley, who was a resident of Hull-House from 1891 to 1899, was responsible for many of Hull-House's early interventions and was most influential in setting the scholarly tone of the *Hull-House Maps and Papers*.

Ellen Gates Starr.
(Chicago History
Museum, DN-0062288,
Chicago Daily News
negatives collection.)

I think you know that we are one of eight groups meeting to discuss ways to strengthen the *Plan of Chicago* that has been drafted by Mr. Daniel Burnham, under the auspices of the Commercial Club of Chicago. Some of the groups offered suggestions on chapters Mr. Burnham wrote for the *Plan.* Our charge is more complicated, since there is little in the *Plan* directly addressing the conditions of immigrants and even less addressing the labor issues that we believe are critical. Nevertheless, by the time we finish our discussion, we will need to develop a few recommendations for additions to strengthen the *Plan.* Then it will be up to the Commercial Club and Mr. Burnham to decide whether to accept our recommendations.

Few issues in Chicago have been as polarizing during the last twenty years as labor issues. Chicago has been the site of some of the nation's most infamous strikes. The influx of large numbers of immigrants to Chicago appeared to some business owners to represent an unorganized and easily manipulated worker pool. Distrust between the many immigrant groups contributed to a divided labor movement and to schisms between native and immigrant workers. The rapid rise of a business class that lacked a culture of civic obligation to other classes certainly exacerbated the polarized state of affairs. A lack of regulatory controls left workers vulnerable to workplace injuries and death. Negroes, women, and children have been especially exploited or used to keep white, male workers' wages low.

In this highly charged atmosphere, the settlement houses were the first institutions to take a somewhat neutral stance. "Neutral" may be a relative term here. Hull-House, which led the settlement movement in developing a policy on labor relations, was clearly on the side of the workers. But our stance can be defined as somewhat neutral because it has tried to see the interests of both sides. Jane Addams has been a friend of labor, but has at times despaired of the militant tactics of some labor leaders.[2] She articulated the view that although settlements were in favor of labor's goals, the settlements should "take a larger and steadier view than is always possible for the workingman . . . or the capitalist."[3]

From the beginning, Hull-House approached labor relations with the same thorough research and deliberative thoughtfulness with which it approached most issues. A very early project, the *Hull-House Maps and Papers* (published in 1895), not only defined issues confronted by labor and immigrants, but also defined scholarly sociological research for many years to come.[4] *Hull-House Maps and Papers* also made clear that Hull-House is aligned with the union perspective. We owe a great debt of gratitude to Florence Kelley, who shaped that early study and set a very high standard of scholarship in its reports.

I would like to read a few sections from *The Spirit of Youth and the City Streets*, a book published just this year, in which Jane Addams interprets the relationship between work, play, and civic life. In the eyes of settlement house leaders, the labor movement is not an end in itself but one component in a full and satisfying life and a healthy city. She says, "It may be illuminating to trace the connection between the monotony

---

2   Deegan, *Men of the Chicago School,* 61.

3   Davis, *Spearheads,* 108

4   Rima Schultz, in an introduction to the 2007 reissue of the Hull-House Maps and Papers says, "This book is important because it is one of the first publications that refuted conservative laissez-faire economics with statistical data on wage labor."

and dullness of factory work and the petty immoralities which are often the youth's protests against them."[5] She goes on to propose solutions that better integrate education and family life with work life:

> Perhaps never before have young people been expected to work from motives so detached from direct emotional incentive. Never has the age of marriage been so long delayed; never has the work of youth been so separated from the family life and public opinion of the community. Education alone can repair these losses. It alone has the power of organizing a child's activities with some reference to the life he will later lead and of giving him a clue as to what to select and what to eliminate when he comes into contact with contemporary social and industrial conditions. And until educators take hold of the situation, the rest of the community is powerless.[6]

Both Mr. Burnham and Miss Addams compare modern industrial cities to classical Greek cities and find them wanting—but for different reasons. Mr. Burnham is enamored of the architecture, the orderly streetscapes, and the monuments. Miss Addams finds that industrial cities have been organized for work, to the exclusion of leisure and learning. She has said, "The classical city promoted play with careful solicitude, building the theater and stadium as it built the market place and the temple," and "Only in the modern city have men concluded that it is no longer necessary for the municipality to provide for the insatiable desire for play."[7]

Before opening this discussion I would like to cover two more areas very briefly by way of introduction. The first is to mention some of the people who played a crucial role in formulating a settlement house position on labor and immigrant issues who are not here today. Some are no longer in the city; others are still at Hull-House but are reviewing other sections of this plan. Finally, I would like to suggest some of the topics we will try to cover during our meeting today.

---

5   Addams, *Spirit,* 107.

6   Ibid., 109.

7   Ibid., 4.

Some of you may know contributors to the *Hull-House Maps and Papers* who moved on to other institutions to continue their work, but for the benefit of others I would like to acknowledge them now. Agnes Sinclair Holbrook was responsible for the painstakingly detailed maps showing ethnic group data and wage data by building for the area around Hull-House. Alzina Stevens, who is now deceased, was the co-author with Florence Kelley of the article "Wage-Earning Children" and became a deputy factory inspector under legislative reforms that Florence will describe. In an interesting twist of fate, we have Mr. Burnham to thank for Alzina's introduction to Hull-House. We met her when she represented the Knights of Labor on the Women's Labor Committee of the World's Congress Auxiliary of the World's Columbian Exposition.[8] Alzina, who began factory work at the age of thirteen and lost a finger to an industrial injury,[9] had more than a scholarly interest in factory conditions.

Mary Kenney, a leader of the bookbinders, who has since moved to Boston, was also a deputy factory inspector for the state. Early on Mary was quite skeptical about the motives of Hull-House and its middle-class reformers. She overcame her reservations while working with Miss Addams to start the cooperative apartments that came to be called the Jane Club. Since that time, she has written, "It was that word 'with' from Jane Addams that took the bitterness out of my life. For if she wanted to work with me and I could work with her, it gave my life new meaning and hope."[10]

Finally, while this list is nowhere near exhaustive, I would like to mention a few other people active on the scene today, who contributed to issues of labor and immigration in the course of their work in related areas. These include Julia Lathrop, John Dewey,[11] Mary McDowell, Graham Taylor, and

---

8   Residents of Hull-House, *Hull House Maps and Papers,* 7.

9   Hamilton, *Alice Hamilton, M.D.,* 62.

10   Hayden, *Domestic Revolution,* 167–168.

11   Deegan, *Men of the Chicago School,* 252. Dewey was a frequent visitor to Hull-House during the time he taught at the University of Chicago and joined the Hull-House Board in 1897. The Labor Museum was a project he spearheaded with Addams to help immigrants connect between their homelands and Chicago.

Lucy Flower.[12] Particularly for the settlement residents, there has been a sense of pride in trying to help "settle" some of the worst divisions between employer and employee,[13] or at least to alleviate some of the worst consequences for wage earners.

I know this has been a long introduction and I beg your indulgence just a few more minutes while I suggest some topics we want to cover today. Florence Kelley is prepared to give us some greater insight into relevance of the reports in the *Hull-House Maps and Papers* and to fill us in on the legislative battle for child labor laws and general factory reforms. Agnes Nestor will provide background on the settlement movement's role in nurturing women's unions. May Wood Simmons, who has written on many issues in socialism, has some illustrative background to provide about Jane Addams's relationship with Lucy Parsons, one of the more radical leaders of the labor movement. We have two leaders from immigrant groups representing Russian Jews and Swedes, from whom we can learn a good deal. They are respectively, Bessie Abramovitz and Othelia Myhrman. In addition, Grace Abbott has prepared some background about her work with the Immigrant Protective League. Mary Wilmarth, who has had her hand on the pulse of virtually every issue that has come before Hull-House, will help ensure we consider other unprotected or unpopular groups. Lastly, before we move to fashioning recommendations I would like to provide some examples of published statements by business interests about labor relations to provide context a reasonable scope for our recommendations. Are we ready to move forward? If so, I would like to introduce Florence Kelley, general superintendent of the National Consumer League, who not only guided the production of the *Hull-House Maps and Papers*, but was also the author of the 1893 Illinois Factory and Inspection Act, popularly known as the Sweatshop Act. Kelley's work radicalized other Hull-House residents who were

---

12 Wade, *Graham Taylor*, 75. Taylor and Flower were active through the Civic Federation's Philanthropic Department in assisting with job placement during the depression of 1893–94.

13 Spain, *How Women Saved*, 241.

able to see things they hadn't seen before.[14] I know she will help enlighten us today.

Seeing agreement to move forward among others around the table, Miss Starr nodded to Florence Kelley, who began her overview:

Let me start by saying I think it is highly regrettable that Mr. Burnham is apparently unaware of the information we analyzed fifteen years ago. It has relevance to his inquiry today. I have been told that instead he requested nationality data on the Near West Side from the Chicago postmaster, although I don't know why he had such a high degree of interest in this area when his plan covers the whole region. He also consulted with a University of Chicago professor about immigrant issues, but not one who, to my knowledge, has been involved with Hull-House.[15] We can only conclude that his reliance on sources that are somewhat distant from the reality of life here has limited his understanding of the issues.

Jane Addams was restrained in introducing the report. She said "The residents . . . offer these maps and papers to the public, not as exhaustive treatises, but as recorded observations which may possibly be of value, because they are immediate, and the result of long acquaintance."[16] I believe she was excessively modest, for the cumulative effect of the chapters is very powerful, never having been collected and reported before. In addition to the maps, we documented industrial conditions, the circumstances of three different ethnic groups, and some of the institutions that sought to reform identified problems.

For those of you who are not familiar with the study, let me provide an overview of the sections. The first report includes the maps and the methodology we used for collecting and displaying the information. The maps of nationalities and household wages cover the area from Halsted Street to State Street and from Polk Street to Twelfth Street. One set of maps displays the language group to which every household belongs,

---

14   Residents of Hull-House, *Hull-House Maps and Papers*, 6.

15   Schaffer, *Urban Ideals*, 292–293.

16   Residents of Hull-House, *Hull-House Maps and Papers*, 45.

building by building, for every lot in the area. The other set of maps shows the total weekly wages of families by building, ranging from $5 a week to over $20 a week. The remaining articles fall into three categories: industrial conditions, particularly child labor and the "sweating system"; the experiences of Russian Jews, Bohemians, and Italians living on the Near West Side; topics indirectly related to the labor movement, such as Cook County Charities, the arts, and the settlement movement. The study concludes with an appendix listing the many programs in operation at Hull-House in the mid-1890s. I will focus here primarily on relevant information from the three chapters on industrial relations.

We discovered that there were 162 sweatshops employing men, women, and children in the Nineteenth Ward at the time of the study.[17] The situation for these families was dire. Let me quote to you directly on one of our most disturbing findings:

Children at work in a bottle factory. (University of Illinois at Chicago Library, JAMC_0000_0198_0319, Special Collections and University Archives Dept.)

---

17   Ibid., 66.

"The trade life of the garment worker is probably shorter than any other occupation; and the employees are always on the verge of pauperism, and fall into the abyss with every illness or particularly bad season."[18] We described the tragic example of one man who had worked twenty years, from the age of fourteen, only to fall into illness defined by doctors as "old age" at thirty-four. All four of his children were suffering from pneumonia after a particularly poor work season caused a lack of food in the household. We found that while other industries concentrated and mechanized production, the garment trade has diffused production and reduced living standards and consequently reduced the health of workers. The lone technical innovation—the button-hole machine—became the way to increase child labor, but at a high cost of deformity to the children thus employed.[19] I must admit that we somewhat naively thought that if the public was not shocked by the conditions under which garment workers suffered, they would at least be shocked to discover that even some of the finest quality clothing was produced in quarters that should have been quarantined because of serious disease in the producing household. This included epidemic strains that should not be released on unsuspecting shoppers. Unfortunately, there was no official action to protect the public, much less to help the sweaters. And yes, if you have heard the account about Julia Lathrop and myself entering a tenement with smallpox to carry out and destroy thousands of dollars worth of clothing—it is a true story. The city preferred to deny the existence of smallpox in Chicago rather than antagonize the merchants.[20]

I would like to point out that the essay on "The Sweating System" was written less than a year after passage of the 1893 Workshop and Factories Act, an act which, by the way, required half of the factory inspectors to be women.[21] The results of the act included: fewer small children in shops, the partial separation of home and shop, and partial enforcement

---

18   Ibid., 68.
19   Ibid., 69.
20   Addams, *Lathrop,* 83.
21   Residents of Hull-House, *Hull House Maps and Papers,* 74.

of the eight-hour day for girls and women.[22] Unfortunately, the eight-hour day provision didn't survive a court challenge, and Illinois reformers had to spend over a decade renegotiating a partial victory, a ten-hour day limitation.[23] I understand that progress on child labor has been made, although a somewhat halting progress dependent on cooperation from many entities including truant officers and school administrators.

In a separate article on "Wage-Earning Children" we found that the argument for using child labor where workers are scarce is a spurious one. Using national census information from 1890 we found that children are used where competition for jobs is most fierce, as a way to keep wages low. For example, Nevada has 620 employees for every one child worker; Pennsylvania has only 23. This dichotomy between older, industrial states and newer, less industrial states held constant.[24] It is the populous states, with large available labor pools, that are most likely to employ children in factories.

I'm sorry to say that the Illinois Bureau of Labor Statistics, which was established in 1879, never produced a report on child labor. After passage of the 1893 law, we published the first annual report in December of 1893, with statistics from July 15 to December 15. In those five months we visited 12 percent of the state's manufacturing businesses and found 6,576 children laboring in factories, although the 1890 census reported only 5,426 children employed in factories throughout the state.[25]

Let me briefly report some of the obstacles to enforcement. Many children were not covered under the law, since it applied only to factory work. Newsboys, bootblacks, and children who did piecework at home were not covered, nor were children holding retail jobs. Although the schools were provided with lists of all children under fourteen years of age who were removed from factories, the truant officers were not able to follow up to get them all into school. While I am sympathetic to the overworked truant officers, I have been highly critical

---

22   Ibid., 72.

23   Schultz and Hast, *Women Building Chicago*, 625.

24   Residents of Hull-House, *Hull-House Maps and Papers*, 74

25   Ibid., 74.

of the Board of Education for failing to provide more truant officers to see that children removed from factories are actually enrolled in school. In fact the system often worked in the reverse. Principals expelled eleven-year-olds as incorrigible and come to us, expecting us to give the children work permits so they can enter the factory system![26]

Another challenge is that Illinois still has no law requiring machinery to be safeguarded. Children and adults work with dangerous machines and inspectors are helpless to change their circumstances.[27] Fortunately or unfortunately, child wage earners usually exhibit very unstable employment patterns, rarely spending more than two months on a given job. This instability may save them from the worst health or injury consequences of a given job, but prevents them from learning a viable livelihood.[28] Before leaving this subject, let me draw you a picture from a caramel factory right here in the Nineteenth Ward that employs up to two hundred children. It is far from the worst example. Although it is well lit and ventilated, the towering six-story building has only one wooden staircase and no fire escapes. Since the 1893 Factory Law, the work week during the busiest holiday season was reduced from eighty-two hours a week to a *mere* forty-eight hours![29]

It is not only the factory owners who benefit from the work of children. Some children work because their fathers don't earn enough, or are injured or dead. But we also found that some families, especially some Italian, Bohemian, and German families, send children to work in order to pay off a mortgage and improve the household's economic status.[30] This is an example of where we need to do more work in our communities helping neighbors understand the long-term consequences of child labor and lack of schooling.

There is much more detail in the articles, and I urge those of you who have not read them to do so, but I hope these examples will serve to introduce the problems. Agnes Nestor

---

26   Herrick, *Chicago Public Schools,* 66.

27   Residents of Hull-House, *Hull House Maps and Papers,* 82.

28   Ibid., 84.

29   Ibid., 77–78.

30   Ibid., 85.

appears to be ready to broaden the discussion to Hull-House's role in assisting working women to organize.

Agnes smiled her thanks to Florence Kelley with obvious respect and deference to her many achievements and stature:

Not all of you know me well, so I would like to give you a few words of background. I began my work life at a glove factory and organized the women workers there. Since 1904 I have been a member of the Chicago Women's Trade Union League and since 1906 a member of the National Women's Trade Union League. The recent, unfortunate discord between local WTUL members who removed the WTUL from its Chicago settlement house roots to lodge the organization more firmly in the labor movement has been painful to watch.

I was glad to hear Miss Starr introduce Mary Kenney's contributions in her overview. Mary is a bookbinder and was a leader of the first all-women union organized in Chicago.[31] As an aside, I should point out that we are in the presence today of the two people who helped bring bookbinding to Hull-House and Chicago as a viable trade for young women. Ellen Gates Starr went to England over a decade ago to learn the skill and bring it back, and Mary Wilmarth was good enough to pay for her trip.[32] Thank you, to both of you, for your important contributions to working women.

Let me return to Mary Kenney's evolution from a skeptic of the motives of the settlement residents to a partner. This came about largely through the development of the Jane Club. Mary was the one who conceived the idea of cooperative housing for working women and received assistance from Hull-House to make it a reality. Mary saw her concept for housing security grow from one apartment to many. Women pooled their money to be able to see each other through periods of unemployment, so that all were safe from destitution and the special vulnerability women are subject to if their housing becomes uncertain. Hull-House helped to furnish the original apartment and continued to provide support as

---

31 Addams, *Twenty Years*, 125.
32 Schultz and Hast, *Women Building Chicago*, 984.

the cooperative expanded. The membership grew to fill a six-unit apartment building at 253 Ewing Street. By the time it reached fifty members it had outgrown the Ewing building. Hull-House helped establish a permanent building within the Hull-House complex, and incidentally created a parallel model for men, the Phalanx Club.[33]

Union activities were not just supported at Hull-House; often they were initiated here. The women shirtmakers and cloakmakers unions were formed here, as was the Dorcas Federal Labor Union, a federation of women's unions.[34] And as we all know, it was Jane Addams and Mary McDowell who opened the Chicago branch of the Women's Trade Union League here in Hull-House several years ago.

We are all aware of the special problems women face in the workplace, requiring labor organizations especially for women. But we are also highly aware of the dangers of dividing the labor front. Women and children enter the labor market to support themselves because the extremely low wages paid to men don't support a family. Women earn just over half of what men earn generally, and children earn a third of a man's pay.[35] Some women are supporting not only their children but a husband who is sick or in the grip of the bottle.

There is no support system for families in which a breadwinner has been injured or killed on the job. Jane Addams describes the public insurance system in Germany in her new book, the same book Miss Starr read from in her opening. She says, "In one year in the German Empire one hundred thousand children were cared for through money paid from the State Insurance fund to their widowed mothers or to their invalided fathers. And yet in the American states it seems impossible to pass a most rudimentary employers' liability act, which would be but the first step towards that code of beneficent legislation which protects the widow and fatherless in Germany and England. Certainly we will have

---

33   Hayden, *Domestic Revolution,* 167–168.
34   Addams, *Twenty Years,* 125.
35   Ashbaugh, *Lucy Parsons,* 48.

to bestir ourselves if we would care for the victims of the industrial order as well as do other nations."[36]

It is not just the industrial setting that has been harsh to women. In recent years, the Chicago federation of teachers, which represents primarily the women elementary school teachers, organized to save their hard-won pension system. Margaret Haley and Catherine Goggin founded the Chicago Federation of Teachers just twelve years ago, in 1897.[37] Since that time they have been under siege one year after the next.

Women working for the public schools are paid less than men, for the same work. The battle to gain and maintain pensions was a particularly maddening assault on the security of current and former teachers. The school board claimed the money wasn't available, but because all the largest businesses in Chicago paid taxes at rates that were pitifully under-assessed, the solution was easily within reach: collect more taxes through a fair system. Newspapers owned by the traction interests, such as the *Chronicle*, went on the attack against the teachers. Traction companies were alleged to be among the worst abusers of fraudulent assessments.[38] The *Chronicle* fought the teachers with a 1905 article saying that a teacher who was a union member couldn't teach character and citizenship since unions teach class hatred. They went so far as to blame teachers and the labor influence for insubordinate behavior in children,[39] as if naughtiness was invented in the past decade!

Miss Starr, I hope this very cursory review of women and unions in Chicago will be of help in our deliberations. There is so much more that could be said, but I know the committee looking at education will also cover some of this territory, particularly with relation to the teachers' union and the current dissent between Miss Addams and the WTUL.

Ellen Gates Starr thanked Agnes for her contribution, assured her it was adequate for the task at hand and introduced the next speaker, writer May Wood Simmons, who began thus:

36 Addams, *Spirit,* 149–150.
37 Flanagan, *Charter,* 41.
38 Davis, *Heroine,* 131.
39 Herrick, *Chicago Public Schools,* 108.

Thank you for the opportunity to join this discussion. Many of these issues are familiar to me from research for my articles. I have had a long-standing interest in the distant but respectful stance Lucy Parsons and Jane Addams mutually established. I think it is illustrative of how women can benefit from focusing on their areas of agreement and mutual benefit, rather than allowing us to be divided by our differences. Miss Parsons is as volatile as Miss Addams is temperate. Her life experience has embittered her, and for good reason. She fought racial discrimination as a Negro woman and bore personal tragedy as the wife of a white Haymarket radical who was executed. Her own radicalism in defense of working people sometimes exceeds that of her late husband, Albert Parsons. Yet it has a touching innocence at other times. Lucy expects that as more and more workers join the ranks of trade unionists, they will enter into agreements to voluntarily manage workplace behavior.[40] She ignores the advice of friends who try to dissuade her from working to organize immigrants and the most oppressed classes, the groups hardest to organize.[41] In this respect, I believe she shares Miss Addams's passion for taking on the hardest tasks, those tasks where the need is greatest.

Like Miss Addams, Miss Parsons is also able to step outside the common understandings we hold about how we arrange our lives and relationships. Just as Miss Addams and Miss Starr conceived of a cooperative living arrangement for Hull-House, Miss Parsons draws on her experience as a colored woman to visualize the world differently than it is. She compares wage slavery to chattel slavery,[42] and finds very little difference between the two. She carries the analogy one step further to point out that a housewife may simply be a servant who receives no wages at all and is bound to a form of sex slavery.[43] While her outlook is decidedly more pessimistic than Miss Addams's they both seek justice and relief for the

---

40   Ashbaugh, *Lucy Parsons,* 174.
41   Ibid., 191.
42   Ibid., 55.
43   Ibid., 202.

oppressed through their analyses of the existing domestic and industrial institutions.

Miss Addams, however, has a circumspect style that belies her strong passions. Lucy has less restraint and has been known to propose offensive measures. Her front-page article in the first issue of the *Alarm* newspaper, which Albert edited at one time, urged tramps who were committing suicide out of desperation to take some wealthy people to their deaths at the same time.[44] While I wouldn't judge Lucy's entire philosophy by her most inflammatory statements, there are many even in the radical labor faction who find her views difficult to tolerate. Mother Jones, when she was in Chicago, professed to be offended by speeches made by the Parsons at rallies on the lakefront.[45]

Miss Addams will defend and has defended Lucy's right to free speech, in spite of the differences in their personal styles and beliefs. As a journalist, and as a socialist, I have to respect that type of openness to ideas that challenge very fundamental notions of right and wrong.

As May Wood Simmons seemed to be completing her remarks, Bessie Abramovitz indicated she wanted to add to this point:

I think part of Miss Addams's openness to other points of view comes from her ability to analyze her own experience and that of those like her, and then broaden that experience to understand others. She compares her own grandfather's ignorance of Illinois to immigrants' difficulty in transferring their European customs and knowledge to Chicago. Her grandfather built a large flour mill in Illinois, just like his Pennsylvania mill, without realizing the distances in the Midwest put the mill too far from markets to operate profitably.[46] The room in which we sit, the Hull-House Labor Museum, is one of many ways the settlement has created a bridge between the knowledge and traditions of many different groups and the customs and practices of America. One of the differences I have with Mr. Burnham's *Plan of Chicago* is that it seems not to respect or

---

44   Ibid., 55.

45   Ibid., 60.

46   Addams, *Lathrop*, 56.

honor the traditions of newcomers. It seems that he would demolish and rebuild our physical communities in a style he calls "well-ordered" and simultaneously destroy the Old World customs that live on here. Some of what he sees as disorder is celebrated here as an evolving blend of American customs and immigrant traditions.

In my own experience, attending night school at Hull-House has been a wonderful opportunity to learn. It will surely help me adapt to American expectations. I *want* to learn American customs, become a citizen, and participate in civic life. But I don't want people who sneer at my community and my neighbors, people who seem to want to tear down this community, to forcibly Americanize me in their own image.

Othelia Myhrman nodded vigorously. Bessie ceded the floor to Othelia to continue providing an immigrant's perspective.

The Swedish community up north does not face such a direct threat from this plan as do the communities closer to downtown, communities that occupy land on which the businessmen have designs. In fact our community is essentially ignored by this plan and perhaps I should be grateful for that. Often our interaction with American customs has had serious consequences for Swedes, as in the situation that originally mobilized me to community service—the cold-blooded shooting of a Swede by police.[47] My effort to find work for unemployed countrymen through the Swedish National Association has helped me understand just how deep is the contempt that runs through some parts of the native-born population toward immigrants.

The settlement houses, on the other hand, offer tools immigrants need to "Americanize" themselves at a pace they choose for themselves. Whether one partakes of cultural celebrations of one or many groups is up to the individual. Whether one comes to hear a lecture or a concert is purely a matter of personal choice. The sixty-year-old grandmother in a family may come once in a while and never learn to speak English, but the children are likely to come as often as possible and to become fluent not only in the language but also in the

47   Schultz and Hast, *Women Building Chicago,* 615.

ways of America. After seeing how immigrants gladly embrace this smorgasbord of cultural amenities when offered without coercion, I can't understand what the businessmen are thinking in trying to force "Americanization" on their terms.

But what is even more surprising to me is that they don't see the value in settlement programs that are a direct service to them. Why is there no proposal in Mr. Burnham's *Plan* to expand kindergartens and crèches[48] so that working parents might labor in serenity knowing that their children are safe and well cared for? Why is there no support for expanding the services of the Visiting Nurses' Association so that public health might be preserved and the workforce be healthier and more productive? What of all the night-school and college-level classes offered at the settlements which enhance on-the-job mechanical and logical skills? As we go about the job-search and job-placement activities at the Swedish National Association, we constantly advise people to take full advantage of the opportunities offered by settlement houses to expand workers' skills.

I can only come to one conclusion about the businessmen's complete disregard for the ways in which settlement programs strengthen their workforce, and that is to postulate that it is the settlements' strong support for worker self-determination, as expressed through labor unions and settlement assistance in establishing labor unions, that blinds the businessmen to their own best interests.[49]

Bessie, you were very patient with my interruption. I don't know if you had finished your comments when I broke in. Please pardon my keen desire to express myself.

Bessie Abramowitz, with dignity and poise that belied her extreme youth, responded kindly:

There is no need to apologize, Mrs. Myhrman. Your points are important and very much in keeping with my own. I was planning to close my remarks with some anecdotes that came to me from or about my own countrymen. Russia can be a

---

48   "Crèche" was the term common for day care at the time. Burnham did include crèches in his draft, but the proposal was removed from the final plan.

49   Spain, *How Women Saved*, 241.

cruel nation. As you may know, the Russian government has demanded extradition of Russian immigrants in Chicago whom it considers to be "revolutionaries." These demands are based on false charges of crimes such as murder or arson, when in fact these people are pursued for political reasons. Abraham Isaak[50] and that Rudowitz fellow are among radicals who were pursued and persecuted on American soil by Russian authorities. Settlement leaders were among the most fervent defenders of their right to avoid such persecution, even to the point that Hull-House and Chicago Commons were vandalized in retaliation.[51]

It is not just our own countrymen who seek to brutalize us in America. We have seen particularly inflammatory incidents here at the hands of the Chicago police. The Averbuch case, in which an innocent young man was shot by the chief of police, would have been quietly forgotten had it not been for the advocacy of Miss Addams, the lawyer Harold Ickes, and businessman Julius Rosenwald, not to mention a host of other Jewish community leaders. But it was really Miss Addams's article, which was widely published in news accounts across the country that kept the incident from escalating into a full-blown anti-Semitic incident.[52]

Ellen Gates Starr thanked Othelia Myhrman and Bessie Abramowitz for sharing their countrymen's encounters with tragedy and injustice. She then invited Grace Abbott to introduce the group to the Immigrant Protective League and the work it recently started.

Grace Abbott began:

I am honored to speak to this work, but want to begin by emphasizing the number of people who contributed to establishing the Immigrant Protective League. We sought to create a safe haven for women and girls arriving in Chicago without protection of family. This became urgent because of the high rate of females who were expected but never arrived, either disappearing en route to Chicago or disappearing

---

50   Davis, *Heroine,* 117.
51   Deegan, *Men of the Chicago School,* 117.
52   Lissak, *Pluralism and Progressives,* 91–92.

between the train station and the boarding house or shop that expected them. Annual estimates of the numbers of girls and women missing went as high as 20 percent in some years.[53]

The Immigrant Protective League was started less than two years ago, in 1907. Hull-House had a significant role in establishing the league,[54] as did the Women's Trade Union League. We had the support of some of the more compassionate men of the community, including Julian Mack, who served as president of the Board. Julius Rosenwald, who has always taken a great interest in immigrant issues, is also on the board.[55] Our practices include meeting trains that are likely to carry immigrants to Chicago, establishing relationships with women who are alone and visiting them in their new homes.

We built a network of women fluent in the languages of most new immigrants; they greet the trains. It doesn't make any sense to send English-speakers to try to communicate with a frightened and overwhelmed young person. "This method [of dealing with immigrants in English only] of assimilation is not a new one . . . [but] the evidence . . . proves overwhelmingly that this method . . . is not only cruel but unsuccessful." We find that "the devotion to their own languages is strongest among the Bohemians, Poles, Slovaks, Lithuanians, and others who came from countries in which because they struggled for years to resist the efforts of the government to stamp out their language and to substitute German, Russian, or Magyar, freedom of language has come to be regarded by them as an evidence of liberty."[56] So we have as wide as possible a range of native speakers, rather than providing only the dominant European languages.

In the near future we expect to investigate the known exploiters of these vulnerable newcomers and to advocate for legislative change.[57] Our charter is broadly constructed so that we can expand our charge as we expand our networks. The charter obligates us to "apply the civic, social, and

53   Costin, *Two Sisters,* 89.

54   Schultz and Hast, *Women Building Chicago,* xxxiv.

55   Costin, *Two Sisters,* 67.

56   Lissak, *Pluralism and Progressives,* 53.

57   Breckinridge, *New Homes,* 223.

philanthropic resources of the city to the needs of foreigners in Chicago, to protect them from exploitation, to co-operate with the Federal state and local authorities, and with similar organizations in other localities and to protect the right of asylum in all proper cases."[58] We hope ultimately that our advocacy will cause the Federal Immigration Service to reconsider its very restricted role in protecting immigrants. A broader role under the current Federal Immigration Service is "unthinkable, but with a change in personnel and with a wider understanding of the nature of the problem, the apparently impossible might be realized."[59]

Ellen Gates Starr stepped up to transition to the next topic, thanking Grace Abbott for information on this new and very necessary organization. She reminded the group of the next two topics and then the charge to the group:

> We are coming close to the end of our time together and will need to fashion some recommendations before we leave. There are two more areas we set out to cover briefly before turning to recommendations. Those are to look at groups with interests closely allied to immigrants and labor and to review some of the published thoughts of the business community about our topic. Mary, you have many years of experience in this city, at Hull-House, on the boards of the Henry Booth House and the Frederick Douglass Center. I know you can help us to understand the perils facing groups that are pitted against each other rather than part of a common solution. For those of you who don't know Mary well, you need to know that she has infinite tolerance for all shades of opinion and has a long history of bringing together people of diverse opinion. Why in 1891, she even invited University of Chicago president William Rainey Harper to a Hull-House reception for anarchist Peter Kropotkin, a very unpopular event with Chicago's mainstream leadership![60]

---

58   Ibid., 224.

59   Ibid., 226.

60   Schultz and Hast, *Women Building Chicago*, 984.

Mary Wilmarth, a woman in her mid-seventies, looked the part of the experienced matriarch. She began by quoting her close friend, Jane Addams:

Let me begin with some wisdom found in the article from the *Hull-House Maps and Papers*, written by Miss Addams, entitled "The Settlement as a Factor in the Labor Movement." Miss Addams notes that "the discovery of the power to combine was the distinguishing discovery of our time."[61] However, problems arise when sub-groups are pitted against each other fighting for meager benefits. The settlements traditionally played a role in bringing people together across gender and ethnic lines to strengthen the entire labor movement. For instance, women who are forced to enter the sewing trades and work at home, combining their roles as provider and parent, have been seen by male tailors as undercutting wages since women are paid less.[62] On the other hand, women resisted taking part in union meetings because they were always held in saloon halls. Hull-House hosted a first meeting of male and female cloakmakers to bring the factions together. Forty Russian Jewish tailors and several Irish girls, settlement residents, and a male interpreter were in attendance. The girls were socially at ease but less skilled at their trade. They felt safely "chaperoned" by the presence of the residents, but would not have undertaken to meet with unfamiliar men on their own. The Russian tailors were highly skilled at their trade but at a linguistic and social disadvantage. Their attempts to unionize would be much more difficult with "competition" from the girls.[63] It is unlikely that these two groups could have come together without Hull-House acting as an intermediary, in effect strengthening both groups through a collaborative effort.

It is this kind of cross-group solidarity that is so important and yet seemingly so difficult for many of the labor unions to effect. It is not just a question of gender. The city's population

---

61   Residents of Hull-House, *Hull-House Maps and Papers,* 139.

62   Ibid., 140.

63   Ibid., 141.

and neighborhoods are Balkanized, and the labor movement itself is fractured by trade and by ethnic group.[64]

The Chicago Federation of Labor has made some progress in bringing certain labor groups together. Almost half of the city's workforce holds membership in a Federation union. But the business owners retaliated with a drive for open shops, which seem to be gaining some success.[65] Unfortunately the American Federation of Labor stopped organizing Negro workers around the time of the World's Columbian Exposition. The Knights of Labor, which did actively organize Negroes, have waned in influence.[66]

As long as Negroes must stand outside organized labor, every working person is at risk of "divide and conquer" tactics. I don't know if most of you know the lengths to which Jane Addams went when she hired a Negro cook who was unable to join a Chicago union, simply by virtue of race. Grace Abbott, through sheer persistence, was able to get the cook into a Negro local in St. Louis. Although Hull-House is a very benign work environment, these two dynamic women wanted to make sure the Hull-House cook had proper recourse and representation if it was needed.[67]

You all know how rare it is for an employer to safeguard the rights of Negroes. Negro workers are often used as strikebreakers by employers who won't hire them for regular employment. Mary McDowell has seen this first hand in the stockyards, where only one stockyards laborer of twenty thousand was Negro in 1890.[68] Mary has had some small success in first gaining the trust of the packinghouse workers, and then gradually trying to show them the wisdom of admitting Negroes to their unions to thwart the union-busting tactics of the companies.[69] Her progress is dismally slow, but not for lack of trying on her part.

---

64   Feffer, *The Chicago Pragmatists,* 95.

65   Ibid., 212.

66   Ashbaugh, *Lucy Parsons,* 187.

67   Davis, *Spearheads,* 106.

68   Reed, *All the World,* 14.

69   Diner, "Chicago Social Workers," 402.

I have not done this subject justice, but to tell the truth, time is short and additional examples for additional groups would simply be a recitation of similar circumstances in different settings. Let me close by simply taking us back to the statement by Miss Addams that I quoted at the beginning of my remarks. It is the power to combine that will make us all strong, not the power to divide. When women are pitted against men, whites against blacks, Italians against Bohemians, we all end up with less than we would have had if we closed ranks.

Ellen Gates Starr assumed the floor to conclude the discussion:

Mary, I know how difficult it must be for you to make such a brief summary of your many years of commitment to many different people. Your consideration of our time imperatives is just further evidence—if we needed any—of your unselfish devotion to the needs and interests of others.

At this point I hope to be as concise as Mary. Before we move to recommendations in our area of expertise, let us make sure we are aware of the barriers to fundamental change. The business community in Chicago has some uncompromising views of the rest of us. I don't want to make more of this than we should, but we need to be aware of the views in order to formulate reasonable responses. It has been some time now since Pullman, Field, and their types dominated the business scene. We may be seeing a small and gradual evolution in the business community to a more collaborative approach, but the past dies hard.

The Pullman and Field approach to labor was a militaristic one. Their response to labor unrest was to donate or purchase land to build the military bases of Fort Sheridan and Great Lakes Naval Base.[70] When Illinois's governor and Chicago's mayor refused to intercede in the Pullman Strike, the businessmen activated national contacts to ensure that President Cleveland would send troops.[71]

---

70 Flanagan, *Charter*, 29.

71 C. Smith, *Urban Disorder*, 236.

We all know of George Pullman's attempts to control a whole community of employees, including every aspect of their family, religious, and civic life. Indeed, during the debate over annexing the township in which the Pullman Car Company and Pullman town lay, the company fired any resident said to be in favor of annexation.[72] Pullman believed in his right to rule his employees until his dying day. He once responded to Graham Taylor's question about how the company could ensure loyalty to the town's rules with the response that they simply remove "undesirable" tenants.[73]

These are simply some of the excesses that have been most public. Other attempts to put labor at a disadvantage, or extinguish it altogether, have been more clandestine. The one place where business attitudes toward labor have been clear and unequivocal is in some of the newspapers. Thankfully not all of them are resolutely anti-labor. And some, like the *Inter-Ocean* and the *Chronicle* are simply the known mouthpieces of the traction companies. But it is disturbing to see how labor has been portrayed over the years in the *Chicago Tribune,* which asserts its journalistic responsibility. Here are a few examples: After Albert Parsons applied for a reporting job at the *Tribune* and was manhandled and threatened, the *Tribune* wrote: "The world owes these classes rather extermination than a livelihood."[74] It is so much easier to dehumanize those who are unfamiliar, as this quote from the *Tribune* allows and even encourages: "This motley mixture of humanity . . . Bohemian Socialistic slums . . . Scandinavian dives . . . thieves from Halsted, Des Plaines, Pacific Avenue and Clark Street . . . red-headed, cross-eyed and frowsy servant girls."[75] Most disturbing of all I think is this quote: "When a tramp asks you for bread, put strychnine or arsenic on it and he will not trouble you any more and others will keep out of the neighborhood."[76] Frankly, I found Lucy Parsons's article appalling, but it is even more appalling to hear exactly the same call for execution of

72   Karlen, *Crabgrass Communities,* 68.
73   Wade, *Graham Taylor,* 76.
74   Ashbaugh, *Lucy Parsons,* 25.
75   Ibid., 29.
76   Ibid., 57.

innocent people in a mass circulation newspaper that aspires to "respectability."

We touched on a great number of problems. Now we need to begin to consider what solutions we would recommend as part of a forward-looking *Plan of Chicago*. If each of you will write your highest priority on a sheet of paper, we can read them aloud and see how much agreement we already have. Then we can decide on one or more recommendations that we think will enhance the *Plan of Chicago*.

After everyone read their priorities, it appeared that many of them could be grouped under one umbrella recommendation:

The Chicago region should establish a first-of-its kind Labor Institute, governed by a board representing business, labor, settlement, and elected officials. It should be funded by a one-cent tax on every ten employees. The institute will promote public and private initiatives such as insurance for workers injured or killed on the job, vocational and technical education for workers, crèches for children whose parents must work, and public health nurses in workplaces to improve the health and longevity of workers.

10

Public Health

First (middle, maiden) Name	Last Name	Brief Biographical Information	Approximate Age
Margaret Day	Blake	Executive board of Immigrant Protective League, after 1909 was a University of Illinois trustee, co-founder of group that became the League of Women Voters, donor and trustee of the Art Institute of Chicago.	30s
Harriet	Fulmer	Superintendent of Visiting Nurses' Association from 1898; placed nurses in factories, schools, and "baby tents" in neighborhoods.	30s
Alice	Hamilton	Physician, epidemiologist, studied industrial disease, first woman on faculty of Harvard Medical School.	40s
Caroline	Hedger	Physician; published articles on public health in stockyards area and conditions leading to high TB rates and consequences for food production.	30s
Fannie Barrier	Williams	Became major force in founding Provident Hospital and Training School, 1891; active in Frederick Douglass Center, Ida B. Wells Club, Phyllis Wheatley Club, and Phyllis Wheatley Home for Girls; co-founder of National Association of Colored Women.	50s
Rachel Slobodinsky	Yarros	Physician; professor at College of Physicians and Surgeons of Chicago, Obstetrics; language facility helped her work with immigrants; moved to Hull-House in 1907 with husband, Victor.	40s

🖤 THE YEAR IS 1909. The location is the kitchen in the Coffee House and Gymnasium Building at Hull-House. The kitchen is large; two hundred nutritious hot lunches are prepared there each day and sold to working people for ten cents each.[1] The residents and their guests sit around an expansive table covered with oilcloth.

Alice Hamilton, a Hull-House resident, trusted confidant of Jane Addams and physician, began the meeting with a statement of its purpose:

> Miss Addams has asked me to preside over this meeting to discuss issues of public health relevant to the development of a plan for Chicago and environs. Miss Addams is traveling at present and did not want to delay the accomplishment of this important task. Some of you may know of Mr. Daniel Burnham, who oversaw the construction of the World's Columbian Exposition. Mr. Burnham, on commission to the Commercial Club, has drafted a plan for our city's future, which I hope you all took the opportunity to read.
>
> For those of us in the field of health, it is impossible not to notice the absence of substantive public health recommendations in the *Plan of Chicago*. In order to complete our task, we will need to start from nothing and come up with an honest appraisal of the problems and the solutions. Please allow me to suggest a way we may cover the topics that require our attention. We all have depth and breadth of experience to draw on. I suggest we start with a general discussion of public health, the communities hardest hit by sanitation problems, recurring epidemics, and lax enforcement of existing laws. You should all feel free to add issues in this general discussion.
>
> After we set the stage, I would like to call on each of you for expertise in specific areas, beginning with Mrs. Fannie Barrier Williams to brief us on the role of hospitals and health facilities, followed by Harriet Fulmer who will discuss the roles of health professionals. I will provide an overview of industrial health and safety and Caroline Hedger will tell

---

1   *Hull-House Maps and Papers* cites lunches as ten cents in 1895. The price may have increased by 1909.

Alice Hamilton. (Library of Congress, LC-B2-5118-8, Bain News Service, Publisher, Prints and Photographs Division.)

us about some exciting new developments in fighting infant mortality. Finally Rachel Yarros will raise some of the special health concerns centered on women's issues. Margaret Day Blake, who is involved in a variety of reform efforts, can add a broader perspective to some of these topics as we discuss them.

Is this plan agreeable to everyone? I know you were each asked to think about and prepare your individual topics, but I want to ensure that you feel all matters will be considered and adequately discussed.

Alice Hamilton looked around the room and saw she had general agreement from the group. She called on Caroline Hedger first.

Caroline, you have published articles about conditions in the stockyards area. Can you establish the questions and concerns for us?

Miss Hedger responded eagerly:

Certainly, I am honored to do so. I would like to firmly place the discussion in the context of the greater good. So often, our concerns are marginalized as being soft-hearted responses to unpopular immigrant groups who are somehow responsible for their own misery. This is not only wrong—it is dangerous. Festering disease and open sewage systems are a threat to all of us, even if they are out of sight of many prominent Chicagoans. My article for *World's Work* dealt with the potential spread of tuberculosis from untreated food-handling workers in the stockyards area.[2] Upton Sinclair's novel, *The Jungle*, is another treatment of similar problems. Of course, we all remember when Florence Kelley and Julia Lathrop boldly invaded sweatshops during the smallpox epidemic and destroyed thousands of dollars worth of clothing that had been handled by desperately ill workers.[3] This was the same epidemic that William Stead wrote of as being "bequeathed to Chicago" by the congestion of the World's Fair. Too often public health is subordinated to public image, in the interests of marketing the city or its merchandise, and to the detriment of its people.

Fannie Barrier Williams recalled that some public health innovations were introduced at the World's Columbian Exposition:[4]

Ellen Swallow Richards, the first woman to graduate from the Massachusetts Institute of Technology, set up a Rumford Kitchen at the fair to promote a scientific approach to nutrition. The Rumford Kitchen was named for Count Rumford of Germany, who conducted experiments leading to methods of nutritious, economical cooking in large quantities.[5] Shortly after the fair, Mrs. Richards consulted here at Hull-House on the design of the kitchen we sit in today.

As a chemistry professor at MIT, her specialty is public and private sanitation.[6] Her former student, Marion Talbot, carries

---

2   Hedger, "Unhealthfulness," 7507–7509.

3   Addams, *Lathrop,* 83.

4   Mrs. Williams was the only African American woman to serve in any capacity with the Board of Lady Managers of the World's Fair.

5   Spain, *How Women Saved,* 216.

6   Ibid., 203

the torch locally at the University of Chicago, establishing one of the first university departments[7] of what is now beginning to be called "home economics." Mrs. Richards and others are in the process of convening a national association for the study of public and private sanitation. It goes without saying that good public hygiene is essential to a healthful home. Children who must play in garbage-strewn alleys will never be safe, even where their overworked mothers are able to establish healthful home conditions.

Rachel Yarros raised a topic close to the heart of her long-time friend, Alice Hamilton:

Conscientious mothers cannot overcome the risk of infectious disease by healthful home conditions. This is a role for state and municipal leaders, but their achievements thus far have been more often to avoid responsibility than to assume it. Typhoid, smallpox, tuberculosis, diphtheria—each of these scourges visits our communities repeatedly, with insufficient official response. Alice and two other residents of Hull-House presented results of their study of the 1902 diphtheria epidemic to the Chicago Medical Society.[8] The study focused on contamination carried by flies from privies to kitchens. After the study was completed, Alice learned that the epidemic was aggravated by a break in a sewage pipe in the Nineteenth Ward, which contaminated the drinking water for three days before it was discovered and repaired. This one example has many lessons. First, the maintenance and inspection of the few public sanitary facilities in existence is inadequate, especially in poorer neighborhoods. Second, the city is not forthright about sharing information about public facilities with the public. Third, the Health Department is doing too little to uncover and remedy these threats to public health.

Alice Hamilton picked up the thread:

Two years later, we saw that nothing had changed. This time it was a typhoid epidemic that was especially hard-hitting on

---

7   Ibid., 204.

8   Hamilton, *Alice Hamilton, M.D.,* 98–100.

the Nineteenth Ward population and other congested areas. The greatest pity was that laws were in place that should have prevented the outbreak. But the Health Department was lax in enforcing the law. The Chicago Civil Service Commission investigated. Five inspectors were indicted for bribery and four others charged with inefficiency.[9] As most of you probably remember, Jane Addams and Anita McCormick Blaine succeeded in convincing the city to hire Charles Ball from New York as the new chief sanitary inspector for Chicago.[10] However, arguments about bringing in an "outsider" tied his hands until very recently[11] so we have yet to see how much he can accomplish.

Margaret Day Blake reminded everyone how entrenched the current system is, and who benefits:

Politics and patronage rather than professional qualifications are the criteria used to fill important public health positions. I don't see how anyone could plan for the future of our region without addressing these systemic barriers to providing decent, safe, and healthy communities. Let me remind everyone of the battles Lucy Flower, Julia Lathrop, and others waged with Cook County government to provide adequate care in county health facilities. The problem is not that government is unable to do better—it is unwilling because the political benefits of patronage jobs carry weight. The elderly, disabled, and mentally ill residents of county asylums carry no political weight. Many of you probably remember when the county board president, Daniel Healy, tried to rescind the Illinois Training School for Nurses' contract[12] in retaliation for Jane Addams and Lucy Flower exposing patronage abuses at Dunning Asylum. Unfortunately, every public function in Chicago, from health care, to sanitation, to schools, to housing is seen as an opportunity to make money or hire a relative or friend, rather than to provide services to the taxpaying public. It is really almost hopeless!

---

9   Abbott, *Tenements of Chicago,* 63–64.

10   Davis, *Spearheads,* 69.

11   Abbott, *Tenements of Chicago,* 64.

12   Schultz and Hast, *Women Building Chicago,* 275.

Alice Hamilton broke in to prevent Margaret from spiraling into despair:

The task is formidable, but it is not hopeless unless we let it become so. We have too often worked twice as long and twice as hard as we should need to, to thoroughly document what is self-evident to fair-minded observers. And it is true that our gains are often threatened by a change of political leadership, an inept bureaucrat, or an unscrupulous newspaper editor. But we have no choice other than to continue and to draw support from within our own ranks and the ranks of our natural allies.

Harriet Fulmer indicated to Alice that she wanted to open a new avenue of discussion:

My training as a nurse makes me aware of the most essential elements for public health. Clean water is the most crucial of those necessities. I find it amazing that the city that can engineer a change in the flow of the river so that we might send our sewage toward St. Louis and New Orleans can't provide sufficient clean water in our neighborhoods. No discussion of water can be undertaken without deference to Sarah Hackett Stevenson[13] to whom we all owe so much. It was her pithy observation in 1892 that the only place one could find water at public facilities in Chicago was in a saloon, in spite of the city looking out over more than 20,000 square miles of water.[14]

Let me just mention two examples where settlement houses have stepped in to provide healthy water where it was lacking. Chicago Commons residents were horrified to find their neighbors drawing drinking water from a horse trough and tried to get the city to condemn the trough. Not meeting with any success through the city, Chicago Commons built a public drinking fountain on Milwaukee Avenue at its own expense in 1897.[15]

In 1893, the same year the World's Fair opened, Hull-House donated land one block north of the settlement for the first

---

13   Miss Stevenson, who suffered a stroke in 1903, died in 1909.

14   Schultz and Hast, *Women Building Chicago,* 846.

15   Wade, *Graham Taylor,* 124.

public bathhouse in the city. Once Hull-House initiated the project, the city came forth with $12,000 to build the facility, which was named in honor of Mayor Carter Harrison.[16]

Fannie Barrier Williams remembered Sarah Stevenson fondly too:

Miss Stevenson gave an impassioned speech in favor of my membership in the Chicago Woman's Club,[17] which some of you may remember as creating a painful amount of dissention. She also served as a consultant for many years to Provident Hospital, which you know I have long been affiliated with. Her dedication to the cause of justice for Negroes was nearly as large as her service to the causes of public health and medicine.

I think, though, that this is a good time for me to offer my review of the many health institutions women established or helped to establish in Chicago. I dedicate this summary to Sarah Stevenson with fervent wishes for her comfort and well-being.

Seeing that the rest of the group was in agreement with moving to the question of health facilities, Mrs. Williams continued:

There are so many health institutions founded or co-founded by women that I will try to just give a brief chronological account. I do want to say at the outset that not all of these institutions welcome all Chicagoans. Having women as founders is no guarantee of just policies.

In the earliest days, it was religious women who were in a position to build health institutions in Chicago. After the Chicago Fire, women began to provide financial support for hospitals and other institutions as a social rather than religious expression of benevolence. Several hospitals and health-related agencies were established by women before the Civil War, including Mercy Hospital and Orphan Asylum in 1852, St. James Hospital in 1854, both the Magdalene Asylum and the Home for the Friendless in 1858, and Providence for

---

16   Spain, *How Women Saved,* 213.
17   Schultz and Hast, *Women Building Chicago,* 846.

Working Girls in 1859.[18] I am compelled to point out institutions that close their doors to some. For instance, Mercy Hospital's policy is to provide treatment to non-Catholic whites, but refuse treatment to Negroes, even those who are Catholic.[19]

Incidentally, Helen Culver, to whom Hull-House owes so much,[20] took a brief respite from her years in Chicago to serve as manager of a forty-bed hospital in Tennessee during the Civil War.[21] Mary Thompson Hospital of Chicago for Women and Children opened May 8, 1865, through the efforts of Mary Harris Thompson, who followed this achievement by establishing a Women's Medical College.[22] St. Luke's Hospital was also started in this period, partially a response of women to the poor care that had been offered in military hospitals during the war.[23]

Julia Foster Porter founded the Maurice F. Porter Memorial Hospital[24] in 1882 to honor her son, who died of rheumatism at the age of 13.[25] Three Catholic nursing orders established hospitals in Chicago neighborhoods after the war: St. Joseph Hospital in 1868 and, within twenty-five years, St. Elizabeth Hospital and St. Mary of Nazareth.[26]

Nursing schools soon followed the establishment of hospitals. The Illinois Training School for Nurses was founded in 1880. Board members included some names familiar to you, such as Dr. Sarah Hackett Stevenson and Lucy Flower.[27] Five new nursing schools, founded or largely supported by women, quickly followed between 1885 and 1889: Women's Hospital Training School for Nurses, Women and Children's

---

18   Ibid., xxi.

19   According to Thomas Lee Philpott, author of The Slum and the Ghetto: Immigrants, Blacks and Reformers in Chicago, 1880–1930, this was true up through the 1940s, xiii.

20   Culver was the owner of the Hull-House building, which was initially rented to and then donated to the settlement.

21   Schultz and Hast, Women Building Chicago, 202.

22   Ibid., xxviii.

23   K. McCarthy, Noblesse Oblige, 39.

24   Now Children's Memorial Hospital.

25   Schultz and Hast, Women Building Chicago, 713.

26   Grossman, Keating, and Reiff, The Encyclopedia of Chicago, 392.

27   K. McCarthy, Noblesse Oblige, 39–40.

Hospital Nursing School, St. Luke's Training School for Nurses, Lincoln Park Sanitarium Training School for Nurses, and Bethesda Nursing School.[28] The struggle to guarantee professional nurses in county hospitals and asylums began with the first nursing schools and continues to this day.

The small Negro community in Chicago was growing by the 1880s and 1890s, but few health services were available to Negroes. As many of you know, my husband and I worked with Dr. Daniel Hale Williams and others to open Provident Hospital in 1891. Provident Hospital serves white and colored patients, but its nursing school trains only Negroes. It is the only nursing school in the city Negroes can attend.[29] An additional health facility for my community, the Home for Aged and Infirm Colored People opened ten years ago.[30]

Of course, many women of means provided funding and experience as board members to health institutions. Louise de Koven Bowen is remarkable for her breadth of health interests, which included over the years not only the Maurice Porter Memorial Hospital but also St. Luke's and Passavant Hospitals.[31]

I would like to end by reminding all of us of the example of one of the rare men of our generation, a friend to the settlement movement, but also one of the firmest friends of the Negro in Chicago. That man is Julius Rosenwald, a man who has been a major contributor to Provident Hospital,[32] provided scholarships for colored students to attend predominantly white institutions, and has made race relations a major focus of his public life. While I subscribe to the goals of the settlement houses, I think we could all learn from his example to find more complete fulfillment of neighborliness.

Margaret Day Blake suggested a role for Julius Rosenwald in promoting public health issues in the *Plan of Chicago*:

---

28   Ibid., 43.

29   www.Providentfoundation.org/history/index.html.

30   Knupfer, *African American Women's Clubs,* 37.

31   Bowen, *Growing Up,* 54–56.

32   K. McCarthy, *Noblesse Oblige,* 111.

Your mention of Mr. Rosenwald sets me to wondering if we could possibly ask him to promote our public health suggestions, since he is a subscriber to the *Plan*. It is maddening to hear of the many contributions women have made to health and know that the whole topic will be omitted from the plan for our region's future.

Alice Hamilton took the floor to make a transition to the next topic.

Margaret, that is a suggestion with much merit, a strategic suggestion we should perhaps consider for promoting all of the recommendations. We know a few other friends within the ranks of the subscribers who might support specific recommendations with the Plan Committee.

Fannie, thank you for your heartfelt and important reminder that we all have work to do—in the larger world and within our own hearts and minds. Each of those who found a door closed because of our gender should be able to understand exactly why it is so important to open all options to all people.

Harriet, you devoted decades to making sure that public health is protected by trained professionals, whether men or women, white, Negro, or foreign born. Can you give us a summary?

Harriet Fulmer rose to the challenge:

Thank you, Alice. I do want to begin though by acknowledging the struggle of women doctors for positions commensurate with their skills and training. In addition to the physicians assembled here, women such as Gertrude Wellington, Sarah Stevenson, Julia Low, Marie Josepha Mergler, and Cornelia DeBey all struggled with what it means to be a woman and a doctor in Chicago. Doctors Fannie Hagen Emanuel, Anna B. Cooper, and Harriet Rice struggled even harder to find a niche as Negro doctors and women. The opportunity to collectively influence public health in the future is an important challenge to undertake.

I would like to summarize the long and unpredictable battle to ensure that public health is protected by trained professionals. There has been a very unfortunate struggle in Illinois between the forces who see public hospitals as havens for unskilled beneficiaries of political patronage jobs and those of us committed to professional care of dependent patients. Reforms were instituted by progressive leaders, but then lost with the next change of administration. Just as immigrants can be more easily abused in factories and truant children can be more easily ignored in poor districts, poor patients pay a terribly high price for our current system. The logical outcome of the system is that very sick people avoid hospitalization, endangering themselves and potentially the general public.

Governor Altgeld promoted the first and only semi-effective civil service law in Illinois. The 1895 bill was a great help in removing untrained patronage workers from state hospitals.[33] But only six years later, Julia Lathrop was compelled to resign from the State Board of Charities to protest the rapid re-intrusion of the spoils system over the fledgling civic service reforms.[34] More recently, in 1905, Governor Charles Deneen renamed Julia to the Board of State Charities, where she and others worked to reassert professional standards of care.[35] Julia has often warned us of the triple threat of unprofessional patronage workers in public institutions, the minimalist view of municipal responsibility, and the moralism of nineteenth-century charity organizations.[36]

Margaret Day Blake asked leave of the group to bring a message from Julia Lathrop:

Julia asked me to remind you what a difference one honorable official can make. About Governor Altgeld she says, "I know of no man in the public life of Illinois who did so much to give women an opportunity as John P. Altgeld. . . . He did it because he believed it to be right and he modestly never counted it an achievement. One of Governor Altgeld's first official acts was to appoint women on state boards. He was the first Governor to name a woman as one of the trustees of the University of Illinois. He was the first to name a woman factory inspector. He insisted that there be a woman physician

---

33   Addams, *Lathrop,* 68.
34   Ibid.., 77.
35   Ibid., 80.
36   Residents of Hull-House, *Hull-House Maps and Papers,* 25.

in every state institution where women and children were confined. All of these appointments had been swept away by the spoils system."[37]

Harriet, thank you for allowing me to interject this point in the middle of your statement.

Harriet Fulmer continued in a vein similar to Margaret's point:

A similar struggle has been ongoing in Cook County. Not only are workers at the four county health facilities[38] often unskilled, untrained, and uncaring, they change with each election as new county board members look for jobs to fill with political supporters. Hospitalized populations most affected are the feebleminded, elderly, and mentally ill[39] who adapt to change or to harsh conditions less well than others. Miss Lathrop, in her extensive investigations of Cook County facilities, has reported that the hospitals are generally clean and says "that in itself is a cheering sign of advancing care, although the polished outside of the cup and platter may be delusive."[40] One of the unsavory practices found at Cook County Hospital in 1894 was that cooking was done on the wards by convalescents themselves. This is a clear threat to public health, a likely way to incubate and spread disease rather than cure disease.[41]

Hull-House and Chicago Commons have been in the forefront of efforts to provide adequate training to health workers, and enlisted students of the greatest educators, like John Dewey, to assist. Miss Lathrop pioneered a class at Chicago Commons for attendants at insane asylums using games, crafts, hobbies, and occupational therapy.[42] James Angell, a student of Dewey's offered workshops for asylum workers there too.[43]

---

37 Addams, *Lathrop,* 68–69.

38 The four facilities were: Cook County Hospital, the asylum, the infirmary, and the "detention hospital" (the latter hospital receives patients in the throes of psychotic episodes, while awaiting a commitment hearing).

39 Residents of Hull-House, *Hull House Maps and Papers,* 124.

40 Ibid., 127.

41 Ibid., 126.

42 Wade, *Graham Taylor,* 170.

43 Feffer, *The Chicago Pragmatists,* 160.

I would like to digress to quote Julia Lathrop again while she is on our minds, in the context Mrs. Williams so earnestly brought to our attention. In the course of visiting every one of Illinois's 102 county poor houses as a member of the State Board of Charities,[44] Julia admonished, "A state institution which discriminates unjustly against one colored man alienates from the state of Illinois the affections of hundreds of colored citizens."[45] I share your sense of the injustice done to the Negro race, Fannie. I also admire Julia's ability to turn a phrase to gain the acceptance of the broadest audience. She shows the injustice as an injury to the state itself, not just to the individual, which I hope forces more eyes to open.

Now back to the task at hand. We know there is more than adequate evidence of the need for professionals in the health care field. We need food and nutrition professionals, physical and occupational therapists, epidemiologists, and industrial disease specialists. I am dumbfounded that the sponsors of this plan don't see that the region is more likely to succeed by reducing the human and economic cost of epidemics, infant mortality, and industrial accidents. Or that they don't use their influence to insist on state and municipal institutions that rehabilitate rather than inhumanely warehouse vulnerable populations. From a strictly economic point of view, one would think the businessmen would want taxes used to help people prepare to re-enter the laboring class.

Alice Hamilton interrupted Harriet Fulmer briefly to move toward another topic:

Harriet, we will make note that these points should be considered in the *Plan of Chicago*. We will come back to them when it is time to make recommendations. But while you have the floor, please brief us on the work of the Visiting Nurses' Association.

Harriet Fulmer smiled broadly. She was very happy to speak about her life's work:

----

44   Addams, *Lathrop*, 59.

45   Ibid., 66

As some of you know, the Visiting Nurses' Association has been at the forefront of professionalizing health care in public asylums, schools, industry, neighborhoods, and homes. I have had the honor to be superintendent of the Visiting Nurses' Association since 1898.

The Visiting Nurses' Association was established in 1889, after an earlier attempt to set up a nurses' organization failed. I can't say for sure, but always assumed that the involvement of women like Jane Addams, Louise de Koven Bowen, and Florence Pullman[46] on the 1889 board of directors helped to ensure the success of the second attempt. The ties between Hull-House and the Visiting Nurses' Association have always been close, including the establishment of a visiting nurses' office at the settlement.[47]

The visiting nurses continue to benefit from Hull-House and its leaders. Just two years ago Jane Addams, as chair of the Board of Education Management Committee, brought visiting nurses into the schools for the first time. Two nurses' salaries were paid through a private fund and a third was covered by Louise de Koven Bowen.[48] The program grew in 1907. We hope the board will begin to routinely include nurses' salaries along with other professionals. The quality of educational programs will be greatly improved by reducing infectious disease and absenteeism, as well as by improving the physical and mental condition of the learners.

I know that Alice will speak to some ways in which visiting nurses contribute to the new field of industrial medicine, and Caroline will speak of our joint work on a very important public health initiative to reduce the intolerably high rate of summer infant deaths, so I will leave those topics in their able hands. I would like to conclude by putting into the record of our discussion an actual example of a typical day in the life of a visiting nurse. This is less for your benefit, because you are familiar with our organization. My hope is that the businessmen will come to understand that inefficiencies in the way we handle public health are just as costly as inefficiencies

46   K. McCarthy, *Noblesse Oblige*, 132–133.

47   Residents of Hull-House, *Hull-House Maps and Papers*, 169.

48   Bowen, *Growing Up*, 59–60.

in the transfer of goods—perhaps more costly, and certainly crueler.

The primary role of the visiting nurses has been to tend to patients and families in their homes. This work is necessary, particularly because there are so few places where poor and immigrant families can receive medical care. But the work is grueling, the pay is minimal—about $600.49 a year, and the frustrations are many. Let me give you a recent example. Last week one of our nurses found her first patient of the day, a mother with three young children, critical with typhoid pneumonia. The nurse first overcame the patient's resistance to hospitalization, then walked to the drugstore for a phone. After several calls she was fortunate to find a hospital that would take an indigent patient. She had to walk to a physician's office to obtain a permit to summon an ambulance, then call the police to request the ambulance. She returned to the home, helped the patient prepare for the trip, arranged housing for the three children at the Home for the Friendless, then went on to see nine more patients that day.[50]

That concludes my overview of the need for professional health care in schools, institutions, and homes. I hope I adequately summarized the difficulties of providing care under the existing, inadequate public health system.

Alice Hamilton stood to take up the next topic:

It is interesting to hear so many of us start by acknowledging our debt to Hull-House or one of the other settlements. I am no different. My very first night as a resident here left a permanent impression which probably helped steer me toward a new medical frontier. Former governor John Altgeld happened to be a dinner guest that night. I was particularly interested in his role and views on the Haymarket tragedy.[51] Over the years I found myself drawn more and more to what might be called industrial medicine—medicine that tries to prevent some of the worst abuses of the industrial system as we have conceived it in America. One of the other pivotal

---

49   Ibid., 59–60.

50   Schultz and Hast, *Women Building Chicago*, 292.

51   Hamilton, *Alice Hamilton, M.D.*, 60.

moments for me was that tragic incident at the pumping station in the lake. You may remember that a contractor left workers at the pumping station with no means of escape. When a fire broke out, they all drowned. The contractor paid for their funerals and no one expected more.[52] We have all seen—too many times—the long-lasting consequences when a breadwinner is killed or incapacitated.

We all know of children maimed by machinery, men poisoned by industrial exposure to lead, or sewing-trades workers trapped in burning buildings. Even when hazards are not immediately life-threatening, chronic conditions engendered by the factory system affect young and old alike. When Florence Kelley, Alzina Stevens, and other Hull-House residents secured medical exams in 1893 for 135 children in factories who seemed undersized or ill, or worked in dangerous, unsanitary conditions, almost half were found too sick to work.[53] At the time, it was only possible to intervene on behalf of the children because of the new labor law promoted by Hull-House and signed by Governor Altgeld.[54]

The direct threat of injury or disease is of course our greatest fear, but even factories that are relatively benign pose health risks, especially to children. There is a caramel factory near Hull-House that employed large numbers of children. Until the factory law limited the number of hours children could work, eighty-two hours were the norm during weeks of peak production.[55] The statutory limitation to forty-eight hour weeks was an improvement, but the physical consequences of older children making the same repetitive motions over and over for so many hours a week has consequences for the strength of their muscles and bones and for their overall health and fitness.

Margaret Day Blake indicated that she had a point to make:

The business leaders could look within their own ranks for examples of more progressive industrial health practice.

---

52 Ibid., 114–115.

53 Residents of Hull-House, *Hull-House Maps and Papers,* 79.

54 Addams, *Twenty Years,* 122.

55 Residents of Hull-House, *Hull-House Maps and Papers,* 77–78.

Harriet succeeded in placing the first "industrial nurse" at International Harvester in 1903,[56] an innovation we hope will spread to other factories as the benefits of a stable, healthy work force become more evident. The McCormick family, influenced by its matriarch Nettie Fowler McCormick and our good friend Anita McCormick Blaine, has set a higher standard than most in fostering industrial health and safety. Young Cyrus McCormick is on the committee of businessmen developing the plan. I wonder if he would consider promoting industrial medicine in more workplaces. I suspect the businessmen will fear sowing the seeds of "socialism" if they make even the meekest mention of worker health benefits, but perhaps if the suggestion is endorsed by one of their own, they will consider it with more sincerity.

Alice Hamilton continued:

Margaret, that is a very good suggestion. There is one other example of stellar corporate behavior that I want to mention, but while it is instructive, it is not local. "Phossy jaw" is a terrible infection suffered by workers who handle phosphorus in the making of matches. Although the disease is being actively investigated in Europe, virtually nothing can be found in American medical journals about this disfiguring malady. However, in an outstanding act of industrial responsibility, Diamond Match Company will waive its patent rights to a phosphorus alternative so the whole industry can use it.[57]

Industrial medicine is a well-researched specialty in European countries but is scorned as socialist in America, because of the animosity of business. The medical community in America has been so intimidated by the political climate that it has never had a meeting or conference on industrial medicine.[58] Consequently, we are hampered by a lack of information as well as a lack of domestic models of successful programs. Germany has an especially well-developed system of insurance programs for workers who are injured

---

56 Schultz and Hast, *Women Building Chicago,* 292–293.

57 Hamilton, *Alice Hamilton, M.D.,* 117–118. Diamond Match Company took this step in 1909.

58 Ibid., 114–115.

or sickened by industrial processes or products. Charles Henderson, professor of sociology at the University of Chicago, is conducting a study of the German system and will report his results to the governor soon.[59] I hope we can anticipate improvements in the future.[60] Our region can only be made stronger if its workers and families are sure of the means to continue producing and consuming goods in the economy.

After nodding to indicate that Caroline Hedger should prepare to take the floor, Alice Hamilton moved toward her seat while murmurs of approval and agreement with her statements filled the kitchen. Caroline needed no introduction. She had worked with most of them at one time or another in the fight to reduce infant deaths.

We have all heard the heart-rending story of "Little Baby Maloney" who was carried by its father from doctor to hospital to City Hall as it was dying of diphtheria on Thanksgiving Day.[61] In response, the Chicago Woman's Club and prominent physicians—both male and female—mobilized to protect the youngest Chicagoans. This was no small undertaking. At points in the nineteenth century, half of all deaths in Chicago were children under the age of five.[62] Often, as with Little Baby Maloney, it was the epidemics sweeping across the city time after time that took a disproportionate toll on the babies. Some parents kept their children away from doctors and hospitals, either for economic reasons, or because of distrust of institutional care, until it was too late to save the infants from certain death.

Reformers and medical professionals knew they must fight on many fronts to reduce infant mortality. I am happy to say we have had a great deal of success just in the past five years. If I may be immodest, I would like to suggest that the circumstances I am about to recount could become an example for other public health campaigns in our region.

---

59 Ibid., 118–119.

60 Gov. Deneen did appoint an Occupation Disease Commission in 1910. Illinois was the first state to do so.

61 K. McCarthy, *Noblesse Oblige,* 127.

62 Grossman, Keating, and Reiff, *The Encyclopedia of Chicago,* 156.

The Children's Hospital Society[63] was formed in 1903 in order to fight childhood disease and death. Much of the credit for founding the society belongs to the Visiting Nurses' Association, but fortunately they did not struggle alone. For example, the organizing memo for the Civic Federation stated its intent to make Chicago "the best governed, the healthiest city in this country."[64] In that vein, the Civic Federation investigated food-borne illnesses and the quality of city inspection of perishable foods, especially meat and milk. They found city inspections to be lax and ineffective.[65]

The quality of the milk supply was one of the first public health issues the Children's Hospital Society tackled. This was a multi-pronged effort to counteract the annual scourge of infant deaths each summer. Milk could become infected during production, during storage or transport, and after it reached homes. In addition to questions of corporate responsibility, there were questions of municipal responsibility and potential

Baby hammocks, like those used in this sanitarium, were also used in neighborhood tents. (Chicago History Museum, DN-0005123, Chicago Daily News negatives collection.)

---

63   Later the Infant Welfare Society.
64   Davis, *Spearheads*, 188.
65   Sutherland, *Fifty Years*, 27.

corruption of inspection systems. Education of parents and consumers was another front, since the growth of bacteria was poorly understood and few families had proper facilities to refrigerate milk even if they understood the consequences of leaving milk on the shelf. Above all, the reformers had to gain the trust of parents in order to preserve the babies' health. That was not going to happen if parents had to bring children to hospitals or other "suspect" institutions where, in their minds, babies went to die.

I am happy to say that Chicago pioneered a response that had immediate and significant results. Here is how we accomplished such a feat. We set up the first "fresh air station for sick babies" at Northwestern University Settlement in 1905. Rather than asking parents to bring their child into a hospital setting, we brought nurses and doctors to them, using tents. Distrust of institutions was not a factor in the open, in the neighborhoods. The fresh air was beneficial for children and mothers who lived in stifling, dark tenements. Mothers, caring for the children side-by-side with nurses, absorbed health care information easily and readily. The cost of two nurses to staff ten to twenty baby hammocks was only $250 for the summer.[66] Other settlement houses quickly followed suit with their own baby tents, sponsored by their own donors.

The number of infant summer deaths has dropped 18 percent since 1903. Health professionals from other cities visited our program in order to bring it to their cities. These results would be remarkable even if they came at high cost. But the truth of the matter is that the costs were very modest, in keeping with the neighborhood-based method of delivering services.

Alice Hamilton prepared the group for the final transition:

Caroline, thank you. The account of the successful baby tents is one I have heard several times before, but am never sorry to hear again. The simplicity and effectiveness of these steps are a lesson to us all, as well as an inspiration.

Now I would like to introduce my good friend Rachel Slobodinsky Yarros to cover one final area of health before

---

66 K. McCarthy, *Noblesse Oblige,* 128.

we move to the question of our recommendations. We all experience the special health burdens women face and the indifference, or even outright hostility, of some men to the special health needs of women. Indeed, "even the attempt to make childbearing less painful met with opposition from the clergy for many years, because it was contrary to Scripture."[67]

Rachel Slobodinsky Yarros, looking grave, indicated she was ready to begin.

Thank you, Alice. You have been a faithful friend for many years, ever since our internship together at New England Hospital for Women and Children.[68] I'm sure you remember as well as I, the horror we felt as inexperienced doctors at the pain some women suffered. Much of it was unnecessary. Much of it came not from physical necessity, but from cultural and religious animosity toward women, or sometimes from sheer indifference.

I have long felt that if women had more information and control over their reproductive health, our families, communities, and nation would be stronger. We all see the consequences of families with too many mouths to feed. Poverty, malnutrition, housing congestion, school failure, and court involvement are all likely outcomes when women have no control over childbearing. Those consequences, dire as they may seem, are suffered by women society considers "respectable."

Another group of women, often through no fault of their own, are captives of the sex trade. Vulnerable girls and women who are drawn into or forced into the sex trade will find it nearly impossible to redeem themselves, so strong is the social disapproval of their circumstances. In many cases, even an innocent victim of rape will be cast into the category of "fallen woman." They may suffer from degrading diseases that represent a public health crisis no one wants to talk about.

It is this secrecy, this shame, that is the biggest obstacle to women's reproductive health, whether for the married woman

---

67   Hamilton, *Alice Hamilton, M.D.,* 110.

68   Ibid., 43.

or the prostitute. We need to link the medical profession with the women's clubs and unions to create a massive public education campaign about birth control and social hygiene.[69]

Alice Hamilton sensed that Rachel was drawing to a close and resumed her role as chair of the meeting.

Thank you, Rachel, for your very concise summary of the issues and for the work you have done for many years to relieve women's suffering.

We now come to the most difficult part of our assignment. After putting so many important issues on the table, we need to select the ones we will promote as additions to the *Plan of Chicago*. Let me see if I can list each of them. We discussed the role of hospitals and health providers and the need for professionals rather than patronage workers. We also discussed public health in relation to three specific populations: industrial workers, infants, and women.

If you agree that those are the primary topics we covered, let us take each one in turn and see if we feel a specific recommendation should be offered for inclusion in the *Plan of Chicago*. Once we agree on recommendations, I will forward them to Miss Addams, who will forward the work of all the committees to Mr. Burnham. I will also discuss with her the wise recommendation to work with specific subscribers to the *Plan* to see if we can cultivate a group of supporters to whom the Plan Committee will listen.

The recommendations this group agreed to as its highest priorities were:

In the areas of maternal and child health there are many low-cost, high impact public health programs that would save the city and region many times the amount spent for hospital care. This includes reproductive health information and treatment. It also includes public health initiatives to reduce infant mortality by reducing childhood diseases and epidemics, which disproportionately impact infants. The baby

---

69   Payne, *Reform, Labor, and Feminism*, 134. Yarros went on to found the Chicago Birth Control Committee. By 1915 it was working with the Women's Trade Union League.

tents are an example of high-quality, low-cost, neighborhood-based treatment. Schools and settlement houses in every neighborhood should offer public health programs to the community at large.

Industrial concerns should begin to provide on-site medical care because the policy will pay dividends to the company in terms of worker retention and reduced absence, as well as being a humane principle.

Providing professional care in state, county, and city health agencies is absolutely imperative. All governmental health agencies should employ qualified professionals on a strict civil service basis.

11

Housing & Neighborhoods

PLAYERS

First (middle, maiden) Name	Last Name	Brief Biographical Information	Approximate Age
Edith	Abbott	Co-founder, Chicago School of Civics and Philanthropy; author of *Tenements in Chicago*.	30s
Jesse Florence	Binford	Hull-House resident from 1902 to 1963; active in Juvenile Protective Association, investigated neighborhood conditions leading to court involvement of women and children.	30s
Elizabeth Lindsay	Davis	African American clubwoman, author, journalist, co-founder of Phyllis Wheatley Club and Phyllis Wheatley Home.	50s
Mary	McDowell	Taught Hull-House kindergarten, headed University of Chicago Settlement House, founding member of Women's Trade Union League.	50s
Georgia Bitzis	Pooley	First Greek woman in Chicago, persuaded Greek families to settle near Hull-House, founder of Greek civic groups and a Greek school.	60s
Ina Law	Robertson	Founded Eleanor Clubs in 1898 as safe, respectable, and self-governing housing for working women; eventually housed six hundred women.	40s
Madeleine Wallin	Sikes	Hull-House resident; municipal reform work; Civic Federation education committee; researcher, children's issues; co-wrote *Child Labor Legislation Handbook*; monitored Chicago City Council.	40s

🖤 THE YEAR IS 1909. The setting is the dining room in one of the Jane Club apartments. Hull-House residents Edith Abbott and Jesse Binford just finished giving a tour of the Jane Club apartments to the other women, who are allied with Hull-House, but not residents, although Madeleine Sikes was at one point. Mary McDowell brought the group to order:

> As you know, we come together today to look at a plan that is being developed for Chicago's growth, and to look at it primarily from a housing and neighborhood development point of view. This is one of eight meetings being held here at Hull-House to review specific aspects of the *Plan of Chicago*. Our dear friend, Jane Addams, has asked that I assist and guide the group through a discussion of the *Plan*'s adequacy in this area. We may want to recommend additions or changes based on our discussion.
>
> Our assignment was slightly more complicated than some of the other groups, because Mr. Burnham, the architect who wrote the plan, does not include a chapter on neighborhoods, as he has on parks or the central business area for example. So we had to read through the all of the chapters, trying to glean his ideas on neighborhoods. Has everyone had a chance to review the *Plan*? (The others all nod that they have.) Good.
>
> Let me pose a potential outline for our discussion. I think we should briefly review what is in the *Plan* regarding neighborhoods and then move on to areas that are covered insufficiently or not at all. We might want to consider various aspects of housing in greater detail than he did, particularly in terms of characteristics that matter most to households—for example, sanitation and congestion. We know of several housing studies that could and no doubt should have been referenced in Mr. Burnham's work. Then we should consider the city's attempts to impose reasonable housing and sanitation regulations, or conversely the failure of the city to do so. Does that sound like an acceptable plan? Seeing agreement in your faces, I would like to throw the floor open to hear your impressions of Mr. Burnham's *Plan of Chicago*.

The first one to take the challenge was Jesse Binford:

Mary McDowell. (Library of Congress, LC-USZ62-73253, Copyright by Moffett, Prints and Photographs Division.)

Thank you, Miss McDowell, for leading this discussion. Your work on housing and neighborhood development in the Stockyards District certainly qualifies you to guide us. I would like to say first of all that I found far too little about city neighborhoods in Mr. Burnham's plan. He seemed to jump right over most of them, discussing the downtown district and then describing the suburban town center. Aside from listing desirable physical characteristics of the boulevards, he did not leave us with much of an impression of what a city neighborhood would look like if his plan were implemented.

Georgia Bitzis Pooley was next to speak up:

I am sorry to be so harsh a critic. But I fear that even if he had painted the picture of a city neighborhood, it would have lacked heart and soul, like the rest of his pictures. I don't think I want to live in a neighborhood, or a city, where everything has the same classical style, even if it is based on Greek architecture!

Much of what is missing from this plan is the heart and soul of the city: the strength and resourcefulness of people who left Europe, or their farm, to make a new home in Chicago; the spirit of neighborliness and mutual aid; the institutions that build cohesion and neighborhood security. Those are just some of the factors that form the essence of a community and a city. There is much in the *Plan of Chicago* about the requirements of the freight companies, the comfort of suburban commuters, the preferences of downtown merchants. It seems it is up to us to define what makes strong, supportive communities. *They* are the heart and soul of the city.

Mary McDowell moved the group toward the first task:

Thank you, Jesse and Georgia. You both provided a very succinct statement of the problem we need to address. Let's make a list of the points we noted from the *Plan of Chicago* that are relevant to city neighborhoods. Let's go around the room and if each person would like to cite a section of the *Plan* they think relevant to this discussion, we can move forward from there. Edith, would you go first?

Edith Abbott, a scholarly woman, thought carefully for a moment before responding:

On the rare occasions when Mr. Burnham ventures beyond the downtown district, he seems to find only dirt and disorder. Even in Paris, the city he holds up as epitomizing all Chicago could be in beauty and convenience, he speaks of Napoleon building monuments as an antidote to "dirty, crowded, ill-smelling, narrow, winding streets, the hotbeds of vice and crime."[1] It seems that anything other than wide plazas, boulevards, and monuments is dirty and crowded by his definition.

Once the ice was broken, the others quickly turned to passages they recalled. Madeleine Wallin Sikes was next to reflect on the *Plan*:

I did like his vision of boulevards: lined with fine dwellings, and having very little traffic. The idea of continuous playgrounds for children and some light manufacturing jobs nearby for adults seemed like a nice, self-contained community. The only

---

1   Burnham and Bennett, *Plan of Chicago*, 15–17.

thing I worry about is his emphasis on uniform design of the buildings facing the boulevards. It seems so sterile.[2]

Georgia Bitzis Pooley, who lived on the Near North Side, but knew many Greeks living near Hull-House, spoke with great passion:

Yes, but you know he is not envisioning that kind of thing for our communities. I think he is speaking of our communities when he says, "Here there are no buildings possessing either historical or picturesque value which must be sacrificed to carry out plans necessary to provide circulation for a growing metropolis."[3] In another spot, where I believe he is speaking of buildings built shortly after the fire—in other words, neighborhoods like this one—he says: "The buildings which cover the greater part of Chicago's area beyond the business center are not of a permanent character, and in the natural order of things they must be replaced by others more substantial."[4] With this one sentence he has condemned "the greater part" of all the neighborhoods in Chicago. I do give him credit for proposing that new buildings provide more light and air than existing buildings. But I cannot quiet my fear that his plan wreaks havoc on existing communities, rather than provide a gradual evolution of housing for populations already resident in these older Chicago neighborhoods.

Elizabeth Lindsay Davis was clearly cross about the example Georgia Bitzis Pooley gave:

He also condemns Chicago's neighborhoods to a future of unpaved and unsanitary streets. He says, "On residential streets the city should not be burdened unnecessarily with the cost of street construction and maintenance."[5] This is maddening, since we know the downtown businesses are seriously under-assessed and force the working-class and middle-class taxpayers to shoulder most of the responsibility for paying the city's bills. And yet Mr. Burnham and his friends in the

---

2 Ibid., 85–86.

3 Ibid., 87.

4 Ibid., 97.

5 Ibid., 88.

Commercial Club want the neighborhoods to fund their own streets or to do without!

Jesse Binford added fuel to already simmering opinions:

It is even more maddening to recall that when the city wanted to apply a special assessment on lakefront property to pay for erosion control, the wealthy businessmen who lived there refused to pay it, saying lakefront protection was a public responsibility![6]

Madeleine Wallin Sikes moved to a new topic:

Speaking of the relationship between streets and neighborhood development, I am concerned about his emphasis on diagonals to relieve congestion.[7] Tearing up the city to put in these diagonals will divide and disrupt many existing neighborhoods. They might decrease travel time to the central area by a bit, but at what cost?

After ensuring that everyone else had the opportunity to speak, Mary McDowell read passages of the *Plan* that she found particularly troublesome:

He seems to use road construction as an excuse for clearing areas of the city that he and his sponsors fear. Bear with me while I read his remedy for slums, which is the "cutting of broad thoroughfares through the unwholesome district; and, secondly, the establishment and remorseless enforcement of sanitary regulations which shall insure adequate air-space for the dwellers in crowded areas, and absolute cleanliness in the street, on the sidewalks, and even within the buildings. The slum exists to-day only because of the failure of the city to protect itself against gross evils and known perils, all of which should be corrected by the enforcement of simple principles of sanitation that are recognized to be just, equitable, and necessary."[8] We can agree in principle that cleanliness on the street and fresh air are desirable. But we part company on the question of how to achieve such a state. It is the busi-

---

6   Miller, *City of the Century,* 110.

7   Burnham and Bennett, *Plan of Chicago,* 89.

8   Ibid., 108.

ness community that insists that sanitation remain in private hands, while the various women's groups long advocated municipal control of critical health and safety functions. The businessmen see sanitation as merely another business opportunity, rather than a public health matter.[9]

Georgia Bitzis Pooley spoke with great passion:

Immigrant neighborhoods are under extreme pressure from business, which blames us for the condition of our dilapidated neighborhoods. Meanwhile, businesses are expanding into all the immigrant communities around the central area: the area between Hull-House and downtown, the Plymouth Court area where the Italians live, and south from there. Property is relatively inexpensive because the housing is so poor. Communities on the fringe of the central business district are no match for well-funded commercial ventures. The communities are being decimated and their residents scattered to other neighborhoods.

Edith Abbott said:

I agree with you, Georgia. I think the priorities Mr. Burnham claims for his plan speak volumes about his lack of concern for most of the city and its people. Here are the six priorities he defines: the lakefront; the highway system up to sixty miles outside the city; the terminals and traction system; the outer parks; the street system; and civic, intellectual centers.[10]

But I think we should take his definition of a desirable suburban community configuration and see if it doesn't apply equally well to city neighborhoods. Listen to this description, and where he says "town" simply think "neighborhood": "In each town plan spaces should be marked out for public schools, and each school should have about it ample playgrounds, so that during all the year the school premises shall be the children's center, to which each child will become attached by those ties of remembrance that are restraining influences throughout life. Next to the school, the public library should have place; and here again the landscape set-

9   Flanagan, *Gender,* 1037.

10   Burnham and Bennett, *Plan of Chicago,* 121.

ting should be generous and the situation commanding. The townhall, the engine-house with its lookout tower, the police station with its court of justice, and the post-office, all naturally form a group of buildings that may be located about a common or public square, so as to form the suburban civic center." Why shouldn't there be a plan for Chicago that envisions a common area, civic and cultural buildings, and green spaces for neighborhoods throughout the city? Why is his model offered only for suburban towns?

Ina Law Robertson chuckled and said:

Edith, doesn't the Hull-House complex contain many of the non-governmental civic functions of his suburban town center? Hull-House offers a branch of the library and of the Art Institute. It also offers college extension courses through the University of Chicago.[11] Put a complex like Hull-House in or near a large grassy space, with the local school and library, and you have a model for a neighborhood center that could be reproduced throughout the city. I think when we determine our recommendations, we should merge his suburban vision with our own city-building work and develop a strong model for neighborhood development.

Mary McDowell was clearly eager to make a point:

The group that reviewed the *Plan of Chicago*'s chapter on parks made the same point. Mr. Burnham is not without a vision of an ideal town center or community center. He simply has not applied his vision to Chicago neighborhoods, with the exception of a brief description of those neighborhoods along the boulevards. Ina, I think you made a very prudent suggestion about building on his model in our recommendations. We will certainly return to that. In the meantime, let's make sure we have all the information we need on the table. We have a wide range of experience around this table relevant to the problems of housing in congested areas of the city. I'd like to talk a little about the special problems of the Stockyards District, but before I do, let's talk about some other neighbor-

---

11   Miller, *City of the Century*, 421.

hoods. Edith, would you give us some of the specifics from various neighborhoods that you've studied?

Edith Abbott began with obvious confidence in her data:

We have all seen from the Hull-House maps documented proof that people live at very close quarters in this area. In order to meet expenses, families often double up in housing units with limited space, or take in lodgers who may or may not be family members. The Nationalities Map published in *Hull-House Maps and Papers* covered the area southeast of Hull-House, from Halsted Street to State Street and from Polk Street to Twelfth Street. Language was used to define the ethnicity of individual households. In that small area we found white, English-speaking households to be the minority. The number of colored households was very small and generally found near State Street. The immigrant groups were very diverse, including: Irish, German, Dutch, Russian, Polish, Italian, Swiss, French, French Canadian, Bohemian, Scandinavian, Chinese, Turk, Arabian, Greek, and Syrian.

We know there have been many changes in the occupants of the buildings in the last fifteen years. For instance, the Greeks who numbered less than one hundred in the Nineteenth Ward in 1894, now number more than five hundred.[12] In spite of some shifts in the proportion of various nationalities, I do not believe the essential crowded conditions changed. Many of the narrow lots on the map were colored with three, four, or five colors, representing different language groups. Of course, within any language group one might have found several families, so different colors under-represent the number of households on a given lot.

Please allow me to digress for one moment. I have to object, and object vehemently, to the "shoe-string lot,"[13] the standard twenty-five-foot-wide lot, as inevitably dark and poorly ventilated at the sides. When one looks at the Nationalities Map, it is clear that many families suffer with no light and little ventilation because of the closely constructed buildings. The city, or Mr. Burnham's plan, could easily relieve some of the worst

12   Abbott, *Tenements of Chicago*, 97.
13   Ibid., 171.

consequences of congested neighborhoods by addressing lot size and configuration for future development in the city.

But I digress. Let's return to the *Hull-House Maps and Papers*. The center of the Nationalities Map shows an industrial district with the river and several rail lines running from north to south. The industrial uses include freight houses, a farm machinery works, a sugar refinery, stone works, and docks along the river. No land within this area, from Halsted to State Street, has been set aside as public space.

Of course, this is the area with which I am most familiar, but let me mention challenges facing some of the other neighborhoods. Ancona, the area east of Division and Ashland, is a community of "dilapidated frame cottages" that "look as though they might fall over at any moment."[14] We have already talked about the poor conditions in the Italian neighborhood near Plymouth Court, which is bordered by a Negro area to the East and a Chinese community to the north.[15] Bohemians, Lithuanians, Scandinavians, and Russians each have an identifiable community with greater or lesser degrees of housing deterioration and unsanitary conditions. But nowhere are the problems as great as in the Negro areas, where we found evidence everywhere of inadequate city services, including an excess of unpaved streets, inadequate street cleaning, and alleys full of uncollected garbage.[16] The Negro areas have more renters than immigrant areas and Negroes live in the most dilapidated buildings, buildings that are clearly not being maintained.[17] I suspect the building owners are waiting for the neighborhood property to be purchased for other uses and refuse to invest in their buildings, even to keep them safe and habitable.

Elizabeth Lindsay Davis wanted to add to Edith Abbott's summary:

Edith, I appreciate your concise summary of the extra problems the Negro community faces. I just want to point out one

---

14   Ibid., 106.
15   Ibid., 111.
16   Ibid., 121.
17   Ibid., 123.

additional factor. In spite of inhabiting the poorest quality housing, Negroes usually pay more in rent than other groups. This is a function of the limited supply of housing in the segregated areas of the city. Negroes can't select housing freely throughout the city. The growing Negro population is straining at the boundaries of the "Black Belt" areas. Segregation forces many of us into the poorest housing at the highest prices. I don't imagine we will find Mr. Burnham taking on that complicated issue in his *Plan of Chicago*.

Jesse Binford said:

It is reprehensible that the people who suffer the consequences of poor housing are then unfairly gouged or blamed for the dilapidated conditions. There are a great many myths and falsehoods about tenements, above and beyond the ones we have all heard about the filth being the fault of the residents. There is the myth that Chicago's tenements are less a problem than New York's because the buildings here are smaller, with fewer stories.[18] We found the interiors no less dingy, the privy vaults no less foul, simply because of smaller buildings.

Agnes Sinclair Holbrook, who painted the nationality and wage maps in the *Hull-House Maps and Papers*, made a perceptive observation about the appearance of Chicago's tenements: "The smart frontage (of a large tenement building) is a mere screen, not only for the individual houses, but for the street as a whole. Rear tenements and alleys form the core of the district, and it is there that the densest crowds of the most wretched and destitute congregate. Little idea can be given of the filthy and rotten tenements, the dingy courts and the tumble-down sheds, the foul stables and dilapidated outhouses, the broken sewer-pipes, the piles of garbage fairly alive with diseased odors, and of the numbers of children filling every nook, working and playing in every room, eating and sleeping in every window-sill, pouring in and out of every door, and seeming literally to pave every scrap of 'yard.' In one block the writer numbered over seventy-five children in the open street; but the effort proved futile when she tried to keep the count of

18   Ibid., 54.

little people surging in and out of passage-ways, and up and down outside staircases, like a veritable stream of life."[19]

Mary McDowell moved the conversation in a new direction:

There have been a number of other important studies con-ducted in the last fifteen years relevant to questions of hous-ing and neighborhood development. Elizabeth, will you give us an overview?

Elizabeth Lindsay Davis was clearly pleased to accept the chal-lenge:

There have been at least four studies in recent years directly relevant to any planning for Chicago. It doesn't appear that Mr. Burnham is familiar with any of them. The *Hull-House Maps and Papers* are but one example. I don't know how many of you are aware that the *Hull-House Maps and Papers* were complementary to Florence Kelley's work on behalf of the U.S. Department of Labor. She was the chief investigator for the Chicago portion of a four-city study. The other three cit-ies were New York, Baltimore, and Philadelphia. Chicago was reported to have the worst sanitary conditions out-of-doors.

Indoor conditions were as bad or worse. For example, al-most three-quarters of families surveyed had an unsanitary privy vault in their building. Only 3 percent had bathrooms. Almost one-fifth of individuals lived in rooms so overcrowd-ed they had less than two hundred cubic feet of air per per-son.[20]

You can see the housing survey form used here in Chicago as part of the Labor Department report. It is published in the *Hull-House Maps and Papers*, and was the source for the maps displaying nationalities and wages building-by-building.[21] The data collected by Mrs. Kelley for the U.S. Department of Labor included almost twenty thousand individuals who were mem-bers of almost four thousand households.[22] Even within the

---

19   Residents of Hull-House, *Hull-House Maps and Papers,* 54.

20   Abbott, *Tenements of Chicago,* 31–32.

21   Residents of Hull-House, *Hull-House Maps and Papers,* map plates are between pp. 58 and 59.

22   Abbott, *Tenements of Chicago,* 32.

study district, the degree of congestion and unsanitary conditions varied by nationality. The Italian area at Plymouth Court and Polk Street was the "worst of all the insanitary [sic] and crowded dwellings that we canvassed at any time."[23]

Where sanitary conditions were not extreme, there were often other negative features near residential areas. For instance Sophonisba Breckinridge has pointed out many times that the vice district was located in Negro residential areas,[24] creating an unhealthy environment for families. Dr. Carrie Golden delivered a paper to the Phyllis Wheatley Club in 1900 on "The Sanitary Condition of the City and Its Relation to the Homes." She reported on inspection of six hundred tenements on the South Side, white and Negro. She reported that the Negro homes were "less sanitary,"[25] although it is not clear from oral reports of her speech whether she was speaking of the interiors or the exteriors. We all know from our own experience that Negro neighborhoods receive less attention from the city's sanitation contractors than do other areas of the city. We can fairly assume that municipal sanitation, or the failure to adequately fulfill sanitation contracts in Negro neighborhoods, is a root cause of other problems.

Ina, why don't you pick up the next phase, the origins and work of the City Homes Association?

Ina Law Robertson was happy to comply:

The next thorough report on housing conditions was locally inspired. Representatives of several settlement houses met at Northwestern University Settlement in 1897 to consider how to attack Chicago's housing problem. The City Homes Association was their response, a new organization to focus exclusively on housing issues. Robert Hunter, a Hull-House resident, was retained as lead investigator.[26] The work of the City Homes Association was funded by Anita McCormick Blaine.[27] Anita also chaired the executive committee of the Associa-

---

23 Ibid., 110.

24 Diner, "Chicago Social Workers," 400.

25 Knupfer, *African American Women's Clubs,* 49.

26 Philpott, *Slum and the Ghetto,* 27.

27 Ibid., 94.

tion.[28] They investigated housing in three districts: the Near West Side, the Near Northwest Side (near Division and Ashland Streets), and the Bohemian District in the Lower West Side.[29] Mary, do you want to mention the decision that was made about the Stockyards District?

Mary McDowell gave a wry smile and nodded:

We had hoped to include the Stockyards District in the City Homes Association study. Lord knows we needed to shine a light on the filthy conditions there. But even our friends could not fathom how to include our area. The Stockyards District was considered to be too far from the norm to provide useful information. However, the committee did note that "The Stockyards district and portions of South Chicago show outside insanitary [sic] conditions as bad as any in the world. Indescribable accumulations of filth and rubbish, together with the absence of sewerage, makes the surroundings of every dilapidated frame cottage abominably insanitary [sic]."[30]

In the Stockyards District, the only open space is the "hair field" where hog and cattle skins are spread to dry. Back of the Yards is encircled by unsavory land uses: the stockyards to the east, a municipal dump to the west, railroad tracks to the south, and Bubbly Creek to the north. Bubbly Creek gets its name from the bubbles caused by carbolic acid from decaying animal parts. In summer the surface is solid enough that small animals can walk across the creek.[31]

Ina Law Robertson resumed her narrative:

The report, *Tenement Conditions in Chicago*, was published in 1901. Hunter found inadequate light and air inside tenements, overcrowding, defective plumbing, dark and dank living units in cellars, with almost one-fifth of buildings unfit for human habitation. As far as exterior conditions, "There were badly paved and unclean streets and alleys; dangerous sidewalks; filthy vacant lots, yards, courts, and passages; of-

---

28   K. McCarthy, *Noblesse Oblige,* 116.

29   Grossman, Keating, and Reiff, *The Encyclopedia of Chicago,* 167.

30   Abbott, *Tenements of Chicago,* 130.

31   Miller, *City of the Century,* 218.

fensive stables and manure boxes. Neglect of garbage was prevalent."[32]

Charles Zueblin, in one of the essays in *Hull-House Maps and Papers*, described three types of tenement housing prevalent in 1894: wood shanties built below grade, three- to four-story brick tenements with little light and no baths, and the "deadly rear tenement."[33] Seven years later there had been essentially no improvement, when the City Homes Association conducted its study.

Even more recently, Miss Abbott and her coworkers began a survey of housing conditions this winter at the request of the chief sanitary inspector of the city of Chicago.[34] Would you share your recent experiences with us, Edith?

Edith Abbott was pleased to be asked:

Certainly. We went back to the three original districts of the City Homes Association study, but added five more West Side

Exteriors of dilapidated housing in the Hull-House neighborhood. Hull-House Board member William Deknatel captioned the photo, "Our back yard." (University of Illinois at Chicago Library, JAMC_0000_0000_1054b, Special Collections and University Archives Dept. Photo by Lewis Hine.)

---

32 Abbott, *Tenements of Chicago*, 58–59.

33 Residents of Hull-House, *Hull-House Maps and Papers*, 97–98.

34 Abbott, *Tenements of Chicago*, 73.

neighborhoods and fifteen other North and South Side neighborhoods.[35] We did include the Stockyards District and Back
of the Yards in the recent study. While we have only collected
one year of data in what will be an annual survey, the information would still have been useful to Mr. Burnham in understanding the challenges and needs of city neighborhoods.

I could go into detail on the results of the studies, but I
think the important point is that the work is already done and
Mr. Burnham could have availed himself of the information
in order to craft a more comprehensive and thorough *Plan
of Chicago*. We did not find conditions significantly different
this year than in 1901, but perhaps the lack of improvement
is reason enough to consider a long-range plan for improving
housing and neighborhood conditions. It is incomprehensible
to me that Mr. Burnham could omit this information and fail
to address the sorry state of municipal responsibility for sanitation and public health.

Mary McDowell seized the opportunity to move the group toward
its next, and final, area of discussion before formulating recommendations:

I couldn't agree with you more, Edith. And you brought us
right to the point we need to be now, the discussion of official
action, or inaction, in response to these critical issues. Madeleine, you have spent a great deal of time following the work
of our elected and appointed officials. Will you summarize
their activities in the recent past?

Madeleine Wallin Sikes took the challenge eagerly:

Surely. I thank you for giving me the opportunity. As many of
you know I monitor city council meetings for the Civic Federation and other groups with which I am associated. Although
Chicago has taken some positive steps recently, most notably
in bringing Charles Ball, a bona-fide professional from New
York, to Chicago a few years ago, the official record is a poor
one overall.

In the mid-nineteenth century, Chicago had no sewage system at all. This was not unusual at the time, but because our

---

35   Ibid., 187.

city was built on swampy land, the drainage problems here led to serious health problems, including frequent epidemics. Business leaders were reluctant to invest in improvements that paid no immediate financial dividend. In December of 1854 the public rose up in protest of inaction at a mass meeting, leading to the establishment of a Board of Sewage Commissioners, which was formed the following year. That board brought Ellis Chesbrough, a renowned engineer from Boston, to Chicago.[36] Chesbrough is justly famous for his two biggest projects here: moving the water intake two miles out in the lake to avoid the sewage near the shore, and for reversal of the river, both of which improved the quality of drinking water in Chicago.

A real turning point came in 1885 though, when a devastating flood shattered the illusion of the upper classes that they were protected from water-borne bacteriological infections. For the first time, the business community, specifically the Citizens' Association, pressed for sanitary reforms. The result was a new taxing body, the Sanitary District of Chicago, which eventually built the Sanitary and Ship Canal[37] to move sewage away from the city more rapidly than the river was able. Thus Chicago embarked on its third big construction project in response to water-borne sewage and disease.

Settlement houses began demanding official action on the condition of streets and alleys almost as soon as they were organized. I'm sure most of you have heard of Hull-House's attempts to deal with unsanitary street conditions first through public education. Our friends realized very quickly that the problem was not the local residents, but lax city regulation. They began demanding that the city enforce existing rules or pass new ones. The publicity Jane Addams received when she submitted a bid to take over the garbage inspector's job in her ward forced the mayor's hand. He had to select her as inspector for the Nineteenth Ward, a position that brought her much press coverage.[38] Settlement workers also increased pressure on City Hall by sponsoring an 1893 conference contrasting

---

36 Miller, *City of the Century,* 124–128.

37 Grossman, Keating, and Reiff, *The Encyclopedia of Chicago,* 276.

38 Davis, *Spearheads,* 153–154.

the idealized White City with real slums,[39] which is perhaps
one of the reasons Mr. Burnham has so carefully avoided us
on his current project!

The record on regulation of housing problems has been extremely inconsistent. I suspect this is a result of many business and city leaders being landlords and resisting any regulation of their "rights" as property owners. Responsibility for
housing regulation has bounced between the Department of
Health and the Department of Buildings. Unlike New York,
Chicago has lacked a Tenement House Department, probably
because some would deny that we have a tenement problem.

The Department of Health had responsibility for reporting
on sanitary conditions of tenements as early as 1880,[40] but
little regulatory power. The next important reform was trig-
gered by the World's Columbian Exposition. "Lodging houses,"
where single individuals rented rooms, grew explosively because of the influx of people coming to work at the fair. In
1893, inspections of lodging houses were authorized to prevent the spread of disease.[41]

Privy vaults were next to come under scrutiny. The health
commissioner was given power to demolish any poorly maintained privy vaults in 1897. A new building code and a new
building commissioner also came on the scene at this time.[42]
Thus, responsibility for tenement inspection rested with two
agencies of the city, instead of residing clearly in one.

The City Homes Association published its report in 1901
and began the drive for a tenement ordinance immediately.
Anita McCormick Blaine spoke forcefully for the ordinance
at the 1902 city council meeting where the ordinance was
considered. Although amendments were made to the original
proposal, the bill did pass with a substantial majority of forty-
seven to seven.[43]

Unfortunately, even this partial victory was diluted in its
implementation. Only four months after passage of the new

---

39   Ibid., 187.
40   Abbott, *Tenements of Chicago,* 47–49.
41   Ibid., 53.
42   Ibid., 53.
43   Philpott, *Slum and the Ghetto,* 102.

ordinance, the city had already exempted twenty-eight buildings from the regulations. A short time later, a particularly
virulent typhoid epidemic led Hull-House residents to try to
isolate the source of the infection. Their findings were that
the primary source was the uncovered privy vaults, but the
secondary source was a health department that was either
corrupt or incompetent. Their research was so ironclad that
five heath inspectors were indicted.[44] By 1905 Chicago still
lacked a unified strategy for tenement regulation. Responsibility remained divided between two departments, and no
chief sanitary inspector had been appointed.

Elizabeth Lindsay Davis broke in to make an important point:

This situation has caused dire consequences for some families in the Negro district. Not only are our areas less likely
to have the benefit of regular garbage collection or tenement
inspections, but parents living in poor conditions were sometimes charged with keeping "neglectful homes" by insensitive
authorities.[45]

Madeleine Wallin Sikes resumed her overview:

Thank you, Mrs. Davis. You are absolutely right. While all
congested areas suffered, some suffered more than others,
purely out of prejudice.

After the health department's public humiliation, Jane Addams and Anita McCormick Blaine convinced the city to hire
Charles Ball, chief sanitary inspector of the New York Tenement House Department as Chicago's chief sanitary inspector.[46] There was so much resistance to an "outsider" taking
on this responsibility that it was actually 1907 before he was
able to assume his responsibilities.[47]

Commissioner Ball proposed reworking the tenement ordinance in 1908 and asked "architects, engineers and representatives of various branches of the building industry" to
testify about potential improvements. The City Club formed a

---

44 Abbott, *Tenements of Chicago,* 62–64.

45 Knupfer, *African American Women's Clubs,* 67.

46 Davis, *Spearheads,* 69.

47 Abbott, *Tenements of Chicago,* 64.

committee to look into comparable ordinances in other cities and the advice of individual architects was solicited here in Chicago. A more predictable protocol was established for the benefit of builders as well as residents.[48] As an architect, Mr. Burnham must be aware of this activity. I find it surprising he makes no reference to it.

In the meantime, reformers have been calling for an official census of housing conditions for at least ten years. The City Homes Association survey of three neighborhoods provided the only hard data on the problem. There were at least two dozen communities that should have been surveyed.

In the absence of a city survey of housing conditions, Commissioner Ball asked Edith and her researchers to conduct the first of what promises to be "a long series of house-to-house canvasses in certain deteriorated areas of the city."[49] This is the same study Edith referred to a few minutes ago. This first annual survey examined housing conditions in twenty-four congested neighborhoods in all parts of the city, including Negro districts. Researchers are still sifting through a very large amount of data collected this winter. Once the survey is conducted over several years, Chicago will possess a very detailed look at housing by location and over time. This seems like very important data for developing a long-range plan.

I do want to mention one other group that was active during this time and a woman who took the lead in advocating for better neighborhood conditions. She was not conducting studies, but her advocacy certainly helped to point to the need for more information. Ada Celeste Sweet was among the founders of the Municipal Order League in 1892. From its inception, the Municipal Order League argued against private contracts for street cleaning, insisting that the city should take direct responsibility for such a critical function. Ada and other women from the league, and the league's allies in the Chicago Women's Club applied tenets of municipal housekeeping in their arguments. The Municipal Order League organized neighborhood street-cleaning societies as a citywide

---

48   Ibid., 65–66. Miss Abbott also reports that efforts to evade the 1908 law were
      immediate and continued through 1935, the publication date of her book.
49   Ibid., 73.

force for better sanitation. The *Inter-Ocean* credited her with initiating the city's Department of Street Cleaning in 1892. She later complained that streets downtown were cleaned but the ones in neighborhood were not, making the "victory" hollow. Using her platform as columnist for the *Chicago American*, she advocated for rebuilding substandard housing near the central business district.[50] I'm sorry she was not able to be here today to speak more directly about her achievements. I understand she is assisting on another committee.

Mary McDowell prepared to bring the group to consider the recommendations it would make:

Thank you, Madeleine. That was an excellent summary of a complicated problem. I want to add one more point before we move to develop our recommendations. I would like you all to know that several settlement house leaders, myself included, attended a meeting of the Merchants' Club Executive Committee in 1906,[51] shortly after it became apparent that a plan for Chicago's future would be developed. We were there to protest the omission of housing from their outline of topics to be covered. Obviously our request fell on deaf ears, but I wanted you to know that the businessmen had fair warning long ago that this was an important issue for many in Chicago.

Now I would like you to break into groups of two or three to discuss what you think are the most important recommendations to make about housing and neighborhood development. I don't want to presume to tell you what your conclusions should be, but hope you will all at least consider Ina's suggestion that we build from Mr. Burnham's own plan for a suburban town center. We will reconvene in one half hour to finish our work.

Recommendations:

Recommendation One, Neighborhood Form:

An ideal neighborhood would have at its core the services and institutions proposed in the *Plan of Chicago* for a suburban

50   Schultz and Hast, *Women Building Chicago,* 863.

51   Philpott, *Slum and the Ghetto,* 108.

town center, as well as one or more nearby commercial streets to fulfill daily shopping requirements, such as grocers, butchers, stationers, and the like.

Recommendation Two, Neighborhood Housing:

The city should develop a progressive building code for new and existing construction, especially with regard to health considerations such as light, ventilation, and sanitation. City inspectors should be trained, professional civil service employees.

Recommendation Three, Housing Research:

The city should use data being accumulated over time to assess the success of its housing program or to modify as the need arises and is documented.

12
Education

First (middle, maiden) Name	Last Name	Brief Biographical Information	Approximate Age
Jane	Addams	Founder and head resident of Hull-House, leader of civic and progressive organizations.	40s
Anita McCormick	Blaine	Daughter of Cyrus McCormick, socialist, philanthropist with an interest in progressive education and housing.	40s
Cornelia Bernarda	DeBey	Physician (homeopathic), education reformer, on Board of Education during early 1900s.	40s
John	Dewey	Former University of Chicago education professor closely aligned with Hull-House.	50s
Frances Crane	Lillie	Physician; socialist; Arts and Crafts approach to motherhood; young children in 1909; daughter of Mary Crane, for whom Hull-House Nursery was named.	40s
Alice Whiting	Putnam	One of first to espouse kindergartens, she was teacher or mentor to most early kindergarten teachers in Chicago; her school was at Hull-House from 1894–1902; regular participant in progressive education initiatives.	60s
Eleanor Clarke	Slagle	Chicago School of Civics and Philanthropy student with concern for the institutionalized; influenced by Julia Lathrop; Justice of Peace in Evanston, 1907–1913, to stay near children.	30s

| Anna Wilmarth | Thompson (later Ickes) | Young mother loosely connected to the activist women's circle, daughter of Mary Wilmarth. | 30s |
| Ella Flagg | Young | Highly respected educator who was named Superintendent of the Chicago Public Schools later in 1909. | 60s |

THE YEAR IS 1909. The setting is an art classroom in Hull-House. Eight women and one man are gathered around a large table. There is sculpture and pottery on shelves around the room, evidence of the work of students young and old.

Jane Addams called the group to order:

I want to thank you all for being here today to participate in this important meeting. I especially want to thank my dear friend John Dewey, who has traveled from his post at Columbia University in New York City to be with us today. We have the opportunity and the obligation to give our best thoughts on how the future of public education might be transformed in Chicago and throughout the region. Our recommendations will be forwarded to Mr. Daniel Burnham who has drafted a *Plan of Chicago*. As I think you all know, this plan has been crafted under the direction of the Commercial Club of Chicago, and represents primarily the business point of view. This is our opportunity to broaden that point of view, but we need to be aware of the constraints within which we operate. Our naiveté in school matters ended years ago, when we first approached Alderman Johnny Powers to try to propose that a new public school be built here in the Nineteenth Ward. Instead, Alderman Powers's cronies on the city council education committee substituted a parochial school, effectively excluding those who could not pay tuition.[1] In spite of a long political battle and the assistance of many other reformers, we have been unable to break the hold of politics on schools in this ward, or for that matter, in most of the city.

---

1   Davis, *Heroine,* 121–122.

*Ella Flagg Young.
(Chicago History Museum, DN-0007580,*Chicago Daily News *negatives collection, Chicago Historical Society.)*

In spite of my very strong concern about this topic, I will be unable to stay for all of this meeting because of another commitment. I want to launch it by introducing to you Mrs. Ella Flagg Young, who will chair the meeting in my absence. Mrs. Young has broken each barrier set before her as a career woman, but still manifested a distinctly feminine approach to working with children and teachers. I say "feminine" in the sense of leading not by fiat but by collaboration, consideration, and kindness. Those of you who know Mrs. Young's credentials well, please indulge me while I give a brief biographical sketch for those who don't.

Mrs. Young has held virtually every position within the school system, except that of superintendent.[2] She passed the teacher exam at the age of fifteen and began her career with the schools at the age of seventeen, when Superintendent William Wells offered her a position in the Normal School because she was too young to teach.[3] She later took the principal's test, which men were required to take, but women were not, and

---

2   J. Smith, *Ella Flagg Young,* 1. Ella Flagg Young was selected as superintendent of the Chicago Public Schools on July 30, 1909.

3   Ibid., 12–15. The Normal School was the teacher training program run by the school system.

received the highest score on the test that year.[4] Since that time, she has been the principal of Skinner School,[5] a district superintendent, and both studied and taught at the University of Chicago, under the tutelage of John Dewey.[6] Mrs. Young has always upheld the highest standards of conduct, even when that stance required resigning her position, as she did as district superintendent when Superintendent Albert Lane was demoted for political reasons[7] and when University of Chicago president William Rainey Harper led the university's education department far from the standards set by John Dewey and other progressive educators.[8] She is currently principal of the Normal School, where she has transformed teacher training by situating practice schools within immigrant communities, thus providing new teachers with a more realistic training experience than they had in the past.[9] In an obvious reflection of the esteem in which she is held throughout the state, Mrs. Young has served on the State Board of Education since 1889.[10] Perhaps the trait for which I personally admire her most is her ability to serve in management and still retain the affection of the teachers and the teachers' union. The talent of maintaining cordial relations with the teachers' union has proved to be a vexatious challenge for me.

As Jane Addams finished, the group broke into spontaneous applause, whether in admiration for Mrs. Young or in a show of affection for Miss Addams despite her chagrin at the situation with the teachers' union, was not clear. Perhaps both reasons influenced the display of support.

Ella Flagg Young assumed the mantle of leadership easily and gracefully:

Thank you, Miss Addams, for your kind words and for your multitude of deeds to make Chicago a better place for all of

---

4   J. Smith, *Ella Flagg Young*, 31.

5   Herrick, *Chicago Public Schools*, 115.

6   Feffer, *The Chicago Pragmatists*, 187.

7   J. Smith, *Ella Flagg Young*, 55.

8   Deegan, *Men of the Chicago School*, 211.

9   J. Smith, *Ella Flagg Young*, 102–119.

10   Ibid., 49–50.

us. I am honored to have the responsibility for guiding this discussion and thank you for taking on the task of providing recommendations to improve the *Plan of Chicago*. This seems like a particularly perilous time for the Chicago public schools, although as we look back at history, it seems there have been few times when the schools weren't in peril. This year, however, the Commercial Club succeeded in gaining legislation to extend all leases of Chicago school property for ninety-nine years. That means the schools will be denied the opportunity to renegotiate with businesses that can clearly afford more rent and will continue to struggle with funding deficits. I do pride myself on objectivity, but I feel compelled to put that one fact before you today as evidence that I may be unable to be completely objective about the Commercial Club's planning project.[11]

Anita McCormick Blaine broke in impulsively:

Excuse me, Mrs. Young, but I need to add one sorry point that will make objectivity even more difficult. Mr. Burnham himself has profited from leases of school property. The Rookery Building which his firm designed and in which he was an investor is one of those properties unwisely leased by the Board of Education.[12] I am highly skeptical about the likelihood of the *Plan of Chicago* making any substantive recommendations to improve the situation, but believe we need to document the need for reform nevertheless.

Ella Flagg Young resumed her opening remarks:

I am very sorry to hear about Mr. Burnham's entanglement in that property. It will be difficult to find the right argument to persuade these men to look beyond their own interests. But we must try.

I think we need some perspective on the past in order to consider the full ramifications of the future. Would one of you like to provide some background?

Alice Putnam, a kindergarten teacher, spoke up:

---

11   Ibid., 145–146.

12   Miller, *City of the Century,* 326–327.

Miss Addams anticipated that you would want a thorough overview of the historical record. She asked me to prepare an overview of the first fifty years of the school system. I fear she asked me to do this because I am one of the few in this room who is old enough to have been around for part of those first fifty years!

It is quite plain to see that many of the problems with which the schools struggle today had their antecedents in the earliest chapters of Chicago's history. In fact, one of the schools just north of here, Carpenter School, is named for druggist Philo Carpenter who protested an 1833 plan to sell school land quickly and cheaply[13] rather than hold it in trust for the benefit of the children. Even in Chicago's first year as an incorporated town, graft won out over prudence. The Board of Education originally held eleven square miles of land, donated by the federal government for schools. This was about 6 percent of the total within the town limits, but most of it was quickly sold off to businesses and investors.[14] Within a very short time, that land escalated in value. A school lot at State and Madison that sold for $20 in 1833 was worth $17,500 in 1851 and $40,000 in 1855.[15]

Chicago's charter as a city in 1837 required semi-annual accounting of school funds and a board of seven "inspectors." The charter also authorized trustees to levy taxes on property at a rate of one-half of one percent. Unfortunately, there was no penalty for non-payment, so almost no one paid the taxes.[16] It is not hard to understand how businesses today feel entitled to grossly underpay their tax assessments, when their forbearers were not compelled to pay any taxes!

You will not be surprised to hear that from the beginning, construction of buildings had greater appeal to the city's leadership than did instruction of students. We might be relieved that when the legislature gave the city council rights to set curricula and to control school contracts, our aldermen

---

13   Herrick, *Chicago Public Schools,* 22–24.

14   Stead, 174–175.

15   Herrick, *Chicago Public Schools,* 26.

16   Ibid., 24.

chose to act only on the latter opportunity.[17] Suffice it to say there was little money to be made in curriculum development. Beginning in the 1870s, Chicago couldn't build schools fast enough to keep up with the rising population. School construction was also a source of patronage jobs.[18] Jobs and contracts are a very attractive combination to the political leadership of the city.

During this time, professional qualifications for teachers were almost nonexistent. Average annual teacher salaries in the early days were $200 per year for women and $500 for men.[19] The dismal state of the schools is evidenced by the first annual report offered by the system's first superintendent, John Dore. Mr. Dore proposed in 1855 that students should no longer be required to clean schools and keep fires burning, that there should be a truant law, and that teachers needed training.[20] As you can see from this list, schools were at a very primitive state of organization in the middle of this century.

The school system existed for fifty-some years before a woman was named to the Board of Education. Ellen Mitchell was the first woman to serve, beginning in 1888, but it took a three-year campaign by the Chicago Woman's Club to gain the seat.[21] Today we have the benefit of the experience of three women who are or have been on the Board of Education: Miss Addams, Dr. De Bey, and Mrs. Blaine. Since Miss Addams has to leave momentarily, I believe that either Dr. Cornelia De Bey or Anita McCormick Blaine would be best equipped to carry this summary forward, with their firsthand experience in school board policies and politics.

Cornelia De Bey smiled her acceptance of the responsibility and Anita Blaine indicated her willingness to have Dr. De Bey take the lead:

In the twenty years since this dear house has come to mean so much to Chicago and to reform, we have seen some

---

17   Ibid., 25.
18   Feffer, *The Chicago Pragmatists,* 182–183.
19   Herrick, *Chicago Public Schools,* 22–24.
20   Ibid., 38.
21   Ibid., 57.

improvements in the schools, but they have been slow and hard fought. Oftentimes, progress has been hampered by a confluence of issues having nothing to do with schools that managed nevertheless to divert the strong headwaters of reform. For example, the question of restrictions on liquor sales, which are unpopular with immigrant groups, is often entangled with school reform because some temperance crusaders support both.[22] We were recently encouraged by the possibilities of reform during the all too brief mayoralty of Edward Dunne. Now we suffer the disappointment of slipping back to the old ways under the current mayor, Mr. Busse. I think the most disturbing development, however, has been the schism between the teachers' union and other reform elements in the city. It is a blessing that Miss Addams had to remove herself from the discussion, since I know this subject causes her great pain. Distractions such as these complicated our work. But I am getting ahead of myself. Let me return to the period just after Ellen Mitchell became a board member.

In 1892 there was great consternation in the city when Dr. Joseph Mayer Rice published a study of schools throughout the country. He found the Chicago schools to be the "least progressive," and to use the "most mechanical, antiquated and absurd methods."[23] I am not knowledgeable about the day-to-day administration of the schools almost twenty years ago, and wonder if it would be appropriate at this point to defer to our chair, Mrs. Young, for her observations on what the real and perceived problems are. I would be happy to then continue recounting the policy-level changes we tried to effect at the board level. Mrs. Young, would you be so kind?

Ella Flagg Young smiled and indicated she was willing to provide the information:

I would be happy to provide some service to the group. You function so collaboratively that you hardly need a chair.

It is unfortunately true that all was not well in Chicago schools in the second half of the nineteenth century, although I'm not entirely convinced we were that much worse than

22   Herrick, *Chicago Public Schools*, 61.
23   J. Smith, *Ella Flagg Young*, 44.

all other cities. From mid-century, the schools struggled to reduce class size. At one point in the mid-1840s, classes averaged seventy-two students.[24] In the 1850s and 1860s, the averages ranged between eighty and one hundred students per classroom, and thousands of children who wanted to enroll were being turned away.[25] This was before the great school construction boom of the 1870s.

By the time Illinois passed a statewide compulsory attendance law in the mid-1880s, a school census in Chicago showed there were almost 170,000 children and youth in Chicago between the ages of six and twenty-one years of age. Fewer than half were enrolled in school. In 1888 the Chicago Woman's Club sent a petition to the Board of Education asking for enforcement of compulsory education. Some of the newspapers called compulsory education "preposterous" and said it would cause the closing of factories.[26] Consequently, because of overcrowding, children have been on half-day sessions for most of the late nineteenth century.[27] I do not believe we were the only city in the nation using half-day sessions, but I don't dispute Dr. Rice's contention that the quality of education was very poor at the time, partially because of the abbreviated school day.

There was one additional factor affecting the quality of education in our schools, which I will touch on briefly here. By 1895 there were almost five thousand teachers in the system, but only the 300 high school teachers were likely to hold college degrees. Elementary teachers were most likely to have a high school education although some had attended special training programs at the Normal School. The Normal School was effectively dismantled in the 1870s. Soon Chicago was the only large city system with no provision for teacher training. An even greater problem was that all teachers had to have a political sponsor in order to be employed by the Board of Education.[28] As you can plainly see, the question of teacher

---

24   Herrick, *Chicago Public Schools*, 26.

25   Ibid., 43.

26   Ibid., 63.

27   Ibid., 75.

28   Ibid., 74.

training and assessment has been contested throughout the history of the Chicago Public Schools.

There you have an outline of some difficulties teachers, administrators, and students struggle with in the classroom. I wish I could paint a brighter picture, and I do have some suggestions about how to improve the situation, which I will happily share in due course. Dr. De Bey, please resume your narrative of recent events with the Board of Education.

Cornelia De Bey nodded and began again:

Little progress was made at improving schools through board initiatives until Mayor Dunne came to office in 1905. That year he named Miss Addams, Mrs. Blaine, and myself to the Board of Education. Mrs. W.C.H. Keough, an attorney, had been serving on the board since 1904. This made for an unprecedented four women on the twenty-one member board.[29] Mayor Dunne named additional members, some of whom were considered "radical" from their work in the charter convention and elsewhere. These included long time allies of the settlement house movement like Raymond Robins and Louis Post, editor of a progressive news magazine, Wiley Mills, proponent of municipal ownership of transit, and John J. Sonsteby, president of the garment workers' union. These appointments put reformers in the majority.[30] As you can well imagine, the business community was livid.

The schools were again drawn into controversial issues only peripherally related to education.[31] The charter convention, which went on in two distinct sessions between 1906 and this year, was dominated by business interests. The public was energized by the convention's deliberations on schools. Many petitions were submitted to the convention on that issue. The Merchants' Club supported business control of the schools. The Chicago Federation of Labor (CFL) resisted, but the CFL and a handful of our friends who were delegates to the convention were vastly outnumbered by the business forces.

---

29   Schultz and Hast, *Women Building Chicago,* 215.

30   G. Harrison, *Anita McCormick Blaine,* 124.

31   Flanagan, *Charter,* 77–78.

The battle over schools moved from the charter convention to the mayoral campaign of 1907, pitting the Chicago Federation of Labor against the businessmen. The public was generally opposed to, or at least skeptical of, the businessmen on school issues. The ongoing debate was whether one strong, businesslike superintendent should run schools, or whether teachers and communities should have a say. Mayor Dunne favored a collaborative approach with teachers and the community contributing. This is an approach I know we will hear more about later today, because it is a subject near and dear to the heart of Mrs. Young. The issue of business control versus community control also became entwined with the question of an elected rather than appointed board, which the charter convention and business community viewed with great alarm.[32]

The *Chicago Tribune,* in covering the mayoral election, said Mayor Dunne had named a school board of "single taxers and socialists" who had a "plan to 'democratize' the school government" and "submit all questions of educational policy to the teachers." I've never understood why "democratize" seemed such an offensive charge for the *Tribune* to hurl at the mayor. But they were clear in calling for a businessman to straighten out the mess, and Fred Busse was their man.[33]

Nineteen aught-seven was a year of gains and losses, with more of the latter than the former. Mayor Dunne lost to Mr. Busse, who quickly began to consolidate his control of the Board of Education. On the other hand, when the time came for the referendum on the proposed new city charter, the public voted against the businessmen's vision of governance of the city and the schools by a two-to-one margin.

Thus began one of the most contentious years of my life and of Anita's and Miss Addams's. Anita, would you mind picking up this saga and bringing it to its sad conclusion?

Anita McCormick Blaine looked briefly at Ella Flagg Young to see if she wanted to direct the group differently and then accepted Cornelia De Bey's invitation:

---

32   Ibid., 103–104.
33   Ibid., 104.

I accept the responsibility, but with great reluctance. I have had more than my share of personal and family tragedy but I don't think anything has ever gnawed at me the way this unfortunate display of power and politics has. I refused Mayor Busse's offer to be reappointed to the Board in 1908[34] and can't imagine ever making such a commitment again. As long as you understand the depths of my bitterness, I will continue.

Seven of the twenty-one board members' terms were to expire in July 1907, giving Mayor Busse the opportunity to reshape the board a few short months after his election. However, instead Mayor Busse created a confrontation by notifying twelve members in May of 1907 that their services on the board were no longer needed.[35] I don't know if he was under pressure from the businessmen to show his mettle, but I would say the fiasco backfired. Not only was his hasty decision ultimately overturned by the courts, but I suspect his meddling in the schools had a great deal to do with antagonizing voters right before the charter referendum. At the time however, Mayor Busse though he achieved a victory when he replaced the so-called "radicals" with businessmen from the Merchants' Club and the charter convention, men distinguished by their union-busting antagonism to the Chicago Teachers' Federation.[36]

An ugly division within the ranks of reformers grew out of this discord. In a backdrop to the Board of Education battle, Miss Addams was finding her famed peace-making skills put to their severest test by the Chicago Teachers' Federation. One issue was Superintendent Edwin Cooley's plan for secret evaluations of teachers, an ill-advised plan in response to a genuine need to increase teacher skills and accountability. Miss Addams was strongly criticized by CTF leader Margaret Haley in 1906 for supporting continuous retraining and evaluation of teachers, although Miss Addams did not support Cooley's secret system.[37] As chair of the management committee, Miss

---

34   G. Harrison, *Anita McCormick Blaine,* 127.

35   Ibid., 125.

36   Flanagan, *Charter,* 108.

37   Feffer, *The Chicago Pragmatists,* 209.

Addams encouraged revision of the plan. Tension between Miss Addams and Cooley was exacerbated by inflammatory newspaper articles. Cooley's modified plan was ultimately approved by the board, with Miss Addams being the deciding vote.[38] Incidentally, this controversial plan has been rescinded and then reinstated since the first vote, perhaps an indication of how difficult and divisive a problem it is.

Miss Addams, who has managed to find common ground with all manner of unusual personalities, was hurt and perplexed by the teachers' impatience with her objective view and their accusations that she had thrown away the opportunity for change.[39] Miss Addams was under additional pressure from the Chicago Teachers' Federation on pension fund issues and from both teachers and former board allies like Raymond Robins for her refusal to resign in protest of Mayor Busse's purge.[40] Miss Addams tried, to no avail, to explain the greater good that she hoped to work toward, including the possibility of increasing school playgrounds by forty new facilities. Margaret Haley's response to Miss Addams's broadminded focus was to retort that 400 playgrounds was too high a price to pay compared to teacher control of their pensions.[41] I know that you have all heard of the vote last year to move the Women's Trade Union League out of Hull-House following the school board controversies. I was glad to hear that Raymond Robins and his wife participated in one of the meetings about the *Plan of Chicago*, but I know feelings are still very raw on all sides. With some relief, I now look to Mrs. Young to take the floor from me. This has been quite wrenching.

Ella Flagg Young thanked Anita McCormick Blaine with genuine concern for her distress. She then proposed they move on to consider some of the reform efforts directed at the school system, from within and without:

Alice, you have been very quiet, but I know your long history at the forefront of many progressive education policies. Would

---

38   J. Smith, *Ella Flagg Young,* 135–137.

39   Herrick, *Chicago Public Schools,* 110.

40   Davis, *Heroine,* 133–134.

41   J. Smith, *Ella Flagg Young,* 138.

you begin the discussion of groups and ideas promoting significant reforms from both outside and inside the system? Then I hope Mr. Dewey will grace us with some background on innovations within academia, particularly those developed at the University of Chicago during his time at that institution. I should confess to any who do not already know that Mr. Dewey was my teacher and mentor and someone to whom I will always be in debt.

Alice Whiting Putnam rubbed her hands together as she gathered her thoughts, then set her hands in her lap and began:

There are so many groups that have taken an interest in the schools that it is hard to know where to start. So much starts with Hull-House. Let's deliberately start elsewhere this time. The Chicago Woman's Club would be first on many lists of reform groups.[42] They were the first to advocate that women needed to be represented on the Board of Education and other civic institutions. CWC supports the Chicago Teachers' Federation in its drive for security through a stable pension system, just as they advocated for other groups of working women. They pushed for enforcement of compulsory education laws. They sponsored kindergartens and vacation schools.[43] Their work in related areas like juvenile courts, child protective services, and public health provided not only good ideas to the system, but often the CWC raised funds to pay for services such as visiting nurses or vacation school, expenses that eventually came to be accepted as legitimate expenses of the school system once their utility was proved.

The Civic Federation was an ally of the schools and worked in concert with the Chicago Woman's Club to establish vacation schools.[44] Mrs. Marion Washburne, the chairwoman of their education department, conducted an important study in 1895 of nearly every school, including building conditions like lighting, heating, and sanitary facilities, and educational factors like seating capacity and teaching methods. The Civic

---

42   Flanagan, *Charter,* 40.

43   American, "Small Playgrounds," 2.

44   Sutherland, *Fifty Years,* 20.

Federation strongly encourages parent councils as a way to increase community participation in school affairs.[45]

One superintendent who generally encouraged good ideas from outside the system was Superintendent Albert G. Lane.[46] One of his most successful outside programs originated here at Hull-House, with Ellen Gates Starr's Public Art Society. The society was instrumental in bringing high-quality art to the public schools.[47]

I don't mean to imply that every idea that came from outside was uniformly good. In fact, I think we would all look askance at the William Rainey Harper committee appointed by Mayor Carter Harrison II. As is so often the case, the committee was composed only of men, and they tended to be men with a stake in the status quo. Their 1898 reform report emphasized centralized authority and the application of business models to the operation of the schools. Understandably, it was seen as institutionalizing business control of the schools. It also included pressure for more academic credentials for teachers,[48] which is positive only if the teachers believe it is a proposal made in concert with them rather than "to" them. Proposals in relation to the board and administration of the schools included changes in the size and committee composition of the board; definition of the board's role to set policy and the superintendent to administer; the right of eminent domain and ability to purchase land; freedom from all political influence; six-year terms for superintendents, with the power to determine curriculum and select assistants and other personnel; a business manager to conduct all business affairs for schools; and standards for teachers.[49]

President Harper's report also included school services we have long advocated, like parental schools, vacation schools, relief from overcrowding, and school playgrounds. And he included some progressive ideas that originated with John Dewey and Ella Flagg Young, including teacher councils,

---

45 Ibid., 11.
46 Herrick, *Chicago Public Schools,* 73.
47 Schaffer, *Urban Ideals,* 133.
48 Feffer, *The Chicago Pragmatists,* 184.
49 Herrick, *Chicago Public Schools,* 84.

schools as community centers, and resident commissions to visit and report on local schools.[50]

Given the positive aspects of this report, it is hard to explain why we and others felt skeptical about the motives of the Harper committee. Schools are so important to families in the city. There is immediate suspicion or concern when any change is proposed. That suspicion is only increased among parents and teachers when groups like the Harper committee work in isolation. The opportunities for influencing the deliberations of these men were constrained. For instance, male principals could only make recommendations through their professional group, the George Howland Club, and women principals were to do the same through the Ella Flagg Young Club.[51] Perhaps teachers' skepticism surrounding Harper's effort had to do with his known antagonism to teachers receiving professional pay. He has been known to say that he believes it appropriate that teachers are on a pay scale similar to his wife's maid. He also urged more male teachers and differential rates of pay for male and female teachers.[52] While none of us here are marching in lockstep with the teachers' union, it is certainly easy to understand why this kind of leadership keeps the majority of teachers in a defensive posture at all times.

I suppose the summary of my comments is that outsiders who hope to improve the Chicago schools need to bring at least two kinds of attributes to the task. We need good ideas and progressive models. But beyond that, we need credible, collaborative leadership to create a foundation for trust so that change is possible.

The saga of reforms coming from inside the system is as mixed as that of the outsider efforts. Probably the longest-running, most important, and most contentious initiative has been the question of teacher training, assessment, and accountability. This is an area in which Mrs. Young has been active since the 1870s and has had remarkable success in terms of maintaining the support of the teachers. Rarely has any other administrator had such strong support from

---

50   Ibid., 86–87.

51   Ibid., 94.

52   Feffer, *The Chicago Pragmatists,* 184.

teachers. Do you know that Mrs. Young established teachers' councils in her district before the Harper Committee made that recommendation?[53] Teachers tell me they trust her because she moves to do what she knows is right, rather than waiting to see which way the administration or the political leadership is leaning on any given day.

She has had somewhat less success in preventing the system from making short-sighted decisions. As you know, Mrs. Young entered the system as a teacher at the Normal School and at this point in her career has come full circle to sit as its principal. What happened to teacher training in the intervening years is a sorry tale. Mrs. Flagg moved from a seventeen-year-old teacher of teachers to a twenty-year-old in charge of the board's teacher training program. When the board reduced the program from a six-month course to two weeks, Mrs. Young transferred to a high-school teaching position rather than run an ineffectual program. By 1877, the board closed the training program altogether. At that time they were accused of hiring only for political or personal reasons, rather than for the professional qualifications of the individual.[54]

Many years later, Superintendent Albert Lane tried to address the deficit in teacher training with an after-hours school for teachers. Shortly thereafter, a separate training institution, the Cook County Normal School, was offered to the board in the winter of 1895–96.[55] Francis W. Parker was head of the Normal School but left a few years later, after coming under fire from within the board. The story becomes very unpleasant here. Superintendent Lane was demoted for political reasons.[56] Visionary staff like Colonel Parker and Mrs. Young left the system in large numbers because the situation was untenable under the imperious leadership of the new superintendent, Benjamin Andrews.

Anita, I see that you want to add something. Please go right ahead.

---

53   Herrick, *Chicago Public Schools,* 94.
54   Ibid., 49.
55   Ibid., 74.
56   G. Harrison, *Anita McCormick Blaine,* 77.

Anita McCormick Blaine, always passionate on the issue of education, nodded her thanks to Alice Putnam and bluntly went to her point:

Some of you know I have been a financial supporter of schools here in Chicago and also in New York and New Mexico.[57] I've worked closely with Colonel Parker and with John Dewey to promote and test out educational innovations, usually providing funds to private schools because the public system is so frightened by innovation. Or perhaps it is more accurate to say they are frightened by the newspapers and the charges of educational "frills and fads." The Chicago schools' conduct toward Francis Parker was an abomination and I, for one, believe it contributed to his death in 1902. I am sorry to interject this strong personal statement into our reflections, but the damage to the schools and to the best individuals in the schools was lasting and severe. I'm sorry, Alice, please feel free to go on.

Alice Putnam calmly picked up the threads of her thought:

While Mrs. Young has provided exemplary leadership, I don't want to do an injustice to some of the other people who made substantial leadership contributions. Superintendents William Wells and Albert Lane are the two that stand out most prominently in my mind. Superintendent Wells was a national education leader of great stature, but his tenure as superintendent was abbreviated by ill health. After retirement in 1864, he was appointed to the Board of Education and served as president. He served on the State Board of Education and helped establish the Illinois State Normal School. As an all-around educational leader he also served on the library board, Chicago Academy of Science, and the Chicago Historical Society.[58] I often wonder whether our school history would read differently if he had been able to more firmly leave his mark on the system in those early days.

In more recent history, the internal reformer we most admired was Albert Lane who distinguished himself by

---

57   G. Harrison, *Anita McCormick Blaine,* 123.

58   Herrick, *Chicago Public Schools,* 46.

expanding manual training and absorbing privately-funded kindergartens into the basic school program. He expanded night school, started a parental school for delinquent children, and supported pensions for teachers.[59]

Even our current superintendent, Edwin Cooley, who has created so much consternation among the teachers' union by proposing secret evaluations, has an admirable track record in other areas. He worked to get children out of factories and into schools, often working alongside many of us. He experimented with "continuation" schools for older students and opened seventeen vacation schools this year. It was his policy to build a playground at every new school and to add playgrounds to older schools where possible.[60]

Of course the brevity of this review does an injustice to some others, but I can see that our time is passing quickly and there is still so much to cover. I will turn the discussion back to you, Mrs. Young.

Ella Flagg Young thanked Alice Putnam for her review and for her many years of dedication to teaching. Then, with obvious pleasure she introduced John Dewey:

As I mentioned earlier Mr. Dewey is my mentor and my friend. Most of you need no introduction to him, since he was at one time a trustee of Hull-House. I will let him speak for himself.

John Dewey was only too happy to oblige. He had been scowling during the discussion of the Harper Report:[61]

I think you all know how much I admire Jane Addams, how we both hold education and democracy as core values.[62] "[My] faith in democracy as a guiding force in education took on both a sharper and deeper meaning because of Hull-House and Jane Addams."[63] Miss Addams's ability to make the

---

59   Ibid., 72.

60   Ibid., 113.

61   According to Andrew Feffer (118), Harper, who was autocratic and controlling, forced Dewey's departure from the University of Chicago in 1904.

62   Deegan, *Men of the Chicago School,* 252.

63   Glowacki and Hendry, *Images of America,* 34. This statement was actually written at a later date by Dewey's daughter.

complex plain, simple, and moral is quite astounding. I think her essay comparing George Pullman to King Lear is "one of the greatest things I have ever read both as to its form and its ethical philosophy."[64] But it is also fair to say that beyond our intellectual compatibility, we share a warm friendship, which is even more rewarding.

My work life at Columbia University is more tranquil than my time under President Harper was, but that doesn't begin to compensate for missing all my friends here at Hull-House. My concept of learning by doing is closely aligned with the Arts and Crafts movement that infuses Hull-House. For instance, when we started the Laboratory School at the University of Chicago the curriculum was designed to teach mathematics through carpentry, to teach botany by gardening.[65] Miss Addams has always made the point that the Chicago public schools allow the children too little opportunity for "hand work"[66] so that they can learn with their whole body and being. I hope the experiments initiated at the Laboratory School will not only be successful, but will also filter over to the public schools once it is proved they are not frills and fads.

By the way, I do want to take the opportunity to restate how deeply indebted we all were to Anita McCormick Blaine for her leadership and her resources in starting the school. The opportunity to actually operate an experimental school while our pedagogy department engaged in the teaching of teachers helped us develop a finely honed philosophy of education. We taught manual education practices not so that students could become drones in a factory, but to help achieve a psychological wholeness in mental and manual activity. The demise of the craft worker, who has for generations taken pride in versatile skills, is one of the great tragedies of the industrial age. Much of that work was continued under my friend and colleague, George Mead, after I left the university, thankfully.[67]

It is an unfortunate corollary that the teachers are as tightly regimented as are the students. Let me quote my dear friend

---

64   Feffer, *The Chicago Pragmatists,* 96.

65   Ibid., 118.

66   Addams, *Twenty Years,* 61.

67   Feffer, *The Chicago Pragmatists,* 132.

Jane Addams again on this topic. In 1905 she said: "The teachers inside the system were unfortunately so restricted that they had no space in which to move about freely and the more adventurous among them fairly panted for air. . . . The larger number of teachers in the Federation fretted individually and as an organization against the rigidity of administrative control, low salary rates from 'economy' boards, and their inability to say anything about curriculum."[68] This is another example of Miss Addams's ability to succinctly describe the core issues for classroom teachers. I have given lecture after lecture about the importance of democracy in the schoolhouse, but rarely have I managed to say it as simply and elegantly as she does.

Those of you who know me from my time in Chicago know I can go on at length. You have too much work to do today to be burdened with one of my lectures on educational theory. I am greatly enjoying the opportunity to be an observer of this conversation and hope you will allow me to return to that role.

Ella Flagg Young warmly thanked her former teacher and moved briskly to the next topic:

Eleanor, I understand you are a student at the Chicago School of Civics and Philanthropy and that you have a specific interest in some broader issues in education that you want to bring to the group today.

Eleanor Clarke Slagle nodded and smiled eagerly:

Yes, Mrs. Young, actually there are two different issues I hope to raise here today. The first is my interest in the schools system's responsibility to children who have physical or mental handicaps. I have been working with Miss Lathrop to try to help resolve some of the problems of children who are in need of services from the new Juvenile Psychopathic Institute.[69] I had hoped to say that the schools need to create

---

68 Herrick, *Chicago Public Schools,* 110.

69 Schultz and Hast, *Women Building Chicago,* 82. The Juvenile Psychopathic Institute was the nation's first child guidance clinic. It was funded by Ethel Sturges Dummer, who will appear in the chapter on the courts.

more specialized learning opportunities for these children, some of whom are institutionalized. They are not so terribly ill or handicapped in many cases. Often they are institutionalized because there is no other place for them. The challenge for children with physical handicaps is that there is no classroom where the blind can learn with the sighted or the deaf with the hearing. As I listened to Dr. Dewey, I wondered if his method of teaching by doing could benefit them. I wonder.

The other point I hoped to make very briefly here was to make sure we acknowledge the many women who created educational institutions. With all due deference to Dr. Dewey and Colonel Parker, I am very aware of the women around me in this room who are creating institutions of learning from the ground up, but who do not receive the recognition they should receive. So I want to read some of their names and achievements into the record, so to speak, today. May I?

Ella Flagg Young and the rest of the group nodded vigorously:

Thank you. First of all, as a student at the Chicago School of Civics and Philanthropy[70] I would like to thank Edith Abbott and Sophonisba Breckinridge for their role in helping Graham Taylor establish that important training forum. I would also like to thank Hull-House for being the Chicago School's original home. As important as the Chicago School is to higher education, it is hardly the only institution founded or cofounded by women. I would like us to acknowledge Mary Blood and Ida M. Riley, who started Columbia College as a speech college for women in 1890.[71] May it live on into the next century!

Mary Harris Thompson established the Women's Medical College. A surprisingly large number of health-related schools, colleges, and universities were founded by women. Lucy Louisa Coues Flower founded the Illinois Training School for Nurses. Fannie Barrier Williams helped found the Provident Hospital Training School. In addition to those two schools, four more nursing schools were founded by women in Chicago.

---

70   The Chicago School of Civics and Philanthropy eventually became the School of Social Service Administration at the University of Chicago.

71   Grossman, Keating, and Reiff, *The Encyclopedia of Chicago,* 185.

Then there is the Chicago Kindergarten Training School, founded by Elizabeth Harrison and Alice Putnam.[72] Hannah Greenebaum Solomon and others reorganized the floundering Illinois Industrial School for Girls, expanded it, and renamed it the Park Ridge School for Girls.[73] Neva Leona Boyd has a plan to establish the Chicago Playground Training School, so I believe we will be seeing this list grow in the future. My observation of all the wonderful women a generation ahead of me is that they are so busy building they seldom took time to catalog and celebrate their achievements. I bring this list to you as a token of my great respect and admiration for the women who opened the doors of education to so many.

Ella Flagg Young heartily thanked Eleanor and introduced the next few topics:

Our time is drawing to a close, and we need to prepare some recommendations for Mr. Burnham and the men of the Commercial Club soon. I would like to make time for three more topics before turning to recommendations. We have two young mothers with us today, members of prominent families who imbibed civic duty at the breast and at the breakfast table. They bring us some thoughts on the long-standing debate between business and education leaders about the purposes of education. That will lead to a recap of the great debate over taxation and inadequate assessments. Then I would like to close the discussion with some of my own theories about how education can be integrated more fully into the community and into democratic society.

Let me introduce Anna Wilmarth Thompson first. Anna's mother, Mary, was literally one of the first people to help Jane Addams and Ellen Gates Starr bring their vision of a settlement house to reality. Anna's collaborator is Frances Crane Lillie, daughter of Mary Crane, for whom the Hull-House day nursery is named. As young mothers, they have a very personal interest in education, in addition to their civic and intellectual interest. Ladies, please take the floor.

---

72   The Chicago Kindergarten Training School evolved over the years into National-Lewis University.

73   Schultz and Hast, *Women Building Chicago*, 824.

Anna Wilmarth Thompson spoke first:

I have heard Miss Addams almost in despair about the
unceasing battles at the Board of Education meetings. She
takes a very evenhanded approach. Even though her heart is
with the labor unions she holds both the unions and business
responsible for the high degree of partisanship, which is so
detrimental to the schools. Recently she wrote, "Under the
regime of men representing the leading Commercial Club of
the city who honestly believed they were rescuing the schools
from a condition of chaos, I saw one beloved measure after
another withdrawn . . . the building of smaller schoolrooms
. . . the extension of the truant rooms so successfully
inaugurated, the multiplication of school playgrounds, and
many another cherished plan was thrown out or at least
indefinitely postponed."[74]

Miss Addams, as always, is very tactful, even charitable in
characterizing the business leaders on the Board of Education.
The gulf between titans of the Commercial Club and labor
unions is very wide, very deep. The school unions believed
immediate profit is the only motive for business involvement
in the schools.[75] I would say that businessmen have a
fundamental misunderstanding of the necessary preconditions
for education. While they are trying to impose the same "order"
on the schools that they would on an assembly line, they
fail to see the need for messy experimentation in a learning
environment. They fail to understand that children need to
move around their environment to learn, that they need to
handle and take apart their tools in order to learn how to use
them. In the same vein, teachers need to be actively engaged
in planning curriculum, establishing their own benchmarks
for performance, and in developing partnerships with parents.
I've heard much hand-wringing over the Chicago Teachers'
Federation's emphasis on their role as "laborers" rather than
as "professionals." Until we have the benefit of a board that
treats the teachers as professionals rather than as cogs in a
machine, we should not be surprised when teachers adopt an

---

74   Addams, *Twenty Years,* 194.
75   Shipps, *School Reform,* 17.

aggressively defensive strategy. They have precious few rights to defend, so it is not surprising that they are fierce in holding on to the few they enjoy.

Frances Crane Lillie picked up the train of thought without pause:

Most of you know that my father, Richard Crane, was one of the businessmen engaged in the debate over schools. We had many a heated discussion over the dinner table about his emphasis on manual training. He, Marshall Field, and John Crerar set up a private manual training high school because they were dissatisfied with the public schools' approach.[76] It is interesting to listen to Mr. Dewey, to hear about the Arts and Crafts approach, and to contrast both of those with the approach of my father and other businessmen. Where Mr. Dewey's version of education tries to engage the whole child in learning and producing, using a variety of skill sets, I think I hear the businessmen talking about training people for repetitive, single-skill tasks. Last year Superintendent Cooley, clearly seeing which way the wind is blowing said, "Instruction in the elementary grades of the city schools was hopelessly academic and unable to fit the mass of the children for the vocation upon which they were to enter."[77] "Hopelessly" does not seem like an appropriate adjective for "academic," especially in a school system that was called antiquated and mechanical in the national study Dr. Rice conducted. The City Club, which on many issues is somewhat more tolerant than the Commercial Club, has also taken a hard stance on vocational education, calling dissenters from its view "selfish."[78] Mrs. Young, I believe that concludes our section.

Ella Flagg Young began to introduce a new topic:

Anita, I was very impressed when I heard the tale that you and your mother demanded the assessor revise your taxes to reflect the actual value of your property. I think you earned

---

76   Herrick, *Chicago Public Schools,* 59.

77   Flanagan, *Gender,* 1039.

78   Ibid., 1040.

the right to offer the overview of the vexing situation with taxes, if you would like it.

Anita McCormick Blaine smiled slyly and nodded her agreement:

Yes, Mother and I made some mischief at the expense of the assessor, but the principle of fair taxation is no laughing matter. I accept the responsibility to outline the unfortunate state of affairs and the attempts of the Chicago Teachers' Federation to remedy it.

One problem we haven't talked about is the high rate of turnover of teachers. The primary reason teachers stay in the schools for an average of only seven years[79] is the low rates of pay teachers receive. Until recent years, teachers had no pension system either. That situation has been remedied, but it seems the teachers have to fight each year to maintain their pension system. The right to a secure old age is not a given for teachers.

The reason most often offered for low teacher salaries is as a lack of funds. During an 1899 campaign to increase teacher salaries, which had been stagnant for twenty years, a Chicago Teachers' Federation committee checked tax records and found some large companies, like Pullman, paid no taxes at all.[80] The Chicago Teachers' Federation made a decision to create a campaign for fair taxation, but to focus on the public utility companies, which were not in a position to move their companies out of state.[81] According to their stockholder reports, the utilities had untaxed franchises worth two hundred million dollars. The companies included Union Traction Company, City Railway Company, People's Gas, Light and Coke, Chicago Edison, and Chicago Telephone Company.[82] Former Governor Altgeld told Margaret Haley the battle for fair tax assessments could not be won. He spoke from his own failed experience.[83] Other men were less polite.

---

79   Herrick, *Chicago Public Schools,* 94.

80   Ibid., 101.

81   J. Smith, *Ella Flagg Young,* 120.

82   Herrick, *Chicago Public Schools,* 101.

83   J. Smith, *Ella Flagg Young,* 128.

Assessors, aldermen, and members of the Board of Education attacked the "impertinent, unladylike independence" shown by the federation in fighting for rightful taxes and raises.[84] When Margaret Haley and Catherine Goggin challenged tax assessments, the corporations retaliated with a bill attacking teacher pensions. The Chicago Teachers' Federation was told that "We men took care of you," until the teachers stepped out of their place to attack corporations. The women were told they should expect retaliation.[85]

Several years of frustrating bureaucratic battles followed. The teachers' federation presented its research to county tax assessors, but won no action. The argument was taken to the State Board of Equalization, which declined to act. Finally the Chicago Teachers' Federation took the case through the court system, where ultimately the Supreme Court ruled the assessment was so low it was fraudulent. The State Board of Equalization set a rate so high the utilities went back to court to say it violated the state uniformity clause since other industries weren't paying the rate. Finally the rate was reduced from two hundred million dollars to six hundred

As principal of Skinner School, Young learned to respect the community's interest in schools. (Chicago History Museum, DN0000585, Chicago Daily News *negatives collection.)*

84   Herrick, *Chicago Public Schools,* 102–103.

85   J. Smith, *Ella Flagg Young,* 130.

thousand.[86] What seemed like the final blow to the teachers
was the board's refusal to use the newly available funds for
teachers' raises, in spite of the Teachers' Federation's work to
secure funds the system was due.

But that was not the last insult they would have to endure.
Mayor Dunne replaced enough board members in 1906 to
gain a majority finally willing to vote to use the delinquent
tax dollars for teacher salary increases.[87] But within two
years, Mayor Dunne was out and Mayor Busse was in office.
His board rescinded the teachers' raises, then gave raises
to non-teaching employees and principals. This year, the
board president called Chicago Teachers' Federation leaders
"conspiring rebels."[88]

I can't think of too many other chronicles of mismanaged
public bodies and opportunities lost that compare with this
one. It seems clear to me that there was a virtual conspiracy to
cheat the children and teachers of Chicago. The name-calling
directed at the women simply because they documented the
abuses and presented the information to the proper authorities
rivals any bullying we have seen in the schoolyard. I am very
happy to end this sordid tale and turn the meeting back over
to you, Ella.

Ella Flagg Young prepared to offer a more hopeful end to the
meeting:

I want to thank Anita and everyone here for their thoughtful
and heartfelt contributions to the discussion today. The
situation we face is a very difficult one and I don't want us to
move toward recommendations from our worst fears. Let me
try to paint a different picture—one that respects student,
teacher, and community, so that our recommendations come
from our best impulses, not our worst.

I am very sympathetic to the teachers' desire for basic
wage and pension security. But none of us should overlook
the equally strong desire of the teachers for involvement in
educational policy and social change. This is where teachers

---

86   Herrick, *Chicago Public Schools,* 101.

87   J. Smith, *Ella Flagg Young,* 132.

88   Herrick, *Chicago Public Schools,* 111.

and businessmen least understand each other. While the businessmen focus on the cost of education, the teachers are focused on the promise of education. I think we have to democratize the administration of the schools to fulfill that promise.

The thesis I wrote under John Dewey was called *Isolation in the Schools*. It described the opportunity for democratic councils in schools, councils that included teachers and principals.[89] Teachers need more time with their peers to develop professional skills. To be the only adult in a classroom of children is a very isolating experience. Bad habits can become ingrained and new ideas may pass one by in the hustle and bustle of everyday class work. I did indeed institute teacher councils in my school on an experimental basis, and would like to see the idea expanded throughout the system. The idea of teacher councils is really just a way to organize a respectful and fortifying atmosphere for teachers. It is equally or more important to create that atmosphere for students too, if we want them to enjoy the comfort and confidence to learn to their highest potential. We must stop using competition and sarcasm as ways to humiliate children into learning.[90] Teachers need to create a milieu of cooperation within classrooms that crosses ability, class, and ethnic background if we are to survive as a democratic republic.

Last, but not least, we must give parents and the community the same respect we accord teachers and students. There has been a gradual movement in the past ten years or so to think of schools as community centers, particularly in those communities where there is no settlement house. Think of the many classes and programs Hull-House offers that could easily be offered in a school building: art classes, night school, debate societies, craft classes, college extension courses, the list is limitless. Among the great advantages of a school building as a community center is the fact that it already sits within a community, residents are familiar with it, and it is generally within walking distance of a great many potential students of all ages. My dear friend Mr. Dewey has been a

---

89   Feffer, *The Chicago Pragmatists,* 188–189.

90   Herrick, *Chicago Public Schools,* 118.

leader in forging connections between the settlement model
and the school model.[91] I think this is an avenue with great
promise for the future and look forward to helping it unfold.

Looking around the room, I see a softening in your
faces. I think we put our anger behind us and are ready
to devise some recommendations that come from our best
instincts. Let's see if we have consensus enough to move
directly to recommendations or whether we need to discuss
alternatives.

In very short order the group agreed that two issues stood
out as very significant and as regional in nature.

Recommendation One, Financial Resources:

The school system must be put on a sound financial footing.
Financial security for the system can be attained by ensuring
that all businesses and individuals pay fair and accurate
assessments. Existing law enables the system to derive
significantly more resources than it draws now. A board
of independent auditors should be established to review
assessments and leases and report to the public on the gap
between allowed resources and actual resources. The board
should also make recommendations about how to recoup
resources, including whether leases that were based on
erroneous appraisals can be broken.

Recommendation Two, Teacher Training and Assessment Tools:

The question of teacher training and assessment is a critical
but highly charged issue. All newly hired teachers should hold
a college degree, and financial incentives should be offered
to encourage existing teachers to take college courses. The
Chicago region should establish a nationally renowned teacher
institute at a local university to provide degree programs
and continuing education for city and suburban school
teachers, thereby ensuring a steady stream of highly qualified
professionals to schools in this region. Teachers should be
evaluated annually using assessment tools that have been
developed collaboratively by administrators and teachers.

---

91   Davis, *Spearheads,* 76–77.

13

Justice & the Courts

PLAYERS

First (middle, maiden) Name	Last Name	Brief Biographical Information	Approximate Age
Grace	Abbott	Led investigation of employment agencies and child labor, headed Immigrant Protective League.	30s
Mary	Bartelme	Lawyer; Cook County Public Guardian; first woman judge in Illinois, second in nation.	40s
Ethel Sturges	Dummer	Philanthropist, theorist, Juvenile Protective Association, founder of Juvenile Psychopathic Institute.	40s
Ellen Martin	Henrotin	Vigorous social and labor reformer, advocate of self-sufficiency for women, wife of the stock exchange president.	60s
Julia	Lathrop	Founder of first juvenile court in the nation, first head of the Federal Children's Bureau.	50s
Minnie	Low	Co-founder, Maxwell Street Settlement; worked with Hull-House, Jewish charities; probation officer.	40s
Hannah Greene-baum	Solomon	Chaired Jewish Women's Congress at World's Fair, helped found National Council of Jewish Women, active in Chicago Woman's Club.	50s
Ada Celeste	Sweet	U.S. pension agent in Chicago 1874–1885, journalist, founder and first president of Municipal Order League, municipal housekeeping proponent, insurance agent (Equitable).	50s

| Ida Bell | Wells-Barnett | Journalist, anti-lynching activist, worked with settlement leaders, co-founded Frederick Douglass Center. | 40s |

🖤 THE MEETING WAS CALLED TO ORDER by Julia Lathrop on an overcast day in 1909. The committee met in the Hull-House Coffee House, a frequent lunching spot for judges, probation officers, and other court personnel.[1] Hull-House was across the street from the new Juvenile Court Building, which was constructed in 1907. The majority of the women present were involved in juvenile justice. Mary Bartelme would go on to become the first woman judge in Illinois, and only the second in the nation, but not until 1913. Julia Lathrop began:

> I think you all know the purpose of our meeting today. Mr. Daniel Burnham, at the behest of the business leaders of Chicago, is developing a plan for our region's future. While his *Plan of Chicago* covers many physical aspects of the region in detail, there is a remarkable dearth of information on important topics like justice, education, and public health. I hope you all had the opportunity to skim Mr. Burnham's report so that you understand the context for this meeting. However, we will not be limited by his failure to address the important issues of justice for adults and children. We have a wealth of knowledge in this room from which to fashion recommendations that can only improve his plan. My only regret is that Lucy Flower, who was so instrumental in the formative days of the Cook County Juvenile Court is not with us today. Lucy was one of the first to recognize the causes of juvenile delinquency and take steps to completely overhaul the court system to better serve children. Unfortunately, because of her husband's chronic illness, Lucy moved to Colorado in 1902. I will be sure to write her to fill her in on our work. She will be pleased to hear that we are recommending long-term improvements to the system.
>
> We are fortunate in having only two focal areas. Some of the other groups had a wide range of topics to cover. We will look

---

1   Addams, *Lathrop,* 96.

Julia Lathrop. (Library of Congress, LC-USZ62-111462, George Grantham Bain Collection, Prints and Photographs Division.)

briefly at the role of the police in maintaining order and then we will look at the purpose and promise of the juvenile court. I believe that Ida Wells-Barnett, Grace Abbott, and Ada Celeste Sweet are prepared to speak on the issue of police.

Ida B. Wells-Barnett spoke first:

As most of you know, my energies have been directed primarily at the evil of lynching in this nation. I am not an expert in the problem of illegal police behavior. However, I am aware that there is a culture of violence against unpopular groups in this nation. When the police abuse people, or when the public senses that the police will not come to the aid of certain groups, the insecurity of the "outsider" groups is increased.

The local business community, in its concern for protecting property, has at times, exercised its power to distort the administration of justice. Their reaction to strikes has not been to improve work conditions, but to create garrisons. For instance Fort Sheridan and the Great Lakes Naval Training Station were both built with resources donated by businessmen, as insurance against striking workers.[2] In addition to guaranteeing that federal troops would be nearby, the business-led Citizens' Association raised over one hundred

---

2   Flanagan, *Charter*, 29.

thousand dollars a year for several years after the Haymarket affair, in order to stamp out what they saw as "anarchy."[3] When the police department relies on private business for a substantial amount of funding, the citizens are less likely to see justice dispensed impartially.

We have seen how the powerful even overrule elected officials when it comes to directing or protecting renegade police officers. Captain John Bonfield evaded mayoral directives in two very high-profile incidents. In 1885 Bonfield was charged with indiscriminately beating passersby, the elderly, ditch diggers at work, and shop owners on their way to work during a streetcar strike. The only "crime" these people had committed was to be in the vicinity of a labor demonstration. One thousand people signed a petition demanding Bonfield's removal. Despite Mayor Harrison's initial agreement to remove him, powerful forces intervened behind the scenes and he was promoted instead.[4]

In another incident, Mayor Harrison was known to have pronounced the Haymarket demonstration peaceful, and left the scene expecting order to prevail. Speculation still circulates that Bonfield operated under unofficial instructions when he ordered police to charge the crowd, directly contradicting the mayor's order. The group most often identified as countermanding the mayor is the Citizens' Association.[5]

It took a long while, and many more innocent citizens were injured by the actions of this man, but by the late 1880s Bonfield finally got his due. It was not the police department that restrained him however. The *Chicago Daily News* ran an exposé of the Des Plaines Street Station showing that Bonfield and other commanders were running bribery, extortion, and gambling rings and offering immunity for prostitution.[6] The same year, police records came to light proving that police testimony at the Haymarket trial had been perjured. In a second reprimand of Bonfield's tactics, Judge Tuley also ruled in 1889 that the anarchists at Haymarket had a right to free

---

3   Ibid., 31.

4   Ashbaugh, *Lucy Parsons,* 60–61.

5   Ibid., 77.

6   Ibid., 61–62.

speech.[7] The cascade of serious charges forced the renegade captain's dismissal from the police force.

Everyone in this room understands that Bonfield's misdeeds were not unique. However, they were so egregious that they attracted attention. Unfortunately, abuse continues to this day. The more downtrodden the community, the more likely it is to experience police abuse. I know this from the number of incidents in the Negro neighborhoods. I know that Grace has several more examples and will defer to her shortly, but first want to make the point that one antidote to official misconduct would be to have a police department that more accurately reflected the population of the city. In 1894 there were only twenty-three Negroes on the police force.[8] That was more than a four-fold increase in ten years, but it still dramatically under-represented the population. The census of 1890 found there were fifteen thousand Negroes in Chicago and we know the population has been growing dramatically.[9] We need more Negro police officers.

Grace, please feel free to bring your expertise to the group. I know you have faced similar problems in the immigrant communities.

Grace Abbott skillfully segued from Ida's last point to her own points:

Ida, your point about who serves on the police force is well taken, although it may not be the only reform needed. Certainly our experience here at Hull-House, where we hear of or become directly involved in protesting police abuses against immigrants, lends credence to your suggestion that a more representative police force might be better able to understand community members and forestall violent confrontations.

In recent years, the police have killed a number of innocent immigrants. In the Averbuch case, the chief of police killed a Russian Jew out of irrational fear that the young man intended to assassinate him. The chief let his own lack of familiarity with immigrants grow into a fear with fatal consequences.

---

7 Ibid., 164.

8 Reed, *All the World,* 15.

9 Knupfer, *African American Women's Clubs,* 30.

This was such an outrageous case that many prominent people contributed to a fund[10] to clear Averbuch's name. Harold Ickes, a good friend of Hull-House, made a powerful and successful case for Averbuch's innocent intent.

In an earlier case involving two Italians who were shot by a Polish policeman while sitting on a garbage box, Hull-House tried to enlist the aid of Clarence Darrow, who declined, since his practice was one of defense, not prosecution.[11] We turned to Mr. Ickes that time too. We have been very grateful for Mr. Ickes's very competent representation of the interests of these victims. Of course you may have noted the paradox in this case of the victims and the police officer all being of immigrant stock, although from different groups. More police officers from among the immigrant groups would be helpful, but it will not be a panacea. Immigrant police officers do not always understand the customs of other immigrant groups. In some cases immigrant officers may carry animosity toward other groups that is just as virulent as that of native-born officers.

The murders of immigrants are the cases that are covered prominently in the newspapers, but we hear on a regular basis of other rough treatment by police that exceeds the definition of reasonable force needed to restrain suspects. Or we hear of people who become suspects simply because of the way they look rather than because of any reasonable suspicion of their involvement in a crime. We may not be able to overrule human nature, but we must establish governmental systems that restrain illegal behavior, particularly on the part of government officials.

At this point, I would like to turn the report over to Ada Celeste Sweet who has taken an interest in and brought about improvement in the treatment of women by police.

Ada Celeste Sweet was obviously pleased to be asked to participate:

I want to thank you all for inviting me to this important meeting. As a businesswoman and newspaper columnist, I don't get out to Hull-House as often as I would like. I spend

10   Lissak, *Pluralism and Progressives,* 91–92.

11   Hamilton, *Alice Hamilton, M.D.,* 76–78.

too much time downtown. This is a perfect opportunity to get some background for future articles about your work and hopefully to contribute some useful information to your effort too.

I agree with Mrs. Wells-Barnett about the dangers of police who are beholden to private groups for resources to do their work. But I must "confess" that I organized a fundraising effort to equip and purchase the city's first police ambulance, back in 1890.[12] As with so many innovations, the authorities were skeptical about how effective such a vehicle would be. With tight resources every budget cycle, city departments tend to continue whatever they have been doing and to discount new ideas. I believe the ambulance proved its value; they have since purchased additional ambulances without asking me to raise the funds!

But that information was just a "disclaimer" about my role as a benefactor of the police department. I assure you I was given no right to countermand official orders and would not have exercised such a right had it been offered. Unfortunately, not all the members of the business committee hold to such scruples.

I believe the reason I was asked to join you today was to talk about some of the advocacy I have undertaken on behalf of another group that is too frequently abused by police—women. Women are vulnerable to abuse for a variety of reasons. Some may be immigrants; ethnic prejudice and gender prejudice may work together. Some of the women who come into contact with police are in the vice trades, often unwillingly trapped in a life they never intended. Their status as prostitutes leads some police to believe that sexual abuse is acceptable on the street and in the station.

My response, working in concert with other women from the Chicago Woman's Club, has been to campaign for matrons in prisons and police stations. It really isn't possible for male police officers to search women without creating the sensation of sexual abuse, even if the officer has no ill intention. The campaign for matrons was successful. Now the chief matron also sits on the Police Trial Board to hear cases where women

12   Schultz and Hast, *Women Building Chicago,* 863.

charge abuse by the police.[13] It is not a perfect system, but it is a significant improvement. We do need to continue to support and monitor the matrons. They must maintain a delicate balance to preserve the respect and collaboration of their fellow officers but still adequately watch over the rights of female suspects or inmates.

I thank you for letting me make these points and look forward to hearing the discussion of the juvenile court. I hold great admiration for the women present here today who created a model for the humane and effective treatment of children in distress.

Julia Lathrop helped the group make the transition to the next topic:

Thank you, Ada Celeste. I was not as familiar with your work as perhaps I should have been. I appreciated hearing of your success. I hope the implementation of the new policies will live up to your highest expectation. I also thank you for organizing the funds to purchase the first police ambulance. We are aware in the course of our work in the community of the lives that have been saved by rapid transport to medical care. We could, and perhaps should, write a book on the number of times women initiated and paid for civic improvements that were initially dismissed as unnecessary but quickly proved their value. Without thinking about it very hard, I can come up with several other examples: vacation schools, school nurses, baby tents to reduce infant mortality, and Chicago's first playground (which was initiated by Hull-House but partially paid for by businessman William Kent). With that said, let us move to the discussion of the juvenile court, the role women had in creating the court, and in funding its staff and facilities for almost a decade.

As context for our discussion of the juvenile court, I would like to remind you of one of the central tenets Lucy Flower held regarding institutional care of children. She saw institutions as stopgap measures, to be used only up to the point where children could be reunited with their families.[14] The debate continues even today about when children should be removed

---

13   Ibid., 864.
14   Ibid., 275.

from their families and for how long. As we all know, some decisions about removal of a child from his or her family are shaped by prejudice against the norms of immigrant groups. As Ida has reminded us, prejudice against Negro families can be even more harmful than the bias against immigrants.

Lucy was a strong advocate of the compulsory school attendance bill that was enacted in 1897, just two years before the juvenile court bill. She wisely saw school attendance as an alternative to delinquency. She went on to lead the drive for a juvenile court bill and helped form the Juvenile Court Committee, of which I was the first president and Jane Addams the second president. The Juvenile Court Committee raised money for probation officer salaries and arranged housing for children in detention.[15]

Even though Lucy is not present today, we will benefit from the representative array of the skills and interests that brought this great project to fruition. Think of it! We created the first juvenile court in the nation in 1899. By 1902 Milwaukee, New York City, Cleveland, and Baltimore followed suit. In 1903 nineteen more cities founded courts including St. Louis, Philadelphia, Minneapolis, Pittsburgh, San Francisco, and New Orleans.[16] Rarely in the history of institution-building has an innovation been adopted so swiftly and so universally.

I always believed our endeavor was successful for two reasons. First there was an evolution of the law regarding children in the late nineteenth century, a move away from the ownership rights of the father, toward the concept of the "best interest of a child."[17] Subsequent legislation to end child labor and require school attendance focused additional attention on optimal treatment of children. The best interest of the child was an important conceptual framework for reform, but required skillful and creative intervention to bring new institutional structures to fruition.

That's where you contributed. The second catalyst for the Juvenile Court of Cook County was the high level of skill, commitment, and diversity of knowledge you each brought to

---

15   Ibid., 275–276.

16   Getis, *The Juvenile Court,* 50.

17   Ibid., 23.

the issue. Ethel was our theoretical muse. Minnie was "in the trenches" so to speak, working directly with troubled children. Ellen had a wide range of interests in encouraging women and girls to be self-sufficient and avoid being victimized. Grace's work with immigrant populations helped us understand the special problems of children and families who were struggling to assimilate into the larger culture. And almost all of us brought some skill at legislative strategy to bear on the rapid adoption of this idea.

But I am getting ahead of myself. I would like to turn the discussion over to some of the others who were instrumental in the early days of the juvenile court. Ellen, would you start the review of how we brought the juvenile court to life?

Ellen Henrotin replied with enthusiasm:

I would be happy to start, Julia. I know you are far too modest to do your own leadership role justice, so I relish the opportunity to do that myself! The Chicago Woman's Club, through the efforts of Adelaide Groves, was aware of the conditions of children in prison during the mid-1880s. Adelaide tried to convince the superintendent of the Chicago House of Correction to physically separate incarcerated boys from men. That attempt failed, but she was allowed to begin a school for boys within the jail. She and her friends paid the teacher's salary and the teacher lived in Adelaide's home. The county did build a school building in 1896, but child inmates still lived with adults until 1899, when a boy's cell-house was built.[18]

Of course, these children had all been incarcerated under existing laws, which treated children as no different from adults in terms of their culpability for a crime, or their likelihood of being redirected and rehabilitated more easily than adults. Largely through the efforts of Julia, Lucy, Cook County Public Guardian Mary Bartelme, and Louise de Koven Bowen,[19] a larger group of us became aware of the need to keep children out of the jail in the first place through a more humane and appropriate court system.

---

18   Ibid., 32–33.

19   Schultz and Hast, *Women Building Chicago,* 101.

The first step was to build support for such an endeavor outside of our own circle of like-minded settlement houses and women's club networks. Julia, Ethel, and Lucy took a scientific approach, gathering data and expert testimony, visiting institutions in Illinois and elsewhere to get firsthand information.[20]

Now, Julia, you are the person in this room with the greatest firsthand experience in creating the juvenile court. I think you really must provide the details to follow my introduction.

Julia Lathrop smiled and assented:

You may remember that the Chicago Woman's Club had an early bill drafted in 1895 that would have established a separate court and probation system, but its constitutionality was questioned so we abandoned the project. "However, interest was only stimulated by defeat. The concern became more general. Judges and prison wardens and other officials, public-spirited physicians, lawyers and clergymen, settlements, the State Board of Charities, the State Federation of Clubs, the principal child-caring societies, the Bar Association, showed a common desire to help."[21]

The Annual State Conference of Charities meeting in 1898 was devoted to this topic. "From this Conference emerged the committee which drafted the Illinois Juvenile Court Act. . . . I think all who were associated in any way with the period during which the act was drafted would agree that though others gave much aid two great figures stand forth, Mrs. Lucy L. Flower and Judge Harvey B. Hurd. They worked together with perfect accord, yet in their respective fields . . . Judge Hurd was a jurist of distinction. His fairness and skill are illustrated by the ingenuity with which, in writing the bill, he was able to overcome the constitutional difficulty which earlier had appeared to others to be insuperable.

After the bill was drawn its passage through the legislature required authoritative support and here undoubtedly no other single influence aided so much as that of the Chicago Bar Association. . . . If there were dissensions at any point

---

20 Shipps, *School Reform,* 1.

21 Anniversary Papers, 293.

in securing passage of the bill, time has amiably obliterated them from my mind and I recall only an extraordinary degree of that cooperative work in a good cause, for which the men and women of Chicago have long been distinguished. . . . Inevitably I omitted much that is of interest. But I believe the foregoing brief outline suggests the modernizing influences which led to the making of the Juvenile Court."[22]

Ellen Henrotin asked leave to add a few points she felt Julia had explained too briefly or too modestly:

Julia neglected to mention that it was her shrewd guidance that led to our eventual success. She had cautioned: "This is a legal matter. It must not go to the Legislature as a woman's measure; we must get the Bar Association to handle it."[23] We worked hard to make sure this wasn't seen as just a "women's" issue or a maternal concern for children. It was good public policy and we presented it that way. The Chicago Woman's Club appointed myself and Julia Lathrop to watch over the progress of the bill in the legislature. The Woman's Club decided to defer action that year on another important legislative struggle, the fight for women's suffrage, to avoid any confusion of one issue with the other. It was that important to us, to pass the Juvenile Court bill.[24]

When the time for the vote came in 1899, it was overwhelmingly supportive. The Senate voted 32 to 1 for the law and the vote was unanimous in the House. True to form, the newspapers reported on the testimony of the men who supported the bill, but our work on behalf of the law was omitted from published reports. Our consolation was that the bill was effective within just a few months, on July 1, 1899.[25]

While the strong support for the bill made for a resounding success, key implementation steps were not addressed in the legislation. The primary problem was that while the court was established, there was no appropriation for services required

---

22   Ibid., 294–295.
23   Getis, *The Juvenile Court*, 28.
24   Ibid., 41.
25   Ibid., 41–42.

to support it. In fact, the Juvenile Court law specified that probations officers could receive "no compensation from the public treasury."[26]

Julia, would you like someone else to take up the discussion here?

Julia Lathrop nodded and smiled:

Yes, Ellen, thank you for bringing us to this point. I would like to call on some of the people involved in the formation of the Juvenile Court Committee, which was founded in 1898, even before the law was passed, to support the functions of a juvenile court. Minnie Low, a co-founder of the Maxwell Street Settlement can give us a good overview of its work. Miss Low, please take the floor.

Minnie Low gladly obliged:

I was fortunate to work with the Juvenile Court Committee from its early days under Lucy Flower, Julia Lathrop, Jane Addams, and Louise de Koven Bowen, all of whom held leadership positions on its board. Through the efforts of these women and others, one hundred thousand dollars was raised between 1898 and 1907 to support the juvenile court system.[27] Such a large sum was necessary because the enabling legislation for the juvenile court did not include any money for probation officers or facilities for children awaiting trial or detained after trial. The committee worked with other organizations to increase the number of probation officers. Hannah Solomon and I were instrumental in founding a charity called the Bureau of Personal Service (BPS), and I became the executive director. The BPS provided funds for three probation officers' salaries, with a focus on Jewish children.[28] Julia, I believe at this point it would be good to defer to others to discuss the special problems faced by other populations in providing probation services.

Julia Lathrop nodded and turned to Ida B. Wells-Barnett:

---

26 Knupfer, *African American Women's Clubs,* 72.

27 Schultz and Hast, *Women Building Chicago,* 276.

28 Ibid., 520.

Ida, I know you are somewhat familiar with the challenges the Negro community faces in the administration of juvenile justice in Cook County. Would you mind speaking of the special circumstances your community faces?

Ida B. Wells-Barnett replied:

Not at all, although I do want to remind you that I am relying on the firsthand reports of others, not on my own direct involvement. As a group, Negroes faced a complicated situation in dealing with the court. On the one hand, we had to tolerate inadequate, segregated facilities for our children. On the other hand, as a community we want to retain some control over traditions and practices in child care that may be lost if our children are absorbed into the larger system.[29] The most difficult problem thus far with the court has been the harsher treatment of Negro women than white. The court is often insensitive to the multiple challenges Negro mothers face and more likely to find Negro mothers "unfit," "neglectful," or "immoral."[30]

Elizabeth McDonald, the first female Negro probation officer, and a volunteer since there was initially no funding for her position, was dissatisfied with the inadequate services available to Negro children coming through the courts. She set up alternatives to compensate for that unequal treatment. In response, she established the Louise Juvenile Home, which eventually became the Louise Juvenile Industrial School.[31]

The first annual report of the Cook County Juvenile Court in 1900 said there were six probation officers paid by private sources and "one colored woman who devotes her entire time to the work, free of charge, and whose services are invaluable to the court as she takes charge of all colored children." Fortunately, by 1903 Elizabeth McDonald was receiving financial assistance from the Chicago Woman's Club and private donors.[32]

---

29   Knupfer, *African American Women's Clubs,* 14–15.

30   Ibid., 66.

31   Ibid., 66.

32   Knupfer, *African American Women's Clubs,* 71–72.

I know from that point on, the Juvenile Court Committee increased the number of paid probation officers, but am not familiar with the details. Perhaps one of you can do that topic more justice than can I.

Mary Bartelme spoke up:

I would be happy to. The Juvenile Court Committee increased the number of probation officers over time to the point where it was funding twenty-two probation officers by its final year. The committee met frequently with the probation officers, here at Hull-House. With no models to follow, the group had to "fall back on our own knowledge of human nature and on our best guess as to their duties," as Louise de Koven Bowen has said.[33] Paying salaries of probation officers took a substantial portion of the one hundred thousand dollar total we spent to support the juvenile court in its early days. But that was not the only expense we needed to shoulder. The law also specified that children could not be confined in jails or police stations, but gave no guidance or resources for where they would be confined. The Juvenile Court Committee acquired an old house on West Adams Street formerly used as a detention home by the Illinois Industrial Association. For seven years, with some help from the city and county, we maintained the house for the benefit of children awaiting trial or in need of protective supervision. Twenty-six to twenty-eight hundred children passed through it each year. The city gave eleven cents a day per child for food. The county gave medical care, transportation to courts, and some other essential services.[34] But all other expenses to maintain the house and care for the children were paid for by the Juvenile Court Committee.

The various women's clubs supported and took a great interest in the home, visited frequently, and monitored conditions closely.[35] In fact, our involvement was so great that two members of the Juvenile Court Committee always sat next to the judge to assist in determining what services were

---

33 Bowen, *Growing Up,* 104.
34 Ibid., 104–106.
35 Ibid., 107.

The "new" Juvenile Court building. (Chicago History Museum, DN-0005149, Chicago Daily News *negatives collection, Chicago Historical Society.)*

available.[36] The juvenile court from the beginning has been blessed with excellent judges, starting with Judge Tuthill and then Judge Mack, who not only made excellent decisions, but conducted a campaign to help the public understand why the juvenile court was important and necessary.[37]

Finally, it was clear that the juvenile court had outgrown its quarters in the regular court building. After a great deal of work on the part of Louise de Koven Bowen, the city eventually donated land on Ewing Street and the county gave $150,000 to build the Juvenile Court Building and Detention Home.[38] It was, in most respects, a relief to turn the responsibility over to the proper authorities. However, turning responsibility for the court to the county does not mean we are without a role. We must increase our efforts to ensure that political patronage does not begin to influence the administration of justice or the quality of care and treatment the children receive.

---

36   Ibid., 112.
37   Ibid., 113–114.
38   Ibid., 113.

Julia Lathrop assumed the floor briefly to transition to the next topic:

Mary, thank you for your summary and for your constant vigilance, on behalf of the children, as Public Guardian for Cook County. I would like to call on Hannah Solomon to outline the next phase of our work in support of the juvenile court. Hannah, would you be good enough to tell us about your work with the Juvenile Protective Association?

Hannah Solomon was happy to take part in the discussion:

Once the funding of the juvenile court became a matter of governmental responsibility, the Juvenile Court Committee disbanded. That was in 1907. Many of their able leaders joined forces with the Juvenile Protective Association, which was led by Judge Julian Mack, Miss Minnie Low, and myself.[39] Now that we had a more self-sustaining juvenile court, we focused energy on keeping children from entering it. We conducted and published studies of the causes of delinquency, usually in pamphlet format for wide circulation. We investigated public dance halls, theaters, liquor, prostitution, and street peddling, all of which were inducements to delinquent behavior.[40] Louise de Koven Bowen is also preparing a study of the effect of prejudice on the Negro population of the city, although that study will not be ready for a good while yet.[41]

Let me tell you a bit about what we learned about the lure of the streets. The energy and curiosity of young people will lead them to explore and engage in activities without much sense of discrimination. We know that children clamor for a part in Hull-House plays by Shakespeare, Moliere, or Schiller, even though it means weeks of rigorous practice. Even those who frequent the five-cent theaters enjoy the courtly manners and the comprehensive story of the play. But there are only a handful of opportunities to act in a play and hundreds of opportunities to attend the five-cent theaters. For youth

---

39   Schultz and Hast, *Women Building Chicago,* 101–103.

40   Ibid., 103.

41   Ibid., 102.

without access to other resources, the five-cent theaters are their only entertainment.[42]

Miss Addams has just published a book in which she ably demonstrates how the lack of productive activities leads to behavior the court must supervise. She says, "'Going to the show' for thousands of young people in every industrial city is the only possible road to the realms of mystery and romance; the theater is the only place where they can satisfy that craving for a conception of life higher than that which the actual world offers them. In a very real sense the drama and the drama alone performs for them the office of art . . . infinitely more real than the noisy streets and the crowded factories."[43] Miss Addams goes on to say, "Seldom, however, do we associate the theater with our plans for civic righteousness, although it has become so important a factor in city life." She quotes a study of 466 theaters on a winter Sunday evening; one-sixth of the city's population was estimated to have attended, and revenge was the theme in over half the shows.[44] Is it any wonder that the number of cases coming to the juvenile court increases over time?

The situation is even worse in some of the dance halls or the billiard halls. In those businesses, "the drinking, the late hours, the lack of decorum, are directly traceable to the commercial enterprise which ministers to pleasure in order to drag it into excess because excess is more profitable," Miss Addams wisely points out.[45] These businesses do even more harm than the five-cent theaters, because rather than wanting to move one ticketed group out and another in, they want to keep customers all evening long, to the point of drunken and reckless conduct.

Now that we have removed children from the inappropriate trials, detention, and sentencing in the adult courts, the next step is to try to keep children from seeing the inside of the court room in the first place. I would like to take a moment to commend Ellen, who has been active for more than two

---

42   Addams, *Spirit,* 86–89.
43   Ibid., 75.
44   Ibid., 83–84.
45   Ibid., 98.

decades through the Protective Agency for Women and Children. Their work has helped women and children who are victims of abuse or desertion, which can be precursors to delinquency in children. This is very important preventive work. Even more important, perhaps, was her work to raise the age of consent in Illinois from ten years to fourteen years, to reduce the legalized abuse of very young girls.[46]

Julia Lathrop moved to direct the conversation to a new topic:

We have so many achievements among us and I salute you all for past and future successes. I do want to give you a glimpse of some new and very exciting work Ethel Sturges Dummer has begun to investigate. I think it has a great deal of relevance for the future of the juvenile court and for our related efforts to keep children out of the courts altogether. Ethel, would you please tell us of your latest investigations and research?

Ethel Sturges Dummer was modest, but intense, about her work:

I know we do not all agree upon the value of psychiatric treatment for delinquent children, and I fully acknowledge it may not be appropriate or useful in all cases. I think we will be in a better position to judge what is most effective if we investigate all avenues fully. For that reason, and at Julia's suggestion, I have undertaken to fund research by the prominent psychiatrist, Dr. William Healy, to investigate the causes of delinquency.[47] I will surely keep you all informed and share any information he provides so that we may all have the benefit of his work.

In addition, I am beginning to visit institutions here in the United States and in Europe to systematically understand the latest and most effective methods of working with the most troubled of young people.[48] While we do not know the full extent of the problem, we do know that some children coming through the juvenile court struggle with more than simple

---

46   Schultz and Hast, *Women Building Chicago,* 376–377.

47   Ibid., 237.

48   Shipps, *School Reform,* 1.

delinquency. Some of them suffer serious mental maladies that require substantial intervention. The question of which children will benefit from mental health treatment and which will benefit from structured, supportive supervision is of great importance to the success of the court's work and credibility. Julia and I are establishing a Juvenile Psychopathic Institute, under the direction of Dr. Healy, to work intensively with the most seriously troubled children.[49] We will certainly keep you informed of developments in that area also.

I think it is very important for us to approach the question of rehabilitating young people with as many tools and techniques as possible. Julia has been a leader in creating new models of treatment, such as the class she pioneered at the Chicago School of Civics and Philanthropy for attendants of patients detained in asylums.[50] Identifying the reasons for extreme misbehavior of children will be fruitless until we are assured of adequately trained staff to care for and restore the health of detained children.

I have one more important announcement I would like to make on a matter related to our local efforts to better understand the role of mental health in delinquent behavior. Julia has just become a founding member of the National Committee for Mental Hygiene, a group which will advocate for better research for and treatment of persons suffering from irrational or delusional behavior. She is the only woman among the twelve founders.[51] I'm sure her continuing discourse with this esteemed group of professionals will help to maintain and inform our efforts at the forefront of juvenile care in the nation.

Julia Lathrop assumed the moderator's role one more time to bring the group to closure:

We have considered a good deal of information and personal experience today. I thank each of you for sharing your recollections and ideas. Now we need to fashion one or more recommendations in the area of justice to recommend

---

49   Addams, *Lathrop*, xv.

50   Wade, *Graham Taylor*, 170.

51   Addams, *Lathrop*, xvi.

for inclusion in the plan for our region's future. May I presume to direct us on one specific pathway? We have adequately discussed the hope and promise represented by the juvenile court. We did not dwell on, or often mention, the disappointments we experienced with other institutions that were sullied by politics. My own personal knowledge, from attempts to establish and support a civil service system[52] at the State Board of Charities, lead me to believe that political patronage is the greatest threat to the juvenile court system. Others have had similar experiences with the Illinois State Training School for Nurses, the county asylum, the county detention hospital, and the public schools. I hope whatever recommendation we make will take into account the need for a qualified, independent staff to carry out the juvenile court's promise.

Why don't we list our possible recommendations and then decide which are our highest priorities? Who would like to suggest the first?

The group needed little time for discussion. Julia Lathrop's suggestion was immediately adopted and expanded to the need for highly qualified, well-trained police officers and guards in the adult justice system. The recommendation they offered was:

In order to rehabilitate adult and juvenile offenders, and return them to productive lives, Cook County should establish high standards for police and court personnel. These personnel should be hired without regard to political patronage or political favoritism and be protected by civil service. Professional training courses should be offered to improve the skills of the police, court, and detention workers. Finally, to ensure that no person in detention is mishandled, there needs to be an independent board of review to investigate any charges of brutality or abuse. The independent board should be selected by the governor from nominations made by a committee of lawyers, judges, and social workers.

---

52   Ibid., 77–80.

If Jane Addams had written a letter summarizing the work of the eight committees, it might have been composed as follows:

Hull-House
335 South Halsted Street
Chicago, Illinois

May 1, 1909

Mr. Daniel Burnham
The Santa Fe Building
224 South Michigan Avenue
Chicago, Illinois

Dear Mr. Burnham:

The residents of Hull-House and other settlements, as well as the members of the Chicago Woman's Club, would like to take this opportunity to thank you for sharing with us your final draft of the Plan of Chicago. The Plan is an ambitious undertaking, a very impressive effort to describe many of the challenges we will face in the future.

As with any groundbreaking endeavor, discussion might be had not only about the conclusions drawn in the Plan, but also about the questions asked. If there is one way to characterize differences we have with the Plan, it is that we would have included additional elements. Specifically, we would have included more elements proposing improved government functions, public institutions, and human welfare. A physically appealing region without prudent and solvent governance is a feeble victory. It may be worse than a "victory" if it offers the misleading impression that all is well when important institutions are corrupt or crumbling.

The enclosed recommendations are offered within that spirit. We had extensive and lively discussions of each topic but attempt to offer a limited number of recommendations. We understand your deadline

for the final report is near and do not want to burden you with an
unwieldy number of potential additions.

It is our fervent hope that future planning efforts will
commence with earlier public discussion and with a broader range of
participants, so that you do not face so many potential additions at
a late stage in the planning process. While we made every attempt to
include a broad range of views and backgrounds in the people reviewing
the Plan, we know our efforts fall short of truly representing the
diversity of this region.

Thank you again for the opportunity to review your inaugural
plan for Chicago. We look forward to working with you in the future
for the betterment of our region.

With kind regards,

Jane Addams

RECOMMENDATIONS

PARKS
Recommendation One, Neighborhood Parks:
The Plan of Chicago should promote a park of two to five acres
for each square mile of the city that is primarily residential. This
park is to be modeled on the South Park Commission model with field
houses, similar to those designed by Mr. Burnham, offering a full
palette of recreational and cultural activities. Wherever possible, the
park and field house should be adjacent to the local grammar school and
library, in order to create a cultural complex. The staff of the park
and field house will be well-trained civil service employees competent
in numerous disciplines.

Recommendation Two, Municipal Taxation:
The Plan of Chicago must address the complicated issues of
taxation and municipal self-determination if it is to have any value to
future generations. The statewide incorporation act for municipalities
with more than two thousand in population is outdated and detrimental
to a city the size of Chicago. We urge the Commercial Club to work with
the Civic Federation and other groups to build a broad coalition to

secure municipal legislation for a twentieth-century region. We offer our own networks and organizing skills as resources in winning these reforms.

STREETS AND TRANSPORTATION

The Plan of Chicago, with respect to transportation and streets, should consider investments in order by size and expense, with the goals of nurturing neighborhoods and the central business district and providing transportation options that are inexpensive and accessible for users. The first priority should be to maintain or upgrade existing public infrastructure, including basic sanitation practices. The second priority should be for safe travel by means that have no cost to the user and little cost to the public treasury. This includes making all areas safe for bicycling and walking, or providing separate right of way for walkers and cyclists. For those who must travel some distance to work, school, recreation, health care, and other necessities of life, the public transportation system should be coordinated, especially with regard to fares. Where bicycling, walking, and transit are not feasible travel options, and in order to provide delivery vehicles access to businesses and homes, the judicious use of new thoroughfares is the option of last resort, given the high construction cost, impact on community cohesion and high cost to purchase private vehicles for use on public roads. The citizens of Chicago will see their taxes used much more efficiently and their lives enriched by completing the simplest and least expensive improvements first.

HEART OF CHICAGO

Recommendation One, Taxation:

Convene a new charter convention that is truly representative of the city as a whole to propose an adequate and fair system of taxation, and to give municipal government more authority and responsibility for municipal services. Include a strong civil service system to abolish patronage hiring. Publish the terms of all contracts, including the ownership of all businesses benefiting from each contract.

Recommendation Two, Business Culture:

Establish a business-labor-community consortium at the Armour Institute or another university to promote harmonious relations and to work out practical solutions to potential conflicts between business and other groups.

Recommendation Three, Arts:

Apply Charles Hutchinson's model of disseminating art throughout the city to other areas such as the performing arts and literature. Create a cultural commission to uncover or create opportunities for cross-fertilization between downtown arts institutions and neighborhood institutions.

LABOR AND IMMIGRANTS

The Chicago region should establish a first-of-its kind labor institute, governed by a board representing business, labor, settlement, and elected officials. It should be funded by a one-cent tax on every ten employees. The institute will promote public and private initiatives such as insurance for workers injured or killed on the job, vocational and technical education for workers, crèches for children whose parents must work, and public health nurses in workplaces to improve the health and longevity of workers.

HEALTH

In the areas of maternal and child health there are many low-cost, high-impact public health programs that would save the city and region many times the amount spent for hospital care. This includes reproductive health information and treatment. It also includes public health initiatives to reduce infant mortality by reducing childhood diseases and epidemics, which disproportionately impact infants. The baby tents are an example of high-quality, low-cost, neighborhood-based treatment. Schools and settlement houses in every neighborhood should offer public health programs to the community at large.

Industrial concerns should begin to provide on-site medical care, because the policy will pay dividends to the company in terms of worker retention and reduced absence, as well as being a humane principle.

Providing professional care in state, county, and city health agencies is absolutely imperative. All governmental health agencies should employ qualified professionals on a strict civil service basis.

HOUSING and COMMUNITY DEVELOPMENT
Recommendation One, Neighborhood Form:

An ideal neighborhood would have at its core the services and institutions proposed in the Plan of Chicago for a suburban town center, as well as one or more nearby commercial streets to fulfill daily shopping requirements, such as grocers, butchers, stationers, and the like.

Recommendation Two, Neighborhood Housing:

The city should develop a progressive building code for new and existing construction, especially with regard to health considerations such as light, ventilation, and sanitation. City inspectors should be trained, professional, civil service employees.

Recommendation Three, Housing Research:

The city should use data being accumulated over time to assess the success of its housing program or to modify as the need arises and is documented.

EDUCATION
Recommendation One, Financial Resources:

The school system must be put on a sound financial footing. Financial security for the system can be attained by ensuring that all businesses and individuals pay fair and accurate assessments. Existing law enables the system to derive significantly more resources than it draws now. A board of independent auditors should be established to review assessments and leases and report to the public on the gap between allowed resources and actual resources. The board should also make recommendations about how to recoup resources, including whether leases that were based on erroneous appraisals can be broken.

Recommendation Two, Teacher Training and Assessment Tools:

The question of teacher training and assessment is a critical but highly charged issue. All newly hired teachers should have a college degree, and financial incentives should be offered to encourage existing teachers to take college courses. The Chicago region should establish a nationally renowned teacher institute at a local university to provide degree programs and continuing education for city and suburban school teachers, thereby ensuring a steady stream of highly qualified professionals to schools in this region. Teachers should be evaluated annually using assessment tools that have been developed collaboratively by administrators and teachers.

JUSTICE AND COURTS

In order to rehabilitate adult and juvenile offenders and
return them to productive lives, Cook County should establish high
standards for police and court personnel. These personnel should be
hired without regard to political patronage or political favoritism
and be protected by civil service. Professional training courses should
be offered to improve the skills of the police, court and detention
workers. Finally, to ensure that no person in detention is mishandled,
there needs to be an independent board of review to investigate any
charges of brutality or abuse. The independent board should be selected
by the governor from nominations made by a committee of lawyers,
judges, and social workers.

14

Can We Recover What We Lost?

JANE ADDAMS AND HER COLLEAGUES, FEMALE AND MALE, would have offered a broad, humanistic approach to planning, based on their formidable achievements in city-building. Even if we can't know each nuance of their opinion about the Burnham *Plan of Chicago*, we can plainly see that had they been asked, they would have enhanced and expanded on the limited physical aspects Burnham's plan included. Their abiding support of fair taxation, fair contracts, equitable services, limits on patronage abuses, and a commitment to justice in all aspects of life would have made this region, and perhaps the state, a very different place.

Before closing this story, we will take a very brief look at some specific examples of how our limited view of planning has hampered the region for the past one hundred years. But first, consider just the past thirty to forty years. In recent memory, most of the public assets the city-building women cared deeply about have been so badly administered that court action or some other kind of federal intervention was required. The federal Gautreaux court decree was necessary in the 1970s to overturn systematic racial segregation on the part of the Chicago Housing Authority, the agency that should have protected poor and minority Chicagoans from housing abuses. In the 1980s, the Chicago Public Schools signed a "consent decree" in a racial segregation suit brought by the U.S. Department of Justice, which allowed them to avoid a verdict in return for compensatory actions on behalf of minority students. Another series of 1980 court cases, including one by the U.S. Department of Justice, accused the Chicago Park District of providing inferior or no facilities in minority communities. The agency agreed to spend $60 million for parks in minority communities over several years. Meanwhile, the Cook County Juvenile Court—the crowning glory of the women's institution-building efforts—has lumbered under federal oversight for decades, including charges of child abuse by patronage employees who are supposed to ensure the health and safety of the children.

Many of these abuses continue thirty years after attorney Michael Shakman sued the city and several other units of government to reverse years of wasteful, destructive patronage hiring that interferes with essential governmental services. Although most of these problems and abuses are specific to Chicago or Cook County, the collar counties bear a good deal of responsibility for the amassing of poor, minority, and immigrant residents in Cook County. Many outlying communities traditionally used zoning policies that prohibit a mix of uses or a mix of housing types and sizes, effectively excluding segments of the population.[1]

If we had honored the city-building women's work, if Burnham had developed a plan for everyone, a plan that addressed the systemic corruption already endemic in his time, would we have a region that worked for all its residents? This author believes it would have made a very big difference and that we need to work very hard now to recapture some of what we've lost. Let's peel back the layers and see how far we have come from the ideal.

TRANSPORTATION PLANNING AS ONE LENS

I spent a decade, roughly 1997–2007, mastering the arcane world of regional transportation planning, looking from the outside in. A new job at the Center for Neighborhood Technology (CNT) allowed me to expand my organizer skills from schools, parks, housing, and neighborhoods into a new and much more complex domain, transportation planning. Transportation mattered to me a great deal because it neatly tied economic development, environmental improvement, and equity into a tidy package. It was a quintessentially urban issue.

---

1   An interesting consequence of exclusionary housing policies is the growing number of older householders who would like to remain in their community in downsized housing. The prohibition of smaller units in many suburbs means that long-time residents have to start over in a new community or remain in a too-large house. This is a problem destined to grow larger as the population of seniors increases dramatically.

What I found as I dug into the culture and customs of regional transportation planning was a system run by and for bureaucrats, with little regard for the taxpayers. In fact, the regional engineers and planners steadfastly refused to even refer to "the taxpayers," preferring the amorphous "the public" if they spoke of stakeholders at all. Taxpayers were people who had, or should have had, ownership of their investments and a right to say what they wanted. That wasn't the way it worked in northeastern Illinois.

Until organizations like CNT and Chicago Metropolis 2020 began to actively engage taxpayers on the question of transportation priorities, no one knew what "the public" really cared about. It turned out there was remarkable consensus for more transit and for safe, walkable communities. Creating civilized roads that could be traveled and traversed safely was a priority. "Safe Routes to Schools" and "Context Sensitive Design" were ideas offered to reduce the excesses of the bigger, faster projects that seemed to make neighborhoods unsafe and unlivable.

How did we get to the point where transportation planning was so out of sync with the public? If transportation planning was out of sync with the public, how did it come to dominate all other forms of planning, to the detriment of our region? How can we recapture the promise and potential of planning and harness it for our communities? Or can we?

"MAKE NO LITTLE PLANS . . ."
AND COMPETE OVER THOSE WE MAKE

Why does this mantra captivate us so? Why not make small plans when they will effectively do the job? Has anyone questioned that statement in the one hundred years since Burnham is purported to have made grandiosity a goal in itself? Even if corruption, patronage, and mismanagement were not ever present, isn't there a good chance that as a region we could have achieved greater good with judiciously targeted small investments, where and when appropriate? Has anyone stopped to consider whether the taxpayers want to pay for grandiose plans and projects that are excessive? Recent experience suggests that over-the-top plans for highways, airports, and world's fairs have proven very controversial in this region.

There is no doubt that part of Chicago's success is due to its physical assets, especially its transportation assets. This is not a suggestion that we build nothing. It is a plea for planners, voters, and elected officials to consider whether every problem requires expensive "hardware" as a solution. For example, in today's planning parlance, the "jobs-housing" imbalance is an important issue to be resolved. Among the "solutions" offered is the building of new highways, probably the most expensive potential expenditure of public funds. New highways "allow" workers to spend more hours a day on the road, consuming more gas and consuming more family resources that would otherwise be used for housing, education, food, and medical care. Rather than having people travel for long periods and long distances every day, we should make a serious effort to locate new businesses where there is a lack of jobs, and create affordable housing where jobs are plentiful and workers are scarce. This plan might be considered "small" because it involves sprinkling a liberal number of businesses and residences where they are most needed, without creating the visibility of a single big construction project. Its impact might be greater than the new highway, though, if done properly.

In order to agree on a fair balance of jobs and housing, we need regional processes based on collaboration, rather than the current competitive atmosphere. Again, the collaboration the city-building women excelled at became a lost art in our region, under the legacy of the business-influenced Burnham plan. As the region has grown, municipalities competed for high-end housing and for taxable commercial development, but avoided a balanced approach to the workers who must travel in and out every day. Our region lacks the skills, policies, and institutions required for collaboration, negotiation, and network building—just those skills Jane Addams and her colleagues successfully applied to a range of thorny problems in human affairs.

As we've seen in this book, many of the city-building women's innovations could be considered "small" in terms of resources, but visionary and broad-reaching in terms of impact. In the present-day example given above, the potential impact of bringing people closer to jobs, and vice versa, would certainly enhance quality of life in ways that having a breadwinner spend two extra hours a day on the highway cannot. But what this region seems to know best, unfortunately, is how to build highways, rail lines, skyscrapers, airports, and water diversion facilities to the exclusion of other approaches. So that is what we do, regardless of the cost. If all you have is a hammer . . .

TURNING A BLIND EYE TO PROBLEMS

The region has had accomplishments of which it is justifiably proud. Public and private entities here excel at engineering feats— reversing the river or building skyscrapers, for example. The region has done a good job of preserving open space, for which the Burnham plan deservedly is given much credit. The Burnham plan shares responsibility for the configuration of some of the region's highways. It was agnostic toward the transit system, putting much more focus on highways and wide thoroughfares.

However, Burnham's approach to inequity was a far cry from that of Anita McCormick Blaine, who insisted on paying her fair share of taxes. The plan on which we based our future not only accepted inequity, it promoted the notion that general funds should be used for improvements to benefit business, but not to benefit taxpayers on their own residential streets. The *Plan* accepted that "civic leaders" would pillage public school funds. It turned a blind eye to the inefficiency and incompetence of patronage workers staffing health institutions because the businessmen needed the help of corrupt Chicago aldermen, men like John "Bathhouse" Coughlin, to force its plan on the city.

The *Plan of Chicago* avoided the double dilemma of how taxes were collected and how they were spent. Remarkably, it didn't address the need for a new charter for Chicago, which had the same autonomy as any other Illinois city of two thousand, but no more. A new city charter was one of the most important questions of the day. The question of how the city and region were governed and taxed were fundamental questions for the region's future. Failure to address tax inequities between counties continues to plague the region to this day. School funding is heavily reliant on property taxes, so children in Chicago and lower-income suburbs are likely to receive an inferior education. Chicago is heavily dependent on the regressive sales tax, which at 10.25 percent is the highest in the nation.

Not all of this should necessarily fall on Daniel Burnham's shoulders. Kristen Schaffer has shown that Burnham would have included some public health, education, and social features in his plan if he had been given a free hand. But the plan that we have to work with is devoid of those human factors. We can only assess the plan handed down to us, not the plan that might have been.

With the *Plan of Chicago* as the guiding spirit for the Chicago region, we turned our attention to anything that could be "built"[2] and turned our backs on the complicated human element, the relationships and networks that Jane Addams and her cohorts excelled at creating and nurturing. The business sponsors of the *Plan of Chicago* had reason to eliminate the human elements in planning. They were in a state of open hostility toward the laboring classes and existed in a world that believed diversity was in effect when businessmen came from a variety of clubs. They were unable and unwilling to reach beyond their class, gender, and ethnicity. But perhaps more importantly, the spoils system of patronage jobs, questionable contracts, undervalued leases of school property, and inequitable taxation—the exact problems the women found most vexatious—benefited the businessmen as much as they benefited corrupt politicians.

As we will see in this final chapter, what began as a narrow plan for parks, transportation, and downtown development was further constricted. Transportation planning was separated from what came to be called "land-use planning." Land-use planning agencies in the Chicago region have been woefully weak throughout history. At critical points in the last century, the Chicago region shifted regional planning authority to transportation agencies, and then more narrowly to highway agencies. By the late 1950s, a little-known and unchartered regional transportation agency was beginning to dominate the official land-use planning agency of the Chicago region (these agencies, with a summary of their purpose and origins, will be introduced shortly). Land-use planning is in the physical realm too, but responds to environmental and human welfare more than transportation planning. In many regions, comprehensive regional planning agencies are actively involved in housing, taxation, intergovernmental collaboration, and other areas well beyond strict land use. A variety of planning agency structures and powers is possible. Our region has evolved from Burnham's day until our own to be narrowly defined by major transportation projects more than by any other facet.

Theoretically, in order to reach a regional policy or apply a policy, a deliberative planning body would apply an appropriate mix

---

2   Even parks require a certain amount of construction and provide long-term maintenance jobs.

of tools, analyses, laws, and infrastructure to achieve a given end. But in the Chicago region, a series of weak land-use agencies were forced to respond to transportation projects rather than being in a position of sufficient strength to recommend how to fulfill land-use priorities. Planning efforts were solely within the arena Burnham established in the chapters of his plan: transportation vs. land use (parks, open space, the central business district).

In the decades-long struggle to put land use at the forefront of regional planning, human services such as education, labor relations, immigration, public health, and justice were weakly or intermittently addressed, dependent more on the interests of progressive staff than on institutional commitment. Housing was addressed by land-use agencies, but most often in terms of supply and location. When leadership of the land-use agencies approached controversial topics like racially restrictive covenants or fair housing, they had to do so very carefully because they lacked authority and had no incentives to offer.

The analysis of how and why the land-use agencies in this region were denied authority, and the implications of that restriction, are complicated matters. This final chapter does not pretend to be a comprehensive analysis. There are other unmet challenges in planning that other authors could detail; this is simply the best-known example to this author of the loss of our capacity to build and sustain institutions that make a critical difference to our quality of life.

BUSINESS AS USUAL

Early business leaders worked hard to promote their private plan as having official stature. They were fairly ruthless in pushing any opposing opinion out of the way. The first construction project developed under the *Plan of Chicago*, the widening of Twelfth Street, was an exercise in political intimidation, as will be explained in a few pages. Women were ignored or pushed out of the way, not only in city-building but also in planning and academic circles. Women remained outside the civic governing structure, even after full suffrage in Illinois.

Efforts to promote the *Plan of Chicago* began even before it was completed. Charles Norton[3] proposed a permanent committee to

---

3   Charles Norton and Franklin McVeagh, two of the people most responsible for

pursue implementation of the *Plan* in January 1908, saying, "The City Plan is a business proposition and it should be developed under the direction and control of businessmen."[4] However, their implementation strategy was totally dependent on public funding. They realized they needed to present the appearance of a public body. A Chicago Plan Commission of three hundred members was appointed by Mayor Fred Busse. The twenty-six-member executive committee was the actual power center of the Chicago Plan Commission, however. The executive committee was composed of members of the Commercial Club and aldermen like John Coughlin and John Powers, both of whom had been targets of reform elements in the city for years. Charles Wacker was appointed chairman of the commission.[5] The businessmen promoted the *Plan* as a general vision for the city when the Commercial Club presented the *Plan of Chicago* at a dinner in honor of the new commission on January 8, 1910.[6]

A ninety-three page popular summary of the *Plan of Chicago* preceded the better-known *Wacker Manual*. The summary's title was *Chicago's Greatest Issue: An Official Plan,*[7] a title that seems presumptuous in defining a plan as the "greatest" issue the city faced at the time. Jane Addams and her colleagues would likely have listed a host of other problems as the "greatest" issues of the time, including the state of the schools, courts, health institutions, worker protections, and housing.

The centerpiece of the Commercial Club's promotional campaign was the *Wacker Manual*. The *Wacker Manual* was distributed through the Chicago Public Schools, headed by Ella Flagg Young. Walter D. Moody (the manual's author) offers thanks to a number of men who presumably offered advice or assistance on the manual.[8] If Ella Flagg Young had a role in developing the manual that the club distributed through her schools, it is not recorded in the document. Moody reported to the Commercial Club in 1911 that

---

initiating the idea of a plan, moved to Washington during development of the plan, to serve as assistant secretary and secretary of the treasury.

4   McCarthy, "Chicago Businessmen," 247.

5   Ibid., 248.

6   Ibid., 249.

7   Smith, *Plan*, 122–123

8   Moody, *Wacker's Manual,* v.

one hundred sixty-five thousand copies of the *Wacker Manual* were being disseminated.

Meanwhile, the first project the city implemented from among those proposed in the *Plan of Chicago* was the widening of Twelfth Street. Charles Wacker was a leader in promoting the widening, saying Chicago would fall behind Cleveland and St. Louis without this improvement. Alderman John J. Brennan, who represented voters on the south side of the street, opposed it, saying his immigrant constituents were "not financially situated to pay for such an expensive improvement." Property owners along Twelfth Street organized in opposition to the widening. Alderman Johnny Powers, nemesis of the Hull-House leaders and many other reformers, represented the north side of Twelfth Street. When the project was constructed, all new right-of-way was taken from the south side of the street.[9] In spite of the lofty ideals portrayed in the *Plan*, the summary, and the *Wacker Manual*, the first message to the public about the reality of Burnham's *Plan of Chicago* was that opposition to any of its powerful proponents was dangerous.

At approximately the same time, the profession of planning was being severed from any connection to the settlement movement or to sociology. Although the 1909 National Conference on Planning was closely tied to settlements, subsequent national conferences turned exclusively to City Beautiful principles, choosing "form over function" in the words of historian Mary Corbin Sies.[10] She goes on to say, "Grandiose civic center plans were useless if the city was not planned so as [to make it comfortable and workable in other ways]." The settlements and sociologists never regained a place in the planning field. We are left to speculate on how the *Hull-House Maps and Papers* might have added value not only to Burnham's Plan but to the field of urban planning. The emphasis of the *Maps and Papers* on neighborhood composition, strengths, weaknesses, ethnic diversity, and economic status could only have been an asset in a broad, humanistic view of city planning.

Women secured the right to vote in Illinois in 1913, but in Chicago that didn't translate to inclusion. No woman would sit on the Chicago City Council until 1971.[11] The one woman who headed

---

9   McCarthy, "Chicago Businessmen," 249–253.

10   Sies and Silver, *Planning,* 74.

11   Anna Langford was the first woman alderman.

a city department following adoption of the *Plan*, the Commissioner of Public Welfare, was paid a salary half that of her male counterparts.[12] The absence of women likely had a direct affect on policy. Since the late 1920s, Chicago focused its budget priorities on "common functions"—buildings, highways, waste disposal, and police and fire departments. It ignored or deflected responsibility for public health, hospitals, and welfare, functions that came to be defined as "poor people's services."[13]

In spite of having an elegant plan, Chicago still lacked a governance structure to match its size and complexity, or that of the region.[14] The question of a new charter stalled and then faded. According to Maureen Flanagan, by the 1930s the new Chicago "machine" brokered a peace pact between the male Chicago unions and businessmen, a three-way relationship that became the *de facto* mode for governing. The triumvirate had no room for women. The school board remained in the hands of male business and labor leaders, and schools were operated to maximize their economic aims.[15] The fate of the school system was not very different from the other institutions the women had created or reformed three decades before.

In the 1920s, the Chicago Regional Planning Association, a quasi-official agency, began to offer research and population forecasts for a fifteen county area of Wisconsin, Illinois, and Indiana. The Chicago City Club made the original call to organize such an agency, proposing a broad scope, including many of the activities of concern to the settlement leaders, such as sanitation, housing, schools, and government. Once the organization was in operation, though, most of its actual work was restricted to physical planning for land uses, streets, parks, sewers, water, and utilities. The regional agency did contribute analyses of industries and guidance on zoning and local plan commissions, both of which were planning innovations at the time.[16]

---

12   Flanagan, *Hearts,* 183.

13   Ibid., p. 194

14   Charter reform was attempted one more time, in 1914, and failed again. It was 1970 before a state constitutional convention redefined municipal authority.

15   Flanagan, *Hearts,* 189.

16   DuCharme, *Fifty Years,* 4–5.

MID-CENTURY PLANNERS HEED BURNHAM

In the middle of the twentieth century, two regional planning entities were created under very different circumstances, yet they both borrowed heavily from the *Plan of Chicago*. For five decades, the Northeastern Illinois Planning Commission (NIPC) and the Chicago Area Transportation Study (CATS) made significant progress in promoting and implementing green space (NIPC) and highways (CATS). The two agencies were authorized, composed, and tasked very differently. Both were dominated by male staff and boards, although as women began to gain elective office around the region, the NIPC commissioners became slightly more representative (most NIPC commissioners were either elected officials or representatives of organizations like park or water management agencies). By 1982 NIPC had its first female board president.

The Northeastern Illinois Planning Commission was officially created by statute in the state of Illinois as the region's land-use planning agency. NIPC was established with a geographically balanced board, a majority of whom were elected officials. As a state-chartered agency, NIPC followed the Open Meetings Act and operated with a high degree of transparency. However, it had no power to bring about change, even through incentives.

NIPC used its advisory powers to influence and, where possible, guide development of parks and greenways. It advocated fair housing practices, transit-oriented development, brownfield redevelopment, and many other best practices related to physical planning. It had little effect on education, justice, immigrant and race relations, labor practices, and public health. Partly by its own inclination, but partly because Chicago mayors were not open to the "meddling" of regional planners, NIPC turned most of its attention over time to newly developing suburbs on the farthest fringes of the region. This had less impact on the city of Chicago, with all its resources, than on the Cook County suburbs, which first experienced growth when the interstates were built. Growth was followed by disinvestment as developers and households sought "greener" pastures in the collar counties with each successive extension of the highway system. Many of the suburbs in the first ring outside Chicago—especially those on the south and west portions of the region—experienced job loss, racial change, and disinvestment simultaneously but had no strategy or staff to respond to these developments.

Almost simultaneously with NIPC's birth, the City of Chicago, Cook County, and the Illinois Department of Public Works[17] created the Chicago Area Transportation Study (CATS). As the word "study" suggests, CATS was organized to be a temporary organization, but lived on until 2005.

CATS was not authorized by state statute, but was designated (on an interim basis) by Governor Dan Walker in 1974 as the official recipient of federal transportation funds,[18] giving it immense power over the region and its municipalities. CATS succeeded in promoting many of the highways proposed in the Burnham plan, particularly in its earliest years, but ran into significant public opposition with highway plans in more recent years. Controversial examples include the never-built Fox Valley Freeway, Crosstown Expressway, Lake County tollway extension (IL-53), and Prairie Parkway.

CATS was a department of the Illinois Department of Transportation [IDOT] for all of its life, limiting its ability to respond nimbly to regional needs and concerns. Its governing board was primarily transportation implementers, rather than elected officials. During the 1970s, NIPC and the City of Chicago proposed a restructured transportation-planning agency, one that would be governed by a more representative board and have more independence.[19] The state firmly quashed that proposal, although a committee established by Governor James Thompson recommended that NIPC and CATS share responsibility.[20] The effort to reorganize planning agencies did result in an interagency agreement between CATS, NIPC, IDOT, and the Regional Transportation Authority outlining which agency had responsibility for various regional functions. These functions were all within the domain of physical planning or transportation operations.

Until the 1990s, CATS operated with little public scrutiny. In 1991 the U.S. Congress overhauled federal transportation policy, requiring transportation agencies that receive federal funds to so-

17   Plummer, *Chicago Area Transportation Study*, 6.

18   Governor's Committee, *Final Report*.

19   City of Chicago, *Transportation Planning*.

20   Governor's Committee, *Final Report*.

Those who approved the 2030 Regional Transportation Plan were primarily engineers. (Center for Neighborhood Technology.)

licit and consider public input, among other new mandates. This was a significant challenge for CATS. The 1991 law had a special provision, relevant only to Los Angeles and Chicago, encouraging the two regions to restructure their planning agencies because of serious deficits. Los Angeles restructured almost immediately; it was fourteen years before Chicago took similar steps.

In the meantime, CATS and NIPC collaborated or competed, depending on the issue. NIPC's greatest successes came in developing regional environmental plans such as the Greenways Plan, water supply and water quality plan, and the Biodiversity Recovery Plan. Land-use plans developed under the leadership of Executive Director Larry Christmas in the 1990s went beyond physical planning to address complex social issues. Due to NIPC's advisory nature and the resistance of local elected officials to any sharing of authority for local policies, the socially responsive plans were doomed.

CATS operated as a private planning process rather than a public one during most of this time. Until activists began to insist in the mid-1990s that the process of spending public funds be opened up, as required by federal law,[21] billions of dollars of investment were allocated in a closed room. Policy-makers and elected officials were notably absent from the deliberations. It was mid- and upper-level bureaucrats who divided the region's transportation "pie." All decision-makers were dependent in one form or another on the Illinois Department of Transportation. All CATS staff were IDOT employees, giving IDOT a monopoly on all policy, procedure, and practice in the region.

---

21   The Center for Neighborhood Technology took the lead in demanding public accountability in the 1990s.

A DISSATISFIED REGION

By the turn of the twenty-first century, civic and business leaders alike were expressing much dissatisfaction with the state of planning in the region. The dissatisfaction was broader than that of the 1970s, which had been a "family fight," an internal dispute among planners. Land-use planning was suffering. Transportation planning led, rather than served, land-use planning, and transportation plans were developed by engineers and technicians, with little public involvement or consideration of public policy. Consider these implications: If a highway agency leads planning, the only solutions possible are transportation solutions. A problem the community expresses as a lack of local jobs is answered not with an effort to create local jobs, but with a roadway to reach jobs elsewhere. The land-use impacts of the new road may or may not be addressed by the land-use agency, but their land-use recommendations will be determined by the highway type installed (strip malls along a multi-lane road, gas stations and chain restaurants at interstate interchanges, or "main street" type development along modestly sized roads). No planning function existed in the Chicago region to effectively respond to the quality-of-life concerns originally expressed. No entity was equipped or empowered to work with the community to determine whether the most effective response to the original concern about jobs was best met by a highway, by vocational training to enhance local job skills, by incentives for business to locate nearby, or by a housing program to help people relocate near jobs. In other words, there has been no way to respond through regional planning to human concerns. Consequently, citizen groups organized in opposition to highway projects they felt were destroying their communities. Civic groups were concerned not only with the plans that were proposed, but with the problems left unsolved. The business community was equally concerned.

The Commercial Club was one of the organizations that stepped forward. The Commercial Club created an organization called Chicago Metropolis 2020 (CM 2020) to address the need for a new plan. The Center for Neighborhood Technology was already soliciting broad-based public sentiment on the region's transportation plan from a more grass-roots constituency.[22] Clear consensus arose from these disparate efforts that residents and the business leadership of the region were in favor of more emphasis on transit and walkable communities, with an approach that addressed equity and quality-of-life concerns rather than simple mobility.

To its credit, *The Chicago Plan for the Twenty-First Century* by Chicago Metropolis 2020 goes far beyond transportation, land use, and physical planning, tackling many of the complex problems the 1909 *Plan of Chicago* avoided. It addresses governance, taxation, segregation, poverty, housing, and economic development. Significantly, the plan begins with a chapter on "Public Education and Child Care." Jane and her compatriots would have found much in that plan to favor.

The official regional planning agencies, in response to these and other pressures to provide plans that were more meaningful to taxpayers, improved the appearance and readability of their plans (NIPC's publications were always much more readable than CATS's, which historically read like the technical reports they were). But their basic formulae were not significantly changed. CATS produced a plan in 2003[23] that acknowledged "common themes" raised by the public, including more and better integrated public transit,[24] better land-use and transportation integration, more bicycle and pedestrian options, better services for seniors and people with disabilities, improved freight management, safety with special reference to pedestrians, and improved traffic congestion management. But it didn't shift any of the sixty billion dollars the region was likely to spend over twenty years to achieve the public's goals. NIPC followed the transportation plan with a land-use plan[25] that did include some elements beyond the physical, such as affordable housing and diversity, but its recommendations were advisory. NIPC had neither the authority to enact a plan nor incentives for sound planning practices.

---

22   Metzger, *Changing Direction*.

23   Chicago Area Transportation Study, *2030 Regional Transportation*.

24   CATS listed increased transit as its first theme for a reason. Transit was found to be a high priority in public involvement processes conducted by CATS, CNT, CM2020, and NIPC. Although CATS acknowledged strong support for transit, the funding allocations for highways and transit did not change in response.

25   Northeastern Illinois Planning Commission, 2040 Regional Framework Plan.

My community organizer role at CNT offered the opportunity to refute the experts' contention that transportation planning was too important and too technical to be shared with the public in any significant way. Federal law was now on the side of open, collaborative planning. It was harder and harder for bureaucrats to justify excluding the public. My job was to translate the deliberately obscured choices into user-friendly, actionable choices for the taxpayers and encourage them to believe in their right and ability to make good choices. As an organizer, there was much more to do: build coalitions, bring diverse people to the same table, and provide meaningful information in digestible chunks. But the essence of the work was to respectfully ask people to provide their genuine expertise on the quality-of-life questions the transportation system could and should address: how to access a job or health care, whether the transportation system supported or prevented physically active travel, whether children could travel safely in their own neighborhoods.

CNT methodically documented the results of meetings with over five hundred people in 2001 and 2002, meetings that showed that the official planning process—the "make no little plans" approach—was seriously out of sync with the taxpayers. Three hundred people came together to launch CNT's report of its eighteen-month public engagement process, *Changing Direction: Transportation Choices for 2030*. Almost simultaneously, Metropolis 2020's *Plan for the Twenty-First Century* was released. Both called for restructuring the regional planning agencies as well as focusing more on the region's quality-of-life challenges such as safety, environmental improvement, community economic development, and transportation choices. Other civic organizations joined in calling for a restructured planning agency, and by 2005, the agency now known as the Chicago Metropolitan Agency for Planning (CMAP) absorbed CATS and NIPC staff under a new state law. However, CMAP is only a partial restructuring. The Metropolitan Planning Organization (MPO), the entity with the power to grant or withhold federal transportation funds, is not wholly integrated into CMAP. Transportation bureaucrats still maintain authority over billions of regional dollars, in spite of the new "comprehensive" agency. In a worst-case scenario, the MPO could take official action contrary to CMAP's preferred direction and policy. While the CMAP board is carefully balanced to reflect the population and geography of the region, the MPO continues to be composed primarily of transportation planners and bureaucrats with narrow expertise.

CMAP is now charged with developing an integrated plan for 2040 that brings together land use and transportation planning. CMAP indicates that there will be some attention given to education, public health, and culture, although really contentious issues like taxation, criminal justice, workplace safety, and racial and ethnic discrimination do not appear to be within its sights.

WE CAN DO BETTER

This book serves in part as a strong challenge to CMAP to deliver a better plan than we have had in the past—a plan for everyone, not just a plan to enrich businessmen. This author is one of those skeptical that CMAP can deliver a truly comprehensive plan. CMAP does enjoy some assets, including a bright and committed young staff. However, the people who set the direction of the agency—the executive director and four of the five deputies (exclusive of the deputy for Finance and Administration)—are all men from CATS or the Illinois Department of Transportation. One needn't question their willingness to step outside the transportation domain. Even if they are willing, the capacity and knowledge to go beyond transportation planning doesn't exist at the leadership levels of the agency.

Many people predicted that a merger of CATS and NIPC would result in the demise of the functions NIPC performed for the region. Their fears have come true. Although NIPC never had the budget or influence CATS had, its work particularly in the area of environment and open space was highly regarded. While many of the new, junior staff of CMAP are qualified planners performing analyses of land-use questions, their lack of experience and seniority renders them unable to challenge senior managers, the transportation planners.

The Burnham model suggests that we should continue building bigger projects so more people can experience longer commutes to a greater number of places, at significant cost to the environment and to family cohesion. Federal transportation law does not require this approach. In fact, since 1991, federal transportation law has encouraged a flexible use of funds, acknowledging that quality-of-life considerations take priority for many voters and taxpayers now. In response to the clear mandate from the public for walkable communities and traffic safety, the Chicago region could significantly increase its expenditures on human-scale transportation like walking and bicycling and still barely dent the budget for big projects.

We could do much better at finding ways to encourage and pay for healthful, human-scale transportation, and still have a great deal of money left over for more carefully selected large projects, particularly the transit projects people throughout the region are requesting. We would have to check the impulse—deeply ingrained in this region—that bigger, wider, and faster is always better.

In recent times, the region generally spent *one half of one percent* of its transportation funds on pedestrians and bicyclists.[26] Additional constraints tend to discourage policy-makers from choosing small, inexpensive, and *effective* transportation investments. For instance, IDOT requires local communities to provide a 50 percent match of construction funds for bicycle and pedestrian projects, but local communities need only chip in 20 percent for road construction. Although road projects are a great deal more expensive than pedestrian and bicycle projects, they appear to be a better "deal" because municipalities leverage proportionally more dollars with roads. If Jane Addams et al. were calling the shots, would we be likely to see a system so stacked against small, practical transportation options that can be used for *free* while promoting physical activity and causing virtually no fatalities? And remember, we have been discussing only one facet of planning for most of this chapter, that of transportation. What if we had been making strategic investments in education, health, housing, and other areas for the past hundred years, judging the quality of the investment not on whether it is big or small, grandiose or modest, but on whether it was *effective*?

THE ROAD NOT TAKEN

In 1909 the city and the nation was at a crossroads that would determine the direction of planning for the next hundred years. We could have adopted the planning model proposed by Mary Simkhovitch and the other New York City settlement women who promoted

---

26   Metzger, *Changing Direction,* 4.

the idea of a first national planning conference to deal with housing "congestion." We could have followed the lead of local settlement house leaders who wrote articles promoting city planning as a way to resolve some of the threats to health, safety, and good citizenship with which they struggled. But in both the city and the nation, leaders of the planning movement chose to narrow the focus to the visual and physical manifestations of a city. They chose the City Beautiful movement over the City Livable movement. Documents like the *Hull-House Maps and Papers*, the New Yorkers' research on housing congestion, and the many articles on urban issues in journals like *Charities and Commons* were disregarded in favor of architectural and engineering models of planning.

It is especially ironic that Chicago became one of the most extreme examples of planning without people. The region followed Burnham's plan in putting its greatest energy into transportation and green space (the latter took a sliver of total investment compared to the transportation projects). Urban institutions that served people and that also play a role in strengthening regions—schools, public health programs, courts, and justice systems—were poorly funded and in many cases drew national attention for the incompetence or corruption of their leadership.

It will be difficult to recoup what we lost when we discarded the model of the collaborative, honest, and civic-minded network of women of all classes and races. How will we learn to do a better job of educating the young, rehabilitating the wayward, shielding immigrants from industrial injuries, reducing infant mortality or reforming the tax system if we don't honor their example? Is it possible for our regional agency to quickly learn and lead us in planning for people? Can we overcome one hundred years of neglect, even if CMAP's leadership gives a full effort to learning what we've lost? Do they want to give that full effort?

What would Jane or Julia or Ellen, or any of the other women who worked so hard one hundred years ago to improve the lives of the region's residents say if they saw what was left of their work today? Juveniles in Cook County suffer under a court system that is a mockery of the fine institution Julia Lathrop, Lucy Flower, and other women created. What would Ella Flagg Young have said twenty-some years ago when U.S. Secretary of Education William Bennett called Chicago's public schools the worst in the nation? Infant mortality is still higher in this region than in most; how deeply

The original Hull-House building was the only part of the complex to survive construction of the University of Illinois-Chicago. (University of Illinois at Chicago Library, JAMC_0000_0123_0922, Special Collections and University Archives Dept.)

grieved would Alice Hamilton be to know we have made such little progress? Housing continues to be a vexatious problem, one that is being "solved" in the city by moving former Chicago Housing Authority residents into Cook County suburbs and to other cities like Gary, Indiana. What would Edith Abbott make of the disruption in the lives of former CHA residents?

Would they remind us that attention to some small plans paid large dividends, like the 18-percent reduction in infant mortality that the settlements and the visiting nurses accomplished with several neighborhood "baby tents," each of which cost $250 a summer? Would they wonder why we honor a plan crafted to benefit private interests at public expense and dishonor or destroy the contributions of those who paid for essential public services from their own pockets? Would they shudder to see that today's tax system is only marginally improved from a hundred years ago? Or to see that the patronage system lives on in spite of court decrees?

If we can't know what Jane Addams and her associates would say, we can at least honor her work, and that of the other city-building women. Each time we are asked to consider a new plan, policy, or project we can ask, *What would Jane say?*

Appendix A

Women Included as Participants in Meetings

MUCH OF THE BASIC BACK-GROUND INFORMATION about the women included in the speculative conversations came from *Women Building Chicago: 1790–1990* (Schultz, Hast, et. al.), although the content of the conversations came from many other sources.

First (middle, maiden) Name	Last Name	Brief Biographical Information	Approximate Age
Grace	Abbott	Led investigation of employment agencies and child labor, headed Immigrant Protective League.	30s
Edith	Abbott	Co-founder, Chicago School of Civics and Philanthropy; author of *Tenements in Chicago*.	30s
Bessie	Abramovitz (Later Hillman)	Arrived in United States in 1905 from Russia as a teen; attended night school at Hull-House; organized a walkout at coat factory in 1908, blacklisted; after 1909 organized Hart, Schaffner & Marx strike (1910).	late teens
Jane	Addams	Founder and head resident of Hull-House, leader of civic and progressive organizations.	40s
Mary	Bartelme	Lawyer; Cook County Public Guardian; first woman judge in Illinois, second in nation.	40s
Enella	Benedict	Hull-House resident, artist, link between Art Institute of Chicago and Hull-House, involved in Arts and Crafts Movement.	50s

Jesse Florence	Binford	Hull-House resident from 1902 to 1963, active in Juvenile Protective Association, investigated neighborhood conditions leading to court involvement of women and children.	30s
Anita McCormick	Blaine	Daughter of Cyrus McCormick, socialist, philanthropist with an interest in progressive education and housing.	40s
Margaret Day	Blake	Executive board of Immigrant Protective League, after 1909 was a University of Illinois trustee, co-founder of group that became the League of Women Voters, donor and trustee of the Art Institute of Chicago.	30s
Louise de Koven	Bowen	Probably the largest donor to Hull-House, inherited a fortune from pioneer grandfather who owned much of what became the central business district; involved in a wide range of civic reform efforts; early proponent of racial justice.	50s
Neva Leona	Boyd	Chicago Kindergarten Institute graduate; settlement volunteer; set model for park activities, starting in 1909 at Eckhart Park; established Chicago Training School for Playground Workers in 1911.	30s
Helen	Culver	Donated Hull-House building and land, subscriber to the *Plan*, real estate developer with progressive business and racial practices.	70s
Elizabeth Lindsay	Davis	African American clubwoman, author, journalist, co-founder of Phyllis Wheatley Club and Phyllis Wheatley Home.	50s
Cornelia Bernarda	De Bey	Physician (homeopathic), education reformer, on Board of Education during early 1900s.	40s
Ethel Sturges	Dummer	Philanthropist, theorist, Juvenile Protective Association, founder of Juvenile Psychopathic Institute.	40s
Fannie Hagen	Emanuel	Physician, supported Frederick Douglass Settlement, founded Emanuel Settlement .	30s

Harriet	Fulmer	Superintendent of Visiting Nurses' Association from 1898; placed nurses in factories, schools, and "baby tents" in neighborhoods.	30s
Rose Marie	Gyles	Hull-House resident, first gymnasium director at Hull-House (1893–1907), taught high school gym in Berwyn after 1907.	40s
Alice	Hamilton	Physician; epidemiologist, studied industrial disease; first woman on faculty of Harvard Medical School.	40s
Caroline	Hedger	Physician, published articles on public health in stockyard area and conditions leading to high TB rates and consequences for food production.	30s
Ellen Martin	Henrotin	Vigorous social and labor reformer, advocate of self-sufficiency for women, wife of the stock exchange president.	60s
Mary Wood	Hinman	Introduced dance at Hull-House, promoted folk dance as a new art.	30s
Florence	Kelley	Social scientist, first woman factory inspector in Illinois, head of National Consumers' League, headquartered in New York after 1899 but retained strong ties to Hull-House.	50's
Julia	Lathrop	Founder of first juvenile court in the nation, first head of the Federal Children's Bureau.	50s
Frances Crane	Lillie	Physician; socialist; Arts and Crafts approach to motherhood; young children in 1909; daughter of Mary Crane, for whom Hull-House Nursery was named.	40s
Minnie	Low	Co-founder, Maxwell Street Settlement; worked with Hull-House, Jewish charities; probation officer.	40s

Marion Lucy	Mahony (Griffin)	Second woman to graduate MIT architecture school, a "community planner," shared work space with Pond brothers, was primary designer for Frank Lloyd Wright.	30s
Annette E. Maxson	McCrea	Landscape architect of railroads and depots.	50s
Catherine Waugh	McCulloch	Friend of Jane Addams from Rockford Female Seminary; admitted to Illinois bar in 1886; represented women (Rockford); helped write 1905 law on rape and age of consent; Justice of Peace in Evanston, 1907–1913 to stay near children.	40s
Mary	McDowell	Taught Hull-House kindergarten, headed University of Chicago Settlement House, founding member of Women's Trade Union League.	50s
Ada	McKinley	Founder of South Side Settlement House,1918.	40s
Rosamond	Mirabella	From the Clark/Polk Italian neighborhood; attended Froebel Kindergarten College, graduated 1906; taught kindergarten in Bohemian neighborhood.	20s
Harriet	Monroe	Poet laureate of World's Columbian Exposition, briefly a resident at Hull-House, started *Poetry* magazine in 1912.	40s
Anna	Morgan	Drama and speech teacher, helped found (1890s) an arts club called the Little Room—members included the Pond Brothers, Howard Van Doren Shaw, Jane Addams, and Harriet Monroe.	50s
Elizabeth Chambers	Morgan	Immigrated to Chicago from England in 1869; worked to protect women and children from industrial abuses and to increase requirements for compulsory school attendance; investigated sweatshops, labor conditions in prison industries, abuse of prostitutes by legal system, and poor work conditions of teachers.	50s

Othelia Mork	Myhrman	Co-founder of Swedish National Association (1893) after a Swede was killed by police without provocation (police were found guilty); ran the Swedish Free Employment Bureau during and after the depression of 1893–94; supported bureau with ethnic festivals, cultural celebrations.	50s
Edith	de Nancrede	School of the Art Institute student, then Hull-House resident in 1898, led Boys' Club; directed Hull-House plays, including a play (1905) by Harriet Monroe.	30s
Agnes	Nestor	Organized female glove makers; joined Chicago Women's Trade Union League in 1904, elected to national WTUL board by 1906; third president of Chicago WTUL and first from working class; involved in suffrage and educational advocacy as routes to improve worker status.	20s
Mollie	Netcher	Chicago's "Merchant Princess," owner of the Boston Store—almost 4,000 employees, some benefits uncommon at the time, such as generous commission (small salary), lunchrooms, classrooms, tennis court on roof.	40s
Anna	Nicholes	Resident of Neighborhood Settlement House (Southwest Side) from 1899; social worker; president of Federation of Chicago Settlements, 1901.	40s
Georgia Bitzis	Pooley	First Greek woman in Chicago, persuaded Greek families to settle near Hull-House, founder of Greek civic groups and a Greek school.	60s
Alice Whiting	Putnam	One of first to espouse kindergartens, she was teacher or mentor to most early kindergarten teachers in Chicago; her school was at Hull-House from 1894–1902; regular participant in progressive education initiatives.	60s
Ina Law	Robertson	Founded Eleanor Clubs in 1898 as safe, respectable, and self-governing housing for working women; eventually housed six hundred women.	40s

Margaret Dreier	Robins	President, Women's Trade Union League, Executive Board of Chicago Federation of Labor from 1908.	40s
Madeleine Wallin	Sikes	Hull-House resident; municipal reform work; Civic Federation education committee; researcher, children's issues; co-wrote *Child Labor Legislation Handbook*; monitored Chicago City Council.	40s
May Wood	Simons	Socialist, publisher of "Woman and the Social Problem" (pamphlet), friend of Jane Addams and Mary McDowell, many socialist publications, resident of Evanston.	40s
Eleanor Clarke	Slagle	Chicago School of Civics and Philanthropy student with concern for the institutionalized; influenced by Julia Lathrop; Justice of Peace in Evanston, 1907–1913, to stay near children.	30s
Hannah Greenebaum	Solomon	Chaired Jewish Women's Congress at World's Fair, helped found National Council of Jewish Women, active in Chicago Woman's Club.	50s
Ellen Gates	Starr	Co-founder of Hull-House, teacher, arts supporter, labor activist.	50s
Ada Celeste	Sweet	U.S. pension agent in Chicago 1874–1885, journalist, founder and first president of Municipal Order League, municipal housekeeping proponent, insurance agent (Equitable).	50s
Marion	Talbot	Home economist, University of Chicago professor, sent students to settlements, sanitary scientist with a focus on public and home sanitation.	50s
Lee	Taylor	Daughter of Graham Taylor, grew up at Chicago Commons (founded 1894), assistant to her father through 1910s when she began research on her own.	20s
Anna Wilmarth	Thompson (later Ickes)	Young mother loosely connected to the activist women's circle, daughter of Mary Wilmarth.	30s

Harriet	Vittum	Political activist, head resident of Northwestern University Settlement House from 1904–1947, pasteurized milk for babies.	30s
Ida Bell	Wells-Barnett	Journalist, anti-lynching activist, worked with settlement leaders, co-founded Frederick Douglass Center.	40s
Fannie Barrier	Williams	Became major force in founding Provident Hospital and Training School, 1891; active in Frederick Douglass Center, Ida B. Wells Club, Phyllis Wheatley Club, and Phyllis Wheatley Home for Girls; co-founder of National Association of Colored Women.	50s
Mary	Wilmarth	One of earliest supporters of Hull-House, first president of Hull-House Board, involved in many civic and social justice causes, subscriber to the *Plan of Chicago*.	70s
Rachel Slobodinsky	Yarros	Physician; professor at College of Physicians and Surgeons of Chicago, Obstetrics; language facility helped her work with immigrants; moved to Hull-House in 1907 with husband Victor.	40s
Ella Flagg	Young	Highly respected educator who was named Superintendent of the Chicago Public Schools later in 1909.	60s

Bibliography

Abbott, Edith. *The Tenements of Chicago, 1908–1935*. Chicago, IL: University of Chicago Press, 1936.

Addams, Jane. *Democracy and Social Ethics*. New York: The Macmillan Company, 1902.

———. *My Friend, Julia Lathrop*. Urbana and Chicago: University of Illinois Press, 1935.

———. *The Spirit of Youth and the City Streets*. Urbana and Chicago: University of Illinois Press, 1972.

Addams, Jane. *Twenty Years at Hull-House*. Urbana and Chicago: University of Illinois Press, 1990.

American, Sadie. "The Movement for Small Playgrounds." *American Journal of Sociology* (September 1898): 159–170.

Annual Reports of the West Chicago Park Commissioners for the Years Ending 1890–1908.

Art Institute of Chicago. "Marion Lucy Mahoney Griffin – Timeline." Supplement to The Magic of America: Electronic Edition. http://www.artic.edu/magicofamerica.

Ashbaugh, Carol. *Lucy Parsons, American Revolutionary*. Chicago: Charles H. Kerr Publishing Company, 1976. (Published for the Illinois Labor History Society)

Avrich, Paul. *The Haymarket Tragedy*. Princeton, NJ: Princeton University Press, 1984.

Bachrach, Julia Sniderman. *The City in a Garden*. Placitas and Santa Fe, NM: The Center for American Places, 2001.

Bernstein, Fred A. "Rediscovering a Heroine of Chicago Architecture." *New York Times,* January 1, 2008.

Bowen, Louise de Koven. *Growing Up With a City*. New York: The Macmillan Company, 1926.

Breckinridge, S.P. *New Homes For Old*. New York and London: Harper & Brothers Publishers, 1921.

Burnham, Daniel H., and Edward H. Bennett. *Plan of Chicago*. Ed. Charles Moore. New York: Princeton Architectural Press, 1993.

Burroughs, Nannie. "Black Women and Reform." *The Crisis* (August 1915): 187.

Chicago Area Transportation Study. *2030 Regional Transportation Plan for Northeastern Illinois*. 2003.

"Chicago Vacation School" (pamphlet), Playground Committee of Chicago Women's Clubs.

The Child, the Clinic and the Court. Anniversary Papers. New York: The New Republic, 1925.

City of Chicago, Department of Planning and Development. *Transportation Planning in Northeastern Illinois: The Metropolitan Planning Organization and the Federal Regulations*. 1977.

Corwin, Margaret. "Mollie Netcher Newbury: The Merchant Princess." *Chicago History* (Spring 1977).

Costin, Lela B. *Two Sisters for Social Justice*. Urbana and Chicago: University of Illinois Press, 1983.

Cranz, Galen. *The Politics of Park Design: A History of Urban Parks in America*. Cambridge, MA: MIT Press, 1982.

Cronon,William. *Nature's Metropolis: Chicago and the Great West*. New York, London: W.W. Norton & Co., 1991.

Davis, Allen F. *American Heroine: The Life and Legend of Jane Addams*. Chicago, IL: Ivan R. Dee, 1973.

———. *Spearheads for Reform: the Social Settlements and the Progressive Movement: 1890–1914*. New York: Oxford University Press, 1967.

Deegan, Mary Jo. *Jane Addams and the Men of the Chicago School, 1892–1918*. New Brunswick, NJ: Transactions, Inc., 1988.

Dewey, John. *The School and Society*. Chicago and London: University of Chicago Press, 1899.

Diner, Steven. "Chicago Social Workers and Blacks in the Progressive Era." *The Crisis* (December 1970): 393–410.

Domer, Marilyn A., et al. *Walking With Women Through Chicago History*. Chicago: Self-published, 1981.

DuCharme, Robert et. al. *Fifty Years of Regional Planning by the North-eastern Illinois Planning Commission 1957–2007*. Chicago: Draft of book to be published, 2008.

Elshtain, Jane Bethke, ed. *The Jane Addams Reader*. New York, NY: Basic Books (Perseus Book Group), 2002.

Feffer, Andrew. *The Chicago Pragmatists and American Progressivism*. Ithaca and London: Cornell University Press, 1993.

Flanagan, Maureen A. *Charter Reform in Chicago*. Carbondale and Edwardsville: Southern Illinois University, 1987.

Flanagan, Maureen A. "Gender and Urban Political Reform: The City Club and the Woman's City Club of Chicago in the Progressive Era." *American Historical Review* (October 1990): 1032–1050.

———. *Seeing With Their Hearts: Chicago Women and Their Vision of the Good City, 1871–1933*. Princeton and Oxford: Princeton University Press, 2002.

Getis, Victoria. *The Juvenile Court and the Progressives*. Urbana and Chicago: University of Illinois Press, 2000.

Glowacki, Peggy, and Julia Hendry. *Images of America: Hull House*. Charleston, Chicago, Portsmouth, San Francisco: Arcadia Publishing, 2004.

Governor's Committee on the Metropolitan Planning Organization. *Final Report*. 1979.

Green, Paul M., and Melvin G. Holli, eds. *The Mayors: The Chicago Political Tradition*. Carbondale and Edwardsville: Southern Illinois University Press, 1995.

Griffin, Marion Mahoney. *The Magic of America: Electronic Edition*. Art Institute of Chicago: n.d.

Grossman, James R., Ann Durkin Keating, and Janice L. Reiff. *Encyclopedia of Chicago*. Chicago and London: University of Chicago Press, 2004.

Hamilton, M.D., Alice. *Exploring the Dangerous Trades: The Autobiography of Alice Hamilton, M.D.* Fairfax, VA: American Industrial Hygiene Association, 1995.

Harrison, Carter Henry, II. *Stormy Years*. Bobbs, 1935.

Harrison, Gilbert A. *A Timeless Affair: The Life of Anita McCormick Blaine*. Chicago and London: University of Chicago Press, 1979.

Hayden, Delores. *The Grand Domestic Revolution: A History of Feminist Designs for American Homes, Neighborhoods and Cities*. Cambridge, MA, and London: MIT Press, 1981.

Hedger, Caroline. "The Unhealthfulness of Packingtown." *World's Work* (May 1906): 7507–7510.

Herrick, Mary J. *The Chicago Public Schools: A Social and Political History*. Beverly Hills and London: Sage Publications, 1971.

Hines, Thomas S. *Burnham of Chicago: Architect and Planner*. Chicago and London: University of Chicago Press, 1979.

Hoyt, Homer. *One Hundred Years of Land Values in Chicago*. Chicago: University of Chicago, 1933. Reprinted by Beard Books, Washington, DC, 2000.

Jacobs, Jane. *The Death and Life of Great American Cities*. New York: Random House, 1961.

Karlen, Harvey M. *Chicago's Crabgrass Communities: The History of the Independent Suburbs and Their Post Offices that Became Part of Chicago*. Chicago, IL: Collectors' Club of Chicago, c. 1992.

Knupfer, Anne Meis. *Toward a Tenderer Humanity and a Nobler Womanhood: African American Women's Clubs in Turn-of-the-Century Chicago*. New York: New York University Press, 1996.

Lasch, Christopher. *The New Radicalism in America, 1889–1963*. New York, New York: Afred A. Knopf, 1965.

Leach, William. *Land of Desire: Merchants, Power and the Rise of a New American Culture*. New York, NY: Pantheon Books, 1993.

Lissak, Rivka Shpak. *Pluralism and Progressives: Hull House and the New Immigrants, 1890–1919*. Chicago: University of Chicago Press, 1989.

Longo, Nicholas V. *Why Community Matters*. Albany, NY: State University of New York Press, 2007.

Map of Chicago. Chicago: Playgrounds Association, 1907.

McArthur, Benjamin. "The Chicago Playground Movement: A Neglected Feature of Social Justice." *Social Service Review* (September, 1975): 376–395

McCarthy, Kathleen D. *Noblesse Oblige: Charity and Cultural Philanthropy in Chicago, 1849–1929*. Chicago and London: University of Chicago Press, 1982.

McCarthy, Michael P. "Chicago Businessmen and the Burnham Plan," *Social Service Review* (Autumn 1970): 228–256.

Metzger, Janice. *Changing Direction: Transportation Choices for 2030.* Chicago: Center for Neighborhood Technology, 2002.

————. *Planning Matters.* Chicago: Center for Neighborhood Technology, 2004.

Miller, Donald L. *City of the Century: The Epic of Chicago and the Making of America.* New York and London: Simon & Schuster, 1996.

Moody, Walter D. *Wacker's Manual of the Plan of Chicago.* Chicago: Calumet Publishing Company, 1916.

Northeastern Illinois Planning Commission. *2040 Regional Framework Plan.* 2005.

Obituary of Mollie Netcher Newbury, *Chicago Tribune,* December 14, 1954.

Payne, Elizabeth Anne. *Reform, Labor, and Feminism: Margaret Dreier Robins and the Women's Trade Union League.* Urbana and Chicago: University of Illinois Press, 1988.

Philpott, Thomas Lee. *The Slum and the Ghetto: Immigrants, Blacks and Reformers in Chicago, 1880–1930.* Belmont, CA: Wadsworth Publishing Company, 1991. Reprinted from Oxford University Press, 1978.

Plummer, Andrew V. "The Chicago Area Transportation Study: Creating the First Plan (1955–1962)." Unpublished manuscript (http://www.surveyarchive.org/chicago/cats_1954-62.pdf), n.d.

Pregliasco, Janice. "The Life and Work of Marian Mahoney Griffin." Supplement to The Magic of America: Electronic Edition. http://www.artic.edu/magicofamerica. Reprinted from *Museum Studies* (The Art Institute of Chicago) 21, no. 2 (1995): 164–181, 191–192.

Reed, Christopher Robert. *All the World is Here! The Black Presence at White City.* Bloomington and Indianapolis: Indiana University Press, 2000.

Report of the Chicago Relief and Aid Society of Disbursements to the Sufferers by the Chicago Fire. Cambridge, MA: Riverside Press, 1874.

Residents of Hull-House. *Hull-House Maps and Papers.* Urbana and Chicago: University of Illinois Press, 2007.

Roderick, Stella Virginia. *Nettie Fowler McCormick.* Rindge, NH: Richard R. Smith Publisher, Inc., 1956.

Sawislak, Karen. *Smoldering City.* Chicago and London: University of Chicago Press, 1995.

Sawyers, June Skinner. *Chicago Portraits*. Chicago: Loyola University Press, 1991.

Schaffer, Kristen J. *Daniel H. Burnham: Urban Ideals and the Plan of Chicago*. Dissertation to the Faculty of the Graduate School of Cornell University, 1993.

Schultz, Rima Lunin, Adele Hast, et. al. *Women Building Chicago: 1790–1990*. Bloomington and Indianapolis: Indiana University Press, 2001.

Shipps, Dorothy. *School Reform, Corporate Style: Chicago, 1880–2000*. Lawrence, Kansas: University Press of Kansas, 2006.

Sies, Mary Corbin, and Christopher Silver, eds. *Planning the Twentieth-Century American City*. Baltimore, MD: Johns Hopkins University Press, 1996.

Smith, Carl. *The Plan of Chicago: Daniel Burnham and the Remaking of the American City*. Chicago and London: University of Chicago Press, 2006.

———. *Urban Disorder and the Shape of Belief*. Chicago and London: University of Chicago Press, 1995.

Smith, Joan K. *Ella Flagg Young, Portrait of a Leader*. Ames, IA: Educational Studies Press, 1976.

Spain, Daphne. *How Women Saved the City*. Minneapolis and London: University of Minnesota Press, 2001.

Stead, William T. *If Christ Came to Chicago*. Chicago: Laird and Lee, 1984.

Steffens, Lincoln. *The Shame of the Cities*. New York, NY: Hill and Wang, 1904. Reprinted from an earlier version by McClure, Phillips & Co., n.d.

Sutherland, Douglas. *Fifty Years on the Civic Front*. Chicago: The Civic Federation, 1943.

Wade, Louise C. *Graham Taylor: Pioneer for Social Justice, 1851–1938*. Chicago and London: University of Chicago Press, 1964.

Williams, Ellen. *Harriet Monroe and the Poetry Renaissance: The First Ten Years of Poetry, 1912–1922*. Urbana Chicago London: University of Illinois Press, 1977.

Young, David M. *Chicago Transit: An Illustrated History*. DeKalb, IL: Northern Illinois University Press, 1998.

Zueblin, Charles. "Municipal Playgrounds in Chicago." *American Journal of Sociology* (September 1898): 145–158.

Index

A

Abbott, Edith, 26, 28, 91, 245, 251–252, 253–254, 344, 345
Abbott, Grace, 74, 99, 193, 199, 212–214, 297, 301–302, 345
Abramowitz, Bessie. *See* Hillman, Bessie
Addams, Jane, ix, 1, 8, 9, 11, 29, 33, 35, 41, 42, 45, 46n, 60, 71, 73, 77, 81, 82, 84, 86, 87, 88, 91, 94, 96, 97, 98, 111, 113 (photo), 117, 131, 139 (photo), 235, 267, 309, 314, 343, 345. *See also* municipal housekeeping concept; settlement house movement
  achievements, 15–16, 42, 87, 91–92, 261–262
  biographical details, 12–13, 33, 209
  confidantes and co-workers, 74–77
  Daniel Burnham, recorded interactions with, 22–23, 148–149
  Democracy and Social Ethics, 2–3
  If Men Were Seeking the Franchise, 3
  Newer Ideals of Peace, 12
  Settlement as a Factor in the Labor Movement, The, 215
  settlements, pragmatic approach to, 14–15, 29–30, 42, 54, 59, 61, 68, 83, 86, 90
  Spirit of Youth and the City Streets, The, 12
  Subjective Necessity of Settlements, The, 11
  Twenty Years at Hull-House, 12
Addams-Burnham recorded interactions
  use of lakefront, parklands, 22–23
  widening of Halsted Street, 22, 148–149
African-American community, 167–168, 254–255, 257, 263, 301, 305, 310–311, 313
Allerton, Samuel W., 159–160
Altgeld, John, 6, 16, 39, 40, 43, 181, 232–233, 236, 237, 292
annexation, geographic, 26–27
Armour, J. Ogden, 99
Armour, Philip, 32, 40, 100, 179–180
Art Institute of Chicago, 22, 32–33, 95, 134, 171, 190, 221
Arts and Crafts Movement, 43, 76, 78, 94, 150, 171, 286
Associated Charities, 125
Association House of Chicago, ix

B

baby hammocks, 240 (photo), 241
Baer, Geoffrey, viii
Ball, Charles, 226, 260, 263–264
Bancroft, Frederick, 129
Bartelme, Mary, 297, 311–312, 345

Beard, Charles, 96

Benedict, Enella, 171, 175, 181, 345

Bennett, Edward, 23, 112

Binford, Jesse Florence, 245, 246–247, 255, 346

Blaine, Anita McCormick, 45, 80, 82, 96, 125, 185–187, 238, 257–258, 267, 277–279, 286, 291–294, 329, 346

Blair, Henry A., 159–160

Blake, Margaret Day, 221, 223, 346

Board of Lady Managers, World's Columbian Exposition (1893 World's Columbian Exposition), 42, 80

Bonfield, John, 40, 300–301

Boston Store, 182, 183, 184, 184n, 185 (photo)

Bowen, Joseph, 143

Bowen, Louise de Koven, 45, 79, 80, 87, 96, 137, 140, 143–145, 171, 172–173, 173 (photo), 176, 178–179, 183, 230, 235, 306, 309, 311, 312, 313, 346

Boyd, Neva Leona, 111, 127–128, 132, 134, 346

Breckenridge, Sophonisba, 91, 257

Buckingham, Clarence, 119

Bureau of Personal Service (BPS), 309

Burnham, Daniel, v–vi, viii, x, 1, 5, 11, 14, 18, 20–23, 28, 29, 35, 41, 54, 59, 62, 102, 104, 128, 222. *See also* Chicago businessmen; City Beautiful movement; *Plan of Chicago*
city-planning priorities, viii, xi, xiv, 20–21, 140–141, 251
forest and lakefront, preservation of, xi, xiii, xv, xvi, 4, 22–23, 57, 104–108, 114–115, 119

Jane Addams, recorded interactions with, 22–23, 148–149
order, his approach to, xii, 1–2, 17–22, 25, 29–30, 54, 104–107, 114, 248
Plan of Chicago, v, xi
profile of, 17–18

Burnham, Margaret, 17–18

Burnham-Addams recorded interactions
use of lakefront, parklands, 22–23
widening of Halsted Street, 22, 148–149

business, labor, and civic organizations, 1850–1910, 45t

Busse, Fred, 50, 51, 103, 160, 177, 274, 277, 332

C

Center for Neighborhood Technology (CNT), 326–327, 337n, 338, 340

Changing Direction: Transportation Choices for 2030, 340

Charity Organization Society, 38, 44, 45, 69

Charter Reform in Chicago (Flanagan), 48

charter reform process. *See* Chicago, municipal charter of

Chesbrough, Ellis, 261

Chicago, municipal charter of
debate to reform, 16, 46–52, 177
and diversity, 48–50
legislative conventions for, 47, 156–157, 156n, 276–277, 321, 334n14
women activists and, 24, 47, 51, 156–157, 177

Chicago Area Transportation Study (CATS), 335–342

Chicago Arts and Crafts Society, 43

Chicago Bar Association, 307–308

Chicago Board of Education, 6, 15, 97, 125, 177, 181, 207, 271–272, 275–276

Chicago Building Trade Strike, 1900, 89

Chicago businessmen, vi, 4, 18, 21, 103–108. *See also* Chicago, municipal charter of; City Beautiful movement; labor confrontations; *Plan of Chicago*

  private-market opportunity *vs.* social reform, 3–4, 20–21, 24, 33–39, 56–57, 71, 101–104, 249–251, 271, 300

  threats to control of, 48–49, 55–56, 217–219, 299–300

  and underpayment of taxes, 5–6, 100, 124, 124n, 179–181, 207, 249–250, 271–273, 291–293

Chicago City Club, 97, 178, 334

Chicago Commons, 77, 94, 95, 97–99, 131, 227

Chicago Daily News, 98, 300–301

Chicago Federation of Labor, 39, 45, 49, 51, 89, 157, 216, 276–277

Chicago Federation of Settlements, 42

Chicago Fire, 1871, 2, 26, 28, 33, 34 (map), 35, 38, 44, 101

Chicago Housing Authority (CHA), 325, 344

Chicago Institute of Social Science. *See* School of Social Service Administration at the University of Chicago

Chicago Metropolis 2020 (CM2020), 327, 338–339

Chicago Metropolitan Agency for Planning (CMAP), 340–342

Chicago Plan Commission, xvi, 98, 332

Chicago Plan for the Twenty-First Century, The (Chicago Metropolis 2020), 339–340

Chicago Playground Association, 120–121

Chicago Public Schools, 15, 80, 119, 125–127, 268, 271, 276, 280, 286, 325, 332. *See also* public education

Chicago Regional Planning Association, 334–335

Chicago Relief and Aid Society, 35–37, 38, 44, 45, 49, 69

Chicago School of Civics and Philanthropy. *See* School of Social Service Administration at the University of Chicago

Chicago's Greatest Issue: An Official Plan, 332

Chicago's social ills, v, 2–3, 7, 17, 19, 23–24, 25–30, 42–43

Chicago Teachers' Federation, 207 278–279, 290, 292, 294

Chicago Tribune, 6, 38, 49, 100, 181, 218–219, 277

Chicago Woman's Club, 22, 38–39, 45, 51, 64, 81, 86, 125, 157, 239, 273, 275, 280, 306, 308, 310

Chicago Women's Club. *See* Chicago Woman's Club

child labor, 5, 7, 63, 201(photo), 203–205, 237

Child Labor Legislation Handbook, 245

children in prison, 306–310

Children's Hospital Society, 240

Citizen Arbitration Committee, Pullman Strike, 15, 89–90

Citizens' Association, 39, 40, 45, 46, 299–300

City as Home. *See* municipal housekeeping

City Beautiful movement, vi, 2, 12, 54, 57, 59, 60, 62, 93, 101, 113, 122, 166, 333, 343

city-building women. *See* women activists, city-planners

City Club of Chicago, 20, 45, 49, 96, 97, 263–264

City Hall, 80 (photo)

City Homes Commission, 27, 257–264

City Livable theory, 8–9, 23–24, 54–55, 57t, 166, 343

City Made Beautiful, The. See Modern Civic Art (Robinson)

City Social theory, 92–93

Civic Center, as replacement for Hull-House complex, xiv, xv, xvi, 148–149, 175

Civic Federation, 15, 20, 42–43, 45, 46, 49, 98, 124, 125, 147, 177, 180, 240, 280

civil service system, 61, 125, 191, 226, 232, 244, 321

Commercial Club, x, xiii, xvi, 2, 3, 4, 5, 12, 20, 22, 23, 29, 40–41, 45, 47, 65, 100, 101, 103, 104, 138, 332, 333, 338

Committee on Congestion of Population, 92–93

common functions *vs.* poor people's services, 334

Cook County Juvenile Court, v, 5, 31, 44, 307–310

cooperative housekeeping theory, 66–68, 83–84

corrupt assessors/inspectors, 5, 29, 100, 108, 178–182, 185–187, 207, 226, 240, 263, 323

Coughlin, John "Bathhouse," 103–104, 329, 332

Crane, Charles, 52, 95, 96

Crane, Mary, 95, 267

cultural role of downtown Chicago, 32–33, 187–192, 322. *See*

also Art Institute of Chicago; Arts and Crafts Movement

Culver, Helen, 4, 13, 24, 78, 81, 97, 171, 176, 180–181, 229, 346

D

Davis, Elizabeth Lindsay, 245, 249–250, 256–257, 346

De Bey, Cornelia, 99, 267, 273–274, 276–277, 346

Deegan, Mary Jo, 15, 16, 90

Delano, Frederic A., 103

Democracy and Social Ethics (Addams), 2–3

Deneen, Charles, 131, 232

Dewey, John, 96, 97, 178, 186, 198, 233, 267, 270, 281, 285–287

Dorcas Federal Labor Union, 65, 206

Dummer, Ethel Sturges, 96, 297, 315–316, 346

Dunne, Edward F., 178, 274, 277

E

Eckhart, Bernard, 132

Eleanor Clubs, 245

Elshtain, Jane Bethke, 12

Ely, Richard T., 20, 96, 102

Emanuel, Fannie Hagen, 137, 140, 148, 149, 164, 167–168, 346

eminent domain, xvi, 8, 132–133, 174, 281

Etling, Victor, 96

F

Field, Marshall, 24, 32, 37, 40, 41, 64, 100, 141, 159, 179–180

Field, Marshall, Jr., 179

field houses, 120–121, 123, 128, 131–135

First National Conference on Planning, 93

Fisher, Walter, 20, 94, 96, 174, 178, 182

Flanagan, Maureen A., 48, 55, 64, 334

Flower, Lucy, ix, 81, 199, 226, 229, 298, 304–305, 307, 309, 343

Foreman, Milton, 49, 50

Fort Sheridan, 40, 72, 217, 299

Forum, Henry G., 131

Fulmer, Harriet, 221, 222, 227–228, 231–236, 347

G

Gage, Lyman, 41

Gilded Age, 1870-1900, 33, 53, 59

Goggin, Catherine, 207

Golden, Carrie, 257

Goldman, Emma, 99

Great Lakes Naval Training Station, 40, 299

Griffin, Marion Lucy Mahony. *See* Mahony (Griffin), Marion Lucy

Groves, Adelaide, 306

Guerin, Jules, 54

Gyles, Rose Marie, 111, 116–117, 133, 347

H

Hagen, Fannie. *See* Emanuel, Fannie Hagen

Haley, Margaret, 207, 278–279, 292–293

Hall, Peter, 60

Hamilton, Alice, 13–14, 74, 76, 77–78, 221, 222–223, 225, 227, 232 (photo), 236–239, 344, 347

Harper, William Rainey and the Harper Committee, 281–283, 285n61

Harrison, Carter, 40, 43, 129

Harrison, Carter Henry II, 118, 147, 157–159, 180, 281, 300

Harrison, Elizabeth, 81

Hart, Harry, 89

Hart, Schaffner & Marx strike, 1910, 89, 193

Hast, Adele, 74

Hayden, Delores, 85

Hayden, Sophia, 42

Haymarket riot, 25, 39, 41, 43, 82, 300–310

Healy, Daniel, 226

"Heart of Chicago," 172–192

Hedger, Caroline, 221, 222, 223–224, 239–241, 347

Henderson, Charles, 96

Henrotin, Ellen Martin, 80, 86, 297, 347

Hillman, Bessie (Abramowitz), 81, 193, 199, 209–210, 211–212, 345

Hines, Thomas S., 17, 23, 28–29, 41

Hinman, Mary Wood, 111, 116, 127, 134, 347

Holbrook, Agnes Sinclair, 198, 255–256

Home Problems from a New Standpoint (Hunt), 146

Hooker, George, 93, 96, 97, 178

hospitals/health centers and nursing schools, list of, 228–230

housing, 7, 43, 55, 67, 80, 108, 245–266, 325, 326n, 331, 344

How Women Saved the City (Spain), 56, 122

Hoyt, Homer, 26

Hull, Charles, 13, 24, 72

Hull-House, 28, 29, 32, 36, 39, 56, 58, 62, 64, 65, 68, 69, 74, 81, 82, 86, 89, 91, 94, 95, 96, 108, 131, 313. *See also Hull-House Maps and Papers* (Residents of Hull-House); settlement house movement charter of, 13 and Immigrant Protective League, 45, 193, 199, 212–214, 221, 297

and Jane Clubs, 20, 65, 78, 83, 86–87, 198, 205

labor relations, 78, 81, 89–90, 196, 198n, 215

legislation involved with, 16, 199, 237

as living quarters, 59–60, 66, 79, 84–85, 97, 206

neighborhood, housing in, 24, 259 (photo)

and neighborhood development, 78, 85–86, 252

physical facility, vi, xv, 13, 22, 78, 344 (photo)

residents' achievements, 56, 75–77

visiting nurses' office, 235

Hull-House Maps and Papers (Residents of Hull-House), 41, 44, 65, 74, 90–91, 133, 194n, 196, 199–201, 215, 253, 254, 256–257, 333, 343

humanistic city-building. *See* settlement house movement

Hunt, Caroline, 146

Hunter, Robert, 27, 257

Hurd, Harvey B., 307

Hutchinson, Charles, 33, 95, 134, 190, 322

I

Ickes, Anna Wilmarth Thompson, 268, 289–291, 350

Ickes, Harold, 212, 302

Ida B. Wells Club, 42, 45, 221

If Christ Came to Chicago (Stead), 6, 20, 42, 46, 100, 179–181

If Men Were Seeking the Franchise (Addams), 3

Illinois Central Railroad, 101, 103n95

Illinois Department of Transportation (IDOT), viii, 336–338

Illinois Juvenile Court Act, 1899, 307–308

Illinois State Toll Highway Authority, viii

Illinois Training School for Nurses, 81, 226, 229–230, 288

Immigrant Protective League, 45, 193, 199, 212–214, 221, 297

immigrants, 17, 28, 35, 41–42, 193–220. *See also* Hull-House; settlement house movement

as cause of pollution, 55–56

effects of Chicago Fire on, 34–39

mapped by nationality, 252–254

and municipal charter reform, 48, 50

rights of, 7, 48, 108, 193–219, 306

role in cultural life, 85–86, 189–192

as worker pool, 195

Independence League, 49

infant mortality, 239–241, 322

infectious diseases, 202, 224–226, 233, 236, 239–241, 322

International Harvester Company, 186n46, 238

J

Jane Addams and the Men of the Chicago School, 1892–1918 (Deegan), 16–17

Jane Addams Reader, The (Elshtain), 12

Jane Clubs, 20, 65, 78, 83, 86–87, 198, 205

Jensen, Jens, 119, 128

Jungle, The (Sinclair), 25, 44, 96, 224

justice and the courts, 62, 80, 108, 298, 305–309, 311–312

children in prison, 306–310

eminent domain, xvi, 8, 132–133, 174, 281
Illinois Juvenile Court Act, 1899, 307–308
Juvenile Court of Cook County, 305–306, 312 (photo)
politics and patronage, 317
present day abuses, 324–326
Juvenile Protective Association, 245, 297
Juvenile Psychopathic Institute, 287, 297, 316

K

Kelley, Florence, 74, 76, 91, 92, 193, 196, 198, 199, 224, 256–257, 347
Kenney, Mary, 81, 88, 198, 205
Kent, William, 94, 95, 96, 100, 117, 158–160, 177
King, Aurelia, 38
King, Henry, 38

L

labor
   child labor, 5, 7, 63, 201 (photo), 203–205, 237
   Child Labor Legislation Handbook, 245
   and immigrant groups, 195–196
   legislation, 43, 199–203
   movement in Chicago, overview of, 63–65
   unions, 7, 20–21, 39–41, 48, 89, 92, 205–209
labor confrontations
   Chicago Building Trade Strike, 1900, 89
   Chicago Stockyards Strike, 1904, 89
   Hart, Schaffner & Marx strike, 1910, 89, 193
   Haymarket riot, 1886, 25, 39, 41, 43, 82, 300–310

   National Anthracite Strike, 1902, 89
   Pullman Strike, 1894, 16, 25, 39, 46, 217–218
   waitresses' strike, 20
land leases, 5–7, 181, 271, 296, 323, 330
land-use planning and agencies for, 330–344
Lane, Albert, 125, 284–285
Lathrop, Julia, ix, 74, 76, 96, 198, 224, 226, 232, 234, 297, 299 (photo), 304–307, 307–309, 343, 347
Lawson, Victor, 96, 98
Leiter, Levi Z., 159–160
Lillie, Frances Crane, 267, 291, 347
Little Room, 94, 188
Livermore, Mary, 35
Lloyd, Henry Demarest, 77, 96, 158–160
Louise Juvenile Home/Industrial School, 310
Low, Minnie, 81, 297, 309, 313, 347

M

Mack, Julian, 96, 213, 312–313
MacVeagh, Franklin, 103
Mahony (Griffin), Marion Lucy, 137, 139, 149–154, 348
Mary Crane Nursery, 95 (photo)
Mason, Roswell, 35
material feminism, 66–67
Maxson, Annette E., 137
McCarthy, Kathleen D., 32, 33, 52
McCarthy, Michael P., 101, 103
McCormick, Anita. See Blaine, Anita McCormick
McCormick, Cyrus, 186, 238, 267
McCormick, Cyrus, Jr., 32, 52, 186
McCormick, Medill, 96

McCormick, Nettie Fowler, 186–187, 238
McCormick, Stanley, 186
McCrea, Annette, 139, 140, 160–162, 348
McCulloch, Catherine Waugh, 137, 154, 162–164, 348
McDonald, Elizabeth, 310
McDowell, Mary, 76, 81, 87, 89, 99, 111, 117–122, 133–134, 198, 216, 245, 348
McKinley, Ada, 111, 124, 348
McKinley Park lagoon, 121(photo)
Mead, George, 96
Medill, Joseph, 38, 177
Medill, Katherine, 38
Merchants' Club, x, 22, 40, 45, 103, 129
Merriam, Charles, 97
Metropolis 2020 Plan (Commercial Club), vii
Metropolitan Planning Organization (MPO), 340
Mirabella, Rosamond, 111, 124–126, 348
Modern Civic Art (Robinson), 122
Monroe, Harriet, 171, 174–175, 187–192, 187n54, 348
Moody, Walter D., 332–333
Morgan, Anna, 171, 179–180, 188–192, 348
Morgan, Elizabeth Chambers, 193, 348
municipal charter reform. *See* Chicago, municipal charter of
municipal housekeeping concept, 2, 3, 15, 47, 50, 51, 57–58, 57t, 58, 61, 68, 146, 164–167, 264–265
Municipal Improvement League, 45
Municipal Order League, 45, 147, 264–265
municipal ownership campaign, 158–160
Municipal Ownership League, 49

municipal services, responsibility for, 320–321. *See also* Chicago, municipal charter of
Municipal Voters League, 45, 95, 96, 98, 158, 177
Myhrman, Othelia Mork, 193, 199, 210–211, 349

N

NAACP (National Association for the Advancement of Colored People), 65, 87–88
Nancrede, Edith de, 172, 176, 178, 349
National Association of City Planning, 92–93
National Association of Colored Women, 42, 45, 87, 221
nationalities map. *See also Hull-House Maps and Papers* (Residents of Hull-House), 200–201, 253–254
National Playground Association of America, 123
neighborhood-centered park philosophy, 17, 119(nn 11,14), 120, 127–128, 131–132, 134, 135, 320
  field houses, 120–121, 120–123, 128, 131–135
  playgrounds, vi, 31, 60, 92–94, 113, 115–124, 130
Nestor, Agnes, 193, 199, 204–207, 349
Netcher, Mollie, 172, 182–185, 349
Newer Ideals of Peace (Addams), 12
Nicholes, Anna, 55, 68, 138, 140, 145–148, 349
Northeastern Illinois Planning Commission (NIPC), 335–344
Northwest Sanitary Commission, 35–36
Norton, Charles D., 103, 332, 332n3

O

Olmsted, Frederick Law, 134, 167
Olmsted Brothers, 119
One Hundred Years of Land Values in Chicago (Hoyt), 26
organizations: business, labor and civic, 1850–1910, 45

P

Palmer, Bertha, 42
Palmer, Potter, 42, 179
park commission, Lincoln Park, 119, 119n, 128
park commissions, south and west, 17, 22, 119(nn 11,14), 127–128, 131–132, 134, 135, 320
parks and greenways, xiii, 2, 104–105, 111–135, 325, 335
Parsons, Albert, 82, 208–209, 218
Parsons, Lucy, 82, 199, 208, 218–219
Perkins, Dwight H., 119
Phelps, Erskine M., 159–160
Phyllis Wheatley Club, 221, 245
Phyllis Wheatley Home for Girls, 221, 245
Plan of Chicago (Burnham), ix, v, viii, x, 2, 3, 4, 6, 7, 12, 18, 19, 20, 22, 23, 24, 29, 44, 47, 50, 52, 53, 55, 56, 59, 69, 71, 72, 76, 89, 92, 94, 95, 100, 101, 102, 124, 130, 211n48, 332
  appendix to, xv–xvi, 8
  and eminent domain, xvi, 8
  first projects implemented, xvi, 333
  Heart of Chicago, 172–192
  omissions from, found in early draft, 104–107, 329
  priorities of, viii, xi, xiv, xv, 20–21, 104–107, 140–141, 251
  promotion of, 7
  subscribers to, 4, 94, 100, 134, 143, 171, 193, 231
  summary of, xii–xvi
  view of order based on, x–xii, 1–3, 17–22, 25, 29–30, 54, 104–107, 114, 248
  visual description of, xi
Plan of Chicago (Schaffer), 19, 19n26, 23, 104–107, 105, 329
Playground Association of America, 116, 120, 121
playgrounds, coffeehouses, bathhouses, vi, 7, 31, 43, 60, 92–94, 113, 115–124, 130
political corruption and patronage, 1, 6–7, 33, 35, 44, 145, 156–159, 176–179
  abuses at Dunning Asylum, 226
  civil service system, 61, 125, 191, 226, 232, 244, 321
  present day abuses, 325–326
Pond, Allen, 78, 94, 95, 96, 100, 150, 158, 177
Pond, Irving, 78, 150
Pooley, Georgia Bitzis, 245, 249, 251, 349
population growth, rate of, 25–30
Porter, Julia Foster, 229
poverty, debate over causes of, 38, 44, 69, 83, 91
Powers, Johnny, 158, 268, 332, 333
Progressive Movement, 52, 61, 68, 75, 87
Protective Agency for Women and Children, 315
Provident Hospital, 81, 99–100, 168, 221, 228, 230
public education, 3, 7, 100, 106, 119, 175, 207
  businessmen *vs.* educators, 290–291
  Chicago Public Schools, 15, 80, 119, 125–127, 268, 271, 276, 280, 286, 325, 332
  compulsory school attendance bill, 1897, 305

land leases, 5–6, 32, 181, 271, 296, 323, 330

politics and patronage, 32, 268, 270, 272–273

present day funding for, 329

and teacher training, 282–284, 323

visiting nurses in Chicago public schools, 80, 235

public health, vii, 2, 3, 7, 12, 27–28, 55–56, 61–62, 106, 108, 236–240, 239n60, 322. *See also* sanitation systems; Provident Hospital

first city bathhouse, 227–228

and infant mortality, 239–241, 322

infectious diseases, 202, 224–226, 233, 236, 239–241, 260–261, 322

neighborhood-based treatment, 240 (photo), 241–242, 344

politics and patronage, 29, 225–226, 232

practitioners' training, 81, 226, 229, 288

quality of milk supply, 240–241

visiting nurses, 80, 211, 221, 234–235, 240

women's reproductive health, 242–244, 322

Pullman, Florence, 235

Pullman, George, 20, 27, 32, 37, 46, 52, 63, 71, 100, 102, 179–180, 218

Pullman Palace Car Company, 27, 63, 65, 218

Pullman Strike, 1894, 15, 16, 25, 39, 40–41, 63, 96

Putnam, Alice Whiting, 81, 267, 280–283, 349

R

rail transportation, freight and passenger, xiv, xv, 140–141, 143, 159

Reason Why the Colored American Is Not in the World's Columbian Exposition, The (Wells), 42

redemptive space concept, 57, 59–60, 83

reformers, 1, 5, 46, 82, 84. *See also* women activists

regional planning, vii–xi, 5–6, 127, 168, 326–343

Regional Transportation Plan 2030, board members of, 337 (photo)

Richards, Helen Swallow, 164–165, 224

Riis, Jacob, 129

Robertson, Ina Law, 245, 257–259, 349

Robins, Margaret Dreier, 88–89, 97, 138, 140, 164, 168–170, 350

Robins, Raymond, 88, 97, 138, 140, 150, 154–160, 177, 178

Robinson, Charles Mulford, 54, 113, 122

Rosenwald, Julius, 28, 44, 45, 79, 96, 99–100, 212, 213, 230–231

Ryerson, Edward L., 96

Ryerson, Martin, 33

S

Sanitary District of Chicago, 261

sanitation systems, 27, 29, 44, 47, 55–56, 107, 146–147, 165, 176, 224–226, 225, 250–251, 256–265

Schaffer, Kristen, 19, 23, 104–105, 329

Schaffner, Joseph, 89

School of Social Service Administration at the University of Chicago, 44, 91, 96, 245, 316

Schultz, Rima, 69, 74–75

Seeing With Their Hearts: Chicago Women and Their Vision of the Good City, 1871–1933 (Flanagan), 55

Settlement as a Factor in the Labor Movement, The (Addams), 215

settlement house movement, 1, 53, 64–65, 68, 74, 79. *See also* Hull-House; *Hull-House Maps and Papers* (Residents of Hull-House); municipal housekeeping concept

fresh air stations for sick babies, 240 (photo), 241

humanistic city-building, vi, vii, viii, 2–3, 25, 333

men allied with, 94–100

New York settlement efforts, vii, 82, 343

playgrounds, vi, 31, 60, 92–94, 113, 115–124, 130

reciprocal learning environment, 85–86

and redemptive spaces, 57, 59–60, 83

role in Chicago's cultural life, 188–192

Toynbee Hall (London), 13

workers, uniqueness of, 77

Shame of the Cities (Steffens), 102

Shipps, Dorothy, 25

Shoop, John, 62

Sies, Mary Corbin, 93, 333

Sikes, Madeleine Wallin, 245, 248–249, 250

Simkhovitch, Mary, 92–93, 343

Simmons, May Wood, 193, 199, 207–209, 350

Simonds, Ossian Cole, 119

Sinclair, Upton, 96

Skinner School, 293 (photo)

Slagle, Eleanor Clarke, 267, 287–289, 350

Small, Albion, 96

small parks, xiii, 17, 113, 115–134. *See also* playgrounds, coffeehouses, bathhouses

Smith, Carl, 23, 72, 102

Smith, Mary Rozet, 79

sociology, a new discipline, vii, 61, 90–92

Solomon, Hannah Greenebaum, 297, 309, 313–315, 350

Spain, Daphne, 56, 59–60, 122

Special Park Commission, xiiin, 114–115, 118–119

Spirit of Youth and the City Streets, The (Addams), 12, 190, 196–197

Starr, Ellen Gates, 2, 13, 72, 76, 94, 117, 193–200, 195 (photo), 205, 217–219, 281, 343, 350

Stead, William, 6, 20, 32, 41–42, 46, 78, 100–101, 124n, 157, 179–181, 224

Steffens, Lincoln, 25, 102

Stevens, Alzina, 198

Street Paving Committee of the Commercial Club, 147

streets, avenues, and boulevards, xiv, xv, 8, 129–131, 145–149, 166–170, 174, 249–250, 321

Subjective Necessity of Settlements, The (Addams), 11, 13

suburban commuters, xiv, 21, 28, 140, 155, 248

suburbs, 21–22, 115–116, 127, 322–323, 335

suffrage for women, 1, 3, 47–48, 51–52, 82, 87, 194, 308, 331

Sweatshop Act (1893 Illinois Factory and Inspection Act), 199–205

Sweet, Ada Celeste, 147, 264–265, 297, 302–304, 350

Swift, George, 147
Swope, Gerald, 97

T

Talbot, Marion, 138, 164–167, 224–225, 350
taxation
    and assessed property values, 5–6, 100, 124, 177, 179–181, 249–250, 291–293
    and municipal self-determination, 1, 135, 320–321
Taylor, Graham, 76, 96, 97–99, 119, 177, 179, 198, 218
Taylor, Lea, 112, 114–116, 350
Tenement Conditions in Chicago, 258
Tenements of Chicago, 1908–1935 (Abbott), 26
Thompson, Anna Wilmarth. *See* Ickes, Anna Wilmarth Thompson
Thompson, James, 336
Thompson, Mary Harris, 229, 288
Toynbee Hall (London), 13, 13n5
traction companies, traction franchise system, xi, xiv, xv, 139n, 140, 144–145, 156–159, 207, 218
transportation, 138, 140–141, 143, 159, 167–170, 321
    by elevated trains, streetcar lines, and subways, 141, 144, 154–156
    pedestrians and bicyclists, 167, 339, 342
    and public needs, 130, 167–170, 321
    on streets, avenues, and boulevards, xiv, xv, 8, 28, 28n45, 129–131, 145–149, 166–170, 174, 249–250, 321
    traffic movement and transit, xv, 104–105

transportation planning, regional, 326–327
    Changing Direction: Transportation Choices for 2030, 340
    Chicago Area Transportation Study (CATS), 335–342
    Chicago Metropolis 2020 (CM2020), 327, 338–339
    Chicago Metropolitan Agency for Planning (CMAP), 340–342
    2030 Regional Transportation Plan, board of, 337 (photo)
Twenty Years at Hull-House (Addams), 12, 14, 89

U

United Charities. *See* Chicago Relief and Aid Society; Charity Organization Society
Urban Disorder and the Shape of Belief (Smith), 72

V

vacation schools, 125–127, 280
Vaux, Calvert, 134
Visiting Nurses' Association, 211, 221, 234–236, 240
Vittum, Harriet, 76, 81, 112, 126–127, 131, 351

W

Wacker, Charles H., 103, 332
Wacker Manual, xvi, 332–333
Wade, Louise C., 29
Wald, Lillian, 92
Walker, Dan, 336
Walsh, John R., 179
Washington, Harold, ix
Watson, Carrie, 179
Wells, William, 284
Wells-Barnett, Ida B., ix, 42, 88, 298, 309–311, 351
Wheeler, George H., 159–160

White City, x, 25, 41, 54, 59,
    261–262. *See also* World's
    Columbian Exposition
Williams, Fannie Barrier, 42,
    81, 86, 88, 221, 222, 224n,
    228–230, 351
Wilmarth, Mary, 4, 150, 194, 199,
    205, 351
Wilson, Walter H., 103
Woman's City Club of Chicago, 45,
    58 (illustration), 60, 97
women activists, city-planners, v,
    4–5, 31, 79, 82. *See also* spe-
    cific women by name
  backgrounds of, 345–351
  City Livable theory, 8–9, 23–24,
    54–55, 57t, 166, 343
  divided reform movement of,
    44–47
  exposing corruption, 44, 158,
    179, 183, 226
  municipal charter reform, 24,
    47, 51, 156, 177
  personal funding of reforms,
    31, 186–187, 235, 257–258,
    303–304, 310–311
  relief for Chicago Fire victims,
    37–39
  and solidarity regardless of
    class, race/ethnicity, 64, 82,
    84–85, 193–219
  their approach to *Plan of Chi-
    cago*, 5, 7–9, 72–73
  and 1893 World's Columbian
    Exposition, 42
*Women Building Chicago: 1790–
    1990* (Hast and Schultz), 74,
    346
women doctors, list of, 231
women educational leaders, list of,
    288–289
women's reproductive health,
    242–244, 322

women's suffrage, 1, 3, 38, 47, 48,
    51–52, 82, 87, 194, 308, 331,
    334
Women's Trade Union League
    (WTUL), 51, 81, 88–89, 97,
    164, 205, 207, 245
Woolley, Celia Parker, 88
workplace safety, 12, 16, 201–204
World's Columbian Exposition
    (1893 World's Columbian
    Exposition), x, xi, xii, 6, 18,
    24, 32, 39, 41–43, 96, 97,
    102, 107, 147, 154, 155, 180,
    224, 262
Wright, Frank Lloyd, 137, 139,
    149–150

Y

Yarros, Rachel Slobodinsky, 221,
    223, 225, 241–243, 351
Yerkes, Charles T., 157–159, 178,
    179
YMCA, 38, 99
Young, Ella Flagg, 150, 268–275,
    269 (photo), 274–276, 281–
    283, 332–333, 343

Z

Zueblin, Charles, 96, 97, 112, 117,
    119, 128–131, 178, 259

Acknowledgments

❦ IT ALMOST GOES
WITHOUT SAYING that virtually all of
my female friends and colleagues were immediately
intrigued by the concept of this book. A group too large to
mention offered their support and enthusiasm from beginning to
end. I am especially indebted to Gin Kilgore for her thoughtful
comments on the structure, clarity, and readability of the manuscript. I am also very grateful for the work of Therese Newman,
who secured photos and permission for use, which I could not
have done while deeply immersed in the writing. Sharon Woodhouse, Lake Claremont Press's publisher, immediately grasped the
significance of this untold story, for which I am very, very grateful.

But it was men by and large who helped me make the book
happen. First and foremost, my soul mate, John Paige, offered his
twenty-eight years of experience in the field of regional planning
and his substantial library of relevant books on Chicago and Daniel Burnham. In addition to his intellectual contributions, he was
unfailingly patient with the disruptions caused by my total focus
on "Jane and friends" for almost a year, and willing to do virtually
anything he could do help me make this book happen, whether the
task was substantial or mundane.

Two of my sons, Chris and Tim, became my "legs" when health
issues impacted my mobility. They made innumerable trips to the
library for biographies of the women, articles or books written by
my protagonists, and other slices of Chicago history. My boss,
Steve Perkins, was extremely flexible about juggling projects to
allow me a partial sabbatical so this work could be completed in
time for the Burnham Centennial year (our CEO, Kathy Tholin,
was equally supportive of the sabbatical). All of this good will and

great assistance would have been for naught if it wasn't for Dr. Philip Bonomi of Rush University Hospital, who kept me healthy enough to finish the book.

There is a final group whose help was invaluable. Rima Lunin Schultz, co-editor Adele Hast, and the many contributors to *Women Building Chicago: 1790–1990,* provided an enormous amount of necessary background on the lives and achievements of over one hundred women working on city-building at the time of the *Plan of Chicago.* There are only a handful of biographies available even on Jane Addams's closest collaborators (there are, of course, several biographies of Addams herself). Autobiographies (Alice Hamilton and Louise de Koven Bowen, for example) or books written decades ago by friends (Jane Addams's biography of Julia Lathrop) are among the few books available. There is little recent scholarship about the women who formed Addams's inner circle, let alone about other, less prominent, women. The authors of *Women Building Chicago* have done a great service by collecting voluminous amounts of information from firsthand sources like letters, speeches, newspaper clippings, and other difficult to locate documents. The depth and breadth of *Women Building Chicago* was critical to understanding the full range of women and their contributions.

About the Author

JANICE METZGER HAS RESIDED IN CHICAGO almost all of her adult life. When her three sons, Timothy, Andrew, and Christopher, were growing up, she immersed herself in community issues, particularly public school matters. She held a number of voluntary positions with parent-school organizations and was appointed to the Desegregation Monitoring Commission. In 1987, following a forty day teachers' strike, Mayor Harold Washington named Metzger one of four co-chairs of the Parent Community Council of his Education Summit. Although Mayor Washington died shortly after naming the council, the summit went on to propose sweeping reforms of the system, and to win most of the legislative changes needed to enact the reforms. During this period she was also on the board of Association House of Chicago, and was vice president of the first editorial board of *Catalyst*, an education reform journal published by the Community Renewal Society.

Since 1995, Metzger has worked for the Center for Neighborhood Technology, a public policy and advocacy organization located in Wicker Park. She spent a decade monitoring the regional planning agencies, advocating for more public participation (when it didn't happen, she organized a broad-based public involvement process for transportation planning), more attention and resources for physically active travel, and more transit. She and her partner, John Paige, reside in Wicker Park. Her three adult sons all live within three miles and share her passion for Chicago and for urban issues.

Lake Claremont Press

FOUNDED IN 1994, Lake Claremont Press specializes in books on the Chicago area and its history, focusing on preserving the city's past, exploring its present environment, and cultivating a strong sense of place for the future. Visit us on the Web at www.lakeclaremont.com.

SELECTED BOOK LIST

The Politics of Place: A History of Zoning in Chicago

The Chicago River Architecture Tour

The Chicago River: A Natural and Unnatural History

From Lumber Hookers to the Hooligan Fleet: A Treasury of Chicago Maritime History

Rule 53: Capturing Hippies, Spies, Politicians, and Murderers in an American Courtroom

For Members Only: A History and Guide to Chicago's Oldest Private Clubs

Wrigley Field's Last World Series: The Wartime Chicago Cubs and the Pennant of 1945

Graveyards of Chicago

Finding Your Chicago Ancestors: A Beginner's Guide to Family History in the City and Cook County

On the Job: Behind the Stars of the Chicago Police Department

Chicago's TV Horror Movie Shows: From Shock Theatre to Svengoolie

The Golden Age of Chicago Children's Television

Hollywood on Lake Michigan

Carless in Chicago

Oldest Chicago

Today's Chicago Blues

Historic Bars of Chicago